Fourth Workshop on Universal Dependencies (UDW 2020)

Held online due to COVID-19

Barcelona, Spain
13 December 2020

ISBN: 978-1-7138-2841-9

COLING 2020

Fourth Workshop on Universal Dependencies (UDW 2020)

Proceedings of the Workshop

December 13, 2020
Barcelona, Spain (Online)

Preface

These proceedings include the program and papers that are presented at the fourth workshop on Universal Dependencies, held in conjunction with COLING online on December 13, 2020.

Universal Dependencies (UD) is a framework for cross-linguistically consistent treebank annotation that has so far been applied to over 90 languages (http://universaldependencies.org/). The framework is aiming to capture similarities as well as idiosyncrasies among typologically different languages (e.g., morphologically rich languages, pro-drop languages, and languages featuring clitic doubling). The goal in developing UD was not only to support comparative evaluation and cross-lingual learning but also to facilitate multilingual natural language processing and enable comparative linguistic studies.

After three successful editions of the workshop, we decided to continue to bring together researchers working on UD, to reflect on the theory and practice of UD, its use in research and development, and its future goals and challenges.

We received 33 submissions of which 24 were accepted. Submissions covered several topics: some papers describe treebank conversion or creation, while others target specific linguistic constructions and which analysis to adopt, sometimes with critiques of the choices made in UD; some papers exploit UD resources for cross-linguistic and historical analysis, or for parsing, and some develop tools using UD.

We are honored to have an invited speaker: Martha Palmer (Department of Linguistics, University of Colorado at Boulder), with a talk on "Transcending Dependencies" which talks about contextual interpretation in dialogues and the role of Abstract Meaning Representation in this context.

We are grateful to the program committee, who worked hard and on a tight schedule to review the submissions and provided authors with valuable feedback.

We thank Google, Inc. and the National Science Foundation (NSF) for grants which allowed us to cover registration fees of some of the participants.

We wish all participants a productive workshop!

Marie-Catherine de Marneffe, Miryam de Lhoneux, Joakim Nivre and Sebastian Schuster

Workshop Co-Chairs:

Marie-Catherine de Marneffe, The Ohio State University, USA
Miryam de Lhoneux, University of Copenhagen, Denmark
Joakim Nivre, Uppsala Univeristy, Sweden
Sebastian Schuster, Stanford University, USA

Program Committee:

Željko Agić, IT University of Copenhagen, Denmark
Emily Bender, University of Washington, USA
Marcel Bollman, University of Copenhagen, Denmark
Gosse Bouma, University of Groningen, The Netherlands
Marie Candito, Université Paris Diderot, France
Giuseppe Celano, University of Leipzig, Germany
Çağrı Çöltekin, Tübingen, Germany
Valeria dePaiva, Samsung Research, USA
Timothy Dozat, Google, USA
Kira Droganova, Charles University Prague, Czech Republic
Richard Futrell, University of California Irvine, USA
Kim Gerdes, Sorbonne University, France
Carlos Gómez-Rodríguez, University of Coruña, Spain
Michael Hahn, Stanford University, USA
Jan Hajic, Charles University Prague, Czech Republic
Johannes Heinecke, Orange Labs
Sylvain Kahane, Université Paris Ouest - Nanterre, France
Arne Köhn, University of Hamburg, Germany
Natalia Kotsyba, Polish Academy of Sciences, Poland
John Lee, City University of Hong Kong, Hong Kong
Teresa Lynn, Dublin City University, Ireland
Arya McCarthy, John Hopkins University, USA
Stephan Oepen, University of Oslo, Norway
Lilja Øvrelid, University of Oslo, Norway
Guy Perrier, University of Lorraine, France
Tommi Pirinen, University of Hamburg, Germany
Martin Popel, Charles University, Czech Repbulic
Sampo Pyysalo, University of Cambridge, UK
Peng Qi, Stanford University, USA
Alexandre Rademaker, IBM Research, Brazil
Rudolf Rosa, Charles University in Prague, Czech Republic
Tanja Samardžić, University of Zurich, Switzerland
Nathan Schneider, Georgetown University, USA
Francis Tyers, Indiana University, USA
Zdeněk Žabokrtský, Charles University in Prague, Czech Republic
Amir Zeldes, Georgetown University, USA
Daniel Zeman, Charles University Prague, Czech Republic

Invited Speakers:

Martha Palmer, University of Colorado at Boulder, USA

Table of Contents

A small Universal Dependencies treebank for Hittite
Erik Andersen and Benjamin Rozonoyer 1

Parsing in the absence of related languages: Evaluating low-resource dependency parsers on Tagalog
Angelina Aquino and Franz de Leon 8

A Universal Dependencies conversion pipeline for a Penn-format constituency treebank
Þórunn Arnardóttir, Hinrik Hafsteinsson, Einar Freyr Sigurðsson, Kristín Bjarnadóttir, Anton Karl
Ingason, Hildur Jónsdóttir and Steinþór Steingrímsson 16

Corpus evidence for word order freezing in Russian and German
Aleksandrs Berdicevskis and Alexander Piperski 26

Subjecthood and annotation: The cases of French and Wolof
Olivier Bondéelle and Sylvain Kahane 34

Verification, reproduction and replication of NLP experiments: A case study on parsing Universal Dependencies
Çağrı Çöltekin 46

From LFG To UD: A combined approach
Cheikh M. Bamba Dione 57

Identifying and handling cross-treebank inconsistencies in UD: A pilot study
Tillmann Dönicke, Xiang Yu and Jonas Kuhn 67

Composing byte-pair encodings for morphological sequence classification
Adam Ek and Jean-Philippe Bernardy 76

Configurable dependency tree extraction from CCG derivations
Kilian Evang 87

Unifying the treatment of preposition-determiner contractions in German Universal Dependencies treebanks
Stefan Grünewald and Annemarie Friedrich 94

Annotation issues in Universal Dependencies for Korean and Japanese
Ji Yoon Han, Tae Hwan Oh, Lee Jin and Hansaem Kim 99

Exploring diachronic syntactic shifts with dependency length: The case of scientific English
Tom S Juzek, Marie-Pauline Krielke and Elke Teich 109

UDon2: A library for manipulating Universal Dependencies trees
Dmytro Kalpakchi and Johan Boye 120

Annotating MWEs in the Irish UD treebank
Sarah McGuinness, Jason Phelan, Abigail Walsh and Teresa Lynn 126

I've got a construction looks funny – representing and recovering non-standard constructions in UD
Josef Ruppenhofer and Ines Rehbein 140

Universal Dependencies for Manx Gaelic
Kevin Scannell 152

Variation in Universal Dependencies annotation: A token-based typological case study on adpossessive constructions
Kaius Sinnemäki and Viljami Haakana 158

PALMYRA 2.0: A configurable multilingual platform independent tool for morphology and syntax annotation
Dima Taji and Nizar Habash 168

Universal Dependencies for Albanian
Marsida Toska, Joakim Nivre and Daniel Zeman 178

First Steps towards Universal Dependencies for Laz
Utku Türk, kaan bayar, Ayşegül Dilara Özercan, Görkem Yiğit Öztürk and Şaziye Betül Özateş189

Dependency annotation of noun incorporation in polysynthetic languages
Francis Tyers and Karina Mishchenkova 195

Universal Dependency treebank for Xibe
He Zhou, Juyeon Chung, Sandra Kübler and Francis Tyers 205

Workshop Program

Sunday, December 13, 2020

14:00–14:10   Introduction

14:10–15:00   Q&A Session 1

Dependency annotation of noun incorporation in polysynthetic languages
Francis Tyers and Karina Mishchenkova

I've got a construction looks funny — representing and recovering non-standard constructions in UD
Josef Ruppenhofer and Ines Rehbein

Annotating MWEs in the Irish UD treebank
Sarah McGuinness, Jason Phelan, Abigail Walsh and Teresa Lynn

Subjecthood and annotation: The cases of French and Wolof
Olivier Bondéelle and Sylvain Kahane

Annotation issues in Universal Dependencies for Korean and Japanese
Ji Yoon Han, Tae Hwan Oh, LEE JIN and Hansaem Kim

15:00–15:10   Break

15:10–16:00   Q&A Session 2

Variation in Universal Dependencies annotation: A token-based typological case study on adpossessive constructions
Kaius Sinnemäki and Viljami Haakana

Corpus evidence for word order freezing in Russian and German
Aleksandrs Berdicevskis and Alexander Piperski

Parsing in the absence of related languages: Evaluating low-resource dependency parsers on Tagalog
Angelina Aquino and Franz de Leon

Verification, reproduction and replication of NLP experiments: A case study on parsing Universal Dependencies
Çağrı Çöltekin

Composing byte-pair encodings for morphological sequence classification
Adam Ek and Jean-Philippe Bernardy

16:00–17:15   Poster Session

A small Universal Dependencies treebank for Hittite
Erik Andersen and Benjamin Rozonoyer

Universal Dependencies for Albanian
Marsida Toska, Joakim Nivre and Daniel Zeman

Universal Dependencies for Manx Gaelic
Kevin Scannell

Universal Dependency treebank for Xibe
He Zhou, Juyeon Chung, Sandra Kübler and Francis Tyers

First Steps towards Universal Dependencies for Laz
Utku Türk, kaan bayar, Ayşegül Dilara Özercan, Görkem Yiğit Öztürk and Şaziye
Betül Özateş

From LFG to UD: A combined approach
Cheikh M. Bamba Dione

UDon2: A library for manipulating Universal Dependencies trees
Dmytro Kalpakchi and Johan Boye

PALMYRA 2.0: A configurable multilingual platform independent tool for morphology and syntax annotation
Dima Taji and Nizar Habash

Unifying the treatment of preposition-determiner contractions in German Universal Dependencies treebanks
Stefan Grünewald and Annemarie Friedrich

17:15–18:00   Keynote

Transcending dependencies
Martha Palmer, University of Colorado Boulder, USA

Break

18:10–19:00   Q&A Session 3

Exploring diachronic syntactic shifts with dependency length: The case of scientific English
Tom S Juzek, Marie-Pauline Krielke and Elke Teich

Identifying and handling cross-treebank inconsistencies in UD: A pilot study
Tillmann Dönicke, Xiang Yu and Jonas Kuhn

Profiling-UD: A tool for linguistic profiling of texts (cross-submission)
Dominique Brunato, Andrea Cimino, Felice Dell'Orletta, Simonetta Montemagni and Giulia Venturi

Configurable dependency tree extraction from CCG derivations
Kilian Evang

A Universal Dependencies conversion pipeline for a Penn-format constituency treebank
Þórunn Arnardóttir, Hinrik Hafsteinsson, Einar Freyr Sigurðsson, Kristín Bjarnadóttir, Anton Karl Ingason, Hildur Jónsdóttir and Steinþór Steingrímsson

Invited Talk: Martha Palmer, University of Colorado Boulder

Transcending Dependencies

This talk will discuss some of the challenges arising from the Blocks World scenario in the DARPA Communicating with Computers program. The actions are very simple and concrete, such as "Add a block to the tower." However, even in this restricted world, getting the appropriate contextual interpretation of a sentence can be challenging, especially with respect to spatial relations and implicit information. The talk will review the progress we have made so far on collecting useful data that comprises complete 2 person dialogues discussing block structure constructions, and our attempts to achieve the goal of contextual interpretation in the processing of these dialogues. A main focus will be the ways in which we are expanding AMR annotation to encompass spatial relations and the recovery of implicit arguments. Both expansions play into the task of maintaining a discourse structure and producing the predicate logic sentence representations needed by the down-stream planner. The talk will conclude with our current AMR parsing results, our attempts to pass them along to the planner, and our future goals.

Bio

Martha Palmer is the Helen & Hubert Croft Endowed Professor of Engineering in the Computer Science Department, and an Arts & Sciences Professor of Distinction in the Linguistics Department, at the University of Colorado, with a split appointment. She is also an Institute of Cognitive Science Faculty Fellow, a co-Director of CLEAR, an ACL Fellow, and a AAAI Fellow. She was the Director of the 2011 Linguistics Institute in Boulder, CO. Her research is focused on capturing elements of the meanings of words that can comprise automatic representations of complex sentences and documents in English, Chinese, Arabic, Hindi, and Urdu, funded by DARPA, DTRA and NSF. A more recent focus is the application of these methods to biomedical journal articles and clinical notes, funded by NIH. She co-edits LiLT, Linguistic Issues in Language Technology, and has been a co-editor of the Journal of Natural Language Engineering and on the CLJ Editorial Board. She is a past President of ACL, past Chair of SIGLEX, was the Founding Chair of SIGHAN, and has over 300 peer-reviewed publications.

A Small Universal Dependencies Treebank for Hittite

Erik Andersen
Brandeis University
erikandersen@brandeis.edu

Benjamin Rozonoyer
Brandeis University
brozonoyer@brandeis.edu

Abstract

We present the first Universal Dependencies treebank for Hittite. This paper expands on earlier efforts at Hittite corpus creation (Molina and Molin, 2016; Molina, 2016) and discussions of annotation guidelines for Hittite within the UD framework (Inglese, 2015; Inglese et al., 2018). We build on the expertise of the above works to create a small corpus which we hope will serve as a stepping-stone to more expansive UD treebanking for Hittite.

1 Introduction

Hittite is an extinct language of the Anatolian sub-branch of the Indo-European language family. It was the main language of the Hittite kingdom (16th-13th centuries B.C.E.), and is recorded from the 18th to the 12th centuries B.C.E. (Molina and Molin, 2016; Molina, 2016). Knowledge of Hittite reached beyond the boundaries of the Hittite kingdom as far as Egypt. As the earliest attested Indo-European language, it remains vital to Indo-European studies and our understanding of the rest of the Anatolian sub-branch, all of whose languages – Luwian, Palaic, Lycian, Lydian, and Carian – are extinct (Dalby, 2004; Hoffner and Melchert, 2008a; Collins, 2012).

The Hittite empire left behind a wide range of texts, which can be classified according to linguistic time periods – Old Hittite, Middle Hittite, and New Hittite – with Middle Hittite acting more as a transitional period between the two (Melchert, 2007).

Hittite's fragmentary corpus of cuneiform tablets with extensive borrowing of signs from both Akkadian and Sumerian make the language challenging for treebank creation (Molina and Molin, 2016). As a dependable source of unfragmented text, we annotated original Hittite sentences presented in Hoffner and Melchert's tutorial (Hoffner and Melchert, 2008b), and which we had analyzed in a lecture setting. The sentences are drawn from a variety of texts, spanning legal, religious, and mythological, from the three linguistic periods. Despite minor diachronic developments in morphology and syntax (see Section 2), scribal recopying of older texts occasionally obscures a definitive chronological classification for the surviving texts. These considerations swayed us in favor of a single corpus for the three linguistic periods. We include the dating, whenever possible, in the sentence's metadata.

1.1 Grammatical sketch

Hittite is an SOV language that "shows the typical features of an older Indo-European language" in that it is synthetic and suffixing in its derivational and inflectional morphology (Hoffner and Melchert, 2008a). The language employs a rich noun case system and appears to display split-ergativity (see §3.2).

Hittite verbs display two main tenses, present and preterite, but they can be augmented with auxiliary verbs *ḫar(k)-* and *ēš-* to create more complex tenses, such as the analytic perfect. Verbs also display two basic moods: imperative and indicative.

Aspect marking is more complex. The three verbal suffixes *-ške-, -anna/i-, -šša-* appear to act as imperfect markers on verbs (Hoffner and Melchert, 2008a). However, not all verbs displaying incomplete

Proceedings of the Fourth Workshop on Universal Dependencies (UDW 2020), pages 1–7
Barcelona, Spain (Online), December 13, 2020

Category	Example
Hittite Word	*pár-ku-iš*
Hittite Word with Determinative	[d]*A-la-lu*
Sumerogram	MUŠEN
Multiple Character Sumerogram	TA.ÀM
Akkadogram	*EL-LA-AM*
Hittite Word with Sumerian Plural	*up-pé-eš-šar*[MEŠ]

Table 1: Examples of Hittite in narrow transcription

action require them, and it is debatable whether they always act as imperfectives (Inglese, 2015) (see §3.2).

Even more unclear is the exact function of Hittite clausal connectives *nu*, *šu*, and *ta* and the topicalizing or contrasting particle *-(m)a* (see §3.1).

2 Previous work

Inglese (2015) discusses an annotation schema for a Hittite Universal Dependencies treebank. His work primarily concerns sentences originating from the Old Hittite *Zalpa's text*, so our treebank requires some other rules to account for grammatical conventions reflected only in later texts. These include use of the *-za* particle in nominal and "to be" sentences with 1st or 2nd person subject, and pronominal clitic repetition (see §28.32-42 and §30.19 of Hoffner and Melchert, 2008a).

Furthermore, some of Inglese's work must be updated to adapt it to the current Universal Dependencies 2.0, which was released subsequently to his paper.

Inglese et al. (2018) introduce a Hittite treebank in the PROIEL (Pragmatic Resources in Old Indo-European Languages) framework, whose treebanks for Old Church Slavonic and Latin have been mapped into the UD format.

Molina (2016) has done previous work on a large constituency MsSQL corpus of Hittite texts; we do not use it as a guide to our annotation.

3 Annotation

3.1 Orthography and tokenization

Hittite was initially written in cuneiform, with each word separated by space (Hoffner and Melchert, 2008a; Inglese, 2015). There are two common methods for modern transcription: narrow and broad. In narrow transcription, the boundary of each character is clearly delineated, whereas broad transcription more closely reflects the probable pronunciation. In the example below, the top line is provided in narrow transcription, and the second line in broad transcription:

(1) zi-ik   am-me-el É-na   le-e   ú-wa-ši
     zik   ammel   É-na   lē   uwaši
     you   my   house:ALL;SG PROHIB   come:PRS;2SG [1]
     You shall not come to my house. (from KUB 29.1 i 19-20 (OH/NS))

Hittite borrowed extensively from both Sumerian and Akkadian. Sumerograms are represented by non-italicized capital letters, as in the word MUŠEN "bird" or the word for "house" É above, and Akkadograms are represented using capital italic text, such as *EL-LA-AM* "free (ACC)." Hittite words are written using lowercase letters (Hoffner and Melchert, 2008a). Multiple adjacent Sumerograms are separated by a dot.

In Hittite, the determinative, featured only in the written language, is placed before or after a word to codify it as part of a category, and is transcribed with a superscript. For example, the determinative

---

[1]We use the Leipzig conventions for our glosses in this paper.

MUŠEN is used to indicate birds, and the determinative *d* (short for DINGIR) is used for deities. This behavior is also seen in both Sumerian and Akkadian. The Akkadian UD treebank (Kopacewicz, 2018), which uses narrow transcription, does not treat determinatives as separate from the words they qualify but attaches them using hyphens in the position they were found originally. Unlike the Akkadian treebank, we treat determinatives as separate words but include them in a multiword token with the noun that they qualify.

While we use hyphens, as in narrow transcription, to reflect word-internal cuneiform boundaries, we adopt the "=" from broad transcription to signal clitic boundaries. This hybrid approach allows the reader to immediately recognize clitics in the transcription, while being backwards-compatible with the writing system.

The absence of punctuation in Hittite made sentence splitting decisions non-trivial, since a significant number of "sentences" in Hoffner and Melchert's tutorial were comprised of at least two consecutive independent clauses without conventional coordinating conjunctions. Following Inglese (2015) and Molina and Molin (2016), we took the phrase connectors *nu*, *ta*, and *šu* (the last of which does not appear in our corpus) to delineate sentence boundaries whenever they stand at the beginning of an independent clause. Similarly, we exploited the non-emphatic clitics *-wa*, *-(m)a*, *-kan*, *-šan*, *-za*, *-ašta*, *-an*, *-apa* (the last two of which do not appear in our corpus). Whenever these appear at the start of an independent clause which is not the beginning of quoted speech introduced by a verb of saying, they signal a new sentence. All these discourse particles and clitics may be seen as connectives and give us a relatively clean heuristic for sentence tokenization. We did not split independent clauses which were strung together without such discourse connectives, and opted instead to use parataxis.

Employing this method of sentence tokenization, and treating determinatives and clitics as distinct words (including in complex Sumerogram multiword expressions such as DUMU.NAM.LÚ.U$_{19}$.LU-*(l)a-*, which corresponds to Hittite *dandukišnaš* DUMU-*(l)a-* "human being (*lit.* child of mortality)"), the statistics of our corpus come out to 136 sentences, 1309 words, and 970 (whitespace-separated) tokens.

3.2 Morphology and lemmatization

Hittite has the following cases: nominative, accusative, genitive, dative-locative, instrumental, ablative, ergative, allative and vocative. The ergative case appears when a neuter noun is the subject of a transitive verb (Hoffner and Melchert, 2008a). A neuter noun appears in the "absolutive" when it functions as the subject of an intransitive verb or as the direct object of a transitive verb. Hoffner and Melchert package this behavior under the name "nominative-accusative". The ergative does not occur in pronouns or common-gender nouns. Although the ergative case (Erg) does not occur in our corpus, we have annotated neuter nominative-accusative nouns as absolutive (Abs). Melchert (2011) provides a clause where the neuter subject (and corresponding neuter demonstrative) appears in the ergative case:

(2) maḫḫan=ta   kāš   tuppianza   anda wemiyazzi
     when=you   this   tablet:ERG   reach:PRS;3SG
     When this tablet reaches you   (HKM 14:3-5)

In our annotation, we do not include the aspect feature as per Inglese's (2015) proposal. While Hittite uses the imperfective verbal suffixes *-ške-*, *-šša-*, and *-anna/i-*, they are not always used when the aspect is imperfective (see §24 of Hoffner and Melchert, 2008a). These suffixes perform a variety of functions, mostly iterative and durative in nature. In contrast, adverbs such as *kuitman* "while" can sometimes indicate an incomplete action without any contribution from the verb:

(3) nu   ku-it-ma-an A-NA ^{LÚ}-SANGA pa-a-an-zi
     CONN   while   to   priest   go:PRS;3PL
     And while they go to the priest   (from KUB 5.6 i 39-41 (NH))

In (3), the subordinating conjunction *ku-it-ma-an* appears with the verb *pa-a-an-zi*, which does not use an imperfective suffix.

Tag	Count	Percentage
NOUN	387	29.56%
VERB	208	15.89%
PART	164	12.53%
PRON	146	11.15%
CCONJ	88	6.72%
ADV	73	5.58%
PROPN	73	5.58%
ADP	49	3.74%
SCONJ	34	2.60%
NUM	31	2.37%
ADJ	21	1.60%
DET	16	1.22%
AUX	14	1.07%
X	4	0.31%
INTJ	1	0.08%

Table 2: Hittite UPOS tag statistics

Feature	UPOS	Values
Case	NOUN, VERB, PRON, PROPN, NUM, ADJ, DET	Nom, Acc, Gen, Dat, Abl Ins, All, Erg, Voc, Abs
Definite	NOUN	Cons
Gender	NOUN, VERB, PRON, PROPN, NUM, ADJ, DET	Com, Neut, Masc, Fem
Number	NOUN, VERB, PRON, NUM, ADJ, DET, AUX	Sing, Plur
NumType	ADV, NUM	Card, Ord
Person	VERB, PRON, AUX	1, 2, 3
Poss	PRON	Yes
PronType	PRON, DET	Dem, Ind, Int, Prs, Rel, Tot, [Neg]
Mood Tense VerbForm Voice	VERB, AUX	Ind, Imp Pres, Past Fin, Inf, Part, Sup, Vnoun Act, Mid
Language	*any (except X)*	Akk, Sum

Table 3: Feature values for Hittite grouped by UPOS

Out of the official Universal Dependency part of speech tagset, we used all values except for SYM and PUNCT, as Hittite does not make use of special symbols or punctuation like in English. We display the part of speech tags we used, together with the raw counts and percentages in Table 2.

We show the morphological features we used, mostly adapted from Inglese, in Table 3. The *Pron-Type=Neg* feature is included in Inglese (2015), but does not appear in our corpus.

Lemmas are taken from the stem as provided in Hoffner and Melchert's tutorial, and are always in broad transcription (Hoffner and Melchert, 2008b). While using the stem for a lemma is a convention in Hittitology, this results in different verbs being covered by the same lemma in some cases. To avoid this problem, we add *-#1-* or *-#2-* after the stem, following the example of the Hittite PROIEL annotation team (Inglese et al., 2018).

3.3 Dependency Relations

In our treebank, we introduced the following language-specific dependency relations:

acl:relcl – used to introduce relative clauses, subordinates the predicate of a relative clause to nominal that is modified.

Relation	Count	Relation	Count
root	136	dislocated	13
obj	126	expl:pass	13
nmod	107	parataxis	13
clf	97	xcomp	11
nsubj	96	orphan	9
obl	96	appos	8
advmod	89	aux	7
cc	87	cop	7
discourse	67	vocative	7
case	49	compound	6
conj	45	acl:relcl	4
advmod:loc	34	advmod:emph	4
mark	34	dep	4
advcl	30	ccomp	2
discourse:conn	26	csubj	2
nummod	26	expl	2
iobj	22	acl	1
det	15	flat	1
amod	13		

Table 4: Hittite dependency relation statistics

advmod:emph – used for the emphatic particle *-pat* (and *-ila*, which is not in our corpus), which depends on the noun or pronoun it is attached to. For example, in *a-pu-un=pát* "that very one," *-pát* depends on the distal demonstrative *a-pu-un*.

advmod:loc – used to subordinate the local particles *-šan, -kan, -ašta, -an, -apa* (where the last two do not appear in our corpus) to the predicate in the clause (see §28.43-47 of Hoffner and Melchert, 2008a). Inglese (2015) notes the complexity of these motion particles.

discourse:conn - used for the special phrasal connectives *nu, šu* and *ta* when they occur (typically sentence-medially) as discourse clause connectors that are neither subordinating nor coordinating. As per Inglese (2015), **cc** is used when these connectives occur sentence-initially (and act as coordinating conjunctions).

expl:pass – used for reflexive particle *-za* when it embodies a reflexive meaning, rather than change-of-state or first/second-person subject of a copular sentence (see §28.17-31 of Hoffner and Melchert, 2008a). This represents the current UD 2.6 version of Inglese's suggestion to use **auxpass:reflex**.

The **discourse** relation, often used for interjections, is very common. We annotated *-(m)a* as **discourse**, following Inglese (2015). We also used the discourse relation when *-za* acts as a 1st or 2nd person subject indicator in a copular sentence. In (4), the *-za* particle does not act reflexively, but indicates that the subject of the sentence is in the 2nd person:

(4) zi-g=a-a=z   GIŠ-ḫa-tal-ki-iš-na-aš
     You=but=*za*   hawthorn:GEN;SG
     You are like the hawthorn
     (from KUB 33.54 ii 13-14 (OH/NS) [restored version])

We display the count of each dependency relation in Table 4. Out of the official dependency relations, we used all the universal relations except for *list, goeswith, punct, reparandum*, and *fixed*.

While we used Inglese (2015) as a guide, we needed some other relations for distinct phenomena which occur more exclusively in New Hittite. For example, some New Hittite texts sometimes repeat pronouns within the same clause, possibly as a form of emphasis.

(5) nu=wa-r=a-an=za=<u>an</u>   ^{LÚ}-MU-TI₄=YA   i-ya-mi
     CONN=QUOT=him=REFL=<u>him</u>   husband=my   make:PRS;1SG
     (I do not want to take my servant) and make <u>him</u> my husband.   (from KBo 5.6 iv 6-7 (NH))

In (5), the accusative common-gender 3rd person clitic *-an* is repeated twice, though it refers to the same entity. Clitic doubling is not exclusive to Hittite; it can be seen in Bulgarian, whose UD treebank uses the relation **expl** for this phenomenon (Simov et al., 2015).

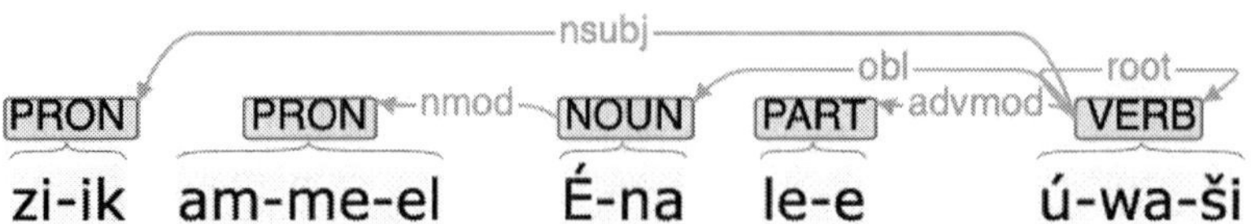

Figure 1: A Hittite UD Annotation of Sentence (1) using WebAnno

4   Implementation of some features proposed by Inglese (2015)

Inglese (2015) underlines the challenge of including philological information within the UD framework, and proposes the following extensions to reflect Hittitological information:

Language=Hitt, Akk, Sum. This feature indicates what language the written word is in. We use the Akk and Sum features, and leave Hittite words unmarked for this feature.

Determinative=1-16. Inglese introduces a Determinative feature which can take a value between 1 and 16, but does not treat determinatives as separate words in his annotation. Since these determinatives most often act as hypernyms, with a grammatical function of categorizing or classifying, we decided that it would be more consistent to have them relate to the head noun with **clf** (similar to numerical measure words in Chinese).

Hlemma (Hittite lemma for a word). We do not use this feature since our lemmatization is Hittite by default. If the underlying Hittite word for a Sumerogram or Akkadogram is not known, we resort to the Akkadian or Sumerian lemma, while retaining as much non-inflectional Hittite morphology in the lemma as possible. For instance, while the full Hittite lemma for the Sumerogram DUMU "son" is unknown, the uninflected stem ends in *-(l)a-*, so we record the lemma as DUMU-*(l)a-*.

Ntrans (Narrow transcription). Since we are working in narrow transcription by default, we do not include a feature for this.

5   Scribal peculiarities

Scribal idiosyncrasies occasionally complicate the annotation process:

(6) da-aš-šu-š=a-a=<u>š</u>-<u>ši</u>   ^d-A-nu-uš   ... pé-ra-an=<u>še-et</u>   ar-ta
     mighty=but=DAT;3SG;MASC   Anu:NOM;SG ... before=GEN;3SG;MASC   stand:PRS;3SG;MID
     while Anu the mighty (foremost of the gods) stands before him.   (from KUB 33.120 i 8-10 (NS))

The original cuneiform of sentence (6) uses NS (New Script), but clearly contains Old Hittite elements. Old Hittite prefers the genitive with postpositions to the dative-locative, sometimes appending the genitive possessive clitic to the postposition, as in *pé-ra-an=še-et* (Hoffner and Melchert, 2008a). However, this sentence also includes the extra New Hittite dative-locative element *-š-ši*, which could be the result of a scribal "correction". In this instance, the postposition *pé-e-ran* appears to govern two co-referential pronominal objects: *=še-et* and *-š-ši* (see §20.23 and §20.26 of Hoffner and Melchert, 2008a). This situation is similar to the clitic doubling, as in Bulgarian (Simov et al., 2015). For consistency, in (6) we have decided to mark the pronoun *-š-ši* as **expl** with respect to the verb in the clause, instead of making use of the **reparandum** relation, because there is no way to prove whether the extra pronoun is indeed a **reparandum**.

6 Conclusion

We have provided a seedling Universal Dependencies corpus for the earliest attested Indo-European language. With a view on making our work as extensible as possible, we have attempted to incorporate both the practical and the philological concerns voiced by Inglese (2015) for treebanking Hittite in the UD framework. We hope that this treebank will serve as a stepping stone for increased computational analysis of Hittite and typological research.

7 Acknowledgements

We would like to extend our gratitude to David Wright, Professor of Bible and Ancient Near East at Brandeis University, for offering his excellent course on Hittite last Spring.

References

Billie Jean Collins. 2012. *The Hittites and Their World*. SBL Press.

Andrew Dalby. 2004. *Dictionary of Languages*. Columbia University Press, Revised edition.

Harry A. Hoffner, Jr. and H. Craig Melchert. 2008a. *A Grammar of the Hittite Language. Part 1: Reference Grammar*. Eisenbrauns.

Harry A. Hoffner, Jr. and H. Craig Melchert. 2008b. *A Grammar of the Hittite Language. Part 2: Tutorial*. Eisenbrauns.

Guglielmo Inglese, Maria Molina, and Hanne Eckhoff. 2018. Incorporating Hittite into PROIEL: a pilot project. In Andrew U. Frank, Christine Ivanovic, Francesco Mambrini, Marco Passarotti, and Caroline Sporlede, editors, *Proceedings of the Second Workshop on Corpus-based Research in the Humanities*, pages 95–104.

Guglielmo Inglese. 2015. Towards a Hittite Treebank. Basic Challenges and Methodological Remarks. In M. Passarotti, F. Mambrini, and C. Sporleder, editors, *Proceedings of the Workshop on Corpus-Based Research in the Humanities (CRH)*.

Kamil Kopacewicz. 2018. UD Akkadian PISANDUB.

H. Craig Melchert. 2007. Middle Hittite revisited. In A. Archi and R. Francia, editors, *VI Congresso Internazionale di Ittitologia*, pages 525–531.

H. Craig Melchert. 2011. The Problem of the Ergative Case in Hittite. In M. Fruyt, M. Mazoyer, and Dennis Pardee, editors, *Grammatical case in the languages of the Middle East and Europe. Acts of the international colloquium Variations, concurrence et evolution des cas dans divers domaines linguistiques*, pages 161–167.

Maria Molina and Alexei Molin. 2016. In a Lacuna: Building a Syntactically Annotated Corpus for a Dead Cuneiform Language (on the basis of Hittite). In *Computational Linguistics and Intellectual Technologies: Proceedings of the International Conference "Dialogue 2016"*.

Maria Molina. 2016. Syntactic Annotation for a Hittite Corpus: Problems and Principles. In *Proceedings of the Workshop on Computational Linguistics and Language Science*.

Kiril Simov, Petya Osenova, and Martin Popel. 2015. UD Bulgarian BTB.

Parsing in the absence of related languages:
Evaluating low-resource dependency parsers on Tagalog

Angelina Aquino and **Franz de Leon**
Digital Signal Processing Laboratory, Electrical and Electronics Engineering Institute
University of the Philippines, Diliman, Quezon City, Philippines
{angelina.aquino, franz.de.leon}@eee.upd.edu.ph

Abstract

Cross-lingual and multilingual methods have been widely suggested as options for dependency parsing of low-resource languages; however, these typically require the use of annotated data in related high-resource languages. In this paper, we evaluate the performance of these methods versus monolingual parsing of Tagalog, an Austronesian language which shares little typological similarity with any existing high-resource languages. We show that a monolingual model developed on minimal target language data consistently outperforms all cross-lingual and multilingual models when no closely-related sources exist for a low-resource language.

1 Introduction

Dependency parsing is a fundamental component of many natural language understanding (Roth and Lapata, 2016; Zhang et al., 2018) and machine translation systems (Ding and Palmer, 2005; Chen et al., 2017). State-of-the-art parsers which annotate syntactic dependencies from raw text have achieved high accuracy for languages with large datasets but continue to yield poor results for low-resource languages which have little to no annotated data (Zeman et al., 2018).

Various methods have been proposed to solve the problem of dependency parsing in a low-resource setting, including cross-lingual transfer (Zeman and Resnik, 2008; McDonald et al., 2011), multilingual modeling (Duong et al., 2015; Ammar et al., 2016), and annotation projection (Hwa et al., 2002; Agić et al., 2016). These methods have been shown to be effective on target languages when datasets (such as treebanks and parallel corpora) are readily available for closely-related source languages; however, would the same hold true in the absence of related language data?

Such is the problem for Tagalog, an Austronesian language of the Philippines with over 25 million speakers worldwide (Eberhard et al., 2020). Despite its widespread use in both spoken and digital domains, it remains largely under-resourced, lacking basic language processing resources such as syntactic treebanks and parsers. Moreover, while dependency treebanks are available for Indonesian, another Austronesian language, the extensive phylogenetic distance between the two languages (Greenhill and Gray, 2009; Reid, 2018) suggests that Indonesian may have too many typological differences to serve as an effective source language for Tagalog.

In this paper, we investigate the performance on Tagalog of three strategies for low-resource dependency parsing: monolingual modeling (using only minimal target language data), cross-lingual modeling (using only data from similar source languages), and multilingual modeling (using data from both target and non-target languages). We present a new Tagalog dependency treebank on which to train and test these approaches together with available treebanks from the Universal Dependencies (UD) project (Zeman et al., 2020), and compare our results to those of previous studies.

2 Related work

To our knowledge, only two dependency treebanks for Tagalog have been created prior to this work. The first is the Tagalog Dependency Treebank (Manguilimotan and Matsumoto, 2011), which includes 2,500

Proceedings of the Fourth Workshop on Universal Dependencies (UDW 2020), pages 8–15
Barcelona, Spain (Online), December 13, 2020

Publication	Treebank	No. of Tokens	Annotation	POS	Feats	Lemm	UAS	LAS
Manguilimotan & Matsumoto (2011)	TDT (Test)	6,557	own native	88.96	—	—	75.90	—
Dehouck & Denis(2019)	TRG	292	UD	—	—	—	70.89	50.38
Kondratyuk & Straka (2019)	TRG	292	UD	61.64	35.27	75.00	64.73	39.38
This work	Ugnayan	1,011	UD	80.54	—	85.47	63.47	55.37

Table 1: Overview of best reported results for dependency parsing of Tagalog treebanks.

sentences annotated with part-of-speech (POS) tags and dependency heads for each word. However, the treebank does not contain labels for dependency relations, nor any other levels of annotation.

The second is the TRG treebank (Samson, 2018) released as part of UD since version 2.2. The treebank contains 55 sentences taken from grammar examples in the Tagalog Reference Grammar (Schachter and Otanes, 1972). Upon inspection, we found that most of these were simple declarative sentences which used the basic predicate-initial word order of Tagalog and contained only one or two arguments. Moreover, the treebank did not contain any examples of other sentence types such as compound sentences, interrogatives, and imperatives, nor of common grammatical components such as adjectival modifiers and plural forms. Table 1 provides a summary of parsing results previously reported for these treebanks.

3 Language data

Tagalog treebank. In order to properly assess the performance of a dependency parser on a target language, we need to have a treebank available in that language which more extensively captures its grammatical complexities and contains universally comparable annotations. Since neither of the previous Tagalog treebanks fulfill both requirements, we developed Ugnayan, a new Tagalog dependency treebank manually annotated in the UD framework. The treebank currently consists of 94 sentences (1011 tokens) taken from educational texts (Almario and Tan, 2016). These sentences include examples of various syntactic phenomena such as compound and complex sentences, clausal modifiers, question forms, and sentence inversion.

Source treebanks. To train the cross-lingual and multilingual models, we also needed to identify which UD languages with available training data are most similar to Tagalog. For this, we used a WALS-reliant distance measure, which compares the typological similarity of a source language S and a target language T based on their features as described in the World Atlas for Language Structures (Dryer and Haspelmath, 2013). We use the distance measure defined by Agić (2017) as the Hamming distance d_h between the WALS feature vectors v_S and v_T for the source and target languages, normalized with respect to the number of features $f_{S,T}$ which are non-empty for both S and T. The resulting WALS measure d_W is given as:

$$d_W(S,T) = \frac{d_h(v_S, v_T)}{f_{S,T}}$$

Using this measure, we found that the five closest source languages for Tagalog included Indonesian (the only other Austronesian UD language), Vietnamese (the only Austro-Asiatic UD language), and three Indo-European languages: Ukrainian, Romanian, and Catalan (see Table 2). Interestingly, we also found that Tagalog was *not* among the five most similar sources for any of the languages above. Unsurprisingly, Ukrainian was much closer to its Slavic neighbors with distances well below 0.2, while Romanian and Catalan were all within distances of 0.3 of other Romance languages. But even among the Asian sources, Indonesian and Vietnamese were much closer to each other, to Mandarin, and even

T	Tagalog	d_W	Indonesian	d_W	Ukrainian	d_W	Vietnamese	d_W	Romanian	d_W	Catalan	d_W
S	Indonesian	0.446	Vietnamese	0.275	Slovenian	0.029	Indonesian	0.275	Italian	0.179	Italian	0.183
	Ukrainian	0.455	Arabic	0.360	Russian	0.054	Mandarin	0.331	Portuguese	0.182	Romanian	0.211
	Vietnamese	0.469	Ukrainian	0.393	Polish	0.087	Ukrainian	0.358	Catalan	0.211	Spanish	0.262
	Romanian	0.471	Mandarin	0.401	Serbo-Croat	0.150	Slovenian	0.385	Bulgarian	0.246	Portuguese	0.267
	Catalan	0.472	Polish	0.416	Estonian	0.175	Portuguese	0.392	Greek	0.256	French	0.297

Table 2: Top 5 most similar source languages S for target languages T, with corresponding WALS distances d_W. Lower d_W indicates higher typological similarity. Distances are symmetric; i.e. $d_W(S,T) = d_W(T,S)$.

Language	Treebank	Train	Dev	Test
Tagalog	Ugnayan			1.0k
Tagalog	TRG			0.3k
Indonesian	GSD	97.5k	12.6k	
Ukrainian	IU	92.4k	12.6k	
Vietnamese	VTB	20.3k	11.5k	
Romanian	Nonstandard	410.4k	18.6k	
Romanian	RRT	185.1k	17.1k	
Catalan	AnCora	416.7k	56.3k	

Table 3: UD v2.6 treebanks used with sizes in tokens.

to other Indo-European languages than they were to Tagalog. This supports the findings by Georgi et al. (2010) that phylogenetic relatedness does not guarantee typological similarity.

For our cross-lingual modeling, we selected all UD v2.6 treebanks with available train and dev sets in the source languages identified above. We also decided to train a model on the Tagalog TRG treebank as a point of comparison. We report the sizes of these data sets in Table 3.

4 Evaluation of parsing models

Methodology. To train parsing models on the treebanks above, we used UDPipe (Straka and Straková, 2017), a pipeline for processing of CoNLL-U treebanks which has served as the baseline system in several CoNLL UD Shared Tasks (Zeman et al., 2017; Zeman et al., 2018). We trained cross-lingual models for each of the identified source treebanks using their specified train and dev partitions, as well as a model using all test data in TRG, and tested these models on all test data in Ugnayan. We performed ten-fold cross-validation to evaluate monolingual models trained on Ugnayan, with a train/dev/test partition of roughly 80/10/10 for each iteration. We also used cross-validation on the multilingual models, which were trained using each of the ten Ugnayan train/dev partitions combined with the individual source treebanks, and tested on the ten Ugnayan test partitions. We used the default settings on UDPipe 3.1 for all training and testing instances.

We then investigated the performance on Ugnayan of the two approaches previously applied to TRG as described in Section 2 by evaluating the pre-trained Indonesian model of Stanza (previously StanfordNLP), a neural pipeline developed by Qi et al. (2020) which reportedly outperforms all submissions to the CoNLL 2018 UD Shared Task for the low-resource categories on all metrics. We selected this as an approximation of the neural parser used by Dehouck & Denis (2019), which was based on the parser of Dozat et al. (2017) currently integrated into Stanza. We also evaluated an updated version of UDify, the multilingual parser by Kondratyuk & Straka (2019).

Results. Table 4 reports the performance of each model tested on the Ugnayan treebank. We recorded

	Parser	Model	Tokenization			Tagging		Parsing	
			Token	Word	Sent	UPOS	Lemm	UAS	LAS
monolingual	UDPipe	tl-ugnayan	**99.27**	**95.67**	95.41	**80.54**	**85.47**	**63.47**	**55.37**
		tl-trg	98.08	86.00	64.04	41.58	65.72	29.23	13.11
cross-lingual	UDPipe	id-gsd	97.40	85.22	90.32	27.45	65.64	18.81	**9.69**
		uk-iu	**97.56**	**85.43**	63.41	12.80	65.55	15.48	8.31
		vi-vtb	74.31	63.81	90.62	22.83	49.44	7.24	3.67
		ro-nonstandard	92.65	81.00	89.80	26.15	39.04	16.56	5.64
		ro-rrt	96.95	84.81	91.98	26.07	48.01	**20.03**	8.15
		ca-ancora	97.40	85.22	94.68	23.70	50.96	14.49	4.89
	Stanza	id-gsd	97.40	85.22	**95.14**	**28.60**	**66.60**	14.88	5.76
multilingual	UDPipe	tl-ugnayan + id-gsd	98.67	94.17	**98.57**	78.16	83.46	48.20	39.73
		tl-ugnayan + uk-iu	99.07	**95.49**	90.46	78.57	**85.32**	**58.54**	48.31
		tl-ugnayan + vi-vtb	98.49	95.13	93.95	**79.28**	84.79	58.05	**48.65**
		tl-ugnayan + ro-nonstd.	98.30	94.69	94.79	71.00	71.18	45.93	34.26
		tl-ugnayan + ro-rrt	**98.71**	95.04	96.42	77.61	80.51	46.70	37.12
		tl-ugnayan + ca-ancora	97.69	94.32	95.23	75.86	80.57	43.01	32.68
	UDify	universal	—*	—*	—*	59.62*	70.92*	51.96*	32.09*

Table 4: F_1 scores on parsing tasks for each parser and model tested on the Ugnayan treebank. Scores for all models trained with Ugnayan data were averaged over 10-fold cross-validation. (*UDify uses gold tokenization.*) **Bold**: highest scores per method. Gray: highest scores across all models.

10

the F_1 scores automatically generated by each of the three parsers on the following tasks: token, word, and sentence tokenization, universal part-of-speech tagging, lemmatization, unlabeled attachment, and labeled attachment. Since the Ugnayan treebank currently does not contain features or language-specific part-of-speech tags, metrics involving those annotations were excluded from the report. For the monolingual and multilingual models trained on Ugnayan data, we present the average scores across ten iterations for cross-validation.

We find that the monolingual Ugnayan models, each trained on less than 90 sentences (or approximately 900 tokens), outperform all other models on the tagging and parsing tasks, and are surpassed only by the Tagalog-Indonesian mixed model on sentence tokenization. These results support the hypothesis by Zeman that "You can actually train a parser and get over 50% accuracy for many languages with just about 100 sentences." (Nivre et al., 2017) which has previously been shown for Indian languages (Ramasamy, 2014), Galician (Garcia et al., 2018), and Faroese (Meechan-Maddon and Nivre, 2019). Garrette and Baldridge (2013) have achieved similar POS tagging performance for Kinyarwanda and Malagasy using similarly limited annotation and graph-based label propagation onto larger amounts of raw text; here we show that supervised modeling using *only* limited annotation can yield good results.

We also observe that the cross-lingual models in particular score much lower than the Ugnayan models or any of the multilingual models on the UPOS, UAS, and LAS metrics. Interestingly, the multilingual models, which use Ugnayan training data together with each of the cross-lingual source treebanks, yield consistently *lower* accuracy than the monolingual models alone. This runs contrary to the findings of Meechan-Maddon & Nivre (2019) who observed that adding related language data to train a multilingual model further improves parsing accuracy. These results suggest that the typological distance between Tagalog and any of its closest UD languages may be too great for the latter to be useful as cross-lingual or multilingual source languages out of the box, and that upweighting of the Ugnayan data may be necessary to account for the size difference between the source and target training corpora.

As for the pre-trained parsers, the Stanza Indonesian model slightly outperforms its UDPipe equivalent on sentence tokenization, POS tagging, and lemmatization, while underperforming on UAS and LAS. Because of the large discrepancy between these results and the 70.89% UAS & 50.38% LAS previously reported for parsing TRG using an Indonesian-only model (Dehouck and Denis, 2019), we further investigated the performance of Indonesians models on both Ugnayan and TRG when gold tokenization and gold tags are made available. We found that UAS and LAS higher than 50% were achievable only with gold tags for both treebanks, and that these results could not be matched when parsing from raw text.

On the other hand, the UDify universal model outperforms all cross-lingual models and even the monolingual TRG model on all tagging and parsing tasks. This is quite remarkable, considering that no annotated Tagalog data was used to train the UDify model, although the availability of gold tokenization may have yielded a performance improvement compared to the other models which parse from raw text. These support the results of Kondratyuk & Straka (2019) which show that UDify's BERT pretraining and multilingual learning produce reasonably high scores even in a zero-resource setting.

5   Extended analysis

Performance on cross-domain data. So far, the experiments we have described above involved the use of Tagalog training and test data from the same corpus (Ugnayan) and domain (educational text). However, as Plank and Agić (2018) have observed, in-domain training naturally results in better performance than the cross-domain scenario for the same amount of data. To test the cross-domain performance of the Ugnayan model, we annotated an additional 7 sentences (265 tokens) of Tagalog news text, and evaluated each of the single-language UDPipe models above on this new dataset. We found that the tagging and parsing results of the Ugnayan model on the news dataset were significantly lower than the in-domain results (see Table 5a). But comparatively, the Ugnayan model still far surpassed any of the other single-language models: Tagalog-TRG achieved the closest scores for each task, followed ID-GSD for UPOS, RO-Nonstandard for UAS, and RO-RRT for LAS respectively. Aside from the dissimilarity of content between domains, the decrease in performance may be attributed to the length of the news sentences—each at least thrice as long as the average sentence in the Ugnayan treebank.

	a. News text (raw)			b. Ugnayan (raw)			c. Ugnayan + POS tags		d. News text + POS tags	
	tl-ugnayan	tl-trg	next-best	es-pud	en-pud	es+en+id	tl-ugnayan	next-best	tl-ugnayan	next-best
UPOS	**64.74**	35.62	28.46 (id-gsd)	25.13	28.98	28.08	—	—	—	—
UAS	**34.22**	18.00	15.83 (ro-nstd)	16.09	13.87	13.05	**74.12**	63.54 (en-pud)	**61.51**	59.25 (en-pud)
LAS	**25.86**	8.22	4.32 (ro-rrt)	5.65	4.81	4.79	**66.89**	49.77 (en-pud)	**52.08**	47.55 (en-pud)

Table 5: F_1 scores for extended analysis experiments. **Bold**: highest scores for each test set.

On historical contact and lexical similarity. In addition to cognates within the Austronesian language family, the Tagalog language is known to have incorporated many loanwords from both Spanish and English as a result of colonial occupation and, in the case of the latter, continued use within the country. To check whether either of these would be viable source languages, we trained single-language UDPipe models using the Spanish and English PUD treebanks. The results were roughly at par with the other source languages tested above (see Table 5b). We also trained a multilingual model using the combination of PUD treebanks for Spanish, English, and Indonesian (to account for Malay cognates), but found no significant improvement. More complex parsing models such as those proposed for code-switching (Partanen et al., 2018; Bhat et al., 2018) may be necessary to effectively utilize these treebanks for Tagalog parsing.

Parsing from gold-tagged data. This paper has largely focused on UD parsing from raw text. In a low-resource context, however, if good POS tagging performance can be achieved for the target language independent of treebank data, delexicalized parsing (which uses only POS tags as input) has been widely thought of as a suitable parsing strategy. In relation to this, we compare the performance of the single-language models when parsing with gold tags available for all test tokens. In contrast, the Ugnayan model achieves the best performance on both in-corpus and news data (see Tables 5c and 5d), outperforming all other single-language models in both cases by a comfortable margin; the next-best source model was English-PUD for both tasks and test sets. These provide partial support for the findings of Falenska and Çetinoğlu (2017), who have demonstrated that lexicalized parsing with limited target data generally outperforms delexicalized parsing with large amounts of source data when no good sources for the target language exist.

6 Conclusion

We have evaluated the performance of monolingual, cross-lingual, and multilingual parsing models on Ugnayan, a new Universal Dependencies treebank for the Tagalog language, given the task of dependency parsing from raw text. We have also identified potential source treebanks for the cross-lingual and multilingual models by measuring the typological similarity between Tagalog and existing high-resource UD languages. We find that a monolingual model trained on roughly 900 tokens of annotated target language data yields better performance than cross-lingual or multilingual models trained on 20,000 or more tokens of annotated data in other high-resource languages if these source languages exhibit low similarity to the target language. We also find that when no annotated training data is available for a target language, a model pre-trained on high-quality multilingual embeddings can give reasonable performance over cross-lingual models trained on individual source languages. We conclude that, when developing a parser for a low-resource language in the absence of any annotations for closely related languages, even a minimal amount of target language annotation greatly improves parsing performance over alternative methods.

We currently plan to expand the Ugnayan treebank in both size and scope, with additional annotations for morphological features and language-specific relation subtypes. Further investigation is warranted on the effects of domain coverage, lexical similarity, and word order differences (Ahmad et al., 2019) on parsing performance, as well as the application of other methods such as data augmentation (Vania et al., 2019) and annotation transfer using parallel corpora (Ma and Xia, 2014) in parser modeling.

Acknowledgements

This work is supported by the U.P. Teaching Assistantship Program. We thank Adrian Vidal, Herlan Benitez, and four anonymous reviewers for their incisive comments and valuable suggestions.

References

Željko Agić, Anders Johannsen, Barbara Plank, Héctor Martínez Alonso, Natalie Schluter, and Anders Søgaard. 2016. Multilingual projection for parsing truly low-resource languages. *Transactions of the Association for Computational Linguistics*, 4:301–312.

Željko Agić. 2017. Cross-lingual parser selection for low-resource languages. In *Proceedings of the NoDaLiDa 2017 Workshop on Universal Dependencies (UDW 2017)*, pages 1–10, Gothenburg, Sweden, May. Association for Computational Linguistics.

Wasi Ahmad, Zhisong Zhang, Xuezhe Ma, Eduard Hovy, Kai Wei Chang, and Nanyun Peng. 2019. On difficulties of cross-lingual transfer with order differences: A case study on dependency parsing. In *Proceedings of the 2019 Conference of the North American Chapter of the Association for Computational Linguistics: Human Language Technologies, Volume 1 (Long and Short Papers)*, pages 2440–2452, Minneapolis, Minnesota, June. Association for Computational Linguistics.

Ani Rosa Almario and Yvette Tan. 2016. *Leveled Readers in Filipino – Isang Kakaibang Araw – Alamin Natin ang mga Anyong-Tubig sa Pilipinas!* Department of Education, Philippines.

Waleed Ammar, George Mulcaire, Miguel Ballesteros, Chris Dyer, and Noah A. Smith. 2016. Many languages, one parser. *Transactions of the Association for Computational Linguistics*, 4:431–444.

Irshad Bhat, Riyaz A. Bhat, Manish Shrivastava, and Dipti Sharma. 2018. Universal dependency parsing for Hindi-English code-switching. In *Proceedings of the 2018 Conference of the North American Chapter of the Association for Computational Linguistics: Human Language Technologies, Volume 1 (Long Papers)*, pages 987–998, New Orleans, Louisiana, June. Association for Computational Linguistics.

Huadong Chen, Shujian Huang, David Chiang, and Jiajun Chen. 2017. Improved neural machine translation with a syntax-aware encoder and decoder. In *Proceedings of the 55th Annual Meeting of the Association for Computational Linguistics (Volume 1: Long Papers)*, pages 1936–1945, Vancouver, Canada, July. Association for Computational Linguistics.

Mathieu Dehouck and Pascal Denis. 2019. Phylogenic multi-lingual dependency parsing. In *Proceedings of the 2019 Conference of the North American Chapter of the Association for Computational Linguistics: Human Language Technologies, Volume 1 (Long and Short Papers)*, pages 192–203, Minneapolis, Minnesota, June. Association for Computational Linguistics.

Yuan Ding and Martha Palmer. 2005. Machine translation using probabilistic synchronous dependency insertion grammars. In *Proceedings of the 43rd Annual Meeting of the Association for Computational Linguistics (ACL'05)*, pages 541–548, Ann Arbor, Michigan, June. Association for Computational Linguistics.

Timothy Dozat, Peng Qi, and Christopher D. Manning. 2017. Stanford's graph-based neural dependency parser at the CoNLL 2017 shared task. In *Proceedings of the CoNLL 2017 Shared Task: Multilingual Parsing from Raw Text to Universal Dependencies*, pages 20–30, Vancouver, Canada, August. Association for Computational Linguistics.

Matthew S. Dryer and Martin Haspelmath, editors. 2013. *WALS Online*. Max Planck Institute for Evolutionary Anthropology, Leipzig.

Long Duong, Trevor Cohn, Steven Bird, and Paul Cook. 2015. Low resource dependency parsing: Cross-lingual parameter sharing in a neural network parser. In *Proceedings of the 53rd Annual Meeting of the Association for Computational Linguistics and the 7th International Joint Conference on Natural Language Processing (Volume 2: Short Papers)*, pages 845–850, Beijing, China, July. Association for Computational Linguistics.

David M. Eberhard, Gary F. Simons, and Charles D. Fennig, editors. 2020. *Ethnologue: Languages of the World*. SIL International, Dallas, Texas, 23 edition.

Agnieszka Falenska and Özlem Çetinoğlu. 2017. Lexicalized vs. delexicalized parsing in low-resource scenarios. In *Proceedings of the 15th International Conference on Parsing Technologies*, pages 18–24, Pisa, Italy, September. Association for Computational Linguistics.

Marcos Garcia, Carlos Gómez-Rodríguez, and Miguel A. Alonso. 2018. New treebank or repurposed? on the feasibility of cross-lingual parsing of Romance languages with Universal Dependencies. *Natural Language Engineering*, 24(1):91–122.

Dan Garrette and Jason Baldridge. 2013. Learning a part-of-speech tagger from two hours of annotation. In *Proceedings of the 2013 Conference of the North American Chapter of the Association for Computational Linguistics: Human Language Technologies*, pages 138–147, Atlanta, Georgia, June. Association for Computational Linguistics.

Ryan Georgi, Fei Xia, and William Lewis. 2010. Comparing language similarity across genetic and typologically-based groupings. In *Proceedings of the 23rd International Conference on Computational Linguistics (Coling 2010)*, pages 385–393, Beijing, China, August. Coling 2010 Organizing Committee.

Simon J. Greenhill and Russell D. Gray. 2009. Austronesian language phylogenies: myths and misconceptions about Bayesian computational methods. In Alexander Adelaar and Andrew Pawley, editors, *Austronesian Historical Linguistics and Culture History: A festschrift for Robert Blust*, chapter 22, pages 375–398. Pacific Linguistics, Canberra, Australia.

Rebecca Hwa, Philip Resnik, Amy Weinberg, and Okan Kolak. 2002. Evaluating translational correspondence using annotation projection. In *Proceedings of the 40th Annual Meeting of the Association for Computational Linguistics*, pages 392–399, Philadelphia, Pennsylvania, USA, July. Association for Computational Linguistics.

Dan Kondratyuk and Milan Straka. 2019. 75 languages, 1 model: Parsing universal dependencies universally. In *Proceedings of the 2019 Conference on Empirical Methods in Natural Language Processing and the 9th International Joint Conference on Natural Language Processing (EMNLP-IJCNLP)*, pages 2779–2795, Hong Kong, China, November. Association for Computational Linguistics.

Xuezhe Ma and Fei Xia. 2014. Unsupervised dependency parsing with transferring distribution via parallel guidance and entropy regularization. In *Proceedings of the 52nd Annual Meeting of the Association for Computational Linguistics (Volume 1: Long Papers)*, pages 1337–1348, Baltimore, Maryland, June. Association for Computational Linguistics.

Erlyn Manguilimotan and Yuji Matsumoto. 2011. Dependency-based analysis for Tagalog sentences. In *Proceedings of the 25th Pacific Asia Conference on Language, Information and Computation*, pages 343–352, Singapore, December. Institute of Digital Enhancement of Cognitive Processing, Waseda University.

Ryan McDonald, Slav Petrov, and Keith Hall. 2011. Multi-source transfer of delexicalized dependency parsers. In *Proceedings of the 2011 Conference on Empirical Methods in Natural Language Processing*, pages 62–72, Edinburgh, Scotland, UK., July. Association for Computational Linguistics.

Ailsa Meechan-Maddon and Joakim Nivre. 2019. How to parse low-resource languages: Cross-lingual parsing, target language annotation, or both? In *Proceedings of the Fifth International Conference on Dependency Linguistics (Depling, SyntaxFest 2019)*, pages 112–120, Paris, France, August. Association for Computational Linguistics.

Joakim Nivre, Daniel Zeman, Filip Ginter, and Francis M. Tyers. 2017. Tutorial on Universal Dependencies: Adding a new language to UD. Presented at the 15th Conference of the European Chapter of the Association for Computational Linguistics, April.

Niko Partanen, Kyungtae Lim, Michael Rießler, and Thierry Poibeau. 2018. Dependency parsing of code-switching data with cross-lingual feature representations. In *Proceedings of the Fourth International Workshop on Computational Linguistics of Uralic Languages*, pages 1–17, Helsinki, Finland, January. Association for Computational Linguistics.

Barbara Plank and Željko Agić. 2018. Distant supervision from disparate sources for low-resource part-of-speech tagging. In *Proceedings of the 2018 Conference on Empirical Methods in Natural Language Processing*, pages 614–620, Brussels, Belgium, October-November. Association for Computational Linguistics.

Peng Qi, Yuhao Zhang, Yuhui Zhang, Jason Bolton, and Christopher D. Manning. 2020. Stanza: A Python natural language processing toolkit for many human languages. In Association for Computational Linguistics (ACL) System Demonstrations.

Logathan Ramasamy. 2014. *Parsing under-resourced languages: Cross-lingual transfer strategies for Indian languages*. Ph.D. thesis, Charles University, Prague, Czech Republic.

Lawrence Reid. 2018. Modeling the linguistic situation in the Philippines. *Senri Ethnological Studies*, 98:91–105.

Michael Roth and Mirella Lapata. 2016. Neural semantic role labeling with dependency path embeddings. In *Proceedings of the 54th Annual Meeting of the Association for Computational Linguistics (Volume 1: Long Papers)*, pages 1192–1202, Berlin, Germany, August. Association for Computational Linguistics.

Stephanie Dawn Samson. 2018. *A treebank prototype of Tagalog*. Undergraduate thesis, University of Tübingen, Germany.

Paul Schachter and Fe T. Otanes. 1972. *Tagalog Reference Grammar*. University of California Press, Berkeley and Los Angeles, California.

Milan Straka and Jana Straková. 2017. Tokenizing, POS tagging, lemmatizing and parsing UD 2.0 with UDPipe. In *Proceedings of the CoNLL 2017 Shared Task: Multilingual Parsing from Raw Text to Universal Dependencies*, pages 88–99, Vancouver, Canada, August. Association for Computational Linguistics.

Clara Vania, Yova Kementchedjhieva, Anders Søgaard, and Adam Lopez. 2019. A systematic comparison of methods for low-resource dependency parsing on genuinely low-resource languages. In *Proceedings of the 2019 Conference on Empirical Methods in Natural Language Processing and the 9th International Joint Conference on Natural Language Processing (EMNLP-IJCNLP)*, pages 1105–1116, Hong Kong, China, November. Association for Computational Linguistics.

Daniel Zeman and Philip Resnik. 2008. Cross-language parser adaptation between related languages. In *Proceedings of the IJCNLP-08 Workshop on NLP for Less Privileged Languages*.

Daniel Zeman, Martin Popel, Milan Straka, Jan Hajič, Joakim Nivre, Filip Ginter, Juhani Luotolahti, Sampo Pyysalo, Slav Petrov, Martin Potthast, Francis Tyers, Elena Badmaeva, Memduh Gokirmak, Anna Nedoluzhko, Silvie Cinková, Jan Hajič jr., Jaroslava Hlaváčová, Václava Kettnerová, Zdeňka Urešová, Jenna Kanerva, Stina Ojala, Anna Missilä, Christopher D. Manning, Sebastian Schuster, Siva Reddy, Dima Taji, Nizar Habash, Herman Leung, Marie-Catherine de Marneffe, Manuela Sanguinetti, Maria Simi, Hiroshi Kanayama, Valeria de Paiva, Kira Droganova, Héctor Martínez Alonso, Çağrı Çöltekin, Umut Sulubacak, Hans Uszkoreit, Vivien Macketanz, Aljoscha Burchardt, Kim Harris, Katrin Marheinecke, Georg Rehm, Tolga Kayadelen, Mohammed Attia, Ali Elkahky, Zhuoran Yu, Emily Pitler, Saran Lertpradit, Michael Mandl, Jesse Kirchner, Hector Fernandez Alcalde, Jana Strnadová, Esha Banerjee, Ruli Manurung, Antonio Stella, Atsuko Shimada, Sookyoung Kwak, Gustavo Mendonça, Tatiana Lando, Rattima Nitisaroj, and Josie Li. 2017. CoNLL 2017 shared task: Multilingual parsing from raw text to universal dependencies. In *Proceedings of the CoNLL 2017 Shared Task: Multilingual Parsing from Raw Text to Universal Dependencies*, pages 1–19, Vancouver, Canada, August. Association for Computational Linguistics.

Daniel Zeman, Jan Hajič, Martin Popel, Martin Potthast, Milan Straka, Filip Ginter, Joakim Nivre, and Slav Petrov. 2018. CoNLL 2018 shared task: Multilingual parsing from raw text to universal dependencies. In *Proceedings of the CoNLL 2018 Shared Task: Multilingual Parsing from Raw Text to Universal Dependencies*, pages 1–21, Brussels, Belgium, October. Association for Computational Linguistics.

Daniel Zeman, Joakim Nivre, et al. 2020. Universal Dependencies 2.6. LINDAT/CLARIAH-CZ digital library at the Institute of Formal and Applied Linguistics (ÚFAL), Faculty of Mathematics and Physics, Charles University.

Yuhao Zhang, Peng Qi, and Christopher D. Manning. 2018. Graph convolution over pruned dependency trees improves relation extraction. In *Proceedings of the 2018 Conference on Empirical Methods in Natural Language Processing*, pages 2205–2215, Brussels, Belgium, October-November. Association for Computational Linguistics.

A Universal Dependencies Conversion Pipeline
for a Penn-format Constituency Treebank

Þórunn Arnardóttir   **Hinrik Hafsteinsson**   **Einar Freyr Sigurðsson**
University of Iceland   The Árni Magnússon Institute for Icelandic Studies

Kristín Bjarnadóttir   **Anton Karl Ingason**
The Árni Magnússon Institute for Icelandic Studies   University of Iceland

Hildur Jónsdóttir   **Steinþór Steingrímsson**
The Árni Magnússon Institute for Icelandic Studies

Abstract

The topic of this paper is a rule-based pipeline for converting constituency treebanks based on the Penn Treebank format to Universal Dependencies (UD). We describe an Icelandic constituency treebank, its annotation scheme and the UD scheme. The conversion is discussed, the methods used to deliver a fully automated UD corpus and complications involved. To show its applicability to corpora in different languages, we extend the pipeline and convert a Faroese constituency treebank to a UD corpus. The result is an open-source conversion tool, published under an Apache 2.0 license, applicable to a Penn-style treebank for conversion to a UD corpus, along with the two new UD corpora.

1 Introduction

The Universal Dependencies (UD) project (Nivre et al., 2016) in version 2.6 consists of 163 treebanks in 92 languages and its standardized annotation scheme makes it an appealing option when creating a treebank. Different methods are available to create a UD treebank, ranging from manual parsing to manual correction of automatic parsing. A UD treebank can also be automatically converted from an existing treebank, which uses a different annotation scheme, as in the present work. We describe a conversion pipeline for a constituency treebank, the Icelandic Parsed Historical Corpus (IcePaHC; Wallenberg et al., 2011; Rögnvaldsson et al., 2011, 2012). We also apply the pipeline to a smaller corpus, the Faroese Parsed Historical Corpus (FarPaHC; Ingason et al., 2012; Ingason et al., 2014), which contains texts in another language but uses the same annotation scheme.[1] With minimal modifications to the pipeline, the conversion is unaffected by linguistic differences in the corpora, which underlines the possibility of using it for other corpora, which use the same scheme.

The conversion uses NLTK (Bird et al., 2009) as a base and it is specific to the annotation scheme of IcePaHC, which itself is based on the Penn Parsed Corpora of Historical English (PPCHE; Kroch and Taylor, 2000; Kroch et al., 2004). Some conversion tools are already available for converting a constituency treebank to the UD scheme, e.g. the PyStanfordDependencies tool[2] and the LTH Constituent-to-Dependency Conversion Tool for Penn-style Treebanks (Johansson and Nugues, 2007).[3] Both tools convert a treebank in the Penn Treebank format to a dependency format. The annotation scheme of the PPCHE is based on the Penn Treebank scheme but the two are not similar enough to be used unaltered with the pre-existing software, so the conversion between the two schemes was deemed to be impractical. Therefore, our conversion tool takes as input an unaltered IcePaHC file and delivers its UD-annotated counterpart. Both IcePaHC and FarPaHC are open-source, published under a CC BY 4.0 license, and we maintain that policy, publishing the conversion tool under an Apache 2.0 license and the resulting UD corpora under a CC BY-SA 4.0 license. The tool is reusable for corpora annotated in the same manner as the constituency treebanks and the source code is available on GitHub.[4] The resulting corpora will be

---

[1]Note that an Icelandic UD treebank (Jónsdóttir and Ingason, 2020) and a Faroese one (Tyers et al., 2018) already exist.
[2]https://github.com/dmcc/PyStanfordDependencies
[3]http://nlp.cs.lth.se/software/treebank_converter/
[4]https://github.com/thorunna/UDConverter

Proceedings of the Fourth Workshop on Universal Dependencies (UDW 2020), pages 16–25
Barcelona, Spain (Online), December 13, 2020

included in the next version of UD, version 2.7, to be released on November 15, 2020.

The paper is structured as follows. Section 2 describes IcePaHC and its annotation scheme and Section 3 compares PPCHE and UD. Section 4 describes the conversion itself, and its stages, i.e. how the files are prepared for the converter (4.1), how the PoS tags and morphological features are mapped (4.2), and how the relational information of heads and dependency are extracted from the IcePaHC format (4.3). Section 5 discusses the FarPaHC conversion, Section 6 considers further use of the converter and the UD treebanks and Section 7 concludes.

2   The Icelandic Parsed Historical Corpus

IcePaHC is a one-million-word, diachronic corpus, which includes texts from the 12th to 21st centuries (Rögnvaldsson et al., 2012). The trees in the corpus have been manually corrected according to the PPCHE annotation scheme, which uses labeled bracketing in the same way as the Penn Treebank. Some minor adjustments were made to adapt the annotation scheme to Icelandic grammar. The PoS tagset used is based on the one particular to the PPCHE, with minor changes to adapt it to Icelandic grammar. The manual IcePaHC annotation process is built on a number of automatic pre-processing steps involving available Natural Language Processing tools for Icelandic, including PoS tagging and shallow parsing in IceNLP (Loftsson and Rögnvaldsson, 2007), and the lemmatizer Lemmald (Ingason et al., 2008).

The IcePaHC scheme splits sentences into matrix clauses and marks their phrases. The phrases and their tokens are marked according to the tagset, which consists of 43 tags and their function tags.[5] Moreover, every token's lemma is displayed along with traces and empty phrases. Figure 1 is an original example from IcePaHC where we show a matrix clause (IP-MAT) with a subject (NP-SBJ), a main verb (VB) in the past tense (D), indicative mood (I), i.e. VBDI, an indirect object (NP-OB2), a direct object (NP-OB1) and a prepositional phrase (PP); the sentence is glossed and translated in (1). This rich annotation scheme makes the conversion to a dependency-based scheme possible.

(1)   Húsbændur-nir   borguðu honum   vatnsburð-inn   á vissum tímum.
        masters.of.house-the.NOM paid   him.DAT water.carrying-the.ACC at certain times
        'The masters of the house paid him for carrying the water at certain times.'

```
( (IP-MAT (NP-SBJ (NS-N Húsbændur$-húsbóndi) (D-N $nir-hinn))
   (VBDI borguðu-borga)
   (NP-OB2 (PRO-D honum-hann))
   (NP-OB1 (N-A vatnsburð$-vatnsburður) (D-A $inn-hinn))
   (PP (P á-á)
      (NP (ADJ-D vissum-viss) (NS-D tímum-tími)))
   (. .-.))  (ID 1883.VOGGUR.NAR-FIC,.37))
```

Figure 1: An example of the IcePaHC format.

The practicality of using a historical (diachronic) corpus for conversion to a descriptive dependency corpus for Icelandic hinges on the fact that Icelandic has changed much less than many other European languages over the last thousand years, syntax included (Rögnvaldsson and Helgadóttir, 2011). This fact by itself supports the use of IcePaHC in the conversion. However, even though Icelandic has changed less than some other languages, it has in fact gone through various syntactic changes. These include changes from OV to VO word order, the emergence of the first position expletive *það* 'it, there' and decreased use of certain types of empty arguments (see Rögnvaldsson, 2005 for an overview).

3   The PPCHE and UD Annotation Schemes

The PPCHE and UD annotation schemes reflect two different ways of parsing a sentence. While the PPCHE scheme denotes phrases by using brackets, the UD scheme connects each token to a single head (Nivre et al., 2016). Every sentence in UD has a root and each dependent relationship a label, but neither are marked in the PPCHE scheme. An obvious difference between the two schemes is how information on a sentence's annotation is displayed. Figure 2 displays the dependency-based counterpart

---

[5]A description of the tagset can be found at `https://linguist.is/icelandic_treebank/Tagset`

to the IcePaHC sentence in Figure 1. Comparing the two, we see that the PPCHE format focuses on phrases while the UD format, which is delivered in CoNLL-U format, lists all tokens in a sentence and gives information on them. The CoNLL-U format consists of ten fields, or columns, as outlined below.

```
ID  FORM           LEMMA        UPOS   XPOS   FEATS                      HEAD  DEPREL  DEPS  MISC
1   Húsbændurnir   húsbóndi     NOUN   NS-N   Case=Nom|Number=Plu...     2     nsubj   _     IFDtag=nkfng
2   borguðu        borga        VERB   VBDI   Number=Plur|Mood=In...     0     root    _     IFDtag=sfg3fp
3   honum          hann         PRON   PRO-D  Case=Dat|Number=Sin...     2     iobj    _     IFDtag=fpkeþ
4   vatnsburðinn   vatnsburður  NOUN   N-A    Case=Acc|Number=Sin...     2     obj     _     IFDtag=nkeog
5   á              á            ADP    P      AdpType=Prep|Degree...     7     case    _     IFDtag=aþ
6   vissum         viss         ADJ    ADJ-D  Case=Dat|Number=Plu...     7     amod    _     IFDtag=lkfpsf
7   tímum          tími         NOUN   NS-D   Case=Dat|Number=Plu...     2     obl     _     IFDtag=nkfþ|
                                                                                             SpaceAfter=No
8   .              .            PUNCT  .      _                          2     punct   _     .
```

Figure 2: An example of the output CoNLL-U format, taken from the Icelandic UD corpus.

- The 1st, 2nd, and 3rd columns contain the word index (ID), the word form (FORM), and the lemma (LEMMA), respectively.

- The 4th column contains the Universal PoS tags (UPOS). This is the UD format tag corresponding to the tag in column 5 and it is discussed further in Section 4.2.

- The 5th column contains the language-specific PoS tags as used in IcePaHC (XPOS).

- The 6th column contains morphological features (FEATS), which give detailed information on a word beyond its UPOS and XPOS tags, for example case, number, tense, voice and person, all depending on word classes. These are discussed further in Section 4.2.

- The 7th column (HEAD) specifies which word the current word is dependent on, by using the head's word index. Each sentence has one root, specified with a '0', on which all other words in the sentence are dependent, whether the relation is direct or through other words.

- The 8th column contains the code for the universal dependencies relation (DEPREL), which states of what kind the relation between a word and its head is, discussed in Section 4.3.

- The 9th column is left blank but it can include information on enhanced dependencies (DEPS).

- Finally, there is a miscellaneous column (MISC). In the case of the Icelandic UD corpus, this column is used for displaying the word's revised Icelandic Frequency Dictionary (IFD) (Pind et al., 1991) morphosyntactic PoS tag, given by the ABLTagger (Steingrímsson et al., 2019), as discussed in Section 4.2.

4 The Conversion

Our method of converting IcePaHC to a UD corpus mainly consists of three steps. The first step involves text cleanup, i.e. removing information not critical to UD. Next is the actual conversion, extracting information on the words and phrase structure and delivering it according to the CoNLL-U format. Lastly, various post-processing is done on the CoNLL-U output files, in order to meet UD format standards. The converter and its resulting treebank have not been evaluated formally but numerous sentences have been checked manually while developing the converter. Systematic evaluation will be carried out in future work.

4.1 Text Cleanup

Since the phrase structure of the sentences in IcePaHC is depicted using brackets, the NLTK CategorizedBracketParseCorpusReader[6] is used. In order for it to operate, some cleanup needs to be carried out on the corpus files. This mostly consists of removing additional information included in the files, e.g. sentence ID tags and the annotators' notes, along with empty lines and extra brackets. In the annotation

---

[6]https://www.nltk.org/_modules/nltk/corpus/reader/bracket_parse.html

scheme, various words that are normally written as one are split into separate tokens, and as the UD format does not follow suit, this process has to be reversed. This includes suffixed articles, e.g. *-in* in *mær-in* 'maiden-the'. These are split from the noun in IcePaHC as separate tokens but appear as a part of the noun in the UD scheme. In addition to these changes, a specific script fixes various minor annotation errors in the corpora themselves, discovered while the converter was being developed.

The second part of this cleanup stage is carried out after the conversion itself, in which the output CoNLL-U files are modified. For example, we transparently portray the cliticization of pronouns to their corresponding verbs in the CoNLL-U output. The annotation scheme splits these pronouns or pronoun clitics from their corresponding verbs such that, e.g., *heyrðu* (imperative 'hear (you)') is split into the imperative form *heyr* 'hear' and the second person singular pronoun clitic *-ðu* 'you'. Keeping consistent with UD annotation guidelines (e.g., for Spanish and German), we adopt the annotation scheme shown in Figure 3, where the word components are shown both combined (ID 1–2) and split (IDs 1 and 2), so that the surface form is apparent but all features and dependency relations of the components are also clear. Included in this last phase of the conversion pipeline is joining together sentences so that a sentence in the final output is defined by a full stop rather than by a matrix clause, to adhere to UD convention.

```
ID    FORM     LEMMA   UPOS
1-2   Heyrðu   _       _
1     Heyr     heyra   VERB
2     þú       þú      PRON
```

Figure 3: An example of a verb-clitic relation marked by index range (further CoNLL-U fields omitted).

4.2 Part-of-Speech Tags and Morphological Features

Information on PoS tags and morphological features is extracted in two ways. To obtain the UD tag, a word's original tag from IcePaHC is used along with handwritten rules, which map each original tag to a corresponding UD tag. The tagset used in the converted corpus consists of 17 tags, displayed in Table 1.

Tags	Description	Tags	Description	Tags	Description
ADJ	adjective	INTJ	interjection	PROPN	proper noun
ADP	adposition	NOUN	noun	SCONJ	subordinating conjunction
ADV	adverb	NUM	numeral	SYM	symbol
AUX	auxiliary verb	PART	particle	VERB	verb
CCONJ	coordinating conjunction	PUNCT	punctuation	X	other
DET	determiner	PRON	pronoun		

Table 1: The UD tags used in the converted corpus.

The mapping from an IcePaHC tag to a UD tag is not always unequivocal since the tagging scheme used in the corpus groups some word classes together, which are kept separate in the UD tagging scheme, and vice versa. An example of this variation is the treatment of quantifiers. They are not included in the PoS categories used in UD but they are included in the IcePaHC tagset, and so an appropriate tag has to be chosen. Some quantifiers are classified as adjectives in UD and some as pronouns, but this distinction is not marked in the original corpus and therefore one tag has to be chosen for all. Since the majority of quantifiers are categorized as adjectives, a decision was made to map quantifiers to adjectives. Another problem of a similar kind is that verbs in IcePaHC can have the same tag whether they are a main or an auxiliary verb, but in UD the tags are different. For example, the Icelandic verb *hafa* 'have' can both act as a main verb, as in (2), and auxiliary verb, as in (3), but it is in both cases tagged as HV in IcePaHC. Therefore, a correct tag has to be chosen based on its context at any given time.

(2)   Hún **hafði** lítinn tíma.
        she   had   little time

(3)   Hún **hafði** notað lítinn tíma.
        she   had   used little time

Although it is thorough, the IcePaHC PoS tagset does not include enough information to display the complete morphological features for all words in the converted corpus, as various grammatical features are omitted from the annotation. For example, grammatical gender (masculine, feminine and neuter) is not present in the tagset, which affects, e.g., nouns and adjectives. This means that a full, automatic conversion from IcePaHC tags to the UD feature scheme, which correctly describes the grammatical features of Icelandic, is not possible in a simple step.

To obtain more information on the tokens, the IcePaHC PoS tags are skipped altogether and the whole text of the treebank is extracted and automatically PoS-tagged using ABLTagger, a state-of-the-art PoS tagger for Icelandic (Steingrímsson et al., 2019). It returns IFD-format PoS tags, mentioned in Section 3, from which morphological features are extracted. The output of this step, although not hand-tagged, is considerably more detailed than the IcePaHC tags, thus providing all necessary morphological features for the output UD corpus, as opposed to the incomplete IcePaHC PoS tags.[7] The tags from the ABLTagger are shown in the miscellaneous (MISC) column in the CoNLL-U format in Figure 2.

4.3   Heads and Dependency Relations

Extracting relational information from the IcePaHC format involves selecting each phrase's head and its dependents and the type of dependency relation. For this, we build on an experimental project carried out by Örvar Kárason.[8] The method of conversion is based on similar work originally done by Magerman (1994) and improved by others (Yamada and Matsumoto, 2003; Johansson and Nugues, 2007).

Each sentence in the given corpus is read with the help of NLTK[9] and information on tags from the original files is also used. A matrix clause is read bottom-up to determine the head of all its subordinate phrases, skipping traces and empty nodes. This head selection is done with handwritten rules that match a phrase tag with its possible heads, which in turn are ordered according to priority so that a correct head is chosen if more than one are possible. The IcePaHC PoS tags are suitable for this task and as they have been manually corrected, no information on phrase type is lost during conversion between tagsets. By selecting phrasal heads bottom-up, we establish a hierarchy where every word or phrase within a phrase is dependent on the head, culminating in the head of the whole sentence, which, according to UD guidelines, is the sentence's root.

When determining the type of dependency relation between two words, information on a phrasal head is used along with the words' PoS tags. Handwritten rules are used to match a tag with its dependency relation, some of which specify the phrasal head's tag to handle ambiguous cases. Again, the detailed tagset of IcePaHC makes this process possible. The dependency relations used can be seen in Table 2. All dependency relations used were crucial for the conversion to be precise and, in most cases, phrasal heads in IcePaHC correspond to a dependency relation. An exception to this are the relations 'acl', 'advcl', 'ccomp' and 'xcomp'. IcePaHC does not make a distinction between 'acl' and 'advcl' on the one hand and 'ccomp' and 'xcomp' on the other, but UD does. These dependency relations are therefore handled specifically and the appropriate relation chosen based on the sentence it appears in.

Not only are the dependency relations important, but their direction is too. Some relations can only go from left to right and others from right to left, and this had to be considered when creating the converter since no equivalent rule is present in IcePaHC. In some cases, the original annotation is changed to adhere to UD rules, for example when a phrase includes two auxiliary verbs, one of them being the phrasal head. The other auxiliary verb cannot be dependent on another auxiliary verb and the relation must therefore be changed, so that both auxiliary verbs are dependent on a main verb.

---

[7]This approach has various issues in itself, both in execution, as it relies on external software, and in output accuracy, as the PoS tagger used is considered state-of-the-art for modern Icelandic, but presumably performs worse as the input texts deviate more from the standard language and orthography. This will eventually be hand-checked and evaluated.

[8]https://github.com/OKarason/venzl

[9]https://www.nltk.org/_modules/nltk/corpus/reader/bracket_parse.html

Dependency relations	Description	Dependency relations	Description
acl	adjectival clause	dislocated	dislocated elements
acl:relcl	relative clause modifier	expl	expletive
advcl	adverbial clause modifier	fixed	fixed multiword expression
advmod	adverbial modifier	flat:foreign	foreign words
amod	adjectival modifier	flat:name	multiword expression with name
appos	appositional modifier	iobj	indirect object
aux	auxiliary	mark	marker
case	case marking	nmod	nominal modifier
cc	coordinating conjunction	nmod:poss	possessive nominal modifier
ccomp	clausal complement	nsubj	nominal subject
compound	compound	nummod	numeric modifier
compound:prt	phrasal verb particle	obj	object
conj	conjunct	obl	oblique nominal
cop	copula	obl:arg	oblique argument
csubj	clausal subject	parataxis	parataxis
dep	unspecified dependency	punct	punctuation
det	determiner	vocative	vocative
discourse	discourse element	xcomp	open clausal complement

Table 2: Dependency relations used in the converted corpus.

5 Extension: Converting a Faroese Treebank

The goal of this project is not to produce a one-shot converter for a specific treebank, but a reusable tool, applicable to treebanks in a similar format. Icelandic and Faroese share a number of linguistic properties that make constituency grammar annotation using the same scheme possible. To demonstrate the reusability of the tool, it was adapted to the Faroese Parsed Historical Corpus (FarPaHC)[10] which uses the same annotation scheme as IcePaHC. It consists of three New Testament translations, i.e. one from the 19th century and two from the 20th century, 53,000 words in total. The 19th century text has not been included in the converted UD treebank yet. Its orthography deviates in many ways from modern spelling; even though the text was modernized for FarPaHC, we decided that before we would add it to the converted treebank, more work on fixing inconsistencies would be needed. A few minor additions were needed for the conversion to be possible, which shows the utility of the conversion pipeline.

The annotation process for FarPaHC is the same as that for IcePaHC; both of them have been manually corrected according to the PPCHE annotation scheme, with some changes to adapt it to Icelandic and Faroese grammar. The tagset used in FarPaHC is for the most part the same as in IcePaHC, which is possible because of the similarities in the languages' grammars. The main difference in the annotation scheme between the two corpora is that lemmas are not shown in FarPaHC. An example of a parsed sentence in FarPaHC is shown in Figure 4, which shows a matrix clause (IP-MAT) with a direct object (NP-OB1), an auxiliary verb (HVPI), a subject (NP-SBJ), a main verb in the past participle (VBN) and two prepositional phrases (PP); the sentence is glossed and translated in (4).

---

[10]https://github.com/einarfs/farpahc

(4)   Hetta havi eg talað til tykkara í líknilsum.
        this   have I said to you.PL in figures

        'I have spoken to you about this figuratively.'

```
( (IP-MAT-SPE (CODE VS:XVI_25J)
    (NP-OB1 (D-A Hetta))
    (HVPI havi)
    (NP-SBJ (PRO-N eg))
    (VBN talað)
    (PP (P til)
       (NP (PRO-G tykkara)))
    (PP (P í)
       (NP (NS-D líknilsum)))
    (.   .-.))   (ID 1936.NTJOHN.REL-BIB,.1310))
```

Figure 4: An example of the FarPaHC format.

Since the two treebanks share an annotation scheme and a tagset, FarPaHC was converted using the methods described in Section 4 with only three modifications. First, the script used to fix various annotation errors in IcePaHC was not used as it did not apply to FarPaHC. No such errors were encountered and such a script was therefore unnecessary. Second, since FarPaHC does not include information on lemmas, neither does the resulting UD corpus. Third, morphological features for FarPaHC were extracted in a different manner. The conversion from IcePaHC relies on an Icelandic high-accuracy PoS tagger for additional information on tokens but no such tagger exists for Faroese. Thus, no third-party software was used for feature extraction and all information was retrieved from the PoS tags themselves. Every component in a tag was mapped to a corresponding morphological feature using handwritten rules, which does not provide all possible features for a given token but does provide more details than solely the tag. These rules can then be built upon if the conversion pipeline is extended for another language with a similar tagset.

The conversion results in a new Faroese UD corpus of 40,000 words to be included in the next UD release. Figure 5 shows the sentence from Figure 4 after having been converted to CoNLL-U. As mentioned, lemmas are not shown, with the exception of the punctuation mark, fewer morphological features are shown and no additional tags are shown in the MISC column. In other respects, all grammatical information represented in the converted Icelandic UD corpus is also represented in the Faroese one.

```
ID  FORM       LEMMA  UPOS   XPOS   FEATS                          HEAD  DEPREL  DEPS  MISC
1   Hetta      _      DET    D-A    Case=Acc                       4     obj     _     _
2   havi       _      AUX    HVPI   Mood=Ind|Tense=Pres            4     aux     _     _
3   eg         _      PRON   PRO-N  Case=Nom                       4     nsubj   _     _
4   talað      _      VERB   VBN    Tense=Past|VerbForm=Part       0     root    _     _
5   til        _      ADP    P      _                              6     case    _     _
6   tykkara    _      PRON   PRO-G  Case=Gen                       4     obl     _     _
7   í          _      ADP    P      _                              8     case    _     _
8   líknilsum  _      NOUN   NS-D   Case=Dat|Definite=Ind|Num...   4     obl     _     SpaceAfter=No
9   .          .      PUNCT  .      _                              4     punct   _     _
```

Figure 5: A sentence converted to UD from FarPaHC.

6   Future Development and Use

IcePaHC currently consists of about one million words but 75,000 additional words were annotated in this project by Kristján Rúnarsson in accordance with the IcePaHC scheme (Rúnarsson and Sigurðsson, 2020). This is done to increase the weight of modern Icelandic in the corpus. These additions, which contain genres not found previously in IcePaHC – parliamentary speeches and sports news texts taken from the Icelandic Gigaword Corpus (Steingrímsson et al., 2018) – will be converted to the UD scheme using the conversion tool described in this paper, making for a close to 1.1 million word corpus. Not only does this enlarge the corpus, but also increases the ratio of modern texts in it.

A possible improvement to the Faroese UD treebank is adding information on lemmas. Since FarPaHC does not include lemmas, a Faroese lemmatizer would have to be used. A few lemmatizers are available for this task (Yildiz and Tantuğ, 2019; Kanerva et al., 2018; Rosa and Mareček, 2018), which would have to be evaluated further in regards to their feasibility.

Compatibility between the current project and the IcePaHC and FarPaHC corpora means that various possibilities exist for future interlinking of projects that make use of the two resources. Firstly, by using the conversion tool for both an Icelandic and a Faroese treebank, we have shown that cross-lingual use is possible. Secondly, with the possibility of user customization, e.g. specifying language-specific rules and parameters, the converter may be applied – with necessary modifications – to various other constituency treebanks to produce new UD corpora for a wide range of languages. These include corpora of Historical Greek (Beck, 2011), Historical Portuguese (Galves, 2018) and Middle Low German (Booth et al., 2020), in addition to PPCHE. Finally, the conversion tool can also be used to convert output from automatic parsers which use the IcePaHC annotation scheme, e.g. IceNeuralParsingPipeline (Arnardóttir and Ingason, 2020), to UD format. Since the original corpus would be automatically created, the UD format output would have to be manually corrected before adding it to the Icelandic UD corpus.

7 Conclusion

In this paper, we have described a rule-based conversion pipeline applicable to the Icelandic Parsed Historical Corpus and the Faroese Parsed Historical Corpus, which results in corpora annotated according to Universal Dependencies. The pipeline is used for converting the two treebanks, delivering a 1 million word Icelandic UD corpus and a 40,000 word Faroese UD corpus. The Icelandic corpus will consequently be among the largest of its type.

We have discussed the benefits of a UD-based corpus for Icelandic and Faroese and why IcePaHC is a good candidate for building the conversion on. The process of converting sentences was described and the methodology behind it, extracting information needed for a UD corpus by using both information included in the IcePaHC annotation scheme and a state-of-the-art PoS tagger for Icelandic. We also discussed some challenges faced because of the different annotation scheme of the original treebank and UD and how these were dealt with. We demonstrated the conversion pipeline's applicability to different languages by converting a Faroese constituency treebank to a UD corpus using the pipeline. Lastly, we discussed further possibilities in using the converter and the UD corpora with available language resources along with the 75,000 word addition to IcePaHC, which will be converted using the pipeline and added to the Icelandic UD corpus.

The benefits of an Icelandic Universal Dependencies corpus are significant, as the UD annotation scheme offers a standard parsing framework across different languages. The information that is annotated in IcePaHC is a superset of what is required by the UD scheme and this makes conversion between the two formats a feasible approach to creating a UD treebank for Icelandic. Furthermore, the open-source policy of IcePaHC as well as the global UD project is important and therefore maintained in this project. The conversion tool is released under an Apache 2.0 license on GitHub[11] and the two UD corpora are included in the next release of UD under a CC BY-SA 4.0 license.

8 Acknowledgements

This project was funded by the Strategic Research and Development Programme for Language Technology, grant no. 180020-5301. The conversion of the Faroese corpus was funded by the Icelandic Student Innovation Fund, grant no. 206457-0091. Thanks are due to Örvar Kárason, whose work was used as a basis for the conversion. We also thank Kristján Rúnarsson for helpful discussions. Finally, we would like to thank two anonymous reviewers for their helpful comments.

---

[11]`https://github.com/thorunna/UDConverter`

References

Þórunn Arnardóttir and Anton Karl Ingason. 2020. A neural parsing pipeline for Icelandic using the Berkeley neural parser. In Costanza Navarretta and Maria Eskevich, editors, *Proceedings of CLARIN 2020*, pages 48–51.

Jana E. Beck. 2011. Penn Parsed Corpora of Historical Greek (PPCHiG). http://ling.upenn.edu/~janabeck/greek-corpora.html.

Steven Bird, Ewan Klein, and Edward Loper. 2009. *Natural Language Processing with Python*. O'Reilly Media, Sebastopol, CA.

Hannah Booth, Anne Breitbarth, Aaron Ecay, and Melissa Farasyn. 2020. A Penn-style treebank of Middle Low German. In *Proceedings of The 12th Language Resources and Evaluation Conference (LREC 2020)*, pages 766–775, Marseille, France. European Language Resources Association.

Charlotte Galves. 2018. The Tycho Brahe Corpus of Historical Portuguese: Methodology and results. *Linguistic Variation*, 18(1):49–73.

Anton Karl Ingason, Sigrún Helgadóttir, Hrafn Loftsson, and Eiríkur Rögnvaldsson. 2008. A Mixed Method Lemmatization Algorithm Using a Hierarchy of Linguistic Identities (HOLI). In *Proceedings of Sixth International Conference on Natural Language Processing*, GoTAL 2008, pages 205–216, Gothenburg, Sweden.

Anton Karl Ingason, Eiríkur Rögnvaldsson, Einar Freyr Sigurðsson, and Joel C. Wallenberg. 2012. Faroese Parsed Historical Corpus (FarPaHC). Version 0.1.

Anton Karl Ingason, Hrafn Loftsson, Eiríkur Rögnvaldsson, Einar Freyr Sigurðsson, and Joel Wallenberg. 2014. Rapid deployment of phrase structure parsing for related languages: A case study of Insular Scandinavian. In *Proceedings of the Ninth International Conference on Language Resources and Evaluation (LREC 2014)*, pages 91–95, Reykjavík, Iceland. European Language Resources Association.

Richard Johansson and Pierre Nugues. 2007. Extended constituent-to-dependency conversion for English. In *Proceedings of the 16th Nordic Conference of Computational Linguistics (NODALIDA 2007)*, pages 105–112, Tartu, Estonia. University of Tartu, Estonia.

Hildur Jónsdóttir and Anton Karl Ingason. 2020. Creating a parallel Icelandic dependency treebank from raw text to Universal Dependencies. In *Proceedings of The 12th Language Resources and Evaluation Conference (LREC 2020)*, pages 2924–2931, Marseille, France. European Language Resources Association.

Jenna Kanerva, Filip Ginter, Niko Miekka, Akseli Leino, and Tapio Salakoski. 2018. Turku neural parser pipeline: An end-to-end system for the CoNLL 2018 shared task. In *Proceedings of the CoNLL 2018 Shared Task: Multilingual Parsing from Raw Text to Universal Dependencies*, pages 133–142, Brussels, Belgium. Association for Computational Linguistics.

Anthony S. Kroch and Ann Taylor. 2000. Penn-Helsinki Parsed Corpus of Middle English. CD-ROM. Second edition. Size: 1.3 million words.

Anthony S. Kroch, Beatrice Santorini, and Lauren Delfs. 2004. Penn-Helsinki Parsed Corpus of Early Modern English. CD-ROM. First Edition. Size: 1.8 million words.

Hrafn Loftsson and Eiríkur Rögnvaldsson. 2007. IceNLP: A Natural Language Processing Toolkit for Icelandic. In *Proceedings of Interspeech – Speech and language technology for less-resourced languages*, Interspeech 2007, Antwerp, Belgium.

David Mitchell Magerman. 1994. *Natural Language Parsing As Statistical Pattern Recognition*. Ph.D. thesis, Stanford University.

Joakim Nivre, Marie-Catherine de Marneffe, Filip Ginter, Yoav Goldberg, Jan Hajic, Christopher D. Manning, Ryan McDonald, Slav Petrov, Sampo Pyysalo, Natalia Silveira, Reut Tsarfaty, and Daniel Zeman. 2016. Universal Dependencies v1: A multilingual treebank collection. In *Proceedings of the Tenth International Conference on Language Resources and Evaluation (LREC 2016)*, pages 1659–1666, Paris, France. European Language Resources Association.

Jörgen Pind, Friðrik Magnússon, and Stefán Briem. 1991. *Íslensk orðtíðnibók [The Icelandic Frequency Dictionary]*. The Institute of Lexicography, University of Iceland, Reykjavík.

Eiríkur Rögnvaldsson and Sigrún Helgadóttir. 2011. Morphological tagging of Old Icelandic texts and its use in studying syntactic variation and change. In Caroline Sporleder, Antal van den Bosch, and Kalliopi Zervanou, editors, *Language Technology for Cultural Heritage: Selected Papers from the LaTeCH Workshop Series*, pages 63–76, Berlin. Springer.

Eiríkur Rögnvaldsson, Anton Karl Ingason, Einar Freyr Sigurðsson, and Joel Wallenberg. 2011. Creating a dual-purpose treebank. *JLCL*, 26(2):139–150.

Eiríkur Rögnvaldsson, Anton Karl Ingason, Einar Freyr Sigurðsson, and Joel Wallenberg. 2012. The Icelandic Parsed Historical Corpus (IcePaHC). In *Proceedings of the Eight International Conference on Language Resources and Evaluation (LREC 2012)*, pages 1977–1984, Istanbul, Turkey. European Language Resource Association.

Eiríkur Rögnvaldsson. 2005. Setningafræðilegar breytingar í íslensku. In Höskuldur Thráinsson, editor, *Setningar. Handbók um setningafræði. Íslensk tunga III*, pages 602–635. Almenna bókafélagið, Reykjavík.

Rudolf Rosa and David Mareček. 2018. CUNI x-ling: Parsing under-resourced languages in CoNLL 2018 UD shared task. In *Proceedings of the CoNLL 2018 Shared Task: Multilingual Parsing from Raw Text to Universal Dependencies*, pages 187–196, Brussels, Belgium. Association for Computational Linguistics.

Kristján Rúnarsson and Einar Freyr Sigurðsson. 2020. Parsing Icelandic Alþingi transcripts: Parliamentary speeches as a genre. In *Proceedings of the Second ParlaCLARIN Workshop*, pages 44–50, Marseille, France. European Language Resources Association.

Steinþór Steingrímsson, Sigrún Helgadóttir, Eiríkur Rögnvaldsson, Starkaður Barkarson, and Jón Guðnason. 2018. Risamálheild: A Very Large Icelandic Text Corpus. In *Proceedings of the Eleventh International Conference on Language Resources and Evaluation (LREC 2018)*, Miyazaki, Japan. European Language Resources Association.

Steinþór Steingrímsson, Örvar Kárason, and Hrafn Loftsson. 2019. Augmenting a BiLSTM tagger with a morphological lexicon and a lexical category identification step. In *Proceedings of RANLP 2019*, Varna, Bulgaria.

Francis M. Tyers, Mariya Sheyanova, Alexandra Martynova, Pavel Stepachev, and Konstantin Vinogradovsky. 2018. Multi-source synthetic treebank creation for improved cross-lingual dependency parsing. In *Proceedings of the Second Workshop on Universal Dependencies (UDW 2018)*, pages 144–150.

Joel C. Wallenberg, Anton Karl Ingason, Einar Freyr Sigurðsson, and Eiríkur Rögnvaldsson. 2011. Icelandic Parsed Historical Corpus (IcePaHC). Version 0.9. http://www.linguist.is/icelandic_treebank.

Hiroyasu Yamada and Yuji Matsumoto. 2003. Statistical Dependency Analysis with Support Vector Machines. In *The 8th International Workshop of Parsing Technologies (IWPT2003)*, pages 195–206, Nancy, France.

Eray Yildiz and A. Cüneyd Tantuğ. 2019. Morpheus: A neural network for jointly learning contextual lemmatization and morphological tagging. In *Proceedings of the 16th Workshop on Computational Research in Phonetics, Phonology, and Morphology*, pages 25–34, Florence, Italy, August. Association for Computational Linguistics.

Corpus evidence for word order freezing in Russian and German

Aleksandrs Berdicevskis
Språkbanken
University of Gothenburg
Gothenburg, Sweden
aleksandrs.berdicevskis@gu.se

Alexander Piperski
School of Philological Studies
HSE University
Moscow, Russia
apiperski@hse.ru

Abstract

We use Universal Dependencies treebanks to test whether a well-known typological trade-off between word order freedom and richness of morphological marking of core arguments holds within individual languages. Using Russian and German treebank data, we show that the following phenomenon (sometimes dubbed *word order freezing*) does occur: those sentences where core arguments cannot be distinguished by morphological means (due to case syncretism or other kinds of ambiguity) have more rigid order of subject, verb and object than those where unambiguous morphological marking is present. In ambiguous clauses, word order is more often equal to the one which is default or dominant (most frequent) in the language. While Russian and German differ with respect to how exactly they mark core arguments, the effect of morphological ambiguity is significant in both languages. It is, however, small, suggesting that languages do adapt to the evolutionary pressure on communicative efficiency and avoidance of redundancy, but that the pressure is weak in this particular respect.

1 Introduction

Languages are optimized for communicative efficiency, at least in some aspects of their structure (Gibson et al., 2019). One manifestation of evolutionary pressures for optimization is the trade-off in core argument marking: languages tend to have either rigid order of subject (S), verb (V) and object (O) or rich morphological marking that shows which argument is the subject and which is the object, rarely both, and never neither (Sinnemäki, 2014). This tendency, long recognized in qualitative linguistic literature (Sapir, 1921; Kiparsky, 1997), has recently received strong quantitative support, both from grammar-based (Sinnemäki, 2014), corpus-based (Futrell et al., 2015; Koplenig et al., 2017; Levshina, 2019) and experimental (MacWhinney et al., 1984; Fedzechkina et al., 2012) studies.

The explanation of the trade-off is quite straightforward. For successful communication, it is convenient to have the semantic distinction between S and O overtly coded. However, one means of coding (either syntactic or morphological) is enough, two are redundant, and languages optimize also by eliminating redundancy (Berdicevskis and Eckhoff, 2016; Fedzechkina et al., 2017).

To consider an example: English is a language with a very rigid word order (SVO) and almost no morphological marking, while Russian is exactly the opposite: there is rich morphological marking (through nominal cases and verbal agreement), and all six word order permutations are grammatically possible. It should be highlighted that both word order freedom and presence of morphological marking are gradual phenomena, not binary. English does have morphological marking for pronominal arguments (both cases and verbal agreement), while Russian word order is not entirely free, as it usually conveys pragmatic and/or stylistic information. A corpus-based approach allows us to adequately quantify these phenomena.

All quantitative typological studies cited above focused on the correlation *across* languages. We test whether an equivalent tendency can be observed *within* a language. In other words, in the previous studies, datapoints were languages, while in ours, datapoints are clauses.

Proceedings of the Fourth Workshop on Universal Dependencies (UDW 2020), pages 26–33
Barcelona, Spain (Online), December 13, 2020

More specifically, we test the following hypothesis: is it true that if a language has relatively free word order, then those clauses where S and O cannot be distinguished by morphological means (due to case syncretism or other kinds of ambiguity) will have more rigid order of S, V and O than those clauses where unambiguous morphological marking is available? This phenomenon has sometimes been dubbed *word order freezing* in the literature (see section 2).

We also make a stronger prediction: in ambiguous clauses, word order will be more often equal to the one which is basic or dominant (most frequent) in the language (for instance, SVO for Russian). Note that the second prediction entails the first, but not vice versa, at least in principle.

2 Word order freezing

One of the earliest explicit wordings of the word order freezing hypothesis belongs to Jakobson (1971, p. 585): "If in a language like Russian the nominal subject and object are not distinguished by morphological means, the relative order SO is compulsory". Since then, word order freezing has been claimed to exist in Russian (Mahowald, 2011), Korean, Bulgarian, Papuan languages (Lee, 2001), Japanese (Flack, 2004), German (Vogel, 2004), Hindi and Urdu (Mohanan, 1994).

There is, however, a dearth of quantitative corpus-based studies. Bouma and Hendriks (2012) demonstrate word order freezing for Dutch, while Øvrelid (2004) does the same for Norwegian. Note, however, that both Dutch and Norwegian have relatively rigid word order (and no case marking on nouns), and virtually the only deviation from the default word order (SVO) that is possible is OVS (which results from object fronting). It is thus unclear whether the results of these studies can be generalized to typologically different languages. In addition, Øvrelid (2004) focuses on a somewhat different facet of word order freezing hypothesis ("word order freezes when properties of the arguments are maximally marked in some sense") and does not directly test the role of morphological ambiguity.

We are interested in directly testing the "morphological ambiguity freezes the word order" hypothesis on two languages, Russian and German, using corpus data from Universal Dependencies (UD) 2.6 (Zeman et al., 2020). The choice of languages is driven by the following considerations: a) languages must have relatively free word order; b) there must be a substantial proportion of nominative-accusative syncretism in the nominal paradigm; c) large treebanks must be available (a pilot study on Russian data suggests that the effect is not visible on smaller datasets). Given the current state of the UD collection, that basically leaves Germanic and Slavic languages, of which we choose one language per group.

We will call a clause containing S, V and O "unambiguous" if S and O can be distinguished from morphological marking and "ambiguous" if they cannot. We will ignore semantic and pragmatic information. In the vast majority of clauses, S and O can be distinguished using context, background knowledge or common sense. For instance, in a German sentence like *Die Zahlung wickelt die Deutsche Bank ab* 'Deutsche Bank is processing the payment', it is clear that *Die Zahlung* 'payment' is the object and *die Deutsche Bank* 'Deutsche Bank' is the subject, because banks normally process payments, and not vice versa. It is, however, extremely difficult to formalize and quantify these factors (besides, they are orthogonal to our hypothesis about formal marking).

Likewise, we ignore other factors that might influence word order, including, for instance, information structure, dependency locality (Futrell et al., 2020), predictability (Ferrer Cancho, 2017), the length (weight) of arguments (Wasow, 1997) etc. Unlike Bouma and Hendriks (2012) and Øvrelid (2004), we will not use animacy and definiteness as predictors. First, the availability of this information varies: German treebanks are not annotated for animacy, while Russian treebanks are not annotated for definiteness. Second, animacy and definiteness strongly overlap with availability of overt morphological marking of syntactic role (in Russian, for instance, animate arguments will almost always be marked), which makes it difficult to reliably estimate their contribution.

3 Materials and methods

For Russian, we concatenate all available UD treebanks, which yields 73K sentences with 1.3M tokens. For German, we concatenate HDT and GSD (excluding the smaller treebanks, PUD and LIT, that lack the necessary annotation[1]), which yields 206K sentences with 3.7M tokens.

We extract all clauses that contain a verb that has a nominal subject (related via NSUBJ) and a nominal object (OBJ). We include both proper and common nouns, but exclude arguments that belong to any other part of speech (pronouns etc.) to avoid adding potential confounds. If there are several coordinated arguments, we include only those that satisfy these criteria. See below for other, language-specific filters.

To establish whether a clause is ambiguous we check whether at least one of the arguments and/or the verb mark which argument is the subject and which is the object. For every argument, all available conjuncts (that pass the filter) are checked, and if at least one of them is marked, then the argument is considered marked. We treat morphological ambiguity/markedness as a binary feature, not trying to quantify degree of markedness. To achieve high accuracy, we do it using a set of language-specific handcrafted rules (see below). We manually check the accuracy of the algorithms on subsample of 100 clauses, randomly drawn from all suitable clauses.

3.1 Russian

We accept only nominative subjects and accusative objects. This filter excludes a small amount of non-canonical arguments (arguments of a negated verb in genitive; experiencer subjects in dative; objects of certain verbs in dative and instrumental; arguments that have a numeral modifier and get their case from the numeral rather from the verb; idiomatic constructions etc.) and misannotations.

An argument is considered non-marked if it is:

1. masculine...
    (a) and inanimate (nominative and accusative are syncretic);
    (b) and animate, and the lemma ends in a vowel other than *-a* or *-ja* (indeclinable with very few exceptions);
2. or feminine...
    (a) and not animate and plural, and the lemma ends in ' (soft sign) (nominative and accusative are syncretic);
    (b) and ends in a vowel other than *-a* or *-ja* (indeclinable);
    (c) and inanimate and plural (nominative and accusative are syncretic);
3. or neuter and not animate and plural (nominative and accusative are syncretic)...
4. or a plurale tantum (nominative and accusative are syncretic).

Otherwise the argument is considered marked, since accusative is different from nominative. If an argument is non-marked according to rules 1b, 2a (singular only) or 2b, but has an adjectival or a pronominal modifier (via AMOD or DET) and the modifier is not an indeclinable possessive pronoun (*ego* 'his', *ee* 'her', *ih* 'their'), then the argument is considered marked, since nominative and accusative are not syncretic for the modifier. This rule may generate a small amount of false positives due to (rarely occurring) indeclinable adjectives.

Russian verbs agree with the subject in number and, in past tense singular, also in gender. Thus, a verb is considered marked iff:

1. it is in past tense singular and subject and object have different genders;
2. subject and object have different numbers. If an argument is in singular, but has at least one conjunct, it is treated as plural, since plural agreement is most likely in such cases.

The manual spotcheck of 100 randomly selected clauses yielded an accuracy of 0.99 at the clause-annotation level. The only error (ambiguous clause labelled as non-ambiguous) is due to a misannotation in the treebank. In addition, two errors in labelling of individual arguments were discovered (but the clause as a whole was still labelled correctly), the rule that generated one of them was corrected in the script, no measures were taken against the other one.

---

[1]LIT lacks morphological features; PUD, unlike the other treebanks, does not have XPOS tags VAFIN and VMFIN, which are convenient for identifying auxiliary verbs.

3.2 German

We aspire to apply the same filter as for Russian, but the situation is complicated by the fact that most nouns in the German treebanks are not annotated for case (German has much less overt case markers on nouns than Russian). For this reason, we adapt the filter, excluding arguments that have any dependent in dative or a dependent preposition in accusative.

In addition, we restrict our analysis to main clauses in German, because in subordinate clauses SOV order is almost obligatory.

An argument is considered non-marked by default, since noun modifiers (articles, pronouns, and adjectives) do not distinguish nominative and accusative in feminine and neuter singular as well as in plural.

An argument is considered marked if it is masculine and singular and has a modifier (via AMOD or DET or their variants, such as via DET:POSS). The rationale is that most nouns except for a small group called "weak declension" (*Löwe* 'lion', *Name* 'name') and substantives derived from adjectives (*Abgeordneter* 'member of parliament') are unmarked for case, and case marking is expressed on dependent words.

German verbs agree with the subject in number. A verb is considered marked if its subject and object have different numbers. If an argument is in singular, but has at least one conjunct, it is treated as plural, since plural agreement is most likely in such cases.

If an argument has a dependent numeral, it is considered plural, even if it is annotated as singular (e.g., *zwei Prozent* 'two percent'). Many proper nouns (30%) lack annotation for number in the treebanks. In such cases, we consider them singular, since proper nouns are most often singular (this is true for 97% of the proper nouns annotated for number).

The manual spotcheck of 100 randomly selected clauses yielded an accuracy of 0.95. The errors are mostly due to incorrect annotation of compounds in the corpus.

4 Results

Our final dataset contains 8,575 clauses for Russian and 53,373 for German (remember that for German we have main clauses only, see section 3.2). Table 1 provides information about the proportion of ambiguous and non-ambiguous clauses and about how exactly the ambiguity is resolved (by marking subject, object, verb or several words at once).

The strategies of morphological marking are clearly different for the two languages. For Russian, the distribution is more uniform. The most frequent strategy is marking subject and verb, but not the object. It is followed by the following strategies: marking subject only; marking verb only; not marking anything; marking everything. The remaining strategies are less common, marking object only is the least frequent one. For German, the two most frequent strategies (marking verb only; not marking anything) account for 71% of all cases, followed by marking object only, the rest are less common, marking everything is virtually non-existent (it happens when both arguments are masculine singular and have a modifier, and in addition one and only one of them is coordinated with other nouns and thus behaves as if in plural). Most importantly for the current study, the proportion of ambiguous sentences is 13% for Russian and 35% for German.

The proportions of different word orders in ambiguous and unambiguous clauses are provided in Table 2. For both languages, the proportion of the basic word order (SVO) is slightly higher for ambiguous sentences, the other word orders either experience small drops in frequency or remain unchanged. Note that the distribution is different across languages: in Russian, SVO accounts for 85% of clauses (across all clauses, both ambiguous and unambiguous), followed by OVS (9%), the other four orders are infrequent, VSO extremely infrequent. In German, SVO accounts only for 56%, followed by VSO (35%), OVS (8%), the other three orders are extremely infrequent.

To quantify word order freedom, we calculate Shannon entropy (in bits) over the six possible word orders, see Table 2. In both languages the entropy is lower for the ambiguous clauses, which is in line with our main prediction. To estimate whether the difference is significant we perform a bootstrap test. We take the set of all clauses, randomly split it into two subsets A (same size as the set of unambiguous clauses) and B (same size as the set of ambiguous clauses), and calculate the absolute difference between word-order entropies for A and B. We repeat the procedure 10,000 times and estimate p-value as the

Subject	Object	Verb	% in Russian	% in German
yes	yes	yes	12	0.2
yes	yes	no	8	3
yes	no	yes	23	6
yes	no	no	16	6
no	yes	yes	8	4
no	yes	no	6	10
no	no	yes	15	36
no	no	no	13	35

Table 1: Proportions of various morphological marking strategies (out of 8,575 clauses for Russian and 53,373 for German); "yes" and "no" denotes whether the respective word disambiguates the clause.

	Russian		German	
	unamb.	amb.	unamb.	amb.
SVO	84.18	87.15	55.38	58.55
SOV	1.27	1.07	0.94	0.90
VSO	0.62	0.36	35.38	33.51
VOS	2.66	2.77	0.25	0.33
OSV	2.28	1.07	0.06	0.07
OVS	8.99	7.58	7.98	6.65
Entropy	0.91	0.76	1.39	1.34

Table 2: Proportions of word orders, in %; entropy of word order.

proportion of splits that yielded the absolute difference larger than or equal to the absolute difference between ambiguous and unambiguous clauses. The resulting p-values are 0.004 for Russian and 0 for German.

To test whether the observed differences for the proportion of the basic word order are significant (i.e. whether our second prediction holds), we apply the same kind of test: p-values are 0.011 for Russian and 0 for German. The bootstrap tests are visualized on Figure 1.

It can be argued that potential word-order preferences of individual verbs should be controlled for in order to ensure more rigorous testing. To do that, we fit a mixed-effects logistic regression model with word order as the dependent variable. To make the model simpler and more interpretable, we treat word order as a binary variable: SO (reference level) or OS. The independent variable is whether the clause is unambiguous (reference level), with by-verb random intercept and random slope. In *lme4* (Bates et al., 2015) notation, the model looks as follows:

$$wo \sim ambiguity + (1 + ambiguity|verb)$$

We performed the calculations in *R* (R Core Team, 2020), using the `lmerTest` package to calculate p-values (Kuznetsova et al., 2017). The summary of the model is presented in Table 3.

For both languages, the coefficient for ambiguity is negative, meaning that in ambiguous clauses the probability of OS word order is lower (and the probability of the basic word order, SO, is higher). For Russian, the significance of the coefficient is slightly higher than the 0.05 threshold, for German, it is much lower.

5 Discussion

Both in Russian and German, both our predictions are confirmed: clauses where subject and object are not marked morphologically have lower word-order entropy and higher proportion of basic word order. According to the bootstrap test, the differences are significant, but according to a mixed-effect logistic

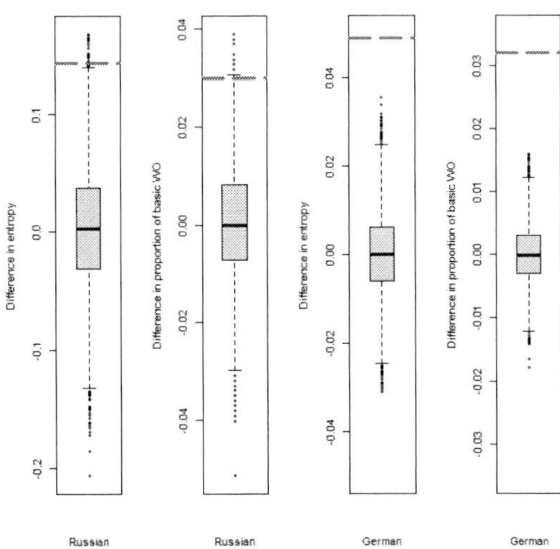

Figure 1: Boxplots showing the distribution of bootstrap test results for difference between word-order entropies and proportions of basic word order. The dashed line denotes the observed difference between ambiguous and unambiguous clauses.

Predictor	Estimate	SE	z value	p value
Russian				
(Intercept)	-2.11	0.06	-34	<0.001*
ambiguous=Yes	-0.58	0.30	-2	0.057
German				
(Intercept)	-2.85	0.07	-44	<0.001*
ambiguous=Yes	-0.25	0.07	-4	<0.001*

Table 3: Summary of the logistic-regression model: word order (whether it is OS) as predicted by clause ambiguity with by-verb random effects. Asterisk denotes significance at the 0.05 level.

regression model with by-verb random slope and intercept the effect of morphological ambiguity is significant only for German, but not for Russian.

Interestingly, Russian and German exhibit considerable differences with respect to how exactly the ambiguity is resolved (by marking subject, object, verb or several words at once) and to the distribution of word orders. Nonetheless, the effect is clearly present in both languages, and in both languages it is small. This implies that the pressure for word-order freezing is relatively weak (and probably mitigated by other factors).

Pace Jakobson (1971), the trade-off is not absolute: morphologically ambiguous clauses where word order is different from the basic one do occur in both languages. We inspected such counterexamples in order to see whether any factors that could explain why these clauses do not have any formal marking of core arguments, but did not discover any patterns. Absence of formal marking, however, is not surprising, given that in most cases the clauses can be disambiguated using semantic and pragmatic information, as well as context and background knowledge.

Further work in this direction might include psycholinguistic experiments (do human beings rely more on word order when interpreting morphologically ambiguous sentences?), diachronic studies (do morphological changes in Russian, German, or other relevant languages that increase or decrease the degree of syncretism affect word order) and machine-learning experiments designed to determine to what extent state-of-the-art parsers rely on morphology and word order (using e.g. ablation techniques à la Berdicevskis and Eckhoff (2016))

The scripts for morphological analysis and statistical tests, as well as detailed results are openly available[2].

Acknowledgements

We are grateful to Andres Karjus for running a pilot study on Estonian (which showed that there is not enough syncretism), to Hanne Eckhoff for advice on Ancient Greek (same conclusion), to a group of high-school students at the educational centre "Sirius" (Sochi, Russia) for performing pilot studies on Russian and German and to teacher assistant Anastasiia Puchkova for supervising them.

References

Douglas Bates, Martin Mächler, Ben Bolker, and Steve Walker. 2015. Fitting linear mixed-effects models using lme4. *Journal of Statistical Software, Articles*, 67(1):1–48.

Aleksandrs Berdicevskis and Hanne Eckhoff. 2016. Redundant features are less likely to survive: Empirical evidence from the Slavic languages. In S.G. Roberts, C. Cuskley, L. McCrohon, L. Barceló-Coblijn, O. Fehér, and T. Verhoef, editors, *The Evolution of Language: Proceedings of the 11th International Conference (EVOLANGX11)*. Online at http://evolang.org/neworleans/papers/85.html.

Gerlof Bouma and Petra Hendriks. 2012. Partial word order freezing in Dutch. *Journal of Logic, Language and Information*, 21(1):53–73.

Maryia Fedzechkina, T Florian Jaeger, and Elissa L Newport. 2012. Language learners restructure their input to facilitate efficient communication. *Proceedings of the National Academy of Sciences*, 109(44):17897–17902.

Maryia Fedzechkina, Elissa L. Newport, and T. Florian Jaeger. 2017. Balancing effort and information transmission during language acquisition: Evidence from word order and case marking. *Cognitive Science*, 41(2):416–446.

Ramon Ferrer Cancho. 2017. The placement of the head that maximizes predictability: An information theoretic approach. *Glottometrics*, 39:38–71.

Kathryn Flack. 2004. Ambiguity avoidance as contrast preservation: Case and word order freezing in Japanese. In Leah Bateman, Michael O'Keefe, Ellen Reilly, and Adam Werle, editors, *University of Massachusetts Occasional Papers in Linguistics 32: Papers in Optimality Theory III*. Booksurge Publishing.

---

[2]https://github.com/AleksandrsBerdicevskis/word-order-freezing

Richard Futrell, Kyle Mahowald, and Edward Gibson. 2015. Quantifying word order freedom in dependency corpora. In *Proceedings of the third international conference on dependency linguistics (Depling 2015)*, pages 91–100.

Richard Futrell, Roger P Levy, and Edward Gibson. 2020. Dependency locality as an explanatory principle for word order. *Language*, 96(2):371–412.

Edward Gibson, Richard Futrell, Steven P Piantadosi, Isabelle Dautriche, Kyle Mahowald, Leon Bergen, and Roger Levy. 2019. How efficiency shapes human language. *Trends in cognitive sciences*, 23(5):389–407.

Roman Jakobson. 1971. *Selected writings [of] Roman Jakobson: Word and language*. Mouton.

Paul Kiparsky. 1997. The rise of positional licensing. In Ans van Kemenade and Nigel Vincent, editors, *Parameters of morphosyntactic change*, pages 460–494. Cambridge: Cambridge University Press.

Alexander Koplenig, Peter Meyer, Sascha Wolfer, and Carolin Müller-Spitzer. 2017. The statistical trade-off between word order and word structure – large-scale evidence for the principle of least effort. *PLOS ONE*, 12(3):1–25, 03.

Alexandra Kuznetsova, Per B Brockhoff, Rune HB Christensen, et al. 2017. lmertest package: tests in linear mixed effects models. *Journal of statistical software*, 82(13):1–26.

Hanjung Lee. 2001. Markedness and word order freezing. In Peter Sells, editor, *Formal and empirical issues in optimality theoretic syntax, volume 5 of Studies in constraint-based lexicalism*. CSLI Stanford, CA.

Natalia Levshina. 2019. Token-based typology and word order entropy: A study based on universal dependencies. *Linguistic Typology*, 23(3):533–572.

Brian MacWhinney, Elizabeth Bates, and Reinhold Kliegl. 1984. Cue validity and sentence interpretation in English, German, and Italian. *Journal of Verbal Learning and Verbal Behavior*, 23(2):127–150.

Kyle Mahowald. 2011. An LFG approach to word order freezing. In Miriam Butt and Tracy King, editors, *Proceedings of LFG11*, pages 381–398. CSLI.

Tara Mohanan. 1994. *Argument structure in Hindi*. Center for the Study of Language (CSLI).

Lilja Øvrelid. 2004. Disambiguation of syntactic functions in Norwegian: modeling variation in word order interpretations conditioned by animacy and definiteness. In *Proceedings of the 20th Scandinavian Conference of Linguistics*, pages 1–17. Helsinki: University of Helsinki.

R Core Team, 2020. *R: A Language and Environment for Statistical Computing*. R Foundation for Statistical Computing, Vienna, Austria.

Edward Sapir. 1921. *Language: An introduction to the study of speech*. Harcourt, Brace and company.

Kaius Sinnemäki. 2014. Complexity trade-offs: A case study. In Frederick Newmeyer and Laurel Preston, editors, *Measuring grammatical complexity*, pages 179–201. Oxford University Press.

Ralf Vogel. 2004. Correspondence in ot syntax and minimal link effects. In Arthur Stepanov, Gisbert Fanselow, and Ralf Vogel, editors, *Minimality effects in syntax*, pages 401–441. Mouton de Gruyter.

Thomas Wasow. 1997. Remarks on grammatical weight. *Language variation and change*, 9(1):81–105.

Daniel Zeman, Joakim Nivre, et al. 2020. Universal dependencies 2.6. LINDAT/CLARIAH-CZ digital library at the Institute of Formal and Applied Linguistics (ÚFAL), Faculty of Mathematics and Physics, Charles University.

Subjecthood and annotation: The cases of French and Wolof[1]

Olivier Bondéelle[1], Sylvain Kahane[2]

[1]Université de Picardie Jules Verne & CERCLL
[2]Université Paris Nanterre & Modyco, CNRS

Abstract

This article considers the annotation of subjects in UD treebanks. The identification of the subject poses a particular problem in Wolof, due to pronominal indices whose status as a pronoun or a pronominal affix is uncertain. In the UD treebank available for Wolof (Dione, 2019), these have been annotated depending on the construction either as true subjects, or as morphosyntactic features agreeing with the verb. The study of this corpus of 40 000 words allows us to show that the problem is indeed difficult to solve, especially since Wolof has a rich system of auxiliaries and several basic constructions with different properties. Before addressing the case of Wolof, we will present the simpler, but partly comparable, case of French, where subject clitics also tend to behave like affixes, and subjecthood can move from the preverbal to the detached position. We will also make a several annotation recommendations that would avoid overwriting information regarding subjecthood.

1.   Introduction

In this article, we explore the identification of the subject in two languages with a rigid SVO order, French and Wolof. While these languages share no genetic relationship, they present similarities at the typological level and the identification of the subject position can become problematic in some constructions. In some languages, especially ergative languages, subject properties can be distributed onto different arguments (Keenan, 1976; Comrie, 1978). This is not the case for the languages we are considering, where the identification of the argument realized as a subject is very clear. What interests us here is the fact that the realisation of the same argument is distributed across several syntactic positions and subjecthood can move from one syntactic position to another. This should not be confused with the cases studied by Cole et al. (1980) for example, where subjecthood moves from one semantic argument to another.

To begin this discussion, we must first give a name to verb argument whose subjecthood we want to discuss. We will name it the *first actant*, following Tesnière (1959, 2015) and Mel'čuk (1988). The first actant is the semantic argument of the verbal form that can be realized as its subject: sometimes it is realized as its subject, but sometimes it is only realized as a pronominal affix in the verbal inflection (especially in pro-drop languages). In the languages we are studying, the first actant is easy to define, while the subject is more difficult to identify, because there are several positions were the first actant can appear. In English for instance, the first actant is characterized by the following set of traits: it can be realized in the preverbal position, it causes the verb to bear an agreement suffix, it controls the object position (*he washes himself*), and it can be realized by specific pronouns such as *she* or *we*.[2] It can appear in three positions as shown in (1), where the first actant of the verb *be* is realized as *my father, he*, and the pronominal index amalgamated in the *is* form of *be*.[3]

---

[1] This work is licensed under a Creative Commons Attribution 4.0 International Licence. Licence details: `http://creativecommons.org/licenses/by/4.0/`

[2] Due to redistributions, such as the passive voice, the first actant is not always the same semantic argument of the verb (the first actant in *John was surprised by Mary* is *John*). Some verbs, such as *seem* in *it seems that Mary left*, do not really have a first actant, because none of their semantic arguments can be realized in the preverbal position.

[3] There is a fourth position where the first actant can appear (our thanks to a reviewer for highlighting this additional problem): a postverbal position in the so-called impersonal construction.

(i) **it** is also desirable **to retain them** [GUM_academic_exposure-5]

Proceedings of the Fourth Workshop on Universal Dependencies (UDW 2020), pages 34–45
Barcelona, Spain (Online), December 13, 2020

(1) "**My father, he's** an anthropologist," she said. [GUM_fiction_veronique-20][4]

Among these three positions, there is one position we will call the *subject*: the preverbal position, because it is obligatory and can be occupied by lexical NPs. The two other positions do not have such properties: one is part of the verb inflection and is not a syntactic position; the other is an optional, prosodically detached position, but always with a pronoun in the preverbal position reflecting it. In other word, the preverbal position is more canonical than the detached position.

We will now explore two languages where the identification of a canonical subject position is less clear: French in Section 2 and Wolof in Section 3. The fact that several positions can theoretically qualify for the subject label in such languages requires a certain degree of caution with regard to treebank annotations. We will also provide several proposals to resolve this issue in our conclusion in Section 4.

2. The case of French

French has a basic structure similar to that of English, with a preverbal position identified as the subject, an SVO order, and a pronominal suffix on the verb in agreement with the subject (identified as s'). However, there are a few differences: pronominal objects (o) are placed before the verb and are cliticized. The pronominal subject is also cliticized on the verb: it has a weak form, which is distinct from the strong/tonic pronominal form in the detached position (D) (2b) and which cannot be separated from the verb (V) (2c,d). We therefore postulate the existence of different positions for the lexical subject (S) and the pronominal subject (s), since a non-cliticized element can be inserted between S and V but not between s and V, which gives us the topological scheme (2a).[5]

(2) a. D S s=o=V-s' O

    b. **lui il** avait passé les quatre nuits ou trois nuits à à ramper dans les décombres
    [Rhap_D0003-18]
      'him, he had spent the four nights or three nights crawling through the rubble'
    c. **le programme** monsieur le premier ministre comporte un certain nombre de projets
      'the program, Mister Prime Minister, includes a number of projects' [Rhap_D2006-1]
    d. * **il** monsieur le premier ministre comporte un certain nombre de projets
      'it, Mister Prime Minister, includes a number of projects'

The pronominal paradigms regarding D, s and s' are provided in Table 1. One may note that the s' agreement suffixes tend to disappear; at present, only the 2PL form is really marked. The *nous* V-*ons* form of the 1PL has been largely replaced by *on* V-Ø in spoken French. The future tense, which is the only tense where agreement is well marked in the s' position, is often replaced by a complex form with the auxiliary *aller* 'go', which is another way to move the agreement to a preverbal position.

This position is analyzed as the subject in UD. This issue falls outside of the scope of this paper, but we think that this annotation is quite problematic because this position does not display the same properties as the preverbal position, and should not be named in the same way according to traditional surface-syntactic criteria (see for instance criterion C in Mel'čuk 1988). In the Surface-Syntactic UD (SUD) annotation scheme, we have analyzed it as an object position (Gerdes et al. 2019).

[4] All our examples are extracted from UD treebanks with their sent_id identifier.

[5] By *topological scheme*, we refer to a linear template corresponding to a syntactic configuration. The topological model was first developed for the modeling of word order in Germanic languages during the 19th century, and was later implemented in dependency grammar (Duchier and Debusmann, 2001; Gerdes and Kahane, 2001).

Table 1. Pronominal indices in French

	D	s	s'
1SG	*moi*	*je*	Ø
2SG	*toi*	*tu*	Ø
3SG	*lui/elle/ça*	*il/elle/ce*	Ø
1PL	*nous*	*nous*	*-ons*
	nous	*on*	Ø
2PL	*vous*	*vous*	*-ez*
3PL	*eux/elles*	*ils/elles*	Ø

It can be noted that non-pronominal subjects are relatively rare in oral French. In the treebank UD_French-Spoken (Kahane et al., 2019), subjects are divided into 12% lexical subjects, 11% relative pronouns subjects and 77% pronominal subjects (we do not have a spoken English treebank for comparison).

French, especially in its spoken form, frequently uses dislocation, which concerns 10% of sentences in UD_French-Spoken. We do not know what proportion of these detached elements are first actants, as they have not been annotated for the moment. It has been argued by some authors (notably Culbertson and Legendre, 2008; Miller and Sag, 1997), that the first lexical actant tends to be realized in position D rather than in position S in spoken French. Data from the UD_French-Spoken corpus shows that S still dominates D in spoken French. Nevertheless, we can imagine a future form of French with a topological scheme D s=o=V O, where the subjecthood has moved to position D and s no longer commutes with S and thus becomes an agreement prefix.

French has several interrogative constructions. In the standard interrogative construction (3a), s and S do not commute either: both positions can be filled simultaneously (3b), s is mandatory, while S is optional (3c) and cannot accept personal pronouns (3d).[6] As only S can accept lexical realisations of the first actant, we consider S to be the subject and the interrogative construction is therefore a pro-drop construction where s has the status of an agreement suffix.

(3) a. interrogative: D S o=V-s'=s O

    b. mais **l'acte d'écrire** est-**il** le prolongement de l'acte de penser ? [Rhap_D2009-9]

      'but is **the act of writing** an extension of the act of thinking?'

    c. mais est-**il** le prolongement de l'acte de penser ?

    d. * mais **il** est-**il** le prolongement de l'acte de penser ?

It is remarkable that French has both pro-drop constructions and non pro-drop constructions.

Currently, the two positions s and S are annotated **nsubj** in the French treebanks. In interrogative constructions, one can thus have two **nsubj** relations. On the other hand, the first actants in position D are annotated **dislocated** and are therefore not distinguished from the other NPs in this position. New proposals will be made in Section 4.

We will see that the situation is more complex in the case of Wolof.

3.   The case of Wolof

Our study of Wolof is essentially based on the analysis of the treebank UD_Wolof-WTB, annotated by Dione (2019). In Wolof, the s position of pronominal subjects must also be distinguished from the S position of lexical subjects. For example, in relative clauses, a very frequent construction in Wolof due to the absence of an adjective class (1739 relatives for 2107 sentences, i.e. 82 relatives for 100

---

[6] In spoken French, s is optional, but not in standard written French. The prosody, as well as the position of the interrogative pronoun, makes possible the distinction between the S and D positions (i a,b).

    (i)   a. S : A qui **Pierre** parle-t-il ? 'Who does Pierre speak to?'

        b. D : **Pierre**, à qui parle-t-il ? 'Pierre, who does he speak to?'

sentences), the order is highly constrained: s is placed before clitic complements o, and S between o and V (4a). [7] Let us develop upon this description of relative clauses in Wolof.

The relative pronouns and determiners of Wolof are constructed with the combination of a nominal class marker (corresponding to the determined or antecedent noun) and one of the three morphemes *a, i* or *u* that structure the entire grammar of Wolof (they are also present in the verbal domain), giving the words CL-*i*, CL-*a* and CL-*u*. There are 10 nominal noun classes: 8 for the singular *(b, k, w, m, g, l, s, j)* and 2 for the plural *(ñ, y)*. The classes *b* and *y* are becoming the default classes for the singular and plural. The morphemes *i* and *a* mark respectively a proximal or distal (4b), while *u* marks an indefinite and tends to become the default marker for the relative pronoun (4c).

Headless relative clauses are very frequent (about 1000 in the corpus). The pronoun can have an anaphoric value and agree with a distant antecedent or be a generic pronoun introducing a new referent. In this case, one of the five noun class markers which designate a human singular (*k*) or plural (*ñ*), an inanimate (*l*) (4d), a temporal (*b*) and a conditional (*s*) (4d) is used. In addition, there are two former nominal classes that indicate location (*f*) and manner (*n*). We gloss the generic marker of the conditional by CND, and the relative and integrative pronouns by REL.

(4)   a.   relative: R=s=o S V O

       b.   jigéen **ji**
            woman CL.DEF
            'the woman (close from me)'

       c.   jigéen **ju**   ko   am-e   [wo_wtb-ud-train-1530]
            woman CL.REL O3sg have-TR
            'a woman who takes care of it'

       d. **li**   nga moom-ul   [wo_wtb-ud-train-1106]
            INA.REL S2SG possess-NEG
             'what you don't possess'

       e. **soo**   ko   yeexe gis   [wo_wtb-ud-train-933]
            CND.S2SG O3SG delay see
            'if you're slow to see it'

       f. buum **bi**   nu   kolonisatëër   bi   nas=oon [wo_wtb-ud-train-1094]
            rope   CL.REL O1PL colonizer   CL.DEF thread=PAST
            'the rope that the settlers put around our necks'

Verbs in a relative clause are always preceded by a subject realized in one of the three possible positions: the relative pronoun (4c), s (4d,e) or S (4f). Relative clauses do not have a D position. The pronominal subject s cliticizes on the relative pronoun and can be amalgamated with it (see (4e), where *soo=su*.S2SG). Positions s and S are distinguished by the position of the pronominal object, which occurs after s (4e) and before S (4f). Wolof has many auxiliaries, but only two of them appear in relative clauses: *di*, the preverbal marker of imperfective, and *woon*, the postverbal marker of past tense. [8]

In contrast to relative clauses, Wolof has several constructions in the main clause, each one controlled by a particular marker, which can be an auxiliary or a verbal suffix (Robert, 1991; Torrence, 2005; Torrence, 2013; Bondéelle, 2015; Martinovic, 2015; Robert, forthcoming). In all these constructions, the first actant can be realized as a pronominal index in position s or in a detached position D, and for some constructions a third position S is available. We will now study the main constructions and discuss the subjecthood for each of them.

---

[7] All our assertions have been verified by requests on UD_Wolof-WTB with grew-match (Guillaume et al., 2012; Bonfante et al., 2018). For instance, we can verify that there are no subject after the verb with a request such as:

    pattern { H -[acl:relcl]-> V ; V-[nsubj]-> S ; V << S }.

[8] The past tense *woon* is only analyzed AUX when it is spelled as a separate word; there are also many verbs with the feature Tense=Past where *woon* is amalgamated with the verb, as in (4f).

There is a minimal SVO construction without an auxiliary used in only 10.4% of sentences (5a). We will mainly focus on constructions with auxiliaries. The auxiliaries of Wolof, other than *di* and *woon*, focalize one of the elements of the verbal construction: *a* focalizes the subject, *la* one of the complements, *na* the verb, and *da* the VP. Negation is marked by the suffix *-u* which attaches to the verb and focalizes it. We leave aside the auxiliary *ngi*, which behaves like *a*, as well as different compound forms which behave more or less like *da*.

3.1 The forms of s

As in French, pronouns realized in position D have a strong form that is different from the form of pronouns in position s. In addition, the s pronouns cliticize on the auxiliary, which produces amalgams and some zero forms in the third person (see for example the zero forms *la* and *na* in columns 5 and 6, and the amalgam *moo* that results from the fusion of the pronoun *mu* and the auxiliary *a* in column 4 of Table 2). The 1PL and 3PL forms are regular for all auxiliaries (the forms *noo = nu.a* and *ñoo = ñu.a* obey a regular morphophonology rule of Wolof). The 1SG forms are quite regular, even if the consonant /m/ disappears with *la* and *na*. On the other hand, the 2SG and 2PL forms are highly irregular, due notably to the disappearance of the particles *la* and *na* and the use of strong pronouns as a basis for *a*. Finally, for 3SG, the index is only expressed for *a*. This is undeniably a sign of a tendency for the s position to become an agreement suffix. The choice of Dione in UD_Wolof-WTB was to analyze s as a subject with *a* (5b-b") and *da* and as a morphosyntactic feature on the auxiliary with *la* (5c-c"), *na* and *-u* (which are the three cases where 3SG has a zero form).

Table 2. Pronominal indices in Wolof

	D	s V	s=a	la=s	na=s	da=s	V-u=s
1SG	*man*	*ma* V	*maa*	*laa*	*naa*	*dama*	V-*uma*
2SG	*yow*	*nga* V	*yaa*	*nga*	*nga*	*danga*	V-*uloo*
3SG	*moom*	*mu* V	*moo*	*la*	*na*	*da(fa)*	V-*u(l)*
1PL	*nun*	*nu* V	*noo*	*lanu*	*nanu*	*danu*	V-*unu*
2PL	*yeen*	*ngeen* V	*yeena*	*ngeen*	*ngeen*	*dangeen*	V-*uleen*
3PL	*ñoom*	*ñu* V	*ñoo*	*lañu*	*nañu*	*dañu*	V-*uñu*

We will now look at the different topological schemes of the auxiliaries and the question of the lexical realization of the first actant. We will see that the S position behaves differently depending on the constructions.

3.2 Verbal constructions in the main clause

Here are the topological schemes of the different constructions in the main clause:

(5) a. minimal construction: D S/s V o O

  b. auxiliary *a* construction (subject focalization): D S/s=a o V O

  b'. **ñoo**   ko   yor=oon.   [wo_wtb-ud-train-3] (*ñoo = ñu.a*)
    S3PL.AUX O3SG possess=PAST
    'They were the ones who detained him'

  b".

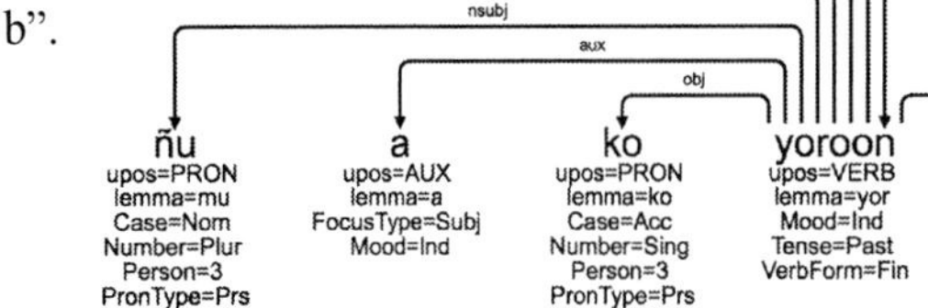

c. auxiliary *la* c: D O! *la*=s o S V O (object focalization of a unique element in O!)

c'. Xar   mu   ndawa-ndaw **laa**   la   jox.   [wo_wtb-ud-train-840]
    portion CL.REL be_tiny   AUX:S1SG O2SG give
    'This is a tiny portion that I gave you'

c''.

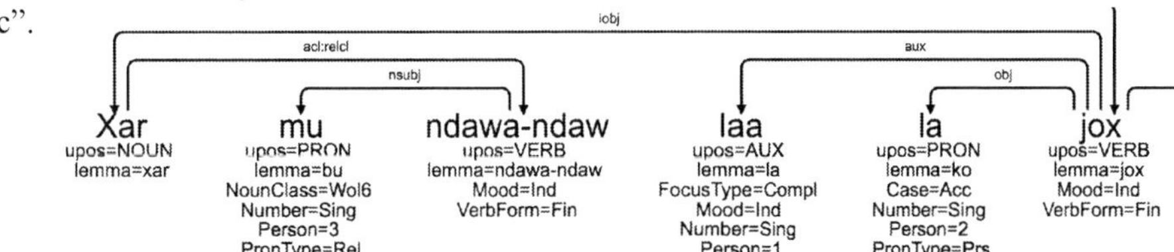

d. auxiliary *na* construction (verb focalization): D V *na*=s o O

e. auxiliary *da* construction (VP focalization): D *da*=s o V O

f. suffix -*u* construction (negation): D V-*u*=s o O

The three assertive constructions with *na*, *da* and -*u* (respectively focalization of V, VP, and negation) block the realization of a lexical subject in position S (there is no possible confusion with position D which, unlike S, can accommodate strong pronouns). In other words, for these constructions, the paradigm of weak subject pronouns, those occupying the position s, no longer commutes with a lexical subject. This leads most authors to consider that weak subject pronouns have become pronominal indices belonging to the verb inflection and that an element in position D co-referring with the index s is therefore the true subject (Sauvageot, 1965; Church, 1981; Diouf, 1985; Ndiaye-Corréard, 1989; Robert, 1991; Fal, 1999; Ndiaye-Corréard, 2003; Guérin, 2016).

Let us see how position D is like a subject. Position S is possible with *a* and *la*. Note that with *a*, the pre-auxiliary position S/s (see 5b) is filled by weak pronouns 81.5% of the time (387 out of 475), compared to 14.5% for NPs and 4% for other pronouns. The proportion of weak pronouns is very high, especially if we consider that *a* focalizes the subject and that it is a written corpus. In comparison, UD_French-GSD and UD_French-FTB have 41% and 33.5% subject pronouns (including relative pronouns) and UD_English-GUM and UD_English-EWT have 53.5% and 57.5% subject pronouns.

The case of *la* (focalization of the object) is particularly interesting, since it opens a position S distinct from s and allows for the realization of a lexical first actant in both the S and D positions. Dione's corpus contains 456 occurrences of the particle *la*, including 115 occurrences of the form *lañu* (*la*=s3PL). None of them contain an NP in position S. On the other hand, we have 78 lexical subjects in position S including 11 with a plural determiner.[9] All are with the form *la*. We conclude from this that it is not possible to have both a pronoun in position s and a lexical subject in position S at the same time. As S is considered a subject position and s is in complementary distribution with S, we must consider that s is a subject in this construction. Example (6) illustrated the case of a plural subject in S: the initial pronoun *moom* 3SG is a strong pronoun in the focalized object position (O! in (5c)) and the position S is occupied by the syntagm *yaakaar yi* 'hopes' whose determiner *yi* marks the plural. The form *la* in this case does not combine with a s3SG zero form and is glossed only by AUX.

---

[9] Nouns without determiners are not marked in numbers. The query to retrieve plural lexical subjects in position S is:

```
pattern { L [upos=AUX, lemma=la] ; V -[aux]-> L ; V -[nsubj]-> S ;
S [upos = NOUN|PROPN] ; S -[det]-> D ; D [Number=Plur] ; L << S }.
```

(6) […] moom **la   yaakaar yi**   tas-e   […]   [wo_wtb-ud-train-488]
    3SG   AUX hope   PL.DEF be_spread-TR
    '[…] it's with him (that) hopes have been dashed […]'

Conversely, there are 16 assertive constructions with the auxiliary *la* where a nominal group in position D is analyzed by Dione as a subject and is therefore the realization of the first actant of the verb: only one has a plural determiner and the form of the auxiliary is *lañu* (*la*=s3PL).

We conclude that the first actants in positions S and D do not behave in the same way with *la*: position S blocks the realization of s and position D requires the realization of s. For constructions with *la*, we would therefore tend to consider that s is the realization of the subject (contrary to the analysis of Dione 2019).

With the negation marker *-u*, the situation is more confusing. Unlike the auxiliaries *a, la, na* and *da* (respectively focalization of subject, object, V, and VP), negation is possible in relative clauses. When the verb is in a relative clause, there is no D position, whereas when the verb is in a main clause, the S position is blocked and the D position is accessible to the first actant. There are 13 occurrences of the first actant of a negative verb being analyzed as a subject by Dione and which have a plural determiner. There are 7 instances where position s is instantiated by *ñu* 's3PL' and 6 where position s is empty. If the situation were the same as for *la*, the first actant would be expected to be in the D position in the first case and in the S in the second. 9 cases behave as expected; for 1 case, after the temporal conjunction *ba*, nothing can be said because both constructions are possible. Some cases are clearly deviant: in (7a), the verb *amag-ul* 'still_have-NEG' is the main verb and s is empty (the *-ul* form of the negative suffixed to V is not marked in number while the syntagm *ay arondismaa* 'boroughs' in position S bears the mark of the plural determiner *-y*); in (7b,c), we have two examples of the same interrogative construction where the verb depends on the verb *tax* 'cause' without a complementizer. In one of these examples, position s is empty (the *-ul* form of the negative in (7b)) while in the other (in (7c)) it is instantiated (the form *-uñoo* = *-u=ñu=a* = NEG=S3PL=PART, where *a* is a subordinating particle).

(7) a. Booba   jamono **ay   arondismaa** amag-**ul**.   [wo_wtb-ud-train-627]
    CL.ANAPH period   CL.IND boroughs   still_have-NEG
    'At that time, there weren't any boroughs yet.'
    b. Lu   tax   **tooñaange yii   yépp**   jur-**ul**   coow? [wo_wtb-ud-train-2007]
    CL.INT cause_that teasing   CL.DEF CL.everything produce-NEG noise
    'Why is it that all the vexations don't make any noise?'
    c. Lu   tax,   **daamar yooyu**   mën-**u**=**ñoo**   daw ci   Senegaal? [ud-train-2048]
    CL.INT cause_that vehicle   CL.ANAPH can-NEG=S3PL:PART run   LOC Senegal
    'Why can't these vehicles circulate in Senegal?'

These deviant cases show a certain wavering in the instantiation of s in relation to *-u* and nevertheless accredit the fact that the functioning of s in relation to the positions S and D tends to harmonize and D to be treated as a subject position equivalent to S.

The correlation between the instantiation of s (presence of *ñu*) and the presence of a comma can be seen in example (7c). One can imagine that this is also correlated with different prosodies. It is probably necessary to distinguish, among the phrases in position D, between those which are actually prosodically detached and those which are prosodically integrated into the verbal nucleus. If the first actants in position D are subjects, it is expected that they are prosodically integrated into the verbal nucleus. It appears from the literature that both situations are possible (Rialland and Robert, 2004). We only have a written corpus and we cannot study prosody, but we can study the presence or absence of a comma after the D position, which is usually the marker of a prosodic boundary. Dione's corpus contains 80 negative verbs which are roots and are preceded by a phrase analyzed as a subject; among them, 7 are followed by a comma. With the root verbs accompanied by the auxiliaries *la* or *na*, we have only 35 subject phrases followed by a comma. Note that there is one case of a comma after a lexical subject in position S with the auxiliary *a* (for 100 without a comma).

We can therefore observe that the first actants in position D of the assertive constructions involving *na*, *la* or negation are rarely followed by a comma (only 10%). For comparison, there are 168 phrases annotated as dislocated (dislocated relation of UD) with the assertive constructions involving *na* and *la* and 73 (i.e. 43%) of them are followed by a comma. Out of 329 adverbial clauses in position D, there are 262 (80%) followed by a comma.

Consequently, it must be considered that there are two types of subjects in Wolof: subjects in position S, which are obligatory and commute with pronouns and do not trigger agreements, and subjects in position D, which are optional and trigger agreements. We are therefore looking at a hybrid system with two subject functions with very different properties.[10] The problem is therefore the analysis of position s which becomes heterogeneous: in constructions where the position S is accessible and in mutual exclusion with s, s must be analyzed as a subject, whereas when the position S is no longer accessible and D is analyzed as a subject, s must be analyzed as an agreement morpheme.

4.   Conclusion

We looked at the issue of subjecthood in three rigidly ordered nominative-accusative SVO languages, English, French and Wolof. In English, the pronominal first actants occupy the same linear place as lexical first actants and are in complementary distribution. In such a case, it is clear that their syntactic position is one and the same. The situation may be more confusing in other languages, such as French or Wolof. The potential problems are as follows:

- the first lexical actant can occur in two different positions, which we have named S and D, position D being a detached position that can be occupied by other NPs;
- position S tends to be used less and less in favor of D, or even to disappear;
- s and S occupy different linear positions;
- s and S can co-occur and are no longer in complementary distribution;
- the forms in position s differ from the pronominal forms in position D (weak vs. strong forms);
- s tends to merge with the verb (or a verbal auxiliary) by becoming inseparable from the verb, resulting in varying forms according to the verb as well as zero forms.

Each of these elements accompanies a shift of the subjecthood from the S position to the D position. It is interesting to note that this shift does not occur homogeneously, but can be faster in some

---

[10] This has already been considered for the SVO and VSO orders of Classical Arabic. With SVO, the verb agrees in gender, person and number with the subject (strong agreement) (El Kassas and Kahane, 2004; Attia, 2008):

   (i) al'awlad   akal**uu**   al-mawz
          DEF-boy.PL eat.PASS.MASC.3PL DEF-banana.PL
          'The boys ate the bananas.'

   (ii) al-banaat   'akal**naa**   al-mawz
          DEF-girl.PL eat.PASS.FEM.3PL DEF-banana.PL
          'The girls ate the bananas.'

But if the order is VSO, the verb agrees only in gender and in person with the subject (weak agreement):

   (iii) 'akal**at**   al-banaat al-mawz
          eat.PASS.FEM.3 DEF-girl.PL DEF-banana.PL
          'The girls ate the bananas.'

There are thus two types of subjects with different agreement properties according to the word order. In the so-called dialectical Arabics, the situation has become simpler. For example, in Egyptian Arabic, both orders (SVO and VSO) are possible (though the SVO order is dominant) and the verb is inflected in the same way in both cases, in gender and number only:

   (iv) el-banaat 'akal**et**   el-moz
          DEF-girl.PL eat.PAST.FEM.PL DEF-banana.PL
          'The girls ate the bananas.'

   (v) 'akal**et**   el-banaat   el-moz
          eat.PAST.FEM.PL DEF-girl.PL DEF-banana.PL
          'The girls ate the bananas.'

(We thank Mohamed Galal for the data.)

constructions and lead to a hybrid system where the first actant can be realized in the S or D positions according to the construction, and where s can function more or less independently from S. Thus in French, in the interrogative construction, s is no longer in complementary distribution with S and becomes an affix, whereas in the basic declarative construction, the realization of the first actant tends to move from S to D. In Wolof, s tends to merge with the various auxiliaries and S has disappeared from some constructions in favour of D. However, in other constructions, such as the relative clause, D is not accessible and s and S are in complementary distribution.

In terms of annotation, our recommendations are as follows.

1) As soon as there is a suspicion of a shift in subjecthood from S to D, it is advisable to use a **dislocated:subj** relation to be able to identify the realizations of the first actant in position D.[11]

2) When there is a suspicion that a pronominal index may not be an affix, it is best to treat it as a pronoun, that is a separate word. One can use the **nsubj** function (and thus sometimes have two subjects), but it may be desirable to distinguish the function of elements in position s (e.g. by an **nsubj:weak** relation), as some pronouns may occupy the position S.[12]

---

[11] Such an annotation may also relate to the object. For example, in Mandarin and Cantonese, the second actant may be detached on the left, without it being clear whether it is a topicalized or dislocated object. This was annotated **dislocated** in UD_Cantonese-HK, making it difficult to study (Wong et al., 2017). A **dislocated:obj** relation would have allowed for a better exploitation of the corpus and comparison with the Mandarin corpus.

[12] As we said Dione has opted for a heterogeneous annotation of s. Despite this, it was possible to identify all occurrences, sometimes at the cost of rather complex queries. The main problem for our study of subjecthood has been the use of **dislocated** regardless of the role of the detached NP.

Abbreviations for glosses

ANAPH: anaphoric   AUX: auxiliary   CL : nominal class
DEF : definite   IMP : imperfective   INT: interrogative
NEG : negative   O : object   PAST : past
PL : plural   REL : relative   S : subject
SG : singular

Abbreviations for topological positions

D : detached item field on the left
o : clitic complements field
O : non-clitic complements field
O! : field accommodating exactly one complement
s : weak pronominal subject field
S : subject field
V : verb field

Acknowledgements

We thank Bernard Caron, Jasmina Milićević and Emmett Strickland, as well as the two reviewers for their comments and suggestions that helped us improve the initial text.

References

Mohamed Attia. 2008. Alternate Agreement in Arabic. *Proceedings of Parallel Grammar Meeting (ParGram)*, Istanbul, Turkey.

Olivier Bondéelle. 2015. *Polysémie et structuration du lexique : le cas du wolof.* Utrecht : LOT.

Guillaume Bonfante, Bruno Guillaume, and Guy Perrier. 2018. *Application of Graph Rewriting to Natural Language Processing*, Wiley-ISTE.

Eric Church. 1981. *Le système verbal du wolof.* Dakar : Université de Dakar.

Peter Cole, Wayne Harbert, Gabriella Hermon, and S. N. Sridhar. 1980. The acquisition of subjecthood. *Language* 56(4) 719-743.

Bernard Comrie. 1978. Ergativity. In *Syntactic typology*, W. P. Lehma (ed.), 329-393. Austin: University of Texas.

Jenny Culbertson and Géraldine Legendre. 2008. Qu'en est-il des clitiques sujet en français oral contemporain ? In Durand J. Habert B., Laks B. (eds.) *Congrès Mondial de Linguistique Française - CMLF'08*. Paris : Institut de Linguistique Française.

Cheikh Bamba Dione. 2019. Developing Universal Dependencies for Wolof, *Proceedings of the Third Workshop on Universal Dependencies (UDW)*, SyntaxFest, Association for Computational Linguistics, 12-23.

Jean-Léopold Diouf. 1985. *Introduction à une étude du système verbal wolof.* Dakar : CLAD.

Denys Duchier and Ralph Debusmann. 2001. Topological dependency trees: A constraint-based account of linear precedence. *Proceedings of the 39th Annual Meeting of the Association for Computational Linguistics (ACL)*, 180-187.

Dina El Kassas and Sylvain Kahane. 2004. Modélisation de l'ordre des mots en arabe standard. *Actes de l'Atelier sur le traitement automatique de la langue arabe, JEP-TALN.*

Arame Fal. 1999. *Précis de grammaire fonctionnelle de la langue wolof.* Dakar.

Kim Gerdes and Sylvain Kahane. 2001. Word order in German: A formal dependency grammar using a topological hierarchy, *Proceedings of the 39th Annual Meeting of the Association for Computational Linguistics (ACL)*.

Kim Gerdes and Sylvain Kahane. 2006. Phrasing It Differently, in Leo Wanner (ed.), *Selected lexical and grammatical issues in the Meaning-Text Theory*, Amsterdam / New-York: John Benjamins, 297-335.

Kim Gerdes and Sylvain Kahane. 2016. Dependency Annotation Choices: Assessing Theoretical and Practical Issues of Universal Dependencies, *Proceedings of Linguistic Annotation Workshop (LAW)*, ACL, Berlin.

Kim Gerdes, Bruno Guillaume, Sylvain Kahane, and Guy Perrier. 2019. Improving Surface-syntactic Universal Dependencies (SUD): surface-syntactic functions and deep-syntactic features, *Proceedings of the 17th international conference on Treebanks and Linguistic Theories (TLT)*, SyntaxFest, Paris.

Maximilien Guérin. 2016. *Les constructions verbales en wolof : Vers une typologie de la prédication, de l'auxiliation et des périphrases*. Thèse de doctorat. Paris, Université Sorbonne Nouvelle Paris 3.

Bruno Guillaume, Guillaume Bonfante, Paul Masson, Mathieu Morey, and Guy Perrier. 2012. Grew : un outil de réécriture de graphes pour le TAL. *Actes de la 12e Conférence annuelle sur le Traitement Automatique des Langues (TALN)*, Grenoble, France.

Sylvain Kahane, Kim Gerdes, and Rachel Bawden. 2019. The microsyntactic annotation, In Lacheret-Dujour A., Kahane S., Pietrandrea P. (eds), *Rhapsodie – A Prosodic and Syntactic Treebank for Spoken French*, John Benjamins, Amsterdam, 49-68.

Edward Keenan. 1976. Towards a universal definition of 'subject'. In *Subject and Topic*, C. N. Li (ed.), 303-334. New York: Academic Press.

Martina Martinovic. 2015. *Feature geometry and head-splitting: Evidence from the morphosyntax of the Wolof clausal periphery*, Doctoral dissertation, University of Chicago.

Igor A. Mel'cuk. 1988. *Dependency syntax: theory and practice.* SUNY press.

Igor A. Mel'čuk. 2013. Syntactic subject, once again. *Proceedings of the 6th International Conference on Meaning-Text Theory*, Prague.

Philip H. Miller and Ivan A. Sag. 1997. French clitic movement without clitics or movement. *Natural Language & Linguistic Theory, 15*(3), 573-639.

Geneviève N'Diaye-Corréard. 1989. Focalisation et système verbal en wolof. *Annales de la Faculté des Lettres et Sciences Humaines,* 19, Dakar, 177-190.

Geneviève N'Diaye-Corréard. 2003. Structure des propositions et système verbal en wolof. *SudLangues,* 3. 163-188.

Annie Rialland and Stéphane Robert. 2004. La focalisation en wolof : morphosyntaxe et intonation. In Anne Lacheret-Dujour, Jacques François (éd.) *Focalisation et moyens d'expression de la focalisation à travers les langues*, Mémoires de la Société de Linguistique de Paris, Peeters, 138-160.

Stéphane Robert. 1991. *Approche énonciative du système verbal : Le cas du wolof.* Paris : CNRS Éditions.

Stéphane Robert. To appear. Wolof: A grammatical sketch. In F. Lüpke (ed.), *The Oxford guide to the Atlantic languages of West Africa.* Oxford University Press.

Serge Sauvageot. 1965. *Description synchronique d'un dialecte wolof : Le parler du Dyolof.* Dakar : IFAN.

Lucien Tesnière. 1959. *Éléments de syntaxe structurale.* Paris : Klincksieck.

Lucien Tesnière. 2015. *Elements of structural syntax*, transl. by T. Osborne and S. Kahane, Amsterdam: John Benjamins.

William H. Torrence. 2005. *On the Distribution of Complementizers in Wolof.* Doctoral dissertation, University of California, Los Angeles.

William H. Torrence. 2013. *The Clause Structure of Wolof: Insights into the Left Periphery.* Amsterdam: John Benjamins.

Tak-Sum Wong, Kim Gerdes, Herman Leung, and John Lee. 2017. "Quantitative Comparative Syntax on the Cantonese-Mandarin Parallel Dependency Treebank" *Proceedings of the Fourth International Conference on Dependency Linguistics*, pp. 266–275, Pisa, Italy, September 2017.

Marina Yaguello. (ed.) 1994. *Subjecthood and subjectivity: the status of the subject in linguistic theory* [proceedings of the Colloquium" The status of the subject in linguistic theory"], London, 19-20 March 1993. Editions Ophrys.

Verification, Reproduction and Replication of NLP Experiments: a Case Study on Parsing Universal Dependencies

Çağrı Çöltekin
Department of Linguistics
University of Tübingen
`ccoltekin@sfs.uni-tuebingen.de`

Abstract

As in any field of inquiry that depends on experiments, the verifiability of experimental studies is important in computational linguistics. Despite increased attention to verification of empirical results, the practices in the field are unclear. Furthermore, we argue, certain traditions and practices that are seemingly useful for verification may in fact be counterproductive. We demonstrate this through a set of multi-lingual experiments on parsing Universal Dependencies treebanks. In particular, we show that emphasis on exact replication leads to practices (some of which are now well established) that hide the variation in experimental results, effectively hindering verifiability with a false sense of certainty. The purpose of the present paper is to highlight the magnitude of the issues resulting from these common practices with the hope of instigating further discussion. Once we, as a community, are convinced about the importance of the problems, the solutions are rather obvious, although not necessarily easy to implement.

1 Introduction

The practice of independent verification of empirical findings has been at the core of the modern science. There have been, however, recent failures of reproduction in many fields (Open Science Collaboration, 2015; Freedman et al., 2015), which also instilled public interest with the popular name *reproducibility crisis* (Fidler and Wilcox, 2018). In computational linguistics and natural language processing (NLP), worries about reproducibility have been voiced for over a decade with a notable increase in recent years (Pedersen, 2008; Fokkens et al., 2013; Mieskes, 2017; Branco et al., 2017; Cohen et al., 2017; Reimers and Gurevych, 2017; Branco et al., 2020; Huber and Çöltekin, 2020, just to name a few).

As some of these studies point out, it is often unclear what is meant by the terms *replication* and *reproduction*. The definitions of these terms are often blurred, and they may even be used in opposite meanings in different studies (Cohen et al., 2018). In this paper, we use the term (exact) *replication* to refer to the activity of running the same code on the same data set with the aim of producing the same measurements reported in the original publication. We use the term *reproduction* to refer to the activity of verifying the claims or findings by varying the experimental settings in meaningful ways. As argued earlier (Drummond, 2009), the scientifically interesting and useful activity is *reproduction*, while *replication* has rather little or no use for the purpose of scientific verification.

The confusion, however, is not only limited to the usage of these terms. In many studies, the aim of the activity is also unclear, or often understood as obtaining the same numbers reported in an original study (in our terms *exact replication*). The emphasis on state-of-the-art scores (even with small increase over the previous state of the art) also motivates the exact, 'fair', comparisons based on a single-best score.

On the other hand, many of the statistical data-driven methods involve a number of inevitable sources of variation. For example, any machine learning method will produce varied results when trained and tested on different parts of the data, and many others are also sensitive to other stochastic processes, such as random initialization of their parameters or the order of training instances. Even though this variation is important for evaluating and comparing statistical models, there has been an increasing emphasis on

Proceedings of the Fourth Workshop on Universal Dependencies (UDW 2020), pages 46–56
Barcelona, Spain (Online), December 13, 2020

exact replication of the published scores. For example, the SemEval 2020 reviewer form includes the following scoring instructions for reviewers (emphasis ours):

> 4 = could mostly reproduce the results described here, although there may be some variation *because of sample variance* or minor variations in their interpretation of the protocol or method.
> 5 = could easily reproduce the results and verify the correctness of the results described here.

Hence, although lightly, not being *exactly* replicable due to sample variation is penalized, encouraging participants to eliminate, or hide, all sources of variation. The same or similar reviewing criteria have recently become standard for major publication venues for computational linguistics.

In this paper, we show that the emphasis on exact replication, in fact, hinders the idea of verification of the results. We support this claim through parsing experiments on Universal Dependencies treebanks (Nivre et al., 2016, UD), investigating the effects of two common or well-established practices that aim to facilitate replication. Namely, fixing random seed of the pseudo random number generator used during experiments, and standard training, development and test set splits.

2   Experimental Setting

Our experiments consist of replicating and reproducing parsing scores reported with version 1.2 of UDPipe (Straka and Straková, 2017; Straka and Straková, 2019) on UD version 2.5 treebanks (Zeman et al., 2019). UDPipe is an open-source pipeline for tokenization, tagging, and dependency parsing designed particularly for the UD annotation scheme. The system obtained near-top results in the recent CoNLL shared tasks on dependency parsing from raw text (Zeman et al., 2017; Zeman et al., 2018). Besides its performance and the ease of use, another interesting aspect of UDPipe for the current study is the fact that maintainers provide pre-trained models for the majority of the UD treebanks, where each model is trained and tested on the standard UD splits. The authors also publish common performance metrics, and provide scripts for replication.[1]

Our experiments consist of (1) exact replication of the reported results using the same code and the standard splits, (2) reproducing the results by varying the random seed, and (3) reproducing the results on random treebank splits. To facilitate exact replication of the published scores, the UDPipe model distribution fixes the random seed used for initializing the model parameters and other sources of variation (e.g., shuffling of training instances). For our main experiments, the UDPipe is modified to set the random seed based on the time stamp (a reasonably random quantity for our purposes). We use the same embeddings distributed with the UDPipe models, and the same hyperparameter settings as the original models. The experiments are run using the scripts provided in the UDPipe 2.5 models package, with slight modifications for parametrizing the input, and parallelizing it with GNU parallel (Tange, 2011). We report results for all treebanks for which a UDPipe 2.5 model was published, except for the largest five treebanks.[2]

For the experiments with different data splits, we simply combine all the sentences from the standard splits, and create 10 versions of each treebank by randomly splitting the sentences into train, dev, and test sets of the same size as the original split. In all cases, since the parser does not use any extra-sentential information, we sample the sentences randomly, without paying attention to document boundaries even if they are marked. In the main text, we only present and compare labeled attachment scores (LAS). Other metrics, including tokenization and tagging scores, are presented in Appendix A.

3   Results

We first verify the exact replication of the published scores. Besides the fixed treebank splits, since original study eliminates all sources of random variation, our results exactly match theirs.

To establish the expected variation of the parser on the same treebank splits, we perform multiple experiments with standard splits after allowing random variation in model initialization. The black bars

---

[1] `http://ufal.mff.cuni.cz/udpipe/models`. The (modified) scripts used in this study are accessible at `https://github.com/coltekin/udpipe-reproduction`.

[2] For the sake of the impact on the environment as well as on the patience of the author. The experiments reported here require over 10 CPU-months on a relatively recent architecture, and 5 additional data points provide little additional support for present discussion, while extending the computational cost considerably.

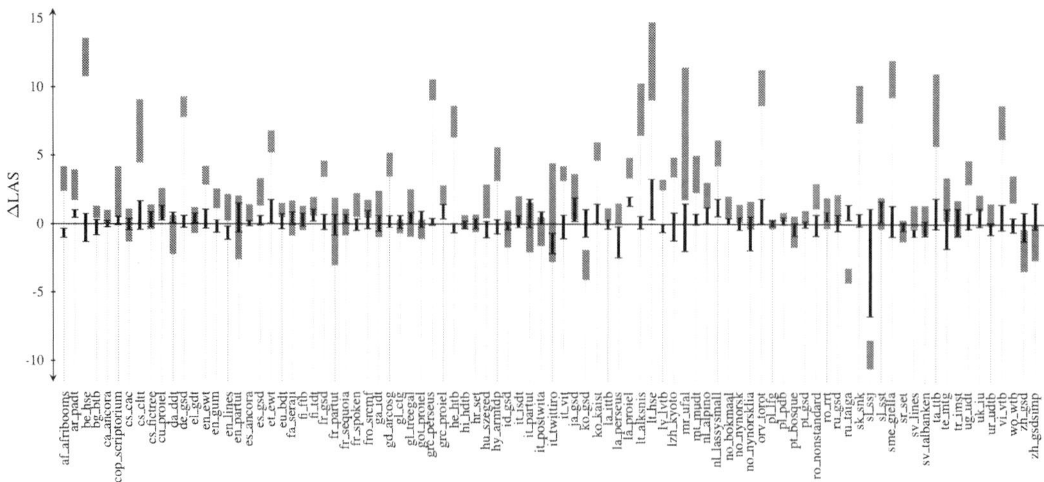

Figure 1: Percent LAS difference from published results and 10 experiments on standard splits (black bars) and 10 experiments with random train/dev/test splits (thick light blue bars). A positive value indicates a score higher than the published score. The bars indicate the complete range of scores.

in Figure 1 present the range of LAS obtained in 10 experiments on the standard splits (all LAS figures presented in this paper are percentages).[3] All scores in Figure 1 are relative to the scores published by the original study, a positive value indicating a score higher than the published score on a particular treebank. The scores do not diverge from the original study substantially. Nevertheless, there is considerable variation. The range of scores are between 0.40 and 7.89 LAS points with an average of 1.30 LAS. The range of LAS scores from 10 experiments with different random seeds do not contain the published result in 21 of the 90 experiments. It is also worth noting that in cases the reported value is within the range, it is not necessarily at the center of the range.

As expected, the range of scores obtained on random treebank splits (shown as light blue bars in Figure 1) indicate an even wider spread. The ranges vary between 0.65 and 9.68 LAS points, with an average of 2.25. The scores of random-split experiments also differ from the published results considerably. The LAS on random splits and the published results differ 2.72 points on average, with a maximum of 12.30. In the majority of the cases, the published results are not within the range of scores obtained on random-split experiments, only 33 out of 90 differences falling within this range. Most differences however, are positive. Minimum LAS obtained in random-split experiments are higher than the published results for 53 treebanks, indicating that standard splits underestimate the success of the parser. This is expected, since most treebanks do not sample test sets randomly, conflicting with the i.i.d. assumption of many machine learning models. The published results are above the random-split range only for 4 treebanks, probably due to the official splits with easier to parse test sets.

4   Discussion

The experiments presented above demonstrate the effects of two sources of variation on parsing scores. The variation displayed in Figure 1 is rarely reported in the literature. Furthermore, common practices promoted for enabling exact replication leads researchers to eliminate this variation from their experiments, reporting single-figure scores without an indication of the expected variation. Such single-figure scores, as demonstrated above, are often biased in an arbitrary direction.

---

[3]The reason for presenting the range is not to amplify the readers' perception of the variation. As an anonymous reviewer pointed out, the standard deviation or the standard error are better, more robust measures of variation from the mean. A study reporting a mean score with its variation over *multiple* experiments should report such a robust measure of variation. However, since the point in question here is the practice of reporting a *single* score from a single model instance, the demonstration of the range is more interesting for our purposes.

The first type of variation we discuss is due to model training and evaluation, e.g., because of random initialization of the model parameters, or random ordering of the data before online or batch training. Any non-trivial statistical model produces different results when trained and tested on the same data. This is typically negligible for convex optimization procedures.[4] The variation is naturally higher for models trained with non-convex optimization, such as neural networks which are the dominant approach to parsing as well as many other NLP tasks. The variation stemming from these two sources is rarely reported in the literature. On the contrary, due to heavy emphasis on replicability in the field (Pedersen, 2008; Wieling et al., 2018, for example), when researchers release their software, they often fix the variation in an arbitrary way, e.g., by fixing the initial random seed used by pseudo random number generators as in our case study above. The point here is not to promote systems with large variation. We want to *reduce* the variation when possible. For example, ensembling or model averaging are useful for reducing the variation. However, there will still be some variation based on initialization differences and sampling, and reporting this variation is useful for understanding the success of the model, as well as for meaningful model comparison.

Our experiments indicate the range of LAS obtained by UDPipe on UD treebanks over 10 random initializations is 1.30 on average, and goes up to 7.89 on individual treebanks. To facilitate a rough comparison, the LAS (averaged over all treebanks) differences between UDPipe and the systems above and below UDPipe in CoNLL 2018 shared task are less than 0.20, indicating that the arbitrary choice of random seed could have made the difference in this ranking.

The solution to this problem is clear. Rather than 'hiding' the variation by settling on a fixed model instance, we should report the variation caused by the inevitable sources of variability. As the quote from the review form in Section 1 demonstrate, reporting results with sampling variation is perceived as a negative property of a paper submitted to many computational linguistics conferences. Hence, to be able to increase chances of acceptance of a paper, the authors are encouraged to fix all sources of (natural) variation of models in an arbitrary manner. The present paper, hopefully, makes it clear that this is wrong. However, since the incorrect behavior is currently being promoted by the community at large. The real solution lies in further discussion of what should really be expected from individual experimental studies.

The second issue we discuss is the adverse effects of standard training, development and test set splits, which has also been brought up by others before (Gorman and Bedrick, 2019). The standard splits are common among all NLP data sets, but tradition is probably older for treebanks, going back to early parsing research.[5] The recent treebanking efforts, e.g., UD treebanks, continued this tradition with official splits of training, development, and test sets. The standard test sets are often justified by replicability of the results obtained on these data sets, and *fair* comparisons between different systems. Another motivation for test split is to avoid 'peeking into test data' (Jurafsky and Martin, 2009, p.189). However, the latter goal is difficult to entertain for a standard test that remains fixed for decades.

Independent of the motivation of the standard splits, the experiments reported above show that the use of standard treebank splits hides a large amount of variation, and it often biases the parsing results arbitrarily. When the scores are calculated over multiple random splits, the variation can be as large as 9.68 LAS and the average scores obtained can differ from the reported results up to 12.30 LAS. Furthermore, for the majority of the treebanks, scores reported in the original study are not in the range of scores obtained in random-split experiments. Clearly, these differences blur model comparisons. More importantly, in any practical use of these tools, the user should be aware of the expected variation. Fortunately, in our experiments, most of the results would come as a pleasant surprise, since we obtained ranges of scores better than the original report. This also means the standard test set splits are biased in certain ways, and, hence, model comparison on these sets may arbitrarily favor certain types of parsers.

The solution is, again, obvious: reporting results (with their variation) on different data splits. In other words, abandoning standard splits. However, this goes against the well-established traditions. Again, true solution require more discussion of the issues in the research community. Many data sets include

---

[4]The most common reason for a potential variance is the convergence criterion based on a fixed threshold. Different initializations may result in stopping at (slightly) different points on the error surface close to the minimum.

[5]As of this writing, a search on ACL anthology for keywords "Penn Treebank" and "section 23" returns over 1000 hits. Many models, most of them parsers, have been compared on this de facto standard test set.

a standard training, development and test set split. As a result, for fair comparison, researchers are encouraged, or sometimes required to report results on a single standard test set. For example, it is unlikely for a paper on parsing to be accepted if it reports results using non-standard splits. Hence, similar to reporting sampling variation, individual authors are forced to follow current practices. The real solution requires community-wide changes to acceptable practices.

The issues discussed above are orthogonal to the issue addressed by statistical significance testing. Although statistical assurances for significant differences have their merits, it is important to note that they indicate statistically significant differences on a *single test set*. Hence, in their typical application, they may even contribute to a false sense of significant difference that disappears when the systems are tested on different test sets, or even the same model trained with different initializations. Interestingly enough, the differences between the minimum and the maximum LAS scores in our experiments conducted on the standard test sets with varying random seeds are statistically significant for all treebanks.[6] Hence, a statistically significant finding reported, e.g., for two alternative training settings, may very well be due to the random initialization at least with a $10\,\%$ chance according to our experiments. The use of above-chance statistical differences are only helpful when the systems are tested on multiple data sets (Dror et al., 2017). However, in most tasks, multiple data sets are not a luxury we enjoy, especially when the research or application at hand is in a particular domain. Using multiple random splits of available data or use of cross-validation is often the closest we can get to a general solution.

Hidden in the issues related to variation with different data splits is the size and quality of the data sets. For many languages or tasks, the data sets are small and sometimes low quality, which eventually affect the models trained and tested on them. Creating, annotating and curating data sets is a labor-intensive, expensive, yet error-prone task. On the other hand, creating more data sets for which there are already existing resources, and improving the existing data sets are not rewarding tasks. Again, to be able to test our models on multiple and better data sets, we, as a community, need ways to encourage and reward creation and maintenance of more and high-quality data sets.

Although our case study is based on parsing results with UDPipe, the problems outlined are neither specific to UDPipe nor parsing. In any statistical, data-driven NLP experiment, some amount of variation is inevitable in experimental results, and the standard test set splits and avoiding variation due to other factors in model training hides this variation.

5   Concluding remarks

This paper presented a demonstration of adverse effects of avoiding variation in the results of NLP experiments. We demonstrate the effects of two sources of variation in NLP experiments: the variation due to sampling and initialization. For sampling variation, a well-established practice in the literature is to use a fixed standard training–test split across different studies. The only clear advantage of using a single standard test set is allowing fair comparisons between different studies. A *fair* comparison is definitely desirable in a competition, but for research we should perhaps emphasize *meaningful* comparisons more. The results presented above demonstrate that comparisons on a single (standard) tests set are not necessarily meaningful. Another, less-established but still common practice is to fix the random seed of the pseudo random number generator used during the experiments. We show that both practices hide the inherent variation in parsing scores, and bias the published results in arbitrary ways. As a result, these practices also defeat their very own purpose, making it difficult to interpret the comparison between different models outside this fixed setting.

The purpose of this paper is to point out the problem and promote further discussion of the topic. Our outcomes indicate that for insightful evaluations, we should acknowledge and report the variation in experimental results, rather than fixing the variation in arbitrary ways. This includes, (1) letting the model initializations vary, and (2) running the experiments on multiple data splits rather than a single training/development/test split. For both cases, reporting the variation based on multiple experiments. However, the implementation of the solutions is not easy. It requires community-wide changes beyond the power of individual researchers.

---

[6]At $p < 0.05$ calculated based on $10\,000$ bootstrap samples.

References

António Branco, Kevin Bretonnel Cohen, Piek Vossen, Nancy Ide, Nicoletta Calzolari, et al. 2017. Replicability and reproducibility of research results for human language technology: introducing an LRE special section. *Language Resources and Evaluation*, 51(1):221–247.

António Branco, Nicoletta Calzolari, Piek Vossen, Gertjan Van Noord, Dieter van Uytvanck, João Silva, Luís Gomes, André Moreira, and Willem Elbers. 2020. A shared task of a new, collaborative type to foster reproducibility: A first exercise in the area of language science and technology with reprolang2020. In *Proceedings of The 12th Language Resources and Evaluation Conference*, pages 5539–5545, Marseille, France, May. European Language Resources Association.

Kevin Cohen, Aurélie Névéol, Jingbo Xia, Negacy Hailu, Lawrence Hunter, and Pierre Zweigenbaum. 2017. Reproducibility in Biomedical Natural Language Processing. In *AMIA Annual Symposium*, Washington, DC, United States, November.

K. Bretonnel Cohen, Jingbo Xia, Pierre Zweigenbaum, Tiffany Callahan, Orin Hargraves, Foster Goss, Nancy Ide, Aurélie Névéol, Cyril Grouin, and Lawrence E. Hunter. 2018. Three dimensions of reproducibility in natural language processing. In *Proceedings of the Eleventh International Conference on Language Resources and Evaluation (LREC 2018)*, Miyazaki, Japan, May. European Language Resources Association (ELRA).

Rotem Dror, Gili Baumer, Marina Bogomolov, and Roi Reichart. 2017. Replicability analysis for natural language processing: Testing significance with multiple datasets. *Transactions of the Association for Computational Linguistics*, 5:471–486.

Chris Drummond. 2009. Replicability is not reproducibility: nor is it good science. In *Proceedings of the Evaluation Methods for Machine Learning Workshop at the 26th ICML*, pages 14–18.

Fiona Fidler and John Wilcox. 2018. Reproducibility of scientific results. In Edward N. Zalta, editor, *The Stanford Encyclopedia of Philosophy*. Metaphysics Research Lab, Stanford University, winter 2018 edition.

Antske Fokkens, Marieke van Erp, Marten Postma, Ted Pedersen, Piek Vossen, and Nuno Freire. 2013. Offspring from reproduction problems: What replication failure teaches us. In *Proceedings of the 51st Annual Meeting of the Association for Computational Linguistics (Volume 1: Long Papers)*, pages 1691–1701, Sofia, Bulgaria, August. Association for Computational Linguistics.

Leonard P. Freedman, Iain M. Cockburn, and Timothy S. Simcoe. 2015. The economics of reproducibility in preclinical research. *PLOS Biology*, 13(6):1–9, 06.

Kyle Gorman and Steven Bedrick. 2019. We need to talk about standard splits. In *Proceedings of the 57th Annual Meeting of the Association for Computational Linguistics*, pages 2786–2791, Florence, Italy, July. Association for Computational Linguistics.

Eva Huber and Çağrı Çöltekin. 2020. Reproduction and replication: A case study with automatic essay scoring. In *Proceedings of The 12th Language Resources and Evaluation Conference*, pages 5603–5613, Marseille, France.

Daniel Jurafsky and James H. Martin. 2009. *Speech and Language Processing: An Introduction to Natural Language Processing, Computational Linguistics, and Speech Recognition*. Pearson Prentice Hall, second edition.

Margot Mieskes. 2017. A quantitative study of data in the NLP community. In *Proceedings of the First ACL Workshop on Ethics in Natural Language Processing*, pages 23–29, Valencia, Spain, April. Association for Computational Linguistics.

Joakim Nivre, Marie-Catherine de Marneffe, Filip Ginter, Yoav Goldberg, Jan Hajič, Christopher Manning, Ryan McDonald, Slav Petrov, Sampo Pyysalo, Natalia Silveira, Reut Tsarfaty, and Daniel Zeman. 2016. Universal dependencies v1: A multilingual treebank collection. In *Proceedings of the Tenth International Conference on Language Resources and Evaluation (LREC'16)*, pages 23–28.

Open Science Collaboration. 2015. Estimating the reproducibility of psychological science. *Science*, (349):943–951.

Ted Pedersen. 2008. Empiricism is not a matter of faith. *Computational Linguistics*, 34(3):465–470.

Nils Reimers and Iryna Gurevych. 2017. Reporting score distributions makes a difference: Performance study of LSTM-networks for sequence tagging. In *Proceedings of the 2017 Conference on Empirical Methods in Natural Language Processing*, pages 338–348, Copenhagen, Denmark, September. Association for Computational Linguistics.

Milan Straka and Jana Straková. 2017. Tokenizing, pos tagging, lemmatizing and parsing UD 2.0 with UDPipe. In *Proceedings of the CoNLL 2017 Shared Task: Multilingual Parsing from Raw Text to Universal Dependencies*, pages 88–99, Vancouver, Canada, August. Association for Computational Linguistics.

Milan Straka and Jana Straková. 2019. Universal dependencies 2.5 models for UDPipe (2019-12-06). LINDAT/CLARIAH-CZ digital library at the Institute of Formal and Applied Linguistics (ÚFAL), Faculty of Mathematics and Physics, Charles University.

Ole Tange. 2011. GNU parallel - the command-line power tool. *;login: The USENIX Magazine*, 36(2):42–47.

Martijn Wieling, Josine Rawee, and Gertjan van Noord. 2018. Reproducibility in computational linguistics: Are we willing to share? *Computational Linguistics*, 44(4):641–649, December.

Daniel Zeman, Martin Popel, Milan Straka, Jan Hajic, Joakim Nivre, Filip Ginter, Juhani Luotolahti, Sampo Pyysalo, Slav Petrov, Martin Potthast, Francis Tyers, Elena Badmaeva, Memduh Gokirmak, Anna Nedoluzhko, Silvie Cinkova, Jan Hajic jr., Jaroslava Hlavacova, Václava Kettnerová, Zdenka Uresova, Jenna Kanerva, Stina Ojala, Anna Missilä, Christopher D. Manning, Sebastian Schuster, Siva Reddy, Dima Taji, Nizar Habash, Herman Leung, Marie-Catherine de Marneffe, Manuela Sanguinetti, Maria Simi, Hiroshi Kanayama, Valeria de-Paiva, Kira Droganova, Héctor Martínez Alonso, Çağrı Çöltekin, Umut Sulubacak, Hans Uszkoreit, Vivien Macketanz, Aljoscha Burchardt, Kim Harris, Katrin Marheinecke, Georg Rehm, Tolga Kayadelen, Mohammed Attia, Ali Elkahky, Zhuoran Yu, Emily Pitler, Saran Lertpradit, Michael Mandl, Jesse Kirchner, Hector Fernandez Alcalde, Jana Strnadová, Esha Banerjee, Ruli Manurung, Antonio Stella, Atsuko Shimada, Sookyoung Kwak, Gustavo Mendonca, Tatiana Lando, Rattima Nitisaroj, and Josie Li. 2017. Conll 2017 shared task: Multilingual parsing from raw text to universal dependencies. In *Proceedings of the CoNLL 2017 Shared Task: Multilingual Parsing from Raw Text to Universal Dependencies*, pages 1–19, Vancouver, Canada, August. Association for Computational Linguistics.

Daniel Zeman, Jan Hajič, Martin Popel, Martin Potthast, Milan Straka, Filip Ginter, Joakim Nivre, and Slav Petrov. 2018. CoNLL 2018 shared task: Multilingual parsing from raw text to universal dependencies. In *Proceedings of the CoNLL 2018 Shared Task: Multilingual Parsing from Raw Text to Universal Dependencies*, pages 1–21, Brussels, Belgium, October. Association for Computational Linguistics.

Daniel Zeman, Joakim Nivre, Mitchell Abrams, Noëmi Aepli, Željko Agić, Lars Ahrenberg, Gabrielė Aleksandravičiūtė, Lene Antonsen, Katya Aplonova, Maria Jesus Aranzabe, Gashaw Arutie, Masayuki Asahara, Luma Ateyah, Mohammed Attia, Aitziber Atutxa, Liesbeth Augustinus, Elena Badmaeva, Miguel Ballesteros, Esha Banerjee, Sebastian Bank, Verginica Barbu Mititelu, Victoria Basmov, Colin Batchelor, John Bauer, Sandra Bellato, Kepa Bengoetxea, Yevgeni Berzak, Irshad Ahmad Bhat, Riyaz Ahmad Bhat, Erica Biagetti, Eckhard Bick, Agnė Bielinskienė, Rogier Blokland, Victoria Bobicev, Loïc Boizou, Emanuel Borges Völker, Carl Börstell, Cristina Bosco, Gosse Bouma, Sam Bowman, Adriane Boyd, Kristina Brokaitė, Aljoscha Burchardt, Marie Candito, Bernard Caron, Gauthier Caron, Tatiana Cavalcanti, Gülşen Cebiroğlu Eryiğit, Flavio Massimiliano Cecchini, Giuseppe G. A. Celano, Slavomír Čéplö, Savas Cetin, Fabricio Chalub, Jinho Choi, Yongseok Cho, Jayeol Chun, Alessandra T. Cignarella, Silvie Cinková, Aurélie Collomb, Çağrı Çöltekin, Miriam Connor, Marine Courtin, Elizabeth Davidson, Marie-Catherine de Marneffe, Valeria de Paiva, Elvis de Souza, Arantza Diaz de Ilarraza, Carly Dickerson, Bamba Dione, Peter Dirix, Kaja Dobrovoljc, Timothy Dozat, Kira Droganova, Puneet Dwivedi, Hanne Eckhoff, Marhaba Eli, Ali Elkahky, Binyam Ephrem, Olga Erina, Tomaž Erjavec, Aline Etienne, Wograine Evelyn, Richárd Farkas, Hector Fernandez Alcalde, Jennifer Foster, Cláudia Freitas, Kazunori Fujita, Katarína Gajdošová, Daniel Galbraith, Marcos Garcia, Moa Gärdenfors, Sebastian Garza, Kim Gerdes, Filip Ginter, Iakes Goenaga, Koldo Gojenola, Memduh Gökırmak, Yoav Goldberg, Xavier Gómez Guinovart, Berta González Saavedra, Bernadeta Griciūtė, Matias Grioni, Normunds Grūzītis, Bruno Guillaume, Céline Guillot-Barbance, Nizar Habash, Jan Hajič, Jan Hajič jr., Mika Hämäläinen, Linh Hà Mỹ, Na-Rae Han, Kim Harris, Dag Haug, Johannes Heinecke, Felix Hennig, Barbora Hladká, Jaroslava Hlaváčová, Florinel Hociung, Petter Hohle, Jena Hwang, Takumi Ikeda, Radu Ion, Elena Irimia, Ọlájídé Ishola, Tomáš Jelínek, Anders Johannsen, Fredrik Jørgensen, Markus Juutinen, Hüner Kaşıkara, Andre Kaasen, Nadezhda Kabaeva, Sylvain Kahane, Hiroshi Kanayama, Jenna Kanerva, Boris Katz, Tolga Kayadelen, Jessica Kenney, Václava Kettnerová, Jesse Kirchner, Elena Klementieva, Arne Köhn, Kamil Kopacewicz, Natalia Kotsyba, Jolanta Kovalevskaitė, Simon Krek, Sookyoung Kwak, Veronika Laippala, Lorenzo Lambertino, Lucia Lam, Tatiana Lando, Septina Dian Larasati, Alexei Lavrentiev, John Lee, Phuong Lê Hồng, Alessandro Lenci, Saran Lertpradit, Herman Leung, Cheuk Ying Li, Josie Li, Keying Li, KyungTae Lim, Maria Liovina, Yuan Li, Nikola Ljubešić, Olga Loginova, Olga Lyashevskaya, Teresa Lynn, Vivien Macketanz, Aibek Makazhanov, Michael Mandl, Christopher Manning, Ruli Manurung, Cătălina Mărănduc, David Mareček, Katrin Marheinecke, Héctor Martínez Alonso, André Martins, Jan Mašek, Yuji Matsumoto, Ryan McDonald, Sarah McGuinness, Gustavo Mendonça, Niko Miekka, Margarita Misirpashayeva, Anna Missilä, Cătălin Mititelu, Maria Mitrofan, Yusuke Miyao, Simonetta Montemagni, Amir More, Laura Moreno Romero, Keiko Sophie Mori, Tomohiko Morioka, Shinsuke Mori, Shigeki Moro, Bjartur Mortensen, Bohdan Moskalevskyi, Kadri Muischnek, Robert Munro, Yugo Murawaki, Kaili Müürisep, Pinkey Nainwani, Juan Ignacio Navarro Horñiacek, Anna Nedoluzhko, Gunta Nešpore-Bērzkalne,

Luong Nguy˜ên Thị, Huy`ên Nguy˜ên Thị Minh, Yoshihiro Nikaido, Vitaly Nikolaev, Rattima Nitisaroj, Hanna Nurmi, Stina Ojala, Atul Kr. Ojha, Adédayọ Olúòkun, Mai Omura, Petya Osenova, Robert Östling, Lilja Øvrelid, Niko Partanen, Elena Pascual, Marco Passarotti, Agnieszka Patejuk, Guilherme Paulino-Passos, Angelika Peljak-Łapińska, Siyao Peng, Cenel-Augusto Perez, Guy Perrier, Daria Petrova, Slav Petrov, Jason Phelan, Jussi Piitulainen, Tommi A Pirinen, Emily Pitler, Barbara Plank, Thierry Poibeau, Larisa Ponomareva, Martin Popel, Lauma Pretkalniņa, Sophie Prévost, Prokopis Prokopidis, Adam Przepiórkowski, Tiina Puolakainen, Sampo Pyysalo, Peng Qi, Andriela Rääbis, Alexandre Rademaker, Loganathan Ramasamy, Taraka Rama, Carlos Ramisch, Vinit Ravishankar, Livy Real, Siva Reddy, Georg Rehm, Ivan Riabov, Michael Rießler, Erika Rimkutė, Larissa Rinaldi, Laura Rituma, Luisa Rocha, Mykhailo Romanenko, Rudolf Rosa, Davide Rovati, Valentin Roșca, Olga Rudina, Jack Rueter, Shoval Sadde, Benoît Sagot, Shadi Saleh, Alessio Salomoni, Tanja Samardžić, Stephanie Samson, Manuela Sanguinetti, Dage Särg, Baiba Saulīte, Yanin Sawanakunanon, Nathan Schneider, Sebastian Schuster, Djamé Seddah, Wolfgang Seeker, Mojgan Seraji, Mo Shen, Atsuko Shimada, Hiroyuki Shirasu, Muh Shohibussirri, Dmitry Sichinava, Aline Silveira, Natalia Silveira, Maria Simi, Radu Simionescu, Katalin Simkó, Mária Šimková, Kiril Simov, Aaron Smith, Isabela Soares-Bastos, Carolyn Spadine, Antonio Stella, Milan Straka, Jana Strnadová, Alane Suhr, Umut Sulubacak, Shingo Suzuki, Zsolt Szántó, Dima Taji, Yuta Takahashi, Fabio Tamburini, Takaaki Tanaka, Isabelle Tellier, Guillaume Thomas, Liisi Torga, Trond Trosterud, Anna Trukhina, Reut Tsarfaty, Francis Tyers, Sumire Uematsu, Zdeňka Urešová, Larraitz Uria, Hans Uszkoreit, Andrius Utka, Sowmya Vajjala, Daniel van Niekerk, Gertjan van Noord, Viktor Varga, Eric Villemonte de la Clergerie, Veronika Vincze, Lars Wallin, Abigail Walsh, Jing Xian Wang, Jonathan North Washington, Maximilan Wendt, Seyi Williams, Mats Wirén, Christian Wittern, Tsegay Woldemariam, Tak-sum Wong, Alina Wróblewska, Mary Yako, Naoki Yamazaki, Chunxiao Yan, Koichi Yasuoka, Marat M. Yavrumyan, Zhuoran Yu, Zdeněk Žabokrtský, Amir Zeldes, Manying Zhang, and Hanzhi Zhu. 2019. Universal dependencies 2.5. LINDAT/CLARIAH-CZ digital library at the Institute of Formal and Applied Linguistics (ÚFAL), Faculty of Mathematics and Physics, Charles University.

A   Further comparisons

This section presents additional scores obtained in our experiments in all stages of the parsing pipeline. Unlike Figure 1 in the main text, the figures presented in this section present absolute values. The scores reported by the original study are indicated by a triangle or diamond on the figures. For ease of interpretation, a blue triangle pointing up indicates that the random-split experiments yielding larger scores than the original report, a orange triangle pointing down indicates random-split experiments that yield results lower than the original report, and a black diamond shape indicates that the original scores fall within the range of scores in random-sample experiments. Similar to Figure 1, the black bars indicate the experiments with standard splits, while the light blue bars represent experiments with random splits.

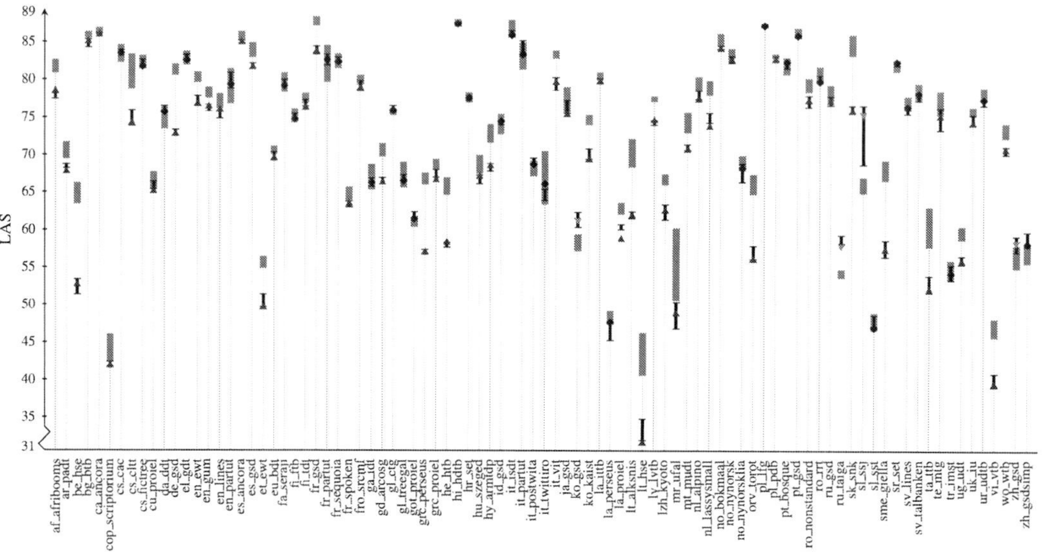

Figure 2: Absolute LAS scores. This figure present the same data in Figure 1, but in an absolute scale rather than relative to the scores published in the original study.

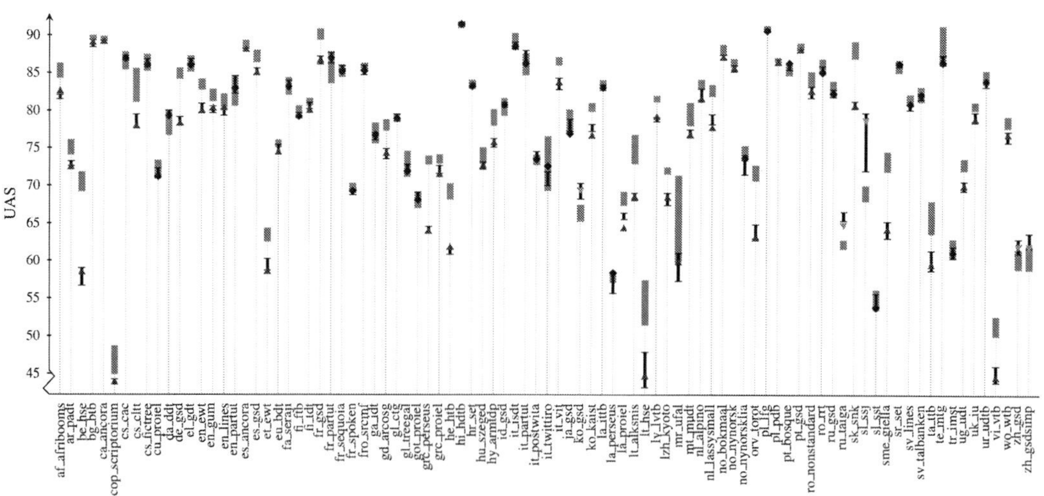

Figure 3: UAS scores.

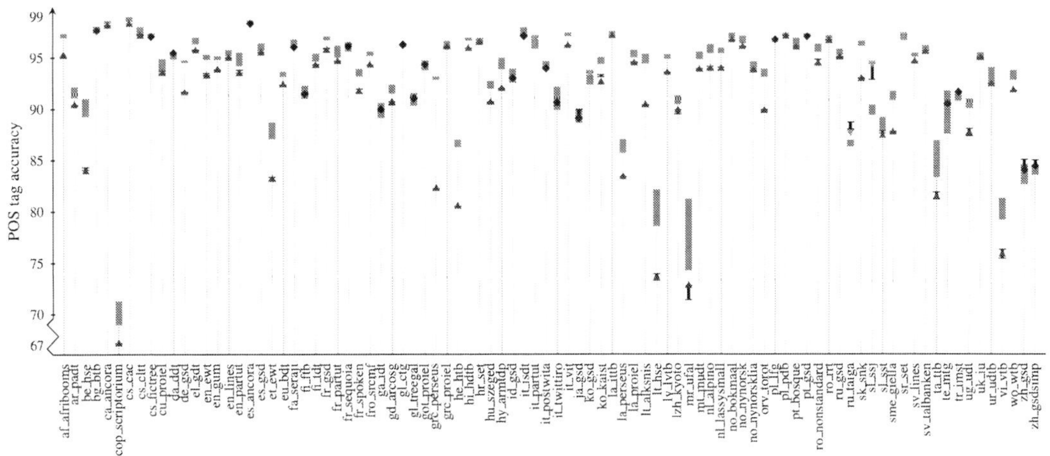

Figure 4: POS tagging accuracy.

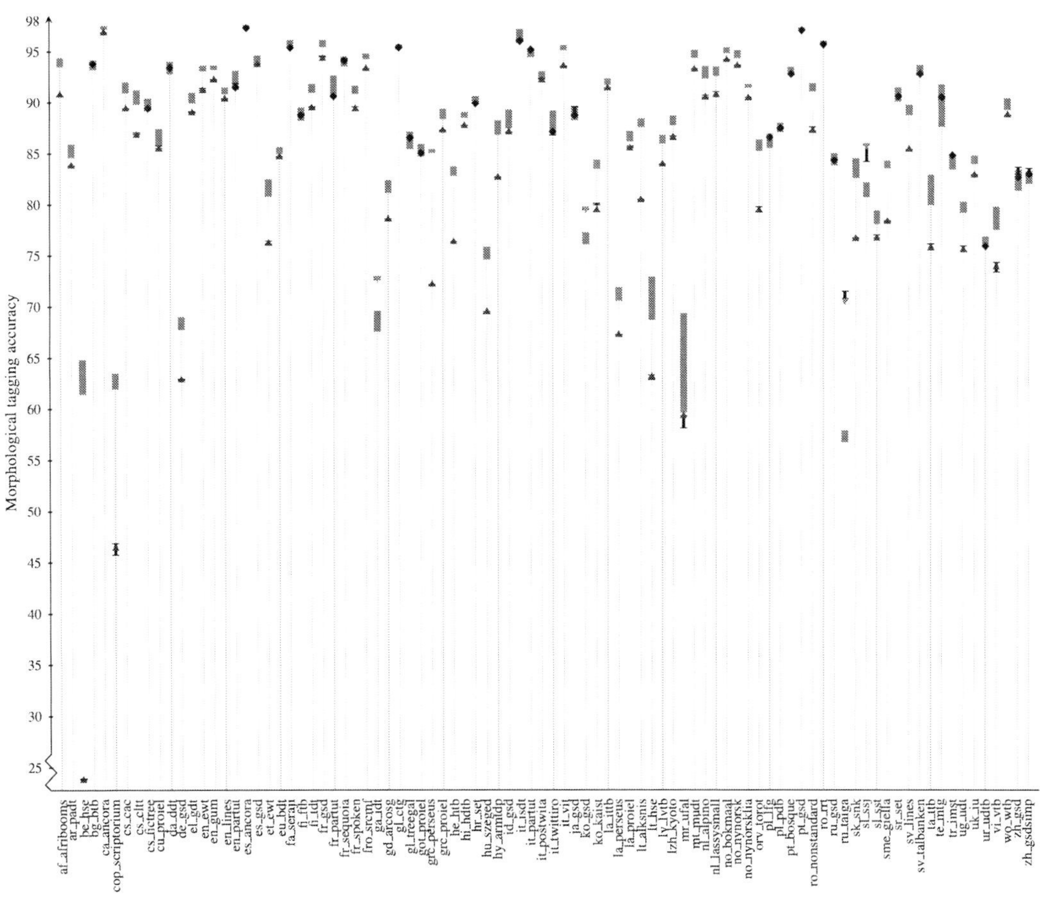

Figure 5: Full morphological tagging accuracy (including POS tags).

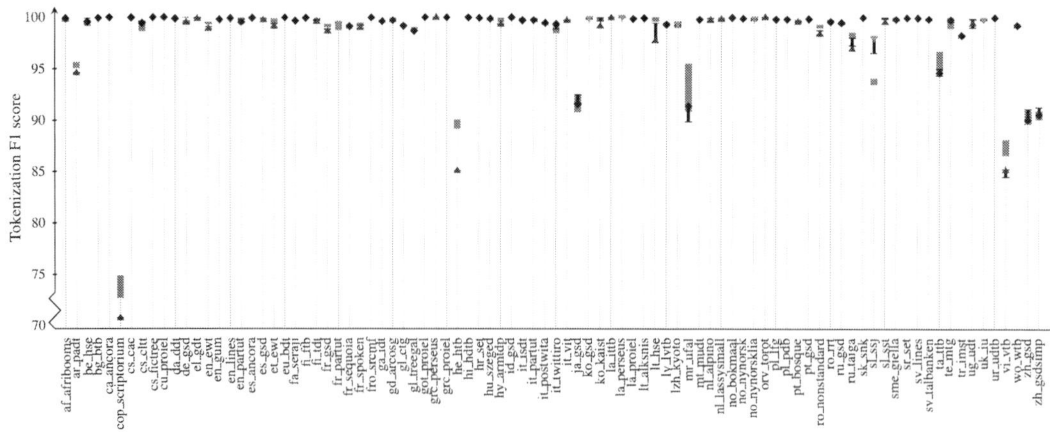

Figure 6: Tokenization F1 score.

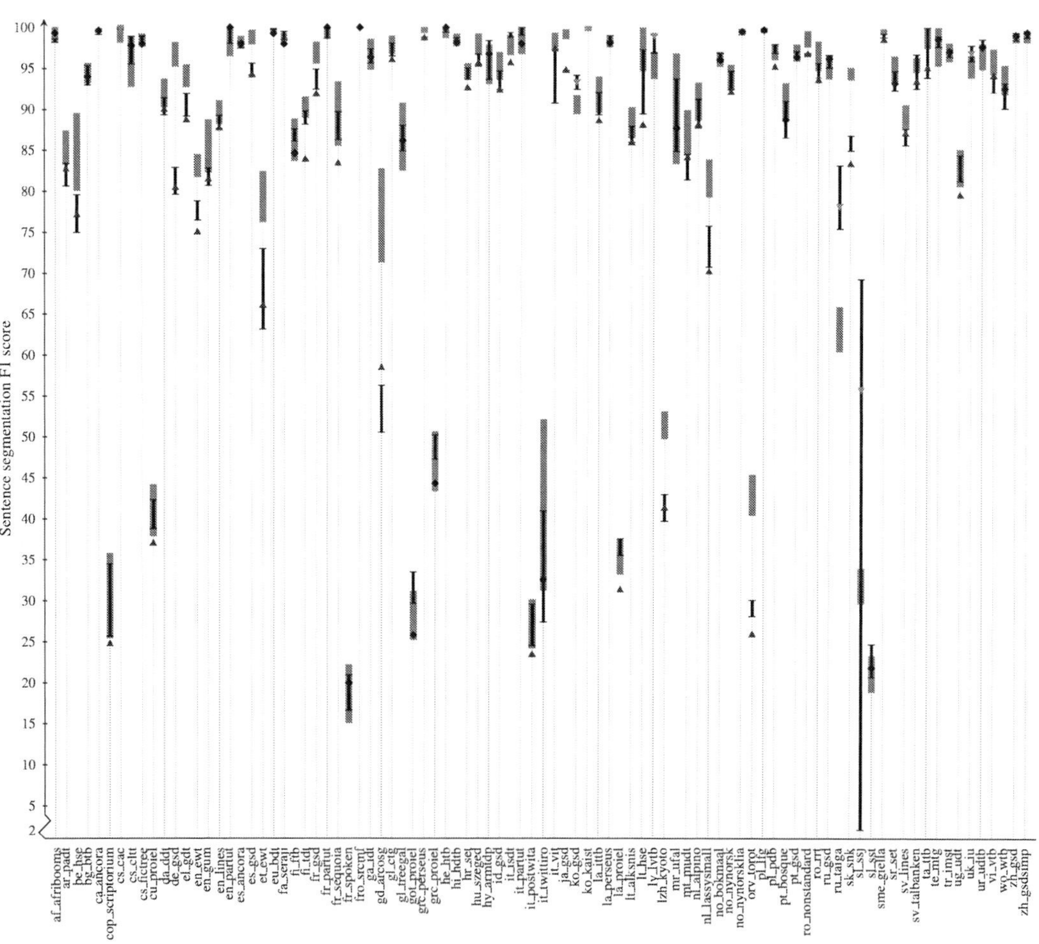

Figure 7: Sentence splitting F1 score.

From LFG To UD: A Combined Approach

Cheikh Bamba Dione

University of Bergen / Sydnesplassen 7, 5007 Bergen

dione.bamba@uib.no

Abstract

This paper reports on a systematic approach for deriving Universal Dependencies from LFG structures. The conversion starts with a step-wise transformation of the c-structure, combining part-of-speech (POS) information and the embedding path to determine the true head of dependency structures. The paper discusses several issues faced by existing algorithms when applied on Wolof and presents the strategies used to account for these issues. An experimental evaluation indicated that our approach was able to generate the correct output in more than 90% of the cases, leading to a substantial improvement in conversion accuracy compared to the previous models.

1 Introduction

This paper describes a methodology to automatically convert Lexical-Functional Grammar (LFG) (Kaplan and Bresnan, 1982) into Universal Dependencies (UD) structures (Nivre et al., 2016). Previous studies in this field (Øvrelid et al., 2009; Çetinoğlu et al., 2010; Meurer, 2017; Przepiórkowski and Patejuk, 2018) show disagreement regarding the structure to start from for the conversion. Meurer (2017) proposed a **lifting algorithm** which performs a step-wise transformation of the c-(onstituent) structure into a dependency tree. In contrast, the **P&P algorithm** (for lack of a better name) proposed by Przepiórkowski and Patejuk (2018) takes f-(unctional) structure as the basis for constructing dependency structures. These algorithms faced several issues when applied to Wolof (see section 3). Accordingly, this paper presents a new approach (discussed in section 4) that combines and extends previous methods.

In LFG, c-structure characterizes the phrase structure tree configurations and f-structure encodes grammatical relations (e.g. subject, object) and features (e.g. person, number). For instance, the Wolof LFG grammar (Dione, 2014) coupled with the Xerox Linguistic Environment (XLE) (Crouch et al., 2019) assigns to the sentence in (1) the c- and simplified f-structure in Figures 1 and 2.

(1)   *Sofoor bi taal na traktër bi.*
     driver the start 3SG tractor the
     'The driver starts the tractor.'

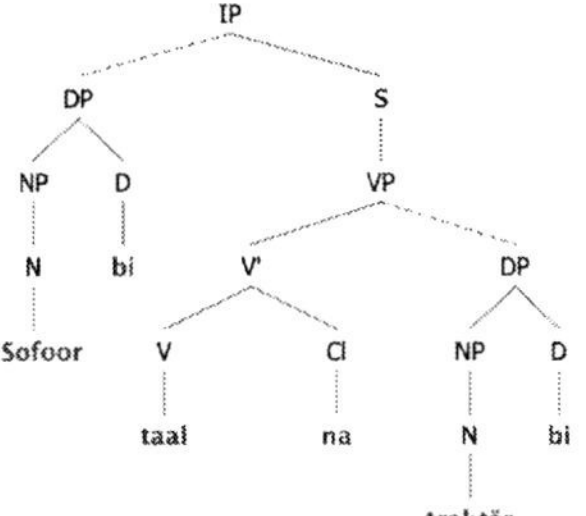

Fig. 1: C-structure of (1)

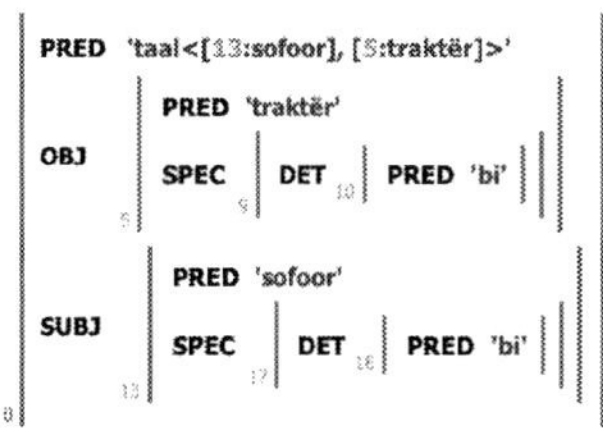

Fig. 2: F-structure of (1)

The f-structure states that the main predicate of (1) is *taal* 'start' and it has two arguments: a subject (SUBJ) and an object (OBJ). Each of these arguments has its own semantic predicate (e.g. *sofoor* 'driver' for SUBJ) and a DET feature embedded under SPEC introduced by the determiner *bi*.

Proceedings of the Fourth Workshop on Universal Dependencies (UDW 2020), pages 57–66
Barcelona, Spain (Online), December 13, 2020

Nonterminal nodes in c-structure are mapped to particular substructures in f-structure via the ϕ (phi) function. Thus, in the c-structure in Fig. 1, the leftmost nodes *DP*, *NP*, *N* and *D* all map to the substructure with index 13 (the value of SUBJ) in the corresponding f-structure. Likewise, the rightmost nodes *DP*, *NP*, *N* and *D* all map to the substructure with index 5 (i.e., the value of OBJ). All the other nonterminals, including *IP*, *S*, *VP*, *V'* and *Cl* map to the entire f-structure with index 0.

A crucial concept is the functional head (FH) (Bresnan, 2001). In LFG, a 'head' of a phrase shares its features with its mother. A solid line between a mother node and its daughter node (DN) in c-structure indicates that DN is a FH of its mother, i.e. they project to the same f-structure.

2 From LFG to dependency structures

Our approach is based on modified versions of both the lifting (Meurer, 2017) and the P&P algorithms (Patejuk and Przepiórkowski, 2018), which are briefly presented in sections 2.1 and 2.2, respectively.

2.1 The lifting algorithm (Meurer, 2017)

This algorithm recursively replaces each non-terminal node X by its functional head (FH) using the following rules. The step-wise derivation of (2) is shown below.

- 1a: If X has no FH, it is replaced by its daughter nodes as direct children of the parent Z of X. Then, the algorithm proceeds as before.
- 1b: If X has more than one FH, the node with shortest or empty embedding path is selected to replace X, taking the remaining nodes as its dependents.
- 1c: As a last resort, if there is still more than one such node, the first (i.e. leftmost) of them is selected as the replacement.
- 2: The edge between node X and daughter node Y is labeled with the minimal f-structure path from $\phi(X)$ to $\phi(Y)$, concatenated with the embedding path of Y.

(2) *Awa dem*
     Awa went

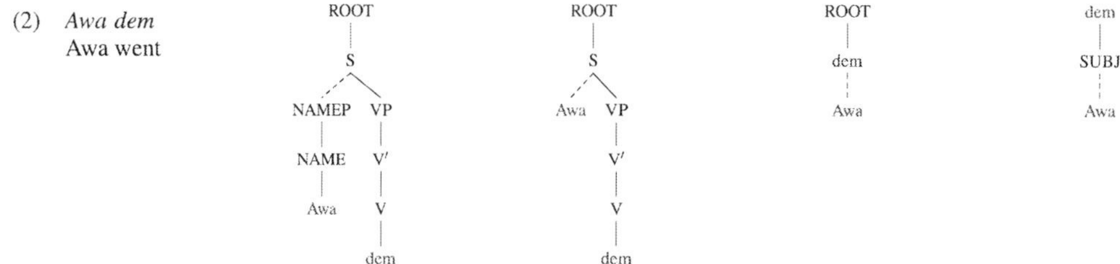

The embedding path indicates how deep the PRED value associated with a c-structure is embedded in the corresponding f-structure. For instance, in Figure 1 the leftmost DP has two functional heads (i.e. NP and D). The functional equation (3) states that the PRED value of the f-structure associated with the *NP* node is the semantic form *sofoor* 'driver'. Hence, the embedding path for N is **empty**, since the PRED value is at the top level of the projected f-structure (eq. 3). In contrast, the path for the determiner *bi* is **non-trivial**, i.e. it is deeper embedded along the path *SPEC DET* in the associated f-structure (eq. (4)). Examples (3-4) contain LFG regular notations by which $\uparrow$ refers to the mother of the node in question.

(3) $(\uparrow \text{PRED})=$'sofoor'   (4) $(\uparrow \text{SPEC DET PRED})=$'bi'

2.2 The P&P Algorithm (Patejuk and Przepiórkowski, 2018)

Unlike Meurer (2017), the approach of the P&P algorithm follows the more standard observation that f-structures provide the most natural basis for dependency relations. The idea is that, besides f-structures, information encoded in terminal and pre-terminal nodes of the constituency tree, together with the standard correspondence between c-structure preterminals and f-structure components, is sufficient to perform the conversion. In other words, the actual constituency information may be completely ignored.

The P&P algorithm was used to derive UD structures from an LFG treebank of Polish. The conversion process occurs in two main steps. First, the LFG structures are converted into 'initial dependencies', i.e.

LFG-like structures that maintain headedness information in c-structures and the names of dependencies
in f-structures. Then, the 'initial dependencies' are converted to 'final UD representations'. The conversion process involves many non-trivial issues, including finding the true heads (i.e. the heads of the
dependency structure). This is particularly challenging, as many c-structure tokens may map to several
f-structures. To find the true head, the P&P algorithm uses information based on POS tag (Patejuk and
Przepiórkowski, 2018, p. 123) as follows:

- *If there is a verbal token among the co-heads, select it as the true head;*
- *otherwise, if there is a nominal or adjectival token, it is the true head;*
- *otherwise, if there is an explicit conjunction, it is the head;*
- *otherwise, if there is a complementiser of the semantic kind, select it as the true head;*
- *otherwise select the final comma as the true head in case there are at most two commas in the
co-head set, or the penultimate comma in case there are more than two commas in the co-head set.*

3   Issues with existing algorithms

When applied on the Wolof data, the existing algorithms faced various issues as discussed below.

3.1   Recovering PRED from f-structures and Issue with Verb inflectional markers

The lifting algorithm heavily relies on the concept of embedding path, but retrieving such a path requires
information encoded in f-structure in terms of PRED values. Crucially, in many cases, there is absolutely
no obvious way to recover the surface form from a PRED value. This is particularly true for morphologically rich languages like Wolof (Ka, 1994; Ndiaye, 1995). For instance, in (5), the verbal root of
the surface form (*feccikuwaatoon*) is *fas* "to tie". The inversive suffix *i* triggered (i) consonant mutation
($s \rightarrow c$), (ii) gemination ($c \rightarrow cc$), and (iii) vowel mutation ($a \rightarrow e$), yielding the stem *fecci* "to untie".
The inversive derivation is followed by the middle derivation (as indicated by *-ku* which is an allomorph
of the *-u* mediopassive (MEDP) marker). In addition, the verbal derivation is also expressed iteratively
(*w* is a glide insertion (GI)) in the past conjugation. The morphological analysis produced by the Wolof
Morphological Analyzer (WoMA) (Dione, 2012) for the form *feccikuwaatoon* in (5) is given in (6).

(5) *Buum gi   fecc-i-ku-w-aat-oon   na.*　　　(6)   feccikuwaatoon ↔ fas+Verb+Invers+MEDP+Iter+PST
　　 rope   the tie-INV-MEDP-GI-ITER-PST 3SG.
　　 "The rope untied itself again."

The c-structure and f-structure associated with (5) are shown in Figure 3. The PRED of the top f-
structure is *fas* "to tie". As this example illustrates, reconstructing the PRED value (*fas*) from the surface
token *feccikuwaatoon* is far from obvious. The inversive and iterative derivation are indicated as lexical
semantic features *LEX-SEM*. Moreover, the f-structure specifies information regarding the mediopassive
voice which subsumes the meaning of the middle voice.

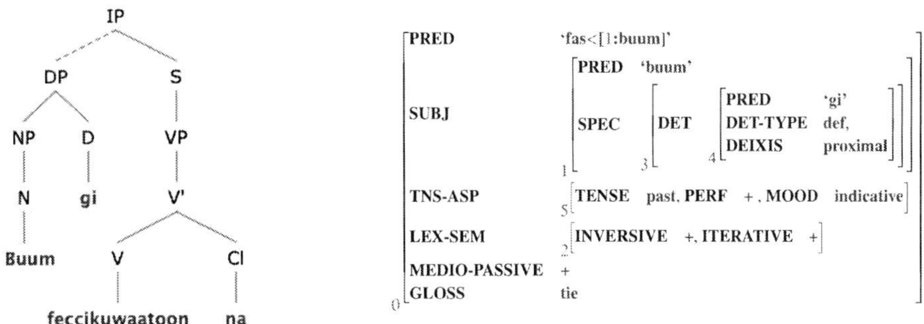

Fig. 3: C-structure and simplified f-structure of (5)

A second issue concerns the treatment of verbal inflectional markers. In imperfective sentences like

(7), the inflectional marker precedes the main verb, but follows it in perfectives sentences like (1).

(7) *Sofoor bi   dina   taal traktër bi.*
driver the.SG IPFV.3SG start tractor the.SG
"The driver will start the tractor."

Figure 4 shows the LFG structures associated with (7). The inflectional marker (*dina*) and the main verb (*taal*) are mapped to the main feature structure (with index 38). Now, a question that existing algorithms need to address is which of these co-heads is the true head.

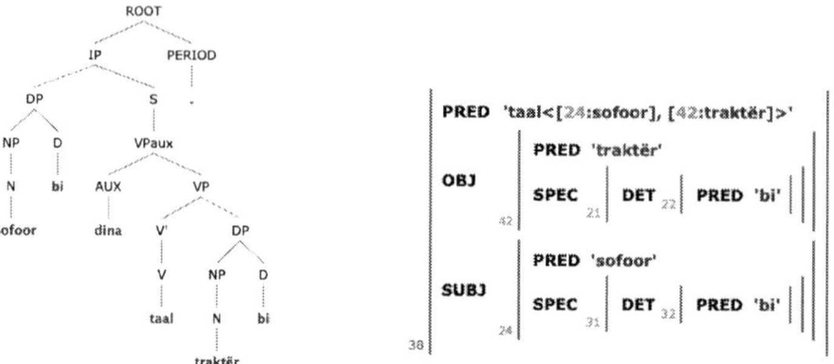

Fig. 4: C-and f-structure of (7)

When trying to answer this question, the lifting algorithm assigns an empty embedding path to both the lexical verb and the inflectional marker. As a consequence, Rule 1b (see section 2.1) cannot settle the matter, since both constituents are associated with an embedding path of the same length. Thus, Rule 1c will select the first node as the true head, yielding incorrect analyses for constructions like (7) where the inflectional marker precedes the main verb. As Figure 5 shows, the auxiliary *dina* is wrongly identified as the head of the clause, taking the lexical verb *taal* and the subject *sofoor bi* as its dependents.

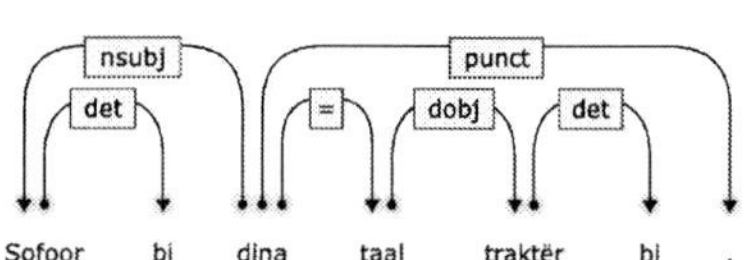

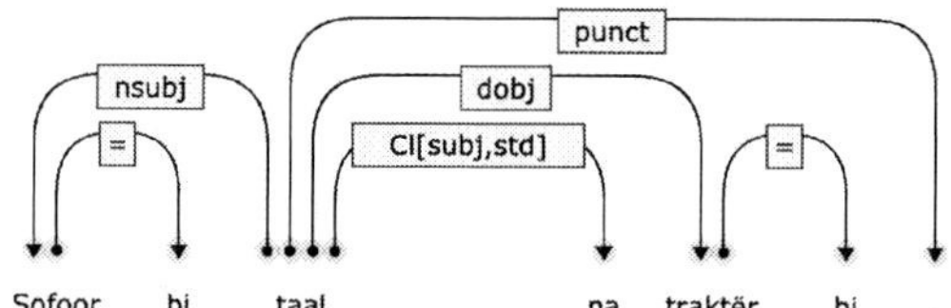

Fig. 5: Dependency of (7) acc. the lifting algo.   Fig. 6: Dependency of (1) acc. the lifting algo.

In contrast, the lifting algorithm produces the correct dependency structure for constructions like (1) where the inflectional marker follows the main verb, as Figure 6 shows. This seems to be an indication that the attachment errors produced by the lifting algorithm when building the dependency structure in Figure 5 stems from an incorrect application of Rule 1c (section 2.1). Both tokens were assigned an empty embedding path and, thus, Rule 1c selected the wrong head based on linear order.

3.2 Free relatives

Another issue concerns the analysis of Wolof free relatives (see the underlined clause in (8)). The relative pronoun *ñi* refers to a nominal that does not appear in the corresponding main clause.

(8) *Xam naa ñi   taal traktër bi   (ñépp).*
know 1SG PRON start tractor the.SG QUANT
"I know ((all) the people) who started the tractor."

Figure 7 shows the c- and simplified f-structure associated with (8). The free relative bears the *OBJ* function of the main clause. As *SUBJ* and *TOPIC-REL* of the embedded verb, the relative pronoun has a pronoun form (*PRON-FORM*) and type (*PRON-TYPE*) feature (not displayed here). Note that the c-structure suggests that none of the daughter nodes of *NP* (i.e. *PRON* and *IPsub*) is a functional head.

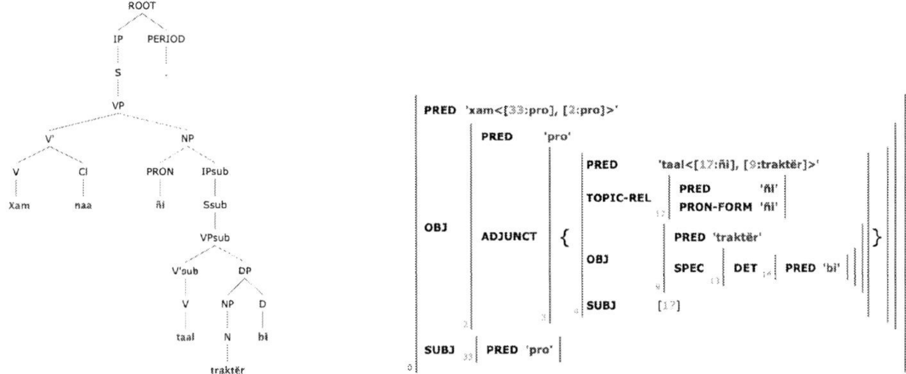

Fig. 7: C- and F-structure of (8)

The quantifier *ñépp* ("all") may surface on the far right edge of the entire free relative clause, in which case it agrees in noun class (e.g. *ñ*) with the free relative pronoun (*ñi*). This constitutes an evidence that free relatives in Wolof, as in English (Butt et al., 1999), behave like nominal phrases and are treated as such in the Wolof UD Treebank (Dione, 2019). The pronoun is analyzed as the head of the free relative, the main verb inside the relative clause being its dependent through the *acl:relcl* relation (see Fig. 8).

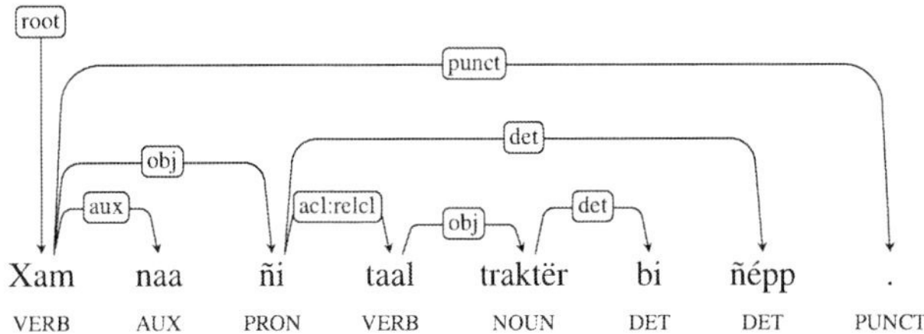

Fig. 8: Final UD representation of (8)

Unlike in LFG, in UD, the relativizer functions as the head of the structure (taking the verb as its dependent). This difference in approach is problematic for the lifting algorithm, because Rule 1c will match and incorrectly choose the verb as the head of the structure. Likewise, for the P&P algorithm, the main verb and the relative pronoun will not immediately enter in competition at the first stage, as they do not directly share the same co-head set. However, at a later stage, when dependencies are added to other co-heads, the verb will compete with and win over the pronoun, leading to an inaccurate UD analysis.

3.3 Constituent dislocation

In LFG, there is structure sharing that arises from discourse functions like *FOCUS* and *TOPIC*. For instance, in (9), the free relative constituent (as underlined) bears both the *TOPIC* and *OBJ* functions of the verb *jël* "to take". The object clitic *ko* is used here as a resumptive pronoun. As the associated f-structure in Figure 10 shows, the topic constituent and the object pronoun share the same index 17.

(9) *Lu des ci xaalis bi, gune yi jël ko.*
    what remain of money the child the take it

    "whatever remains from the money, the children took it."

In principle, this structure sharing can be modeled by means of secondary edges (Meurer, 2017), as is done in some variants of Dependency Grammar to e.g. code functionally bound arguments of the subordinate verb in control constructions. Crucially, the lifting algorithm does not yet implement secondary edges, and therefore typically generates incorrect analyses for structure sharing involving discourse functions: two different arguments are linked to a verb through the same dependency relation, which should be unique. As Figure 11 shows, the main verb *jël* "take" has two direct object arguments (*dobj*), instead of one. Similarly, the P&P algorithm does not include a method that explicitly handles discourse functions, and therefore produces the same error.

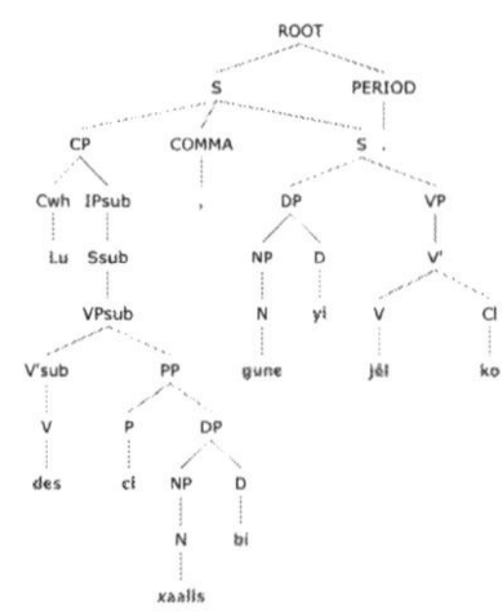

Fig. 9: C-structure of (9)

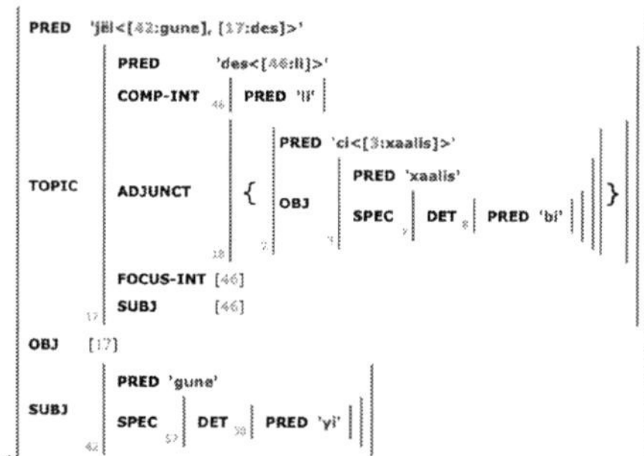

Fig. 10: F-structure of (9)

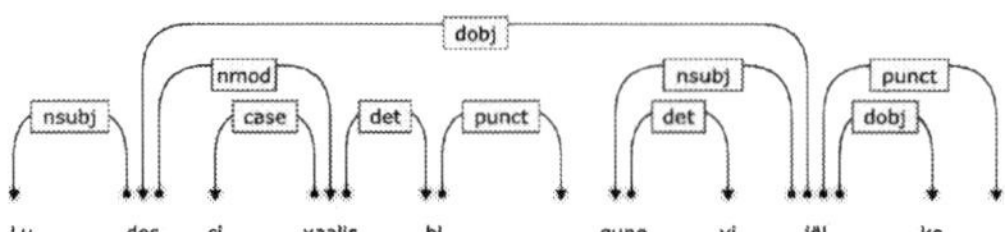

Fig. 11: Analysis of (9) acc. the lifting algo.

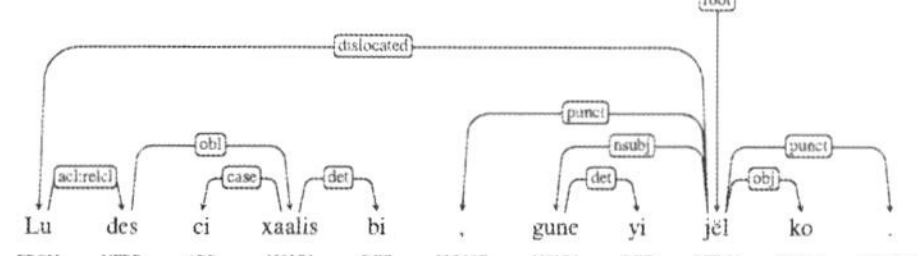

Fig. 12: Correct UD representation of (9)

Following the UD guidelines, the correct dependency relation for the free relative in (9) is *dislocated* (rather than *obj*), which is appropriate for fronted or postposed elements that do not fullfil the usual core grammatical relations of a sentence. The correct UD representation for (9) is displayed in Figure 12.

4 The Combined Approach

Our approach is based on a modified and extended version of existing algorithms. First, the c-structure is transformed step-wise by recursively replacing each non-terminal node by its functional head(s). Then, both the embedding path (as suggested by the lifting algorithm) and the head selection procedure (as suggested by the P&P algorithm) are used to determine the true head. The underlying assumptions of these algorithms were modified where necessary to account for the issues outlined in section 3.

4.1 Selecting the true head

The true head of a structure is selected by combining the strategies suggested by the lifting and P&P algorithms, using their agreement as a validation mechanism. In case of divergence, a decision is made about which one should apply, integrating information from the current configuration and POS tags.

The lifting algorithm assigns an empty path to the c-structure co-heads without a corresponding *PRED* in the f-structure. As this turned out to be problematic for cases involving the lexical verb and the inflectional markers, we did not follow that strategy. Instead, we try to find the path to the *PRED* for each FH that enters in competition, and consider the path to be null (but not empty!) if the *PRED* is not found. Thus, we distinguish between null, empty and non-trivial path.

For instance, if the two functional heads FH1 and FH2 enter in competition, we combine a redefined version of the procedure proposed by the P&P algorithm with the path to the *PRED* for both FH1 and FH2 to determine the true head. Accordingly, we identify three scenarios. If the FHs have both a null path, then the head selection is solely based on POS information. Otherwise, if FH1 has a null embedding path, and FH2 has an empty one (as illustrated in (1)), the latter is selected as the true head, taking the former as its dependent. Finally, if FH1 has an empty path, and FH2 has a non-trivial one (as is the case with DPs), we follow the lifting algorithm by selecting the FH node with shortest or empty embedding path as the true head and treat the other FH as its dependents. We use the P&P POS-tag based selection procedure to validate our choice, and find that the two algorithms almost always produce the same selection.

4.2 Modified lifting algorithm

The modified version of the lifting algorithm proposed in this paper processes one node at a time referred to as the *current nonterminal node* (henceforth **CNN**, highlighted with a box around it in the figures).

For the CNN, we first check two parameters: (1) the number of the functional heads (FHs), and (2) the number of daughter nodes (DNs).

4.2.1 Case 1: One DN, zero FH

In the first case, the CNN has only one DN, but that one is not a FH (see the conjunctive adverbial phrase *CONJadvP* in Figure 13). In this case, the single DN (e.g. *CONJadv*) is trivially promoted as functional head and lifted up to replace CNN.

(10) *Kon, Awa dem*
      thus Awa went

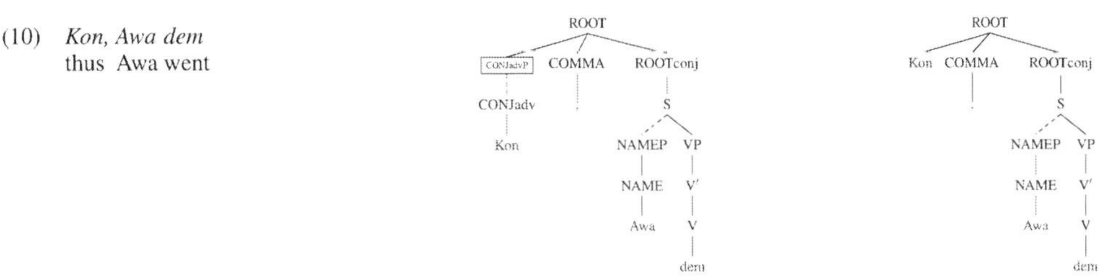

Fig. 13: *CONJadvP* has only 1 DN, and zero FH

4.2.2 Case 2: Many DNs, zero FH

In the second case, the CNN has two or more DNs, and none of them is a FH, as illustrated by the free relative *NP* (*NPrel*) in (11) and its associated c-structure in Figure 14.

(11) *Li   des   ci xaalis bi ...*
      what remain of money the ...
      "what remains from the money ..."

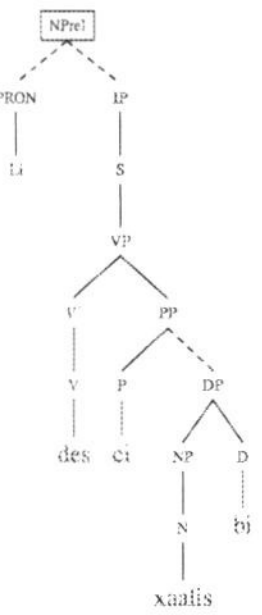

Fig. 14: *NPrel* has 2 DNs, but none of them is FH

In this case, the true head is selected based on the procedure described in section 4.1, which gives the following configuration. First, the noun *xaalis* wins the competition over the determiner *bi* and then over the preposition *ci*. Next, the verb *des* wins over that noun. When, the *NPrel* is processed as CNN, the two daughter nodes in competition are the verb and the free relative pronoun *li*. Finally, we search in the f-structure attributes to check whether the pronoun type is a free relative. If it is the case, we select it as the head and turn the verb into its dependent via the *acl:relcl* relation. Otherwise, the verb wins over the pronoun and is selected as the true head. Accordingly, the head node is lifted up to replace CNN. The step just described is crucial, as it allows to generate the correct analysis for free relatives in section 3.2.

4.2.3 Case 3: Many DNs, one FH

The CNN has two or more DNs, but only one of them is a FH. Instances of this case include coordination (12) and prepositional phrases (e.g. the PP in Figure 14). For instance, the nominal coordination (*NOMCoord*) in Figure 15 has many DNs, but only the conjunction is a FH.

Given this configuration, we first check the type of the phrase, distinguishing four sub-cases. If the structure is a coordination, then we assume the first conjunct to be the true head and append all the other DNs that are not conjunction as its dependents. These dependents are processed in a linear order. For each DN, we check in the node's POS tag whether it is a conjunction, and accordingly, first retrieve the next element of the daughter nodes list to create a dependency relation between that element and the most recent conjunction using the *cc* relation. Otherwise, we connect the first conjunct and that DN via the *conj* relation. Finally, the first conjunct is lifted up to replace the CNN.

Otherwise if the structure is a PP, we then append the FH (i.e. the preposition) as a dependent of one of the other DNs that is selected as the true head based on POS tags (see section 4.1). Otherwise if the structure is a NAMEP, then we inverse the head-dependent relation. In all other cases, we treat the FH as the true head. We turn all but the FH into dependents, and, replace the CNN with the FH.

(12) *Mag   ak gune*
     old.people and young.people
     "Old and young people"

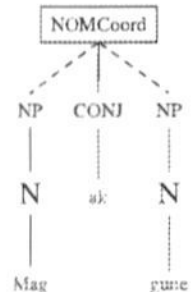
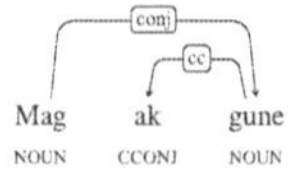

Fig. 15: Handling coordination

4.2.4   Case 4: Many DNs, many FHs

In some cases, the CNN may have up to 5 FHs. For instance, in Figure 16, the *ROOT* node has four FHs: *CONJadvP, COMMA, ROOTconj* and *PERIOD*. Likewise, in Figure 17, all the three conjunctions are FHs of NOMCoord. In this case, we first check whether the structure is a coordination, and, accordingly, apply the coordination rules as explained above. Otherwise, we take the set of FHs and apply the procedure described in section 4.1.

(13) *Kon, ñaari xale ya   agsi.*
     Thus, two   child the.pl arrive
     "So, the two children arrive."

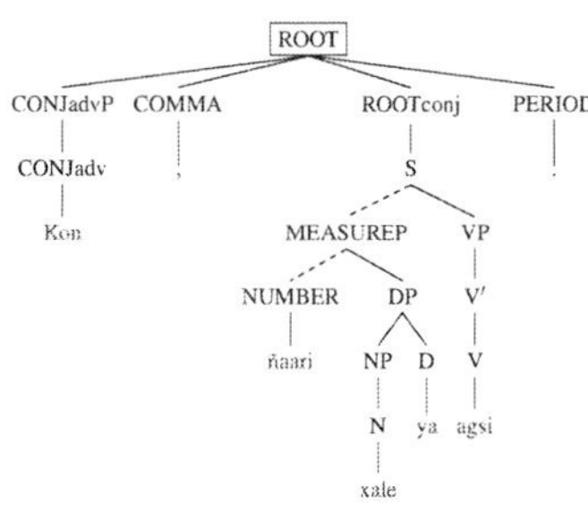

Fig. 16: Example of a root node with four FHs

(14) *Petu   ma   ak   yedd   ya   ak   xuloo ba   ak   lépp*
     meeting the.SG CONJ lecture the.PL CONJ dispute the.SG CONJ QUANT

     "The secret meetings, the lectures, the dispute and all this"
     Lit.: "The secret meetings and the lectures and the dispute and all this"

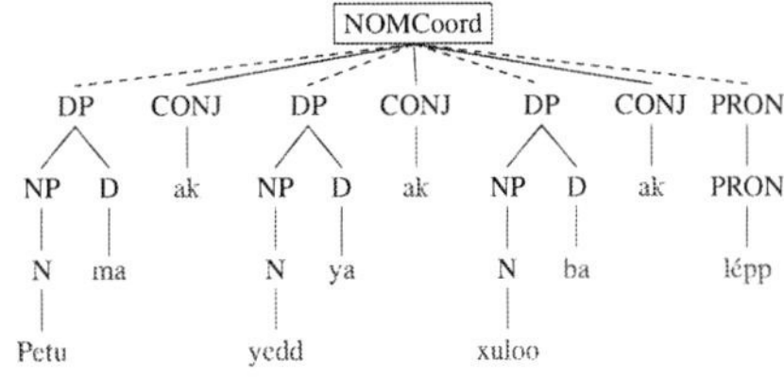
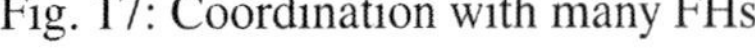
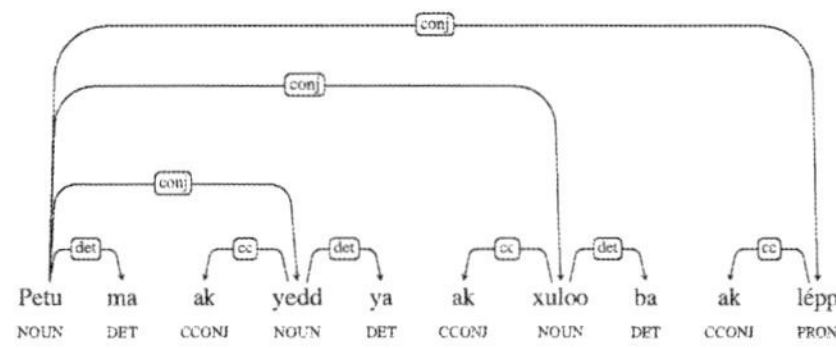

Fig. 17: Coordination with many FHs   Fig. 18: UD analysis of (14)

5   Evaluation

To develop our model, we used a relatively small Wolof corpus that contains 510 sentences: (i) 50 sentences distributed within the ParGram group (Butt et al., 2002), and (ii) 460 sentences drawn from short stories (Cissé, 1994; Garros, 1997). These data were annotated with the Wolof LFG grammar (Dione,

2020) and disambiguated using the LFG Parsebanker (Rosén et al., 2009). This tool supports disambiguation based on discriminants (Carter, 1997). The disambiguated parses in Prolog format were converted to a TigerXML (Brants et al., 2002) file used to generate the c-structure tree and the f-structure graph.

To test our model, we used a different set of 453 sentences extracted from the Wolof LFG treebank (Dione, 2014). These sentences are then annotated semi-automatically in UD v.2 by means of UDPipe (Straka and Straková, 2017). Subsequent to this, the annotations were corrected manually using UD Annotatrix (Tyers et al., 2018) to ensure parsing quality. The final annotations provide the gold standard set used to assess the performance of the combined approach compared to the lifting and P&P algorithms.

Table 1 gives accuracies gained by the different models on the gold standard test set. CLAS computes the labeled score over all relations except relations that relate a function word to a content word (including determiners (*det*), classifiers (*clf*), adpositions (*case*), auxiliaries (*aux,cop*), and conjunctions (*cc,mark*)) as well as punctuations. The *Diff* column indicates the difference in LAS when excluding function words and punctuations. The scores were computed using the CoNLL 2018 script. The results indicate that the combined approach surpasses both the lifting and P&P algorithms on the Wolof data. The most extreme case is the difference in LAS of ca. 25 percentage points between our model and the lifting algorithm. Common mistakes made by the combined approach mostly involve some free relatives and special constructions like ellipses (which are challenging for all the models).

	UAS	LAS	CLAS	Diff
Lifting algorithm	75.02	65.06	69.82	-4.76
P&P algorithm	82.08	74.75	76.78	-2.03
Our model	**91.57**	**89.57**	**89.26**	-0.31

Table 1: Evaluation scores for the Wolof test treebank

The lifting algorithm made an important number of attachment errors involving function words, in particular verb inflectional markers (hence its low performance). This seems to be confirmed by the relatively high difference value (-4.76) observed when comparing the LAS and CLAS scores. There are also many cases involving content words where the algorithm fails to reverse the head-dependent relation. This is particularly true for free relatives. Likewise, the P&P algorithm also committed some mistakes related to function words (e.g. wrong attachment of punctuations). Compared to the lifting algorithm, errors on functional relations have a less significant and differential impact on the score. The LAS score decreases by only 2.03 when these relations are included. Major errors seem to be caused by wrong attachment of content words, e.g. in structures involving free relatives and dislocation.

6   Conclusion

This paper has proposed a new approach to automatic conversion of LFG structures to dependency structures. This approach extends existing algorithms, using their inter-agreement as a validation mechanism. It suggests careful reconsideration of the concept of embedding path to better account for c-structure nodes that lack a PRED value at f-structure. This is particularly true for morphologically rich languages. Likewise, adapting the POS based head selection procedure suggested by the P&P algorithm proved to be essential for selecting the true dependency head. Using f-structure information is crucial for modeling language-specific phenomena (e.g. free relatives in Wolof) that are analyzed following a particular choice of the language's grammar. The combined approach also revisited the concept of structure sharing to enable the analysis of dislocated constituents.

References

Sabine Brants, Stefanie Dipper, Silvia Hansen, Wolfgang Lezius, and George Smith. 2002. The TIGER treebank. In *Proceedings of the workshop on treebanks and linguistic theories*, volume 168.

Joan Bresnan. 2001. *Lexical-functional syntax*. Blackwell, Oxford.

Miriam Butt, Tracy Holloway King, María-Eugenia Niño, and Frédérique Segond. 1999. *A grammar writer's cookbook*. CSLI, Stanford, CA.

Miriam Butt, Helge Dyvik, Tracy Holloway King, Hiroshi Masuichi, and Christian Rohrer. 2002. The parallel grammar project. In *Proceedings of the COLING02 Workshop on Grammar Engineering and Evaluation*, volume 15, pages 1–7. Association for Computational Linguistics.

David Carter. 1997. The TreeBanker: A tool for supervised training of parsed corpora. In *Proceedings of the Workshop on Computational Environments for Grammar Development and Linguistic Engineering*, pages 9–15.

Mamadou Cissé. 1994. *Contes wolof modernes*. L'harmattan.

Dick Crouch, Mary Dalrymple, Ron Kaplan, Tracy King, John Maxwell, and Paula Newman. 2019. *XLE documentation*. On-line documentation, Palo Alto Research Center (PARC).

Cheikh Bamba Dione. 2012. A morphological analyzer for Wolof using finite-state techniques. In *Proceedings of the 8th LREC*. ELRA.

Cheikh Bamba Dione. 2014. LFG parse disambiguation for Wolof. *Journal of Language Modelling*, 2(1):105–165.

Cheikh Bamba Dione. 2019. Developing universal dependencies for wolof. In *Proceedings of the Third Workshop on Universal Dependencies (UDW, SyntaxFest 2019)*, pages 12–23, Paris, France, 26 August. Association for Computational Linguistics.

Cheikh M. Bamba Dione. 2020. Implementation and evaluation of an lfg-based parser for wolof. In *Proceedings of The 12th Language Resources and Evaluation Conference*, pages 5128–5136, Marseille, France, May. European Language Resources Association.

Nataali Dominik Garros, editor. 1997. *Bukkeek "perigam" bu xonq: teeñ yi*. Dakar: SIL; Paris: EDICEF.

Omar Ka. 1994. *Wolof phonology and morphology*. University Press of America, Lanham, Maryland.

Ron Kaplan and Joan Bresnan. 1982. Lexical-functional grammar: A formal system for grammatical representation. In Joan Bresnan, editor, *The mental representation of grammatical relations*, pages 173–281. MIT Press, Cambridge, MA.

Paul Meurer. 2017. From LFG structures to dependency relations. *Bergen Language and Linguistics Studies*, 8(1).

Moussa D. Ndiaye. 1995. *Phonologie et morphologie des alternances en wolof*. Ph.D. thesis, University of Quebec.

Joakim Nivre, Marie-Catherine de Marneffe, Filip Ginter, Yoav Goldberg, Jan Hajic, Christopher D. Manning, Ryan McDonald, Slav Petrov, Sampo Pyysalo, Natalia Silveira, Reut Tsarfaty, and Daniel Zeman. 2016. Universal dependencies v1: A multilingual treebank collection. In *Proceedings of LREC 2016*. ELRA, may.

Agnieszka Patejuk and Adam Przepiórkowski. 2018. *From lexical functional grammar to enhanced universal dependencies*. Polish Academy of Sciences, Institute of Computer Science.

Adam Przepiórkowski and Agnieszka Patejuk. 2018. From lexical functional grammar to enhanced universal dependencies. *Language Resources and Evaluation*, pages 1–37.

Victoria Rosén, Paul Meurer, and Koenraad de Smedt. 2009. LFG parsebanker: A toolkit for building and searching a treebank as a parsed corpus. In Frank Van Eynde, Anette Frank, Gertjan van Noord, and Koenraad De Smedt, editors, *Proceedings of the 7th International Workshop on Treebanks and Linguistic Theories (TLT7)*, pages 127–133, Utrecht. LOT.

Milan Straka and Jana Straková. 2017. Tokenizing, pos tagging, lemmatizing and parsing ud 2.0 with udpipe. In *Proceedings of the CoNLL 2017 Shared Task: Multilingual Parsing from Raw Text to Universal Dependencies*, pages 88–99, Vancouver, Canada, August. Association for Computational Linguistics.

Francis M Tyers, Mariya Sheyanova, and Jonathan North Washington. 2018. UD Annotatrix: An annotation tool for universal dependencies. In *Proceedings of the 16th Conference on Treebanks and Linguistic Theories*.

Özlem Çetinoğlu, Jennifer Foster, Joakim Nivre, Deirdre Hogan, Aoife Cahill, and Josef van Genabith. 2010. LFG without c-structures. In *Proceedings of the Ninth International Workshop on Treebanks and Linguistic Theories (TLT 9)*, page 43–54, Tartu, Estonia.

Lilja Øvrelid, Jonas Kuhn, and Kathrin Spreyer. 2009. Cross-framework parser stacking for data-driven dependency parsing. *TAL*, 50(3):109–138.

Identifying and Handling Cross-Treebank Inconsistencies in UD: A Pilot Study

Tillmann Dönicke
Göttingen Centre for
Digital Humanities
University of Göttingen*
tillmann.doenicke@
uni-goettingen.de

Xiang Yu
Institute for Natural
Language Processing
University of Stuttgart
xiangyu@ims.
uni-stuttgart.de

Jonas Kuhn
Institute for Natural
Language Processing
University of Stuttgart
jonas.kuhn@ims.
uni-stuttgart.de

Abstract

The Universal Dependencies treebanks[1] are a still-growing collection of treebanks for a wide range of languages, all annotated with a common inventory of dependency relations. Yet, the usages of the relations can be categorically different even for treebanks of the same language. We present a pilot study on identifying such inconsistencies in a language-independent way and conduct an experiment which illustrates that a proper handling of inconsistencies can improve parsing performance by several percentage points.

1 Introduction

Merging several available treebanks for the same language is a simple way of obtaining more data – either for training language-specific tools or for systematic corpus studies on the language. This strategy presupposes that each of the merged treebanks adheres to the same annotation scheme; when treebanks to be merged originate from distinct research contexts (which is typically the case in practice), a harmonization process is required. The UD initiative (whose main motivation has been to obtain comparable syntactic annotations *across* languages) has the welcome side effect that whenever several corpora for the same language are included in the UD collection, the amount of consistently annotated treebank data for this language increases – at least in theory. In practice, there can be serious inconsistencies in the way the dependency relations are used in the respective treebanks. This can for instance be the effect of distinct strategies in conversion from a non-UD treebank format, or of idiosyncrasies in the linguistic treatment of a certain construction pursued in one treebanking team. Often such inconsistencies may go unnoticed – in particular when researchers do experiments on large samples of languages from UD – and may lead to problematic conclusions.

Some previous efforts have focused on discovering errors or inconsistencies *within* a treebank, by measuring the patterns based on partially lexicalized dependency relations (Boyd et al., 2008; de Marneffe et al., 2017) or calculating the fitness scores of the dependency relations in a tree (Alzetta et al., 2017). In contrast to these studies, we focus on finding inconsistencies *between* treebanks that are supposed to be annotated in the same way according to a common guideline. Our method builds on the assumption that each individual treebank is already largely consistent within itself, and seeks to identify dependency patterns with contradicting statistics across treebanks.

So far, annotation inconsistencies have been reported for some specific languages, e.g. Korean (Noh et al., 2018) and Russian (Droganova et al., 2018), but there seems to be no comprehensive study addressing these cross-treebank inconsistencies within the UD collection. In our pilot study, we experiment with a dependency-based measure for inconsistency detection that makes no specific language-typological assumptions and appears to be quite effective for detecting various types of inconsistencies. In two experiments, we demonstrate that inconsistencies detected this way can be used as the trigger for a comparatively simple, but effective conversion process on one of the treebanks: a parser trained on the converted treebank achieves higher accuracy on the treebank that is closer to the UD guidelines.

*Work performed while at University of Stuttgart.

[1] https://universaldependencies.org/

Proceedings of the Fourth Workshop on Universal Dependencies (UDW 2020), pages 67–75
Barcelona, Spain (Online), December 13, 2020

2 Methodology

We became aware of inconsistent usages of dependency relations when extracting relative branching directions for another task (Dönicke et al., 2020; Dönicke, 2020) and we reuse this measure here to find potential cross-treebank inconsistencies, without making any prior assumptions what could be a problematic construction in a language under consideration. The measure takes advantage of the fact that the frequency distribution of the directionality of dependencies is by and large independent of domain-specific factors (which will of course differ across treebanks). Moreover, many of the problematic inconsistencies found across treebank schemes go along with the choice of head vs. dependency status and will thus be reflected in the directionality of the arcs for a particular label – even when the label is used fairly infrequently.

The relative frequency of right-branching instances for a dependency relation R in a treebank t is

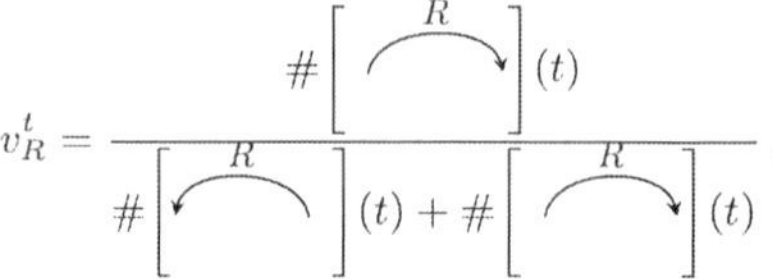

Here, an expression of the form $\#[*](t)$ returns how often the construction $*$ appears in the treebank t. The value ranges between 0 and 1; for example, $v^t_{\mathrm{amod}} = 0$ indicates that adjectival modifiers never follow (i.e. always precede) their governor in t, 1 indicates that they always follow their governor in t, and 0.5 indicates that both orderings are equally common. This measure is very similar to the directional dependency distance of Chen and Gerdes (2017). Our measure only quantifies the average direction of a relation whereas their measure quantifies average direction and distance.

We found that the relative branching direction of a relation sometimes greatly differs among the treebanks of the same language. Therefore, we calculate the maximum branching direction difference (MBD) for a language ℓ as

$$MBD(R, \ell) = \max_{t_1 \in T(\ell)} v^{t_1}_R - \min_{t_2 \in T(\ell)} v^{t_2}_R = \max_{t_1, t_2 \in T(\ell)} v^{t_1}_R - v^{t_2}_R$$

where $T(\ell)$ is the set of all treebanks for ℓ. A higher value indicates that there are at least two treebanks for ℓ in which R shows a different branching behaviour.

3 Inconsistencies among treebanks

We use the MBD to search for inconsistent usages of dependency relations in UD, version 2.5 (Zeman et al., 2019). Table 1 shows languages and relations which have high differences in branching direction between treebanks.[2] We reduced all dependency relations to their base forms (e.g. "csubj:pass" to "csubj") and excluded dependency relations that are very infrequent and tend to have very dissimilar occurrences.[3] We then manually inspected the first 20 cases to evaluate whether they are a real inconsistency or merely a false positive. For the analysis, we mainly used the statistics for individual relations on the treebanks pages (e.g. `https://universaldependencies.org/treebanks/en_partut/en_partut-dep-compound.html`) in combination with the Grew-match tool[4], maintained by Inria, to inspect treebank-specific examples.

We show three examples in the following, two real inconsistencies and one case in which a higher MBD is caused by both consistent and inconsistent use of a relation. The rest of our analysis is provided in the appendix. We are not familiar with all languages of which we analysed treebanks and it is possible that we missed something, making our analysis possibly incomplete. This is also the reason for why we could not analyse the potential inconsistencies for some of the languages (marked by a question mark in the table).

---

[2] Our implementations are available at `https://github.com/tidoe/typology-coling`.
[3] "dep", "discourse", "dislocated", "fixed", "goeswith", "list", "orphan", "parataxis", "reparandum" and "vocative".
[4] `http://match.grew.fr/`

ℓ	R	$MBD(R,\ell)$	v_R^t for all treebanks of ℓ	Incon.
Chinese	clf	1.00	GSD GSDSimp PUD CFL HK 0.00, 0.00 , 0.02, 0.99, 1.00	T
Korean	aux	1.00	PUD GSD Kaist 0.00, 0.83, 1.00	T
Korean	mark	1.00	Kaist GSD 0.00, 1.00	?
Arabic	compound	0.98	PUD NYUAD 0.02, 1.00	T
Galician	cc	0.94	TreeGal CTG 0.00, 0.94	T
Turkish	compound	0.94	PUD GB IMST 0.01, 0.05, 0.95	?
English	csubj	0.90	GUM LinES EWT ESL ParTUT PUD Pronouns 0.10, 0.56, 0.62, 0.73, 0.73 , 0.73, 1.00	F
Old Russian	expl	0.88	RNC TOROT 0.06, 0.93	F
Spanish	compound	0.88	PUD GSD AnCora 0.12, 0.36, 1.00	T
Chinese	compound	0.80	GSD GSDSimp PUD HK CFL 0.00, 0.00 , 0.01, 0.43, 0.80	T
French	csubj	0.80	FTB Spoken PUD GSD ParTUT Sequoia 0.20, 0.20, 0.75, 0.81, 0.97 , 1.0	F
Galician	nummod	0.80	TreeGal CTG 0.18 , 0.98	T
Arabic	nummod	0.75	PUD NYUAD PADT 0.24, 0.47 , 0.99	?
French	cop	0.73	GSD FTB PUD Sequoia Spoken ParTUT FQB 0.02, 0.03, 0.04, 0.05 , 0.05, 0.08 , 0.75	F
Latin	cc	0.72	ITTB PROIEL Perseus 0.04, 0.71 , 0.76	T
Komi Zyrian	cop	0.69	Lattice IKDP 0.12, 0.81	?
French	compound	0.67	PUD Spoken ParTUT 0.33, 0.78, 1.00	F/T
Portuguese	compound	0.63	PUD Bosque 0.37, 1.00	T
German	compound	0.62	PUD GSD HDT LIT 0.34, 0.53, 0.94, 0.96	F
English	compound	0.59	EWT PUD ESL GUM LinES ParTUT 0.09, 0.09, 0.13, 0.13, 0.18, 0.67	F/T

Table 1: Top 20 relations with largest differences in branching direction within a language. The abbreviations written above numbers are the treebank shortcuts. The last column shows whether the difference is a true (T) or false (F) inconsistency or whether the case in unclear (?).

Inconsistent Chinese classifiers (clf)   Figure 1 shows that the annotation for classifiers is categorically different among the Chinese treebanks. The treebanks CFL and HK follow the UD guidelines[5] and attach the classifier to the numeral whereas the other treebanks GSD and PUD attach it to the noun. Note that the annotation of numerals is also different; however, since the branching direction stays the same this cannot be detected by our method.

Figure 1: Chinese annotation scheme for noun phrases with a classifier in CFL/HK (left) and GSD/GSDSimp/PUD (right).

Inconsistent Korean auxiliaries (aux)   All three Korean treebanks have a different usage of the "aux" relation (Figure 2), which is already documented by Noh et al. (2018): Kaist is most closely to the UD guidelines, using the "aux" relation together with the "AUX" tag in around half of its instances (but with a lot of different tags such as "NOUN" and "SCONJ" in the other half), whereas GSD generally uses "flat" and "VERB" to connect auxiliary verbs with their main verbs. In both treebanks, "aux" connects

---

main and auxiliary verbs from left to right. PUD on the other side uses "aux" to connect main and auxiliary verbs from right to left and tags both with "VERB".

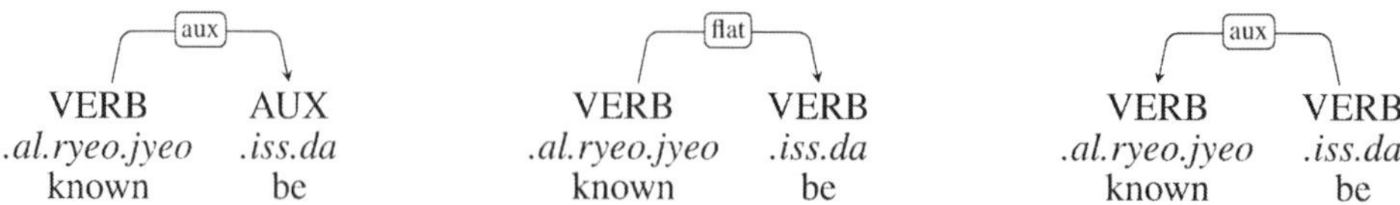

Figure 2: Korean annotation scheme for auxiliary verbs in Kaist (left), GSD (middle) and PUD (right).

In-/Consistent English compounds (compound)   The use of "compound" is only partially inconsistent in English. "compound" connects common-noun compounds right-to-left, whereas "compound:prt" connects verbs and their particles left-to-right, and the ParTUT contains a greater proportion of "compound:prt" instances than the other treebanks. This difference between the treebanks is detected by our method but not an inconsistency. However, the difference is additionally increased by many proper-name compounds in ParTUT that are connected left-to-right with "compound". In the other English treebanks, similar compounds usually show a "flat" relation. Figure 3 shows examples for nominal compounds.

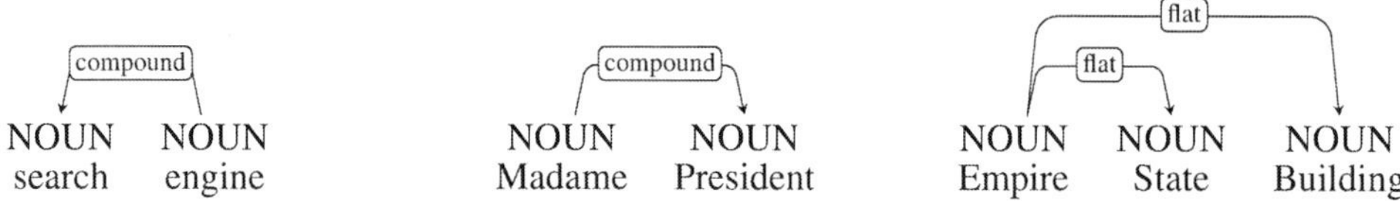

Figure 3: English annotation examples for common-noun compounds (left), proper-name compounds in ParTUT (middle) and proper-name compounds in the other treebanks (right).

4   Experiments

	zh_hk	zh_pud
zh_gsd.orig	48.14	54.97
zh_gsd.clf	50.25	51.51

(a) Traditional Chinese.

	zh_cfl
zh_gsdsimp.orig	43.36
zh_gsdsimp.clf	46.78

(b) Simplified Chinese.

	ko_pud	ko_kaist
ko_gsd.orig	19.10	26.91
ko_gsd.aux	20.13	30.08

(c) Korean.

Table 2: LAS on the test treebanks from models trained on original and converted training treebanks.

Parsing performance of a model trained on one treebank of a language and tested on another treebank of the same language is generally affected negatively by the domain difference, but it will suffer even more seriously in case some of the arc labels are used inconsistently across the treebanks (even though the labels are taken from the fixed UD label set). To empirically demonstrate the impact of annotation inconsistency and verify that our method could alleviate the problem, we perform a pilot experiment on classifiers in Chinese and auxiliaries in Korean, as they are the top two in Table 1.

We designed a set of rules to convert the inconsistent relations in the training treebanks towards the UD guidelines[6]. The target test sets are left as they are, including the ones that are against the general UD guideline (the PUD Treebanks for both languages), since we cannot guarantee the correctness of the automatic conversion. For Chinese classifiers and Korean auxiliaries, there are almost perfect one-to-one correspondences between the annotation schemes which allows a simple conversion of ZH_GSD/GSDSimp and KO_GSD, which is shown in Figure 4.

---

[6]`https://universaldependencies.org/u/dep/`

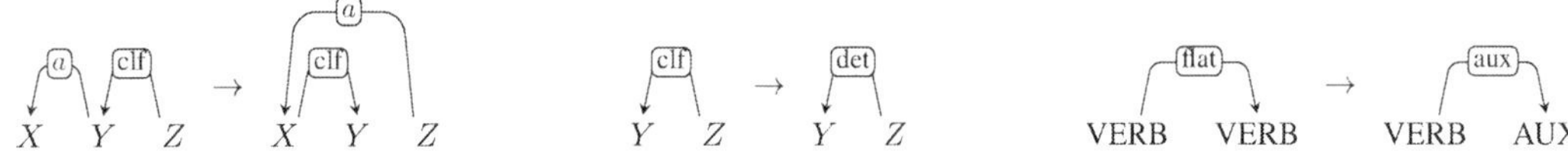

Figure 4: Conversion rules for instances of "clf" with modifier (left) and without modifier (middle) in Chinese, and for instances of "flat" to "aux" in Korean. X, Y, Z and a are variables for any POS tag or dependency relation, respectively.

We use the UDPipe parser (Straka et al., 2016) in our experiments with the default settings. It is based on the Arc-Standard projective transition system using a neural network classifier. It uses predicted POS tags and morphological features by the tagger.

Table 2 shows the Labeled Attachment Scores (LAS) on the test sets by models trained on the original and converted training sets, noted by the suffixes ".orig" and the respective converted relations. For traditional Chinese, converting the classifier relation brings 2.11 points improvements on ZH_HK, while decreases by 3.56 points on ZH_PUD, since ZH_PUD annotates the classifier similar to the original ZH_GSD. For simplified Chinese, the converted model also outperforms the original by 3.42. For Korean, PUD is improved by 1.03 and Kaist by 3.17.

We then break down the parser accuracy on each individual relation. As expected, the F1 score of "clf" in the Chinese treebanks improves from 0 to 69.96 for HK, from 0 to 84.34 for CFL, and from 65.05 to 0 for PUD (since PUD is annotated the same as the original GSD). For Korean, the F1 score of "aux" changes from 0.93 to 63.53 for Kaist, but remains 0 for PUD, since PUD annotates "aux" different from both GSD and Kaist, as explained in Section 3.

Generally, it is clear that by identifying and converting the inconsistencies, the parser model can learn to handle the relations consistent to the target treebank. It improves the parsing accuracy on the particular relations as well as the overall performance.

5   Conclusion and future work

In this pilot study, we show that the measure of relative branching direction applied on two UD treebanks for the same language can be used as a simple, but effective means for detecting candidates for inconsistencies in the usage of UD relation labels – independent of prior assumptions of which relations are particularly problematic. We manually inspected a list of relations with high divergence of branching direction, and as a pilot experiment converted some identified relations and analyze the performance of a parser in the out-of-domain scenario. The experiment confirms the benefit of our identification and conversion of the inconsistent annotation.

Concurrently with this work, Aggarwal and Zeman (2020) propose another method that addresses the identification of cross-treebank inconsistencies by measuring the differences of POS-tag trigrams. However, it focuses on a different type of inconsistency than what our method can identify. Both types of inconsistency can occur independently and a joined approach of the two complementary methods could make further contribution to error detection/correction in the UD treebanks.

References

Akshay Aggarwal and Daniel Zeman. 2020. Estimating POS annotation consistency of different treebanks in a language. In *Proceedings of the 19th International Workshop on Treebanks and Linguistic Theories (TLT 2020)*.

Chiara Alzetta, Felice Dell'Orletta, Simonetta Montemagni, and Giulia Venturi. 2017. Dangerous relations in dependency treebanks. In *Proceedings of the 16th International Workshop on Treebanks and Linguistic Theories*, pages 201–210, Prague, Czech Republic.

Adriane Boyd, Markus Dickinson, and W. Detmar Meurers. 2008. On detecting errors in dependency treebanks. *Research on Language and Computation*, 6(2):113–137.

Xinying Chen and Kim Gerdes. 2017. Classifying languages by dependency structure. Typologies of delexicalized universal dependency treebanks. In *Proceedings of the Fourth International Conference on Dependency Linguistics (Depling 2017)*, pages 54–63, Pisa, Italy, September. Linköping University Electronic Press.

Marie-Catherine de Marneffe, Matias Grioni, Jenna Kanerva, and Filip Ginter. 2017. Assessing the annotation consistency of the Universal Dependencies corpora. In *Proceedings of the Fourth International Conference on Dependency Linguistics (Depling 2017)*, pages 108–115, Pisa,Italy, September. Linköping University Electronic Press.

Tillmann Dönicke, Xiang Yu, and Jonas Kuhn. 2020. Real-valued logics for typological universals: Framework and application. In *Proceedings of the 28th International Conference on Computational Linguistics*.

Tillmann Dönicke. 2020. Evaluation of complex typological universals with language vectors and real-valued logics. Master's thesis, University of Stuttgart.

Kira Droganova, Olga Lyashevskaya, and Daniel Zeman. 2018. Data conversion and consistency of monolingual corpora: Russian UD treebanks. In *Proceedings of the 17th international workshop on treebanks and linguistic theories (TLT 2018)*, pages 52–65.

Youngbin Noh, Jiyoon Han, Tae Hwan Oh, and Hansaem Kim. 2018. Enhancing universal dependencies for Korean. In *Proceedings of the Second Workshop on Universal Dependencies (UDW 2018)*, pages 108–116, Brussels, Belgium, November. Association for Computational Linguistics.

Milan Straka, Jan Hajič, and Jana Straková. 2016. UDPipe: Trainable pipeline for processing CoNLL-U files performing tokenization, morphological analysis, POS tagging and parsing. In *Proceedings of the Tenth International Conference on Language Resources and Evaluation (LREC'16)*, pages 4290–4297, Portorož, Slovenia, May. European Language Resources Association (ELRA).

Daniel Zeman, Joakim Nivre, Mitchell Abrams, Noëmi Aepli, Željko Agić, Lars Ahrenberg, Gabrielė Aleksandravičiūtė, Lene Antonsen, Katya Aplonova, Maria Jesus Aranzabe, Gashaw Arutie, Masayuki Asahara, Luma Ateyah, Mohammed Attia, Aitziber Atutxa, Liesbeth Augustinus, Elena Badmaeva, Miguel Ballesteros, Esha Banerjee, Sebastian Bank, Verginica Barbu Mititelu, Victoria Basmov, Colin Batchelor, John Bauer, Sandra Bellato, Kepa Bengoetxea, Yevgeni Berzak, Irshad Ahmad Bhat, Riyaz Ahmad Bhat, Erica Biagetti, Eckhard Bick, Agnė Bielinskienė, Rogier Blokland, Victoria Bobicev, Loïc Boizou, Emanuel Borges Völker, Carl Börstell, Cristina Bosco, Gosse Bouma, Sam Bowman, Adriane Boyd, Kristina Brokaitė, Aljoscha Burchardt, Marie Candito, Bernard Caron, Gauthier Caron, Tatiana Cavalcanti, Gülşen Cebiroğlu Eryiğit, Flavio Massimiliano Cecchini, Giuseppe G. A. Celano, Slavomír Čéplö, Savas Cetin, Fabricio Chalub, Jinho Choi, Yongseok Cho, Jayeol Chun, Alessandra T. Cignarella, Silvie Cinková, Aurélie Collomb, Çağrı Çöltekin, Miriam Connor, Marine Courtin, Elizabeth Davidson, Marie-Catherine de Marneffe, Valeria de Paiva, Elvis de Souza, Arantza Diaz de Ilarraza, Carly Dickerson, Bamba Dione, Peter Dirix, Kaja Dobrovoljc, Timothy Dozat, Kira Droganova, Puneet Dwivedi, Hanne Eckhoff, Marhaba Eli, Ali Elkahky, Binyam Ephrem, Olga Erina, Tomaž Erjavec, Aline Etienne, Wograine Evelyn, Richárd Farkas, Hector Fernandez Alcalde, Jennifer Foster, Cláudia Freitas, Kazunori Fujita, Katarína Gajdošová, Daniel Galbraith, Marcos Garcia, Moa Gärdenfors, Sebastian Garza, Kim Gerdes, Filip Ginter, Iakes Goenaga, Koldo Gojenola, Memduh Gökırmak, Yoav Goldberg, Xavier Gómez Guinovart, Berta González Saavedra, Bernadeta Griciūtė, Matias Grioni, Normunds Grūzītis, Bruno Guillaume, Céline Guillot-Barbance, Nizar Habash, Jan Hajič, Jan Hajič jr., Mika Hämäläinen, Linh Hà Mỹ, Na-Rae Han, Kim Harris, Dag Haug, Johannes Heinecke, Felix Hennig, Barbora Hladká, Jaroslava Hlaváčová, Florinel Hociung, Petter Hohle, Jena Hwang, Takumi Ikeda, Radu Ion, Elena Irimia, Ọlájídé Ishola, Tomáš Jelínek, Anders Johannsen, Fredrik Jørgensen, Markus Juutinen, Hüner Kaşıkara, Andre Kaasen, Nadezhda Kabaeva, Sylvain Kahane, Hiroshi Kanayama, Jenna Kanerva, Boris Katz, Tolga Kayadelen, Jessica Kenney, Václava Kettnerová, Jesse Kirchner, Elena Klementieva, Arne Köhn, Kamil Kopacewicz, Natalia Kotsyba, Jolanta Kovalevskaitė, Simon Krek, Sookyoung Kwak, Veronika Laippala, Lorenzo Lambertino, Lucia Lam, Tatiana Lando, Septina Dian Larasati, Alexei Lavrentiev, John Lee, Phng Lê Hồng, Alessandro Lenci, Saran Lertpradit, Herman Leung, Cheuk Ying Li, Josie Li, Keying Li, KyungTae Lim, Maria Liovina, Yuan Li, Nikola Ljubešić, Olga Loginova, Olga Lyashevskaya, Teresa Lynn, Vivien Macketanz, Aibek Makazhanov, Michael Mandl, Christopher Manning, Ruli Manurung, Cătălina Mărănduc, David Mareček, Katrin Marheinecke, Héctor Martínez Alonso, André Martins, Jan Mašek, Yuji Matsumoto, Ryan McDonald, Sarah McGuinness, Gustavo Mendonça, Niko Miekka, Margarita Misirpashayeva, Anna Missilä, Cătălin Mititelu, Maria Mitrofan, Yusuke Miyao, Simonetta Montemagni, Amir More, Laura Moreno Romero, Keiko Sophie Mori, Tomohiko Morioka, Shinsuke Mori, Shigeki Moro, Bjartur Mortensen, Bohdan Moskalevskyi, Kadri Muischnek, Robert Munro, Yugo Murawaki, Kaili Müürisep, Pinkey Nainwani, Juan Ignacio Navarro Horñiacek, Anna Nedoluzhko, Gunta Nešpore-Bērzkalne, Lng Nguyễn Thị, Huyền Nguyễn Thị Minh, Yoshihiro Nikaido, Vitaly Nikolaev, Rattima Nitisaroj, Hanna Nurmi, Stina Ojala, Atul Kr. Ojha, Adédayọ̀ Olúòkun, Mai Omura, Petya Osenova, Robert Östling, Lilja Øvrelid, Niko Partanen, Elena Pascual, Marco Passarotti, Agnieszka Patejuk, Guilherme Paulino-Passos, Angelika Peljak-Łapińska, Siyao Peng, Cenel-Augusto Perez, Guy Perrier, Daria Petrova, Slav Petrov, Jason Phelan,

Jussi Piitulainen, Tommi A Pirinen, Emily Pitler, Barbara Plank, Thierry Poibeau, Larisa Ponomareva, Martin Popel, Lauma Pretkalniņa, Sophie Prévost, Prokopis Prokopidis, Adam Przepiórkowski, Tiina Puolakainen, Sampo Pyysalo, Peng Qi, Andriela Rääbis, Alexandre Rademaker, Loganathan Ramasamy, Taraka Rama, Carlos Ramisch, Vinit Ravishankar, Livy Real, Siva Reddy, Georg Rehm, Ivan Riabov, Michael Rießler, Erika Rimkutė, Larissa Rinaldi, Laura Rituma, Luisa Rocha, Mykhailo Romanenko, Rudolf Rosa, Davide Rovati, Valentin Roșca, Olga Rudina, Jack Rueter, Shoval Sadde, Benoît Sagot, Shadi Saleh, Alessio Salomoni, Tanja Samardžić, Stephanie Samson, Manuela Sanguinetti, Dage Särg, Baiba Saulīte, Yanin Sawanakunanon, Nathan Schneider, Sebastian Schuster, Djamé Seddah, Wolfgang Seeker, Mojgan Seraji, Mo Shen, Atsuko Shimada, Hiroyuki Shirasu, Muh Shohibussirri, Dmitry Sichinava, Aline Silveira, Natalia Silveira, Maria Simi, Radu Simionescu, Katalin Simkó, Mária Šimková, Kiril Simov, Aaron Smith, Isabela Soares-Bastos, Carolyn Spadine, Antonio Stella, Milan Straka, Jana Strnadová, Alane Suhr, Umut Sulubacak, Shingo Suzuki, Zsolt Szántó, Dima Taji, Yuta Takahashi, Fabio Tamburini, Takaaki Tanaka, Isabelle Tellier, Guillaume Thomas, Liisi Torga, Trond Trosterud, Anna Trukhina, Reut Tsarfaty, Francis Tyers, Sumire Uematsu, Zdeňka Urešová, Larraitz Uria, Hans Uszkoreit, Andrius Utka, Sowmya Vajjala, Daniel van Niekerk, Gertjan van Noord, Viktor Varga, Eric Villemonte de la Clergerie, Veronika Vincze, Lars Wallin, Abigail Walsh, Jing Xian Wang, Jonathan North Washington, Maximilan Wendt, Seyi Williams, Mats Wirén, Christian Wittern, Tsegay Woldemariam, Tak-sum Wong, Alina Wróblewska, Mary Yako, Naoki Yamazaki, Chunxiao Yan, Koichi Yasuoka, Marat M. Yavrumyan, Zhuoran Yu, Zdeněk Žabokrtský, Amir Zeldes, Manying Zhang, and Hanzhi Zhu. 2019. Universal dependencies 2.5. LINDAT/CLARIN digital library at the Institute of Formal and Applied Linguistics (ÚFAL), Faculty of Mathematics and Physics, Charles University.

Appendix A. Analysis of other potential cross-treebank inconsistencies

Inconsistent Arabic compounds (compound) In the NYUAD treebank, the "compound" relation is only used to connect numerals (NUM tags) from left to right (in the PUD treebank and the PADT, words tagged as NUM are commonly connected by "nummod"). Whilst the "compound" relation is not used in the PADT at all, there are two usages in the PUD treebank: First, "compound" to connect nouns, also from left to right, but rarely used. Second, "compound:prt" to connect words, mainly verbs (VERB), with their particles (PART). Here, the particle almost always precedes its governor. The labelling of particles is, obviously, handled differently in the PADT and the NYUAD treebank.

Inconsistent Galician coordinating conjunctions (cc) Whilst the TreeGal treebank follows the UD guidelines[7] and combines the "cc" and the "conj" relation, the CTG treebank uses "cc" differently (as shown in Figure 5) and does not use "conj". For conjuncts that are nouns, the "nmod" relation is used instead, which makes the "nmod" relation ambiguous between a nominal modifier and a nominal conjunct. Conjuncts which are not nouns are connected similarly using other relations.

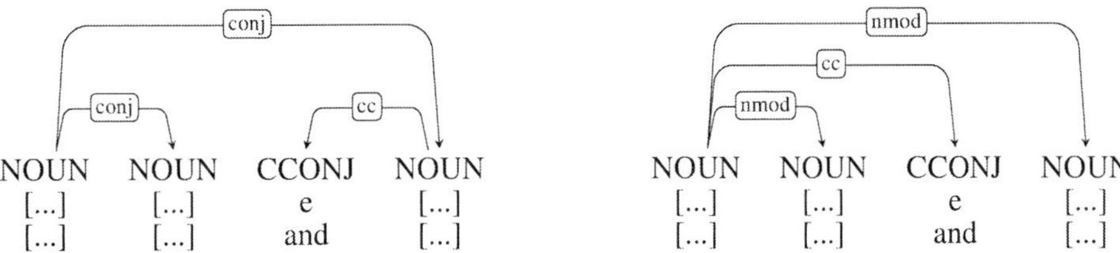

Figure 5: Galician annotation scheme for coordinating conjunctions in TreeGal (left) and CTG (right).

Consistent English clausal subjects (csubj) The presence of an expletive pronoun changes the direction of the "csubj" relation, see Figure 6. The GUM treebank simply contains more sentences with expletives.

---

[7] https://universaldependencies.org/u/dep/cc.html

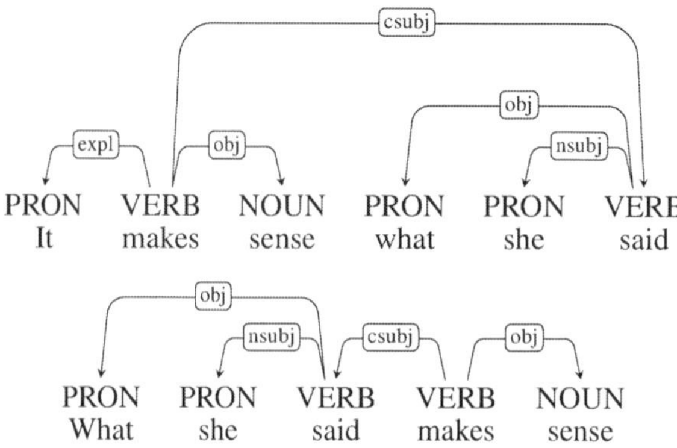

Figure 6: English annotation scheme for clausal subjects with expletive (above) and without expletive (below).

Consistent Old Russian expletives (expl)   The only expletives in the Old Russian treebanks are forms of *sebe/sja* 'oneself'. The TOROT contains over 1,000 examples and in 93% of the cases the expletive follows the verb; the RNC treebank addresses those forms with the subtype relation "expl:rv" and contains only nine examples, in all but one of them the expletive precedes the verb. Furthermore, in the RNC treebank the base "expl" relation is used to connect particles (PART) with their governors and the particle usually precedes its governor.

Inconsistent Spanish compounds (compound)   First of all, the PUD treebank only contains "compound:prt" whereas the GSD treebank and the AnCora treebank only contain "compound". The usage varies in several points, for example with temporal words and reflexive words:

Figure 7: Spanish annotation scheme for temporal words and *pasado* 'last' in AnCora (left) and GSD/ PUD (right).

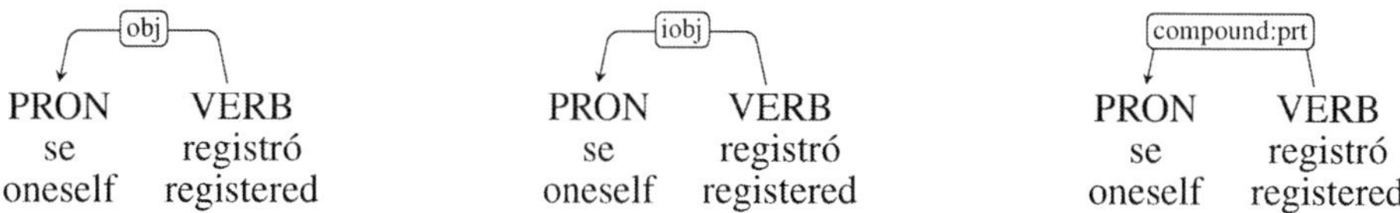

Figure 8: Spanish annotation scheme for reflexive verbs in AnCora (left), GSD (middle) and PUD (right).

Inconsistent Chinese compounds (compound)   All Chinese treebanks use the base "compound" relation and the direction is generally from right to left. However, the HK treebank and the CFL treebank also use "compound:dir", "compound:ext", "compound:vo" and "compound:vv" where the direction is generally from left to right. The extended use of "compound" (by subtypes) in some but not all Chinese treebanks is an inconsistency.

Consistent French clausal subjects (csubj)   In French, the clausal subjects show the same expletive alternation as in English (see above).

Inconsistent Galician numeral modifiers (nummod) The CTG treebank attaches numerals to the determiner instead of the noun (whereas both determiner and numeral should be attached to the noun according to the UD guidelines):

Figure 9: Galician annotation scheme for numeral modifiers in TreeGal (left) and CTG (right).

Consistent French copulae (cop) The FQB contains a lot of questions where fronted forms of *quel* 'which' are the governor of the copula, i.e. the fronted forms change the average direction of the "cop" relation.

Inconsistent Latin coordinating conjunctions (cc) The conjunction is categorically attached to different conjuncts in the Latin treebanks, analogous to Galician (see above).

In-/Consistent French compounds (compound) The "compound" relation is consistently used for common-noun compounds in the PUD treebank, the Spoken treebank and the ParTUT. An inconsistency, however, which cannot be detected by dependency direction difference, is that the other French treebanks mark compounds by other relations, e.g. "nmod".

Inconsistent Portuguese compounds (compound) The Portuguese treebanks show a different use of "compound" and "compound:prt", similar to the Spanish compounds.

Consistent German compounds (compound) The German treebanks differentiate between "compound" and "compound:prt". The former is used for (hyphenated) nominal compounds and usually spans from right to left; the latter is used for verbal particles and mainly goes the opposite direction, from left to right.

Figure 10: German annotation scheme for nominal compounds (left) and particle verbs (right).

Composing Byte-Pair Encodings for Morphological Sequence Classification

Adam Ek and **Jean-Philippe Bernardy**
Centre for Linguistic Theory and Studies in Probability,
Department of Philosophy, Linguistics and Theory of Science,
University of Gothenburg,
{adam.ek, jean-philippe.bernardy}@gu.se

Abstract

Byte-pair encodings is a method for splitting a word into sub-word tokens, a language model then assigns contextual representations separately to each of these tokens. In this paper, we evaluate four different methods of composing such sub-word representations into word representations. We evaluate the methods on morphological sequence classification, the task of predicting grammatical features of a word. Our experiments reveal that using an RNN to compute word representations is consistently more effective than the other methods tested across a sample of eight languages with different typology and varying numbers of byte-pair tokens per word.

1 Introduction

After its introduction, the Transformer model (Vaswani et al., 2017) has emerged as the dominant architecture for statistical language models, displacing recurrent neural networks, in particular, the LSTM and its variants. The Transformer owes its success to several factors, including the availability of pretrained models, which effectively yield rich contextual word embeddings. Such embeddings can be used as is (for so-called *feature extraction*), or the pre-trained models can be finetuned to specific tasks.

At the same time as Transformer models became popular, the tokenization of natural language texts have shifted away from methods explicitly oriented towards words or morphemes. Rather, statistical approaches are favoured: strings of characters are split into units which are not necessarily meaningful linguistically, but rather have statistically balanced frequencies. For example, the word "scientifically" may be composed of the tokens: "scient", "ifical", "ly" — here the central token does not correspond to a morpheme. That is, rather than identifying complete words or morphemes, one aims to find relatively large sub-word units occurring significantly often, while maximizing the coverage of the corpus (the presence of the "out of vocabulary" token is minimized). Approaches for composing words from sub-word units have focused on combining character n-grams (Bojanowski et al., 2017), while other approaches have looked at splitting words into *roots* and *morphemes* (El Kholy and Habash, 2012; Chaudhary et al., 2018; Xu and Liu, 2017), and then combining them.

In this paper, we consider Byte-Pair Encodings (BPE) (Sennrich et al., 2015). BPE has been popularized by its usage in translation and the BERT Transformer model (Devlin et al., 2018). The BPE algorithm does not specifically look for either character n-grams or morphs, but rather it aims at splitting a corpus C into N tokens, where N is user defined. Even though BPE is not grounded in morphosyntactic theory, the characteristics of the sub-word units generated by BPE will be directly influenced by morphosyntactic patterns in a language. In particular, it is reasonable to expect that the statistical characteristics of BPE to be different between languages with different typologies. One issue with this tokenization scheme is that models based on BPE provide vector representations for the BPE tokens (which we call *token embeddings* from now on), while one is typically interested in representations for the semantically meaningful units in the original texts, *words*. In sum, one wants to combine *token embeddings* into *word embeddings*.

Proceedings of the Fourth Workshop on Universal Dependencies (UDW 2020), pages 76–86
Barcelona, Spain (Online), December 13, 2020

Our main goal is to explore how to best combine token embeddings in the context of sequence classification on words, that is, the task of assigning a label to every word in a sentence. Coming back to our example, we must combine the token embeddings assigned to the BPE tokens "scient", "ifical" and "ly" to form a word representation of "scientifically" (as a vector) which we can then assign a label to.

To our knowledge, this is a little-studied problem. For the original BERT model Devlin et al. (2018) simply state that for named entity recognition the first sub-word token is used as the word representation. For morphological sequence classification Kondratyuk (2019; Kondratyuk and Straka (2019) report that only small differences in performance were found between averaging, taking the maximum value or first sub-word token. In this paper we explore the problem in further detail and identify the effect that different methods have on the final performance of a model. Additionally, with the increased interest in multilingual NLP it becomes important to explore how different computational methods perform cross-linguistically. That is, because languages are different morphosyntactically, one can expect various computational methods not to be uniformly effective.

2 Task

To investigate composition methods for token embeddings we focus on the task of morphological sequence classification. The task is to assign a tag to a word that represent its grammatical features, such as gender, number and so on. In addition to the word-form, the system can use information from context words as cues. While the grammatical features primarily are given by the word-form, useful information is also found in the context.

Thus, we have to identify k different tags for a word, each with C_i possible classes, making the task a multi-class classification problem. We simplify the classification problem by combining the different tags into a composite tag with up to $\prod_i^k C_i$ classes (instead of making k separate predictions). This task is suitable for our goal as the output space is large, ranging from 100 to 1000 possible tags for a word, depending on the grammatical features present in the language[1], and is directly linked to the affixes in the word-form. A system must efficiently encode information about the structure of the target words as well as the context words to be able to predict the correct grammatical features.

3 Data

For both training and testing data, we use the Universal Dependencies dataset (Nivre et al., 2018) annotated with the UniMorph schema (McCarthy et al., 2018). We are mainly interested in how the accuracy is influenced by different composition methods, but also consider the type of morphology a language uses as a factor in this task. With this in mind, we consider both languages that use agglutinative morphology where each morpheme is mapped to one and only one grammatical feature, and languages that use fusional morphology where a morpheme can be mapped to one or more grammatical features. The fusional languages that we consider are Arabic, Czech, Polish and Spanish, and the agglutinative languages that we consider are Finnish, Basque, Turkish, and Estonian. We show the size, the average number of BPE tokens per word, and the number of morphological tags for each treebank in Table 1.

The fusional languages were chosen such that two of them (Czech and Polish) have a higher BPE per word ratio than the other two (Arabic and Spanish). We make this choice because one factor that impacts the accuracy obtained by a composition method may be the BPE per word ratio. By having both fusional and agglutinative languages with similar BPE per word ratio we can take this variable into account properly in our analysis.

4 Method

In this section we present the model used for morphological sequence classification, the methods that we use to compose token embeddings, and how the model is trained. [2]

---

[1]For practical reasons, we only consider tag combinations observed in the dataset

[2]Our code is available at: `https://github.com/adamlek/ud-morphological-tagging`

Language	Typology	$\frac{\text{BPE}}{\text{word}}$	Tags	Train	Validation	Test
Basque-BDT	Agglutinative	1.79	919	97336	12206	11901
Finnish-TDT	Agglutinative	1.98	591	161791	19876	20541
Turkish-IMST	Agglutinative	1.73	1056	46417	5708	5734
Estonian-EDT	Agglutinative	1.86	512	346986	43434	43825
Spanish-AnCora	Fusional	1.25	177	439925	55196	54449
Arabic-PADT	Fusional	1.39	300	225494	28089	28801
Czech-CAC	Fusional	1.77	990	395043	50087	49253
Polish-LFG	Fusional	1.75	634	104730	13161	13076

Table 1: Treebank statistics showing the language typology, average number of BPE tokens per word, the number of (composite) morphological tags and the size of the datasets in terms of words.

4.1 Model

Our model is composed of three components, each of them detailed below. First, the input sequence of BPE tokens is fed to a Transformer model, which yields a contextual vector representation for each BPE token. The contextual information here is the surrounding BPE tokens in the sentence. Then, the token embeddings are combined using a composition module, which we vary for the purpose of evaluating each variant. This component yields one embedding per original word. Then we pass the word embeddings through a bidirectional LSTM, which is followed by two dense layers with GELU (Hendrycks and Gimpel, 2016) activation. These dense layers act on each word embedding separately (but share parameters across words). An outline of the model is presented in Figure 1, where f represents the different methods we use to combine token embeddings.

4.1.1 Underlying Transformer Model

To extract a embeddings for each BPE token, we use the XLM-RoBERTa (Conneau et al., 2019) model[3]. XLM-R is a masked language model based on the Transformer, specifically RoBERTa (Liu et al., 2019b), and trained on data from 100 different languages, using a shared vocabulary of 250000 BPE tokens. All the languages that we test are included in the XLM-R model. In this experiment we use the XLM-R$_{\text{base}}$ model with 250M parameters. It has 12 encoder layers, 12 attention heads and use 768 dimensions for its hidden size.

4.1.2 Feature extraction

The XLM-R model uses 12 layers to compute a vector representation for a BPE token. It has been shown in previous research (Kondratyuk and Straka, 2019; Raganato et al., 2018; Liu et al., 2019a) that the different layers of the Transformer model encode different types of information.

To take advantage of this variety, we compute token embeddings as a weighted sum of the layer representation (Kondratyuk and Straka, 2019), using a weight vector w, of size l, where l is the number of layers in the Transformer model. The weight vector w is initialized from a normal distribution of mean 0 and standard deviation 1. If r_{ji} is the layer representation at layer j and token position i, we calculate the weighted sum as follows:

$$x_i = \sum_{j=1}^{l} \mathsf{softmax}(w)_j r_{ji} \tag{1}$$

Consequently, in end-to-end training, the optimiser will find a weight for extracting information from each layer ($\mathsf{softmax}(w)_j$) which maximizes performance.

4.1.3 Composition of BPE token embeddings

The weighted sum yields a token embedding for each BPE token. We proceed to combine them into words as they appear in the data. The model that we use to combine token embeddings is as follows.

---

[3]We use the huggingface implementation `https://huggingface.co/transformers/model_doc/xlmroberta.html`

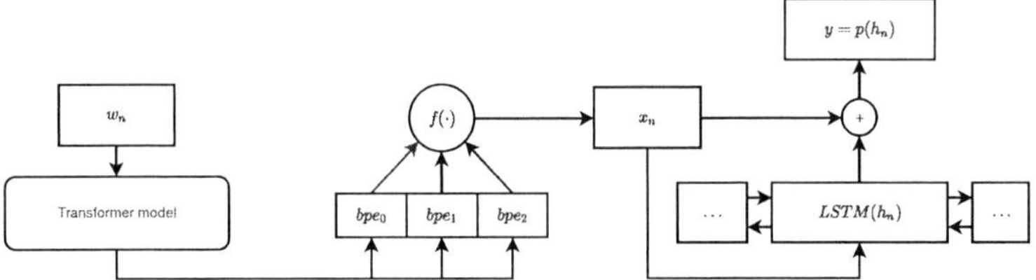

Figure 1: Model outline for one input. A word w_n is tokenized into k BPE tokens. The Transformer model produces one embedding per token per layer. We then calculate a weighted sum over the layers to obtain one representation per token. The resulting token embeddings are then passed to a composition function f that combines the k different token embeddings into a word embedding. The word embedding is then passed to an LSTM followed by a dense prediction layer.

For each sentence we extract n token embeddings x^0 to x^{n-1} from XLM-R$_{\text{base}}$, and then align them to words. We then pass all token embeddings in a word to a function f which combines the tokens into a word embedding.

We consider four methods for composing token embeddings: taking the first token embedding, summation, averaging, and using an RNN. Taking the first token embedding, summation and averaging have been used in previous work (Sachan et al., 2020; Kondratyuk, 2019; Devlin et al., 2018), but using an RNN has not been explored before to our knowledge.

First: The first method is the standard one used by Devlin et al. (2018), which is to use the first token embedding in a word.

Sum: For the Sum method, we use an element-wise sum. That is, we calculate the vector sum of the token embeddings. Assuming that we have T token embeddings in a word X (the word is a matrix of size $(T, 768)$), for dimension i we calculate the word embedding by summing the token embeddings:

$$f(X)_i = \sum_{j=1}^{T} x_i^j \tag{2}$$

Mean: In the mean method we calculate the sum as above and divide by the number of BPE tokens in the word. Thus, for word X we calculate the word embedding by averaging over the sum:

$$f(X)_i = \frac{1}{T} \sum_{j=1}^{T} x_i^j \tag{3}$$

RNN: For this method we employ a bidirectional LSTM to compose the token embeddings. For each word, we pass the sequence of token embeddings through an LSTM and use the final output as the word representation.

4.1.4 Word-level features and classification

The above methods of composing BPE tokens produce one contextual embedding per word. We then pass the word embeddings through an LSTM to take into account the word contexts. While the BPE token embeddings are already contextual, they are conditioned on the BPE token context, not word context. We pass the hidden states for each word to a residual connection with the pre-LSTM representation. We then pass this to two dense layers with GELU activation followed by a dense layer that computes class-scores for each word. We then use a softmax layer to assign probabilities and compute the loss accordingly.

Commonly, systems analyzing morphology use character embeddings as an additional source of information. We opted not to include character embeddings because this would obfuscate the effect of the composition method and may mask some of the effects of the different methods.

4.1.5 Label smoothing

Given that many of the languages have a large number of morphological tags, we want to prevent the model from growing overconfident for certain classes. To address this issue we introduce label smoothing (Szegedy et al., 2016), that is, instead of the incorrect classes having 0% probability and the correct class 100% probability we let each of the incorrect classes have a small probability.

Let α be our smoothing value, in our model we follow (Kondratyuk and Straka, 2019) and use $\alpha = 0.03$, and C the number of classes, then given a one-hot encoded target vector t of size C, we calculate the smoothed probabilities as:

$$t_{smooth} = (1 - \alpha)t + \frac{\alpha}{C} \tag{4}$$

In words, we remove α from the correct class then distribute α uniformly among all classes.

4.2 Training

In our experiments we consider two possible training regimes. In the first regime we finetune the XLM-R model's parameters, in the second we only extract weights for BPE tokens, that is, we use the model as a feature extractor. In all cases, we use end-to-end training.

When finetuning the model we freeze the XLM-R parameters for the first epoch, effectively not finetuning at first. When training the model we use a cosine annealing learning rate (Loshchilov and Hutter, 2016) with restarts every epoch, that is, the learning rate starts high then incrementally decreases to $1e-12$ over N steps, where N is the number of batches in an epoch. We use the Adam optimizer with standard parameters, with a learning rate of 0.001 for layer importance parameter (w in Section 4.1.2), the parameters of the Word-LSTM, of the classification layer, and of the BPE-combination module (when an RNN is used). For the Transformer parameters, we use a lower learning rate of $1e-6$. We summarize the hyperparameters used in Table 2.

As an additional regularization in addition to weight decay and adaptive learning rate, we use dropout throughout the model. Generally, we apply dropout before some feature is computed. Initial experiments revealed that a high dropout yielded the best results. We summarize the dropout used as: We replace 20 percent of the BPE tokens with <UNK>. Then, we compute a weighted sum of the layer representations, to regularize this operation we apply dropout on layer representations with a probability of 0.1, that is we set all representations in the layer to 0. We then combine the token embeddings into word embeddings and apply a dropout of 0.4%, and pass these into the Word-LSTM. Before the contextualized representation is passed to the classification layer, we apply a dropout of 0.4%.

Parameter	Value
Epochs	15
Batch size	4 / 32
Word LSTM size	768
Linear transform size	1536
Optimizer	Adam
Learning rate	0.001
Learning rate$_{xlmr}$	1e−6
Weight decay	0.05
Label smoothing	0.03

Table 2: Hyperparameters used for training the model. Slashed indicates the value of a parameter when we finetune or extract features.

5 Results

Even though our aim is to compare the relative performance of various BPE-combination methods rather than to improve on the state of the art in absolute terms, we compare our results against the baseline reported by McCarthy et al. (2019). This comparison serves the purpose of checking that our system is generally sound. In particular, the actual state of the art, as reported by McCarthy et al. (2019; Kondratyuk (2019), uses treebank concatenation or other methods to incorporate information from all treebanks available in a language, which means that results are not reported on a strict per-treebank basis and thus our numbers are not directly comparable. We report the accuracy of prediction morphological tags for each of our composition methods, and for our two training regimes in Table 3.

Our system performs better than the baseline. As a general trend we see that the RNN method tends to perform better than all other tested methods. This trend is consistent across both language families (agglutinative and fusional) and training regimes showing that, while the advantage of the RNN is small,

Treebank	Baseline	Finetuning				Feature extraction			
		First	Sum	Mean	RNN	First	Sum	Mean	RNN
Basque-BDT	.676	.857	.884	.877	**.901**	.759	.789	.780	**.834**
Finnish-TDT	.751	.961	.958	.960	**.965**	.853	.856	.847	**.899**
Turkish-IMST	.620	.848	.859	.855	**.884**	.742	.741	.735	**.775**
Estonian-EDT	.740	.956	.955	.955	**.961**	.855	.856	.853	**.901**
Spanish-AnCora	.842	.977	.977	.977	**.979**	.951	.954	.952	**.962**
Arabic-PADT	.770	.946	.946	.947	**.951**	.920	.923	.920	**.936**
Czech-CAC	.771	.968	.968	.968	**.975**	.863	.887	.881	**.924**
Polish-LFG	.657	.956	.953	.953	**.959**	.828	.844	.840	**.878**
Average	.728	.933	.937	.936	**.946**	.846	.856	.851	**.888**

Table 3: Accuracy for morphological tagging. We show scores both for finetuning the XLM-R model and extracting features.

Treebank	Finetuning				Feature extraction			
	First	Sum	Mean	RNN	First	Sum	Mean	RNN
Basque-BDT	.739	.802	.790	**.835**	.657	.715	.703	**.774**
Finnish-TDT	.940	.946	.946	**.952**	.780	.805	.794	**.861**
Turkish-IMST	.730	.780	.778	**.818**	.653	.683	.664	**.711**
Estonian-EDT	.938	.939	.939	**.949**	.779	.805	.803	**.868**
Spanish-AnCora	.956	.961	.959	**.964**	.922	.937	.930	**.947**
Arabic-PADT	.889	.896	.898	**.907**	.902	.909	.906	**.923**
Czech-CAC	.940	.947	.947	**.959**	.786	.849	.840	**.900**
Polish-LFG	.917	.920	.918	**.927**	.696	.761	.752	**.812**
Average	.881	.899	.897	**.913**	.772	.808	.799	**.849**

Table 4: Accuracy for morphological tagging on all words that are composed of two or more BPE tokens.

it occurs consistently. In general we find that finetuning yields higher accuracy than plain feature extraction, on average the difference is about 5.8 percentage points. This difference is to be expected when finetuning has 250M more parameters tuned to the task than the feature extraction.

Focusing on the finetuning regime only, we see the largest benefits of the RNN method for Basque with an increased performance of 3.25 points, and 2.7 points for Turkish over using mean or averaging. The First method for Basque and Turkish performs worse with a decrease of 4.4 percentage points for Basque and 3.6 points for Turkish compared to the RNN method. In the bare features extraction regime, we see a larger benefit for the RNN, of 3.7 percentage points (Turkish) and 4.95 points (Basque). Again, this is not unexpected: When finetuning the error rate is smaller, and therefore there is a smaller margin for a subsequent phase to yield and improvement.

Table 3 reports average accuracy for every word, including those which are only composed of a single BPE token. To highlight the strengths and weaknesses of each composition method, we also compute the accuracy for longer words only (composed of two or more BPE tokens). The results can be seen in Table 4. We see the same trend for accuracy on words that are composed of two or more BPE tokens, as in the overall accuracy, where the RNN outperforms all other methods. We can also see that the average increase in accuracy when using an RNN is larger. This holds both when finetuning or extracting bare features. Given that the number of BPE tokens per word varies in the different languages, we also look at the accuracy of the different methods given the number of BPE tokens. We show per-language performance with the different methods in Figure 2.

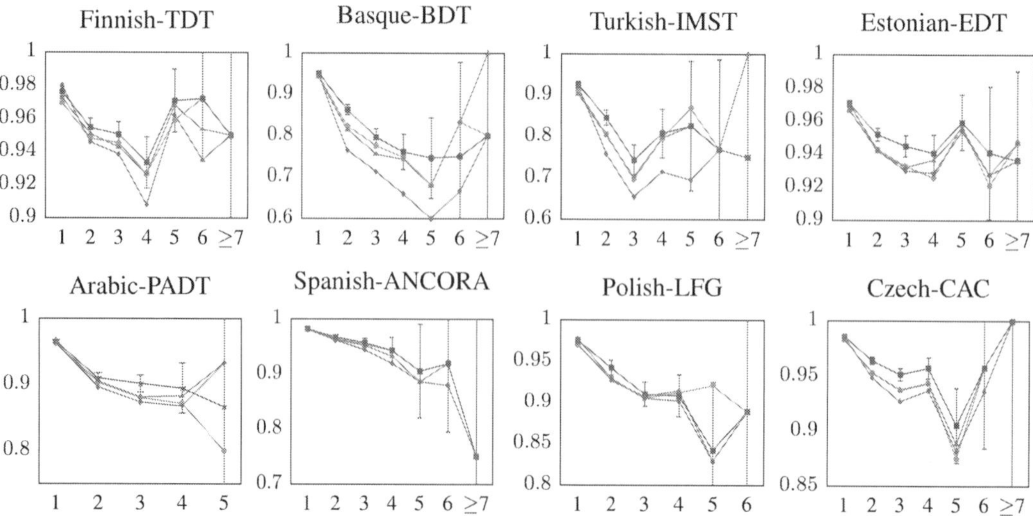

Figure 2: Per-language accuracy on tokens with different numbers of BPE components, for the finetuning training regime. The last data point on the x-axis refers to all tokens composed of seven or more BPE tokens. We indicate the method by encoding First as brown, summation as green, averaging as blue and RNN as red. The accuracy is given on the y-axis. We show the Agresti-Coull approximation of a 95%-confidence interval for the RNN method (Agresti and Coull, 1998). We do not show the intervals for other methods to avoid excessive clutter.

6 Discussion

For predicting morphological features, the RNN method is more effective than the other proposed methods (summing, averaging or taking the first BPE token). This holds regardless of training regime (finetuning versus feature extraction) and across languages with different BPE per word ratios.

As we see it, the advantage of the RNN over commutative methods (Sum, Mean) and taking the first BPE token is that it can take the order of elements into account. In broad terms, information about the order of elements in morphology allows a system to determine what is a stem, prefix, or suffix. Thus allowing a model to collect more predictive information from token embeddings.

We can suspect that the average BPE per word ratio in a language affects the performance of the composition method used. To further control this variable, in Figure 3 we plot the average number of BPE tokens per word in each language (x-axis), and compare this average against the gain in accuracy yielded by using the RNN method over summation (y-axis). For finetuning we see that in general the average number of BPE tokens does not matter that much. The two cases where it does matter is for Turkish and Basque, where we see a substantial improvement of about 3 percentage points. We note however that these are also the languages with the lowest amount of training data. For the other languages the improvements lie in the range .6 to 1.2 percentage points. This indicates that when finetuning, the model can provide information that allows commutative methods to properly compose BPE tokens. However, looking at bare feature extraction we see that there is a larger gap between the low BPE-ratio and the high BPE-ratio languages.

Our sample of languages contain both fusional and agglutinative languages, and the typology does not appear to have an effect in our experiments. We see about the same trends for the fusional languages with a high BPE per word ratio as the agglutinative languages.

6.1 First method

The idea behind the First method is that the Transformer is sufficiently powerful to pool the relevant information into the first BPE token embedding. However, our experiments reveal that it is less efficient than any other method we tested for morphological sequence classification across languages. We see in

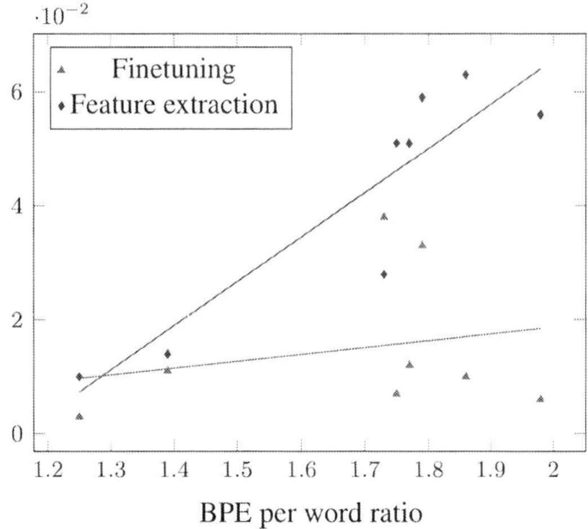

Figure 3: The difference in accuracy between summation and RNN plotted against average number of BPE tokens per word in all languages, with a linear regression line.

Table 3 that the method is, on average, .4 and 1 percentage points lower than the next lowest scoring method for finetuning and feature extraction respectively. This effect is further enhanced when we consider the accuracy of words composed of more than two BPE tokens in Table 4, where the difference is 1.6 and 2.7 points, compared against the next lowest scoring method, for finetuning and feature extraction respectively. When we compare the performance against the RNN this difference only increases, showing a gain of 3.2 percentage points and 7.7 points for finetuning and feature extraction respectively.

While the First method may be effective, primarily because of the expressivity of the Transformer architecture, the method forces the model to push the predictive information of several BPE token embeddings into the first one. This puts an additional burden on the Transformer model, and we believe that this is the reason for the performance degradation which we observe. Besides, putting this burden on the model is not necessary: pooling information from several BPE embeddings can be done effectively using additional layers.

6.2 Sum and Mean

When we consider the commutative methods of combining token embeddings, summation or averaging, we see no clear advantage for either of them over the other one, when doing finetuning. However, when extracting features only we see hints that summation is more effective than averaging. For feature extraction, summation is .5 percentage points better than averaging, and words composed of two or more BPE tokens exhibit an advantage of .9 point for summation.

This discrepancy suggests that by averaging, we are removing some predictive information from the pretrained BPE token embeddings, that is, by reducing the values in the token embeddings uniformly across a sequence of token embeddings we lose useful information. We believe that some token embeddings contain more predictive information than others, and by summing them we retain all the information. But when we finetune, the difference between summing and averaging almost disappears: the model appears to learn how to distribute the information uniformly across the token embeddings that compose a word and is thus able to retain the information better. Interestingly, the model learns to distribute the information across multiple BPE token embeddings more efficiently than pushing the information into the first token. This is shown by the large difference in accuracy between finetuning and feature extraction for the First and averaging method.

6.3 Parameterization of First, Sum and Mean

One question that arises when looking at Figure 2, specifically considering the performance on words composed of only one BPE token is the following: can the superiority of the RNNs be attributed to

		Finetuning				Feature extraction			
Treebank	Baseline	First	Sum	Mean	RNN	First	Sum	Mean	RNN
Basque-BDT	.676	.864	.894	.890	**.901**	.772	.793	.794	**.834**
Finnish-TDT	.751	.958	.959	.961	**.965**	.857	.856	.855	**.899**
Turkish-IMST	.620	.850	.875	.867	**.884**	.742	.722	.729	**.775**
Estonian-EDT	.740	.956	.958	.958	**.961**	.865	.856	.853	**.901**
Spanish-AnCora	.842	.978	.977	.978	**.979**	.953	.954	.952	**.962**
Arabic-PADT	.770	.949	.945	.947	**.951**	.925	.923	.920	**.936**
Czech-CAC	.771	.969	.972	.972	**.975**	.873	.887	.881	**.924**
Polish-LFG	.657	.957	.953	.955	**.959**	.832	.844	.840	**.878**
Average	.728	.935	.942	.941	**.946**	.852	.854	.853	**.888**

Table 5: The accuracy of morphological tagging when we parameterize the First, Sum and Mean method with a non-linear transformation layer.

its ability to take context into account, or simply to containing more parameters and extra layers? We would expect that for the words with only one BPE token, the performance of the model would be the same for all methods. For practical reasons, we push all word embeddings through an RNN, effectively doing a non-linear transformation with tanh activations on the words composed of only one BPE token. Typically, the difference in accuracy between various methods for one-BPE-token words is small (barely visible in Figure 2). But for example in Finnish, we see a larger difference. Although in general if we perform better on longer words consisting of BPE tokens that also appear as words in the data, we could also expect the performance to be better for words of BPE length one, because we will have more accurate representations of the contextual words.

We test this hypothesis by parameterizing the First, Sum, and Mean method. Essentially, we need to increase the capabilities of these methods. This is done by passing all BPE token embeddings through a non-linear transformation with ReLU activation before we compute the Sum, Mean, or select the first BPE-token. Our experiment, whose results are shown in Table 5, shows that while adding parameters to the First, Sum, and Mean method generally improve their performance slightly, ranging between a change of -0.2 and $+0.6$ percentage points, but their performance never exceeds that of the RNN method.

7 Conclusions and Future Work

In conclusion, our results indicate that using an RNN to compose word representations from token representations, obtained from a large Transformer model, is more efficient than two commutative methods, summing and averaging, and also more effective than letting a Transformer model automatically pool the predictive word-level information into the first BPE token embedding. We show this for the task of morphological sequence classification, in eight different languages with varying morphology and word-lengths in term of BPE tokens, as well as for two training regimes, finetuning and feature extraction.

In future work, we want to continue experimenting with the different BPE token embedding composition methods, specifically looking at more complex syntactic and semantic tasks, such as dependency and/or constituency parsing, semantic role labeling, named entity recognition, and natural language inference. We also wish to run our experiments on the hundreds of available UD treebanks to improve the robustness of our results.

Acknowledgments

The research reported in this paper was supported by grant 2014-39 from the Swedish Research Council, which funds the Centre for Linguistic Theory and Studies in Probability (CLASP) in the Department of Philosophy, Linguistics, and Theory of Science at the University of Gothenburg.

References

Alan Agresti and Brent A Coull. 1998. Approximate is better than exact for interval estimation of binomial proportions. *The American Statistician*, 52(2):119–126.

Piotr Bojanowski, Edouard Grave, Armand Joulin, and Tomas Mikolov. 2017. Enriching word vectors with subword information. *Transactions of the Association for Computational Linguistics*, 5:135–146.

Aditi Chaudhary, Chunting Zhou, Lori Levin, Graham Neubig, David R Mortensen, and Jaime G Carbonell. 2018. Adapting word embeddings to new languages with morphological and phonological subword representations. In *Proceedings of the 2018 Conference on Empirical Methods in Natural Language Processing*, pages 3285–3295.

Alexis Conneau, Kartikay Khandelwal, Naman Goyal, Vishrav Chaudhary, Guillaume Wenzek, Francisco Guzmán, Edouard Grave, Myle Ott, Luke Zettlemoyer, and Veselin Stoyanov. 2019. Unsupervised cross-lingual representation learning at scale. *arXiv preprint arXiv:1911.02116*.

Jacob Devlin, Ming-Wei Chang, Kenton Lee, and Kristina Toutanova. 2018. BERT: Pre-training of deep bidirectional transformers for language understanding. *arXiv preprint arXiv:1810.04805*.

Ahmed El Kholy and Nizar Habash. 2012. Orthographic and morphological processing for English–Arabic statistical machine translation. *Machine Translation*, 26(1-2):25–45.

Dan Hendrycks and Kevin Gimpel. 2016. Gaussian error linear units (gelus). *arXiv preprint arXiv:1606.08415*.

Dan Kondratyuk and Milan Straka. 2019. 75 languages, 1 model: Parsing universal dependencies universally. In *Proceedings of the 2019 Conference on Empirical Methods in Natural Language Processing and the 9th International Joint Conference on Natural Language Processing (EMNLP-IJCNLP)*, pages 2779–2795, Hong Kong, China. Association for Computational Linguistics.

Dan Kondratyuk. 2019. Cross-lingual lemmatization and morphology tagging with two-stage multilingual BERT fine-tuning. In *Proceedings of the 16th Workshop on Computational Research in Phonetics, Phonology, and Morphology*, pages 12–18.

Nelson F Liu, Matt Gardner, Yonatan Belinkov, Matthew E Peters, and Noah A Smith. 2019a. Linguistic knowledge and transferability of contextual representations. In *Proceedings of the 2019 Conference of the North American Chapter of the Association for Computational Linguistics: Human Language Technologies, Volume 1 (Long and Short Papers)*, pages 1073–1094.

Yinhan Liu, Myle Ott, Naman Goyal, Jingfei Du, Mandar Joshi, Danqi Chen, Omer Levy, Mike Lewis, Luke Zettlemoyer, and Veselin Stoyanov. 2019b. RoBERTa: A robustly optimized bert pretraining approach. *arXiv preprint arXiv:1907.11692*.

Ilya Loshchilov and Frank Hutter. 2016. SGDR: Stochastic gradient descent with warm restarts. *arXiv preprint arXiv:1608.03983*.

Arya D McCarthy, Miikka Silfverberg, Ryan Cotterell, Mans Hulden, and David Yarowsky. 2018. Marrying universal dependencies and universal morphology. In *Proceedings of the Second Workshop on Universal Dependencies (UDW 2018)*, pages 91–101.

Arya D McCarthy, Ekaterina Vylomova, Shijie Wu, Chaitanya Malaviya, Lawrence Wolf-Sonkin, Garrett Nicolai, Christo Kirov, Miikka Silfverberg, Sebastian J Mielke, Jeffrey Heinz, et al. 2019. The SIGMORPHON 2019 shared task: Morphological analysis in context and cross-lingual transfer for inflection. In *Proceedings of the 16th Workshop on Computational Research in Phonetics, Phonology, and Morphology*, pages 229–244.

Joakim Nivre, Mitchell Abrams, Željko Agić, Lars Ahrenberg, Lene Antonsen, Katya Aplonova, Maria Jesus Aranzabe, Gashaw Arutie, Masayuki Asahara, Luma Ateyah, Mohammed Attia, Aitziber Atutxa, Liesbeth Augustinus, Elena Badmaeva, Miguel Ballesteros, Esha Banerjee, Sebastian Bank, Verginica Barbu Mititelu, Victoria Basmov, John Bauer, Sandra Bellato, Kepa Bengoetxea, Yevgeni Berzak, Irshad Ahmad Bhat, Riyaz Ahmad Bhat, Erica Biagetti, Eckhard Bick, Rogier Blokland, Victoria Bobicev, Carl Börstell, Cristina Bosco, Gosse Bouma, Sam Bowman, Adriane Boyd, Aljoscha Burchardt, Marie Candito, Bernard Caron, Gauthier Caron, Gülşen Cebiroğlu Eryiğit, Flavio Massimiliano Cecchini, Giuseppe G. A. Celano, Slavomír Čéplö, Savas Cetin, Fabricio Chalub, Jinho Choi, Yongseok Cho, Jayeol Chun, Silvie Cinková, Aurélie Collomb, Çağrı Çöltekin, Miriam Connor, Marine Courtin, Elizabeth Davidson, Marie-Catherine de Marneffe, Valeria de Paiva, Arantza Diaz de Ilarraza, Carly Dickerson, Peter Dirix, Kaja Dobrovoljc, Timothy Dozat, Kira Droganova, Puneet Dwivedi, Marhaba Eli, Ali Elkahky, Binyam Ephrem, Tomaž Erjavec, Aline Etienne, Richárd Farkas, Hector Fernandez Alcalde, Jennifer Foster, Cláudia Freitas, Katarína Gajdošová, Daniel Galbraith, Marcos Garcia, Moa Gärdenfors, Sebastian Garza, Kim Gerdes, Filip Ginter, Iakes Goenaga, Koldo Gojenola, Memduh

Gökırmak, Yoav Goldberg, Xavier Gómez Guinovart, Berta Gonzáles Saavedra, Matias Grioni, Normunds Grūzītis, Bruno Guillaume, Céline Guillot-Barbance, Nizar Habash, Jan Hajič, Jan Hajič jr., Linh Hà Mỹ, Na-Rae Han, Kim Harris, Dag Haug, Barbora Hladká, Jaroslava Hlaváčová, Florinel Hociung, Petter Hohle, Jena Hwang, Radu Ion, Elena Irimia, Ọlájídé Ishola, Tomáš Jelínek, Anders Johannsen, Fredrik Jørgensen, Hüner Kaşıkara, Sylvain Kahane, Hiroshi Kanayama, Jenna Kanerva, Boris Katz, Tolga Kayadelen, Jessica Kenney, Václava Kettnerová, Jesse Kirchner, Kamil Kopacewicz, Natalia Kotsyba, Simon Krek, Sookyoung Kwak, Veronika Laippala, Lorenzo Lambertino, Lucia Lam, Tatiana Lando, Septina Dian Larasati, Alexei Lavrentiev, John Lee, Phng Lê H`ông, Alessandro Lenci, Saran Lertpradit, Herman Leung, Cheuk Ying Li, Josie Li, Keying Li, KyungTae Lim, Nikola Ljubešić, Olga Loginova, Olga Lyashevskaya, Teresa Lynn, Vivien Macketanz, Aibek Makazhanov, Michael Mandl, Christopher Manning, Ruli Manurung, Cătălina Mărănduc, David Mareček, Katrin Marheinecke, Héctor Martínez Alonso, André Martins, Jan Mašek, Yuji Matsumoto, Ryan McDonald, Gustavo Mendonça, Niko Miekka, Margarita Misirpashayeva, Anna Missilä, Cătălin Mititelu, Yusuke Miyao, Simonetta Montemagni, Amir More, Laura Moreno Romero, Keiko Sophie Mori, Shinsuke Mori, Bjartur Mortensen, Bohdan Moskalevskyi, Kadri Muischnek, Yugo Murawaki, Kaili Müürisep, Pinkey Nainwani, Juan Ignacio Navarro Horñiacek, Anna Nedoluzhko, Gunta Nešpore-Bērzkalne, Lng Nguy˜ên Thị, Huy`ên Nguy˜ên Thị Minh, Vitaly Nikolaev, Rattima Nitisaroj, Hanna Nurmi, Stina Ojala, Adédayọ Olúòkun, Mai Omura, Petya Osenova, Robert Östling, Lilja Øvrelid, Niko Partanen, Elena Pascual, Marco Passarotti, Agnieszka Patejuk, Guilherme Paulino-Passos, Siyao Peng, Cenel-Augusto Perez, Guy Perrier, Slav Petrov, Jussi Piitulainen, Emily Pitler, Barbara Plank, Thierry Poibeau, Martin Popel, Lauma Pretkalniņa, Sophie Prévost, Prokopis Prokopidis, Adam Przepiórkowski, Tiina Puolakainen, Sampo Pyysalo, Andriela Rääbis, Alexandre Rademaker, Loganathan Ramasamy, Taraka Rama, Carlos Ramisch, Vinit Ravishankar, Livy Real, Siva Reddy, Georg Rehm, Michael Rießler, Larissa Rinaldi, Laura Rituma, Luisa Rocha, Mykhailo Romanenko, Rudolf Rosa, Davide Rovati, Valentin Roca, Olga Rudina, Jack Rueter, Shoval Sadde, Benoît Sagot, Shadi Saleh, Tanja Samardžić, Stephanie Samson, Manuela Sanguinetti, Baiba Saulīte, Yanin Sawanakunanon, Nathan Schneider, Sebastian Schuster, Djamé Seddah, Wolfgang Seeker, Mojgan Seraji, Mo Shen, Atsuko Shimada, Muh Shohibussirri, Dmitry Sichinava, Natalia Silveira, Maria Simi, Radu Simionescu, Katalin Simkó, Mária Šimková, Kiril Simov, Aaron Smith, Isabela Soares-Bastos, Carolyn Spadine, Antonio Stella, Milan Straka, Jana Strnadová, Alane Suhr, Umut Sulubacak, Zsolt Szántó, Dima Taji, Yuta Takahashi, Takaaki Tanaka, Isabelle Tellier, Trond Trosterud, Anna Trukhina, Reut Tsarfaty, Francis Tyers, Sumire Uematsu, Zdeňka Urešová, Larraitz Uria, Hans Uszkoreit, Sowmya Vajjala, Daniel van Niekerk, Gertjan van Noord, Viktor Varga, Eric Villemonte de la Clergerie, Veronika Vincze, Lars Wallin, Jing Xian Wang, Jonathan North Washington, Seyi Williams, Mats Wirén, Tsegay Woldemariam, Tak-sum Wong, Chunxiao Yan, Marat M. Yavrumyan, Zhuoran Yu, Zdeněk Žabokrtský, Amir Zeldes, Daniel Zeman, Manying Zhang, and Hanzhi Zhu. 2018. Universal dependencies 2.3. LINDAT/CLARIAH-CZ digital library at the Institute of Formal and Applied Linguistics (ÚFAL), Faculty of Mathematics and Physics, Charles University.

Alessandro Raganato, Jörg Tiedemann, et al. 2018. An analysis of encoder representations in transformer-based machine translation. In *Proceedings of the 2018 EMNLP Workshop BlackboxNLP: Analyzing and Interpreting Neural Networks for NLP*. The Association for Computational Linguistics.

Devendra Singh Sachan, Yuhao Zhang, Peng Qi, and William Hamilton. 2020. Do syntax trees help pre-trained transformers extract information? *arXiv preprint arXiv:2008.09084*.

Rico Sennrich, Barry Haddow, and Alexandra Birch. 2015. Neural machine translation of rare words with subword units. *arXiv preprint arXiv:1508.07909*.

Christian Szegedy, Vincent Vanhoucke, Sergey Ioffe, Jon Shlens, and Zbigniew Wojna. 2016. Rethinking the inception architecture for computer vision. In *Proceedings of the IEEE conference on computer vision and pattern recognition*, pages 2818–2826.

Ashish Vaswani, Noam Shazeer, Niki Parmar, Jakob Uszkoreit, Llion Jones, Aidan N Gomez, Łukasz Kaiser, and Illia Polosukhin. 2017. Attention is all you need. In *Advances in neural information processing systems*, pages 5998–6008.

Yang Xu and Jiawei Liu. 2017. Implicitly incorporating morphological information into word embedding. *arXiv preprint arXiv:1701.02481*.

Configurable Dependency Tree Extraction from CCG Derivations

Kilian Evang
Heinrich Heine University Düsseldorf
Germany
`evang@hhu.de`

Abstract

We revisit the problem of extracting dependency structures from the derivation structures of Combinatory Categorial Grammar (CCG). Previous approaches are often restricted to a narrow subset of CCG or support only one flavor of dependency tree. Our approach is more general and easily configurable, so that multiple styles of dependency tree can be obtained. In an initial case study, we show promising results for converting English, German, Italian, and Dutch CCG derivations from the Parallel Meaning Bank into (unlabeled) UD-style dependency trees.

1 Introduction

In a world of heterogeneous linguistically annotated resources, the need often arises to convert annotations from one format into another. The purpose may be to extract features, make data available as input for tools that were not designed for it, or to compare heterogeneous tool outputs on an equal footing. For example, sentences annotated with derivations of Combinatory Categorial Grammar (CCG) (Steedman, 2001) must often be converted to dependency graphs or trees. Figure 1 shows an example.

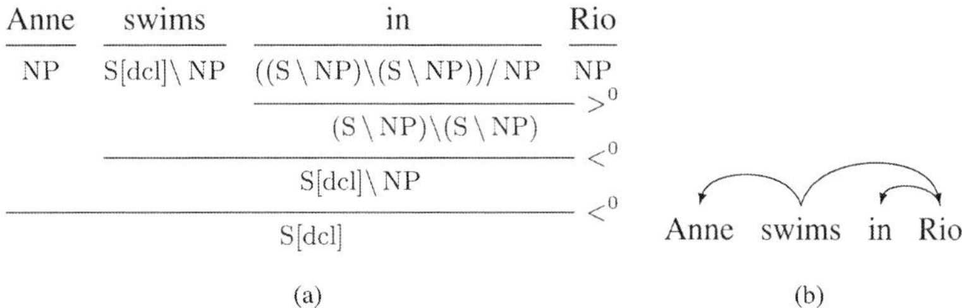

Figure 1: A CCG derivation and corresponding unlabeled UD dependency tree

Clark et al. (2002) define a conversion from derivations to dependency graphs (containing both local and long-range dependencies) by annotating every lexical category that occurs in the English CCGbank (Hockenmaier and Steedman, 2007), specifying the bilexical dependency (or dependencies) that each argument category gives rise to. This annotated inventory of categories and variations thereof have since widely been used to train and evaluate CCG parsers, e.g., Clark and Curran (2007), Zhang and Clark (2011), Lewis and Steedman (2014), Stanojević and Steedman (2019). The obvious drawback of this approach is that each category has to be annotated manually, and adapting the scheme to other languages, other flavors of CCG, or other flavors of dependency graph, is thus labor-intensive.

A simple alternative is to just extract a dependency for each argument category, with the word corresponding to the argument as the dependent, and the word corresponding to the result category as the head. This is, e.g., used for parser training and evaluation for English by Lewis and Steedman (2014) and for English and Japanese by Yoshikawa et al. (2017). Koller and Kuhlmann (2009) define a similar algorithm operating on derivations rather than lexical categories, which however only supports pure

87

Proceedings of the Fourth Workshop on Universal Dependencies (UDW 2020), pages 87–93
Barcelona, Spain (Online), December 13, 2020

first-order CCGs. The main drawback is that only one flavor of dependency tree is supported, in which modifiers and function words such as determiners end up as heads of what they modify due to the way CCG uses functional categories for them. Bisk and Hockenmaier (2013) use a simple algorithm with some tricks to accomodate a variety of different dependency treebank formats, but it only supports a heavily simplified version of CCG with two basic categories, S and N.

In this paper we present a novel approach to extracting dependencies from CCG derivations. It is similar to Clark et al.'s approach in that the lexical categories, augmented with dependency information for each argument category, serve as the basis for the extraction. However, we do not annotate each possible lexical category manually, but rather define a limited and mostly language-independent set of rules to do so automatically, which can be adapted to different dependency flavors easily. Like the other approaches mentioned, we limit ourselves to local dependencies. As a result, the resulting structures are guaranteed to be trees. As a case study, we experiment with converting English, German, Italian, and Dutch derivations from the Parallel Meaning Bank (Abzianidze et al., 2017) to (unlabeled) dependency trees compatible with the annotation guidelines of Basic Universal Dependencies (UD) (Nivre et al., 2016).

2 CCG-to-Dependency Conversion by Argument Category Augmentation

In a CCG derivation, each word is assigned a syntactic *category* that encodes its combinatory potential in terms of syntactic arguments. For example, an English transitive verb like *sees* in *Mary sees John* has the category $(S \backslash NP) / NP$, meaning that it combines with an (object) NP to the right and then with a (subject) NP on the left, and that the resulting constituent is a sentence (S):

(1)   Mary   sees   John
      NP $(S \backslash NP) / NP$ NP

Categories with slashes (i.e., with arguments) are called *functional*, others are called *basic*. We call the basic category that remains after stripping all arguments from a functional category its *top category*, e.g., S is the top category of $(S \backslash NP) / NP$.

The first step in our conversion algorithm is to augment each basic category with a pair of variables X, D, where X represents its identity and D will later be bound to a marker (F or A) that indicates the direction of the dependency:

(2)   Mary   sees   John
      $NP_{A,V}$ $(S_{B,W} \backslash NP_{C,X}) / NP_{D,Y}$ $NP_{E,Z}$

We then unify argument categories of functors with the categories of their arguments (this can be done by traversing the derivation):

(3)   Mary   sees   John
      $NP_{A,V}$ $(S_{B,W} \backslash NP_{A,V}) / NP_{D,Y}$ $NP_{D,Y}$

We now bind the identity variable of the top category of each word to its token number:

(4)   Mary   sees   John
      $NP_{1,V}$ $(S_{2,W} \backslash NP_{1,V}) / NP_{3,Y}$ $NP_{3,Y}$

In the next step, each argument category gets a dependency direction marker. In our example, there are two argument categories, $NP_{1,V}$ and $NP_{3,Y}$, both arguments of the functor category $(S_{2,W} \backslash NP_{1,V}) / NP_{3,Y}$. In this case, the functor-argument relation of CCG corresponds exactly to the head-dependent relation of most dependency grammars. We indicate this by binding the top category of every argument category to F, meaning that the functor is the head:

(5)   Mary   sees   John
      $NP_{1,F}$ $(S_{2,W} \backslash NP_{1,F}) / NP_{3,F}$ $NP_{3,F}$

But the functor is not always the head. Consider the following example:

Remaining category	Head word	New dependency
	3	
$((S_{3,U} \setminus NP_{1,F}) \setminus (S_{2,A} \setminus NP_{E,X}))/NP_{4,A}$	4	$\langle 4,3 \rangle$
$(S_{3,U} \setminus NP_{1,F}) \setminus (S_{2,A} \setminus NP_{E,X})$	2	$\langle 2,4 \rangle$
$S_{3,U} \setminus NP_{1,F}$	2	$\langle 2,1 \rangle$
$S_{3,U}$	2	

Table 1: Conversion of the category of *in* in (7) into dependencies

(6) Anne   swims   in   Rio
      $NP_{1,R}$ $S_{2,S} \setminus NP_{E,X}$ $((S_{3,U} \setminus NP_{1,R}) \setminus (S_{2,S} \setminus NP_{E,X}))/NP_{4,Y}$ $NP_{4,Y}$

Under this CCG analysis, the preposition *in* is a functor that takes two arguments: first, the NP *Rio*, and second, the VP that it modifies (*swims*). However, in a UD tree, *in* would not be the head of either *Rio* or *swims*. Instead, the preposition should become a dependent of its object (*Rio*), which in turn becomes a dependent of the verb that it modifies (*swims*). Thus, the dependency direction markers of the arguments of *in* are bound to A, indicating that the argument is the head. The other argument categories are still marked F:

(7) Anne   swims   in   Rio
      $NP_{1,F}$ $S_{2,A} \setminus NP_{E,X}$ $((S_{3,U} \setminus NP_{1,F}) \setminus (S_{2,A} \setminus NP_{E,X}))/NP_{4,A}$ $NP_{4,A}$

Unfortunately, it is not obvious from this representation between which pairs of words dependencies exist. For example, the presence of $NP_{1,F}$ as an argument category in the category of *in* might suggest that *Anne* depends on *in* when it should depend on *swims*. To correctly convert categories into sets of dependencies, we need to process arguments from outermost to innermost and take into account that the head word we need to attach dependents to changes every time we encounter an A-type dependency.

The process is illustrated in Table 1 for *in*. We start out with word 3 (*in*) itself as the head word, but already the first argument is A-type, so the argument head, word 4, becomes the new head word, and we generate a dependency from it to the former head, word 3. The second argument is A-type as well, so the argument head, word 2, becomes the new head word, and we generate a dependency from it to the former head, word 4. The third argument is F-type, so we generate a dependency from the current head, word 2, to the argument head, word 1. Word 2 remains the final head associated with *in*. Note that when we speak of "argument heads", we mean the final heads associated with argument categories (more properly: with the words whose categories have the same top category), found by recursively processing them.

3   Identifying Modifiers and Function Words

Which arguments to mark with F, and which with A, depends on the style of dependency tree one wishes to obtain. Marking every argument with F would yield very modifier-centric and function-word-centric trees due to CCG's treatment of adjectives, adverbs, adpositions, conjunctions, etc., as functors. Most dependency grammars, however, prefer a modifiee-centric, and to varying degrees also content-word-centric, style. Universal Dependencies (Nivre et al., 2016) is an example of an especially content-word-centric style, treating function words as dependents of content words whenever possible. SUD (Gerdes et al., 2018) is a variant of UD that differs mainly in being less content-word-centric. Non-UD treebanks show considerable variation as to which function words they treat as heads and which as dependents, cf. Gelling et al. (2012).

Our solution is to mark arguments with F by default, but to define a list of rules that identify modifier and function word categories whose outermost argument category should be marked with A. We group the rules into different modules (one for modifiers, one for determiners, etc.) that can be turned on and off individually, so various dependency styles are supported. We base our rules on the CCG category inventory of the Parallel Meaning Bank (PMB) (Abzianidze et al., 2017), a large quadrilingual corpus of sentences annotated with CCG derivations. Our rule inventory is shown in Table 2, where X, Y match

Module	Symbols	Semtags	Category
Coordinating conjunctions		NIL QUE GRP COO	$(X \backslash X)/X$
Modifiers			$X \mid X$
Adjective copulas	be		$(S[X]\backslash NP) \mid (S[adj]\backslash NP)$ $(S[q]/(S[adj]\backslash NP))/NP *$
Noun copulas	be		$(S[X]\backslash NP) \mid NP$ $(S[q]/NP)/NP *$
Adposition copulas	be		$(S[X]\backslash NP) \mid PP$ $(S[q]/PP)/NP *$
Auxiliaries and modals		NOW PST FUT PRG PFT NEC POS NIL	$(S[X]\backslash NP) \mid (S[Y]\backslash NP)$ $(S[q]/(S[X]\backslash NP))/NP *$
Adpositions			$PP \mid NP$ $(X \mid X) \mid Y$
Determiners			NP/N $NP/(N/PP)$
Possessive suffix			$(NP/(N/PP))\backslash NP$
Subordinating conjunctions			$(S \mid S) \mid S[X]$ $(S \mid S) \mid (S \mid NP)$ $((S \backslash NP) \mid (S \backslash NP)) \mid S[X]$ $((S \backslash NP) \mid (S \backslash NP)) \mid (S[X] \mid NP)$ $((S/NP) \mid (S/NP)) \mid S[X]$ $((S/NP) \mid (S/NP)) \mid (S[X] \mid NP)$
Complementizers			$S[em]/S[dcl]$ $(S[to]\backslash NP)/(S[b]\backslash NP)$
Relativizers			$(N \backslash N)/(S[dcl] \mid NP)$ $(NP \backslash NP)/(S[dcl] \mid NP)$ $((N \backslash N)/(S[dcl] \mid NP))/N$ $((NP \backslash NP)/(S[dcl] \mid NP))/N$
Fronted *wh*-words			$S[wq]/(S[q]/(S[adj]/NP))$ $S[wq]/X$ $(S[wq]/X)/Y$

Table 2: Simplified rule inventory

anything and $\mid$ matches both $/$ and $\backslash$.

Not in all cases are categories sufficient for identifying function words, so we use the PMB annotations of symbols (language-independent generalization of lemmas) and semantic tags in some rules. Copulas, auxiliaries, and modals in verb-first (question) sentences have the problem that our algorithm attaches them to the subject, rather than the complement, due to the inverted order of arguments. We mark them specially and reattach them automatically in postprocessing. The affected categories are marked with an asterisk. The rule inventory shown here is simplified for space reasons. The full inventory is released with our data and code.

4 Case Study: Converting the PMB to UD-style Dependencies[1]

To initially develop and test our conversion algorithm, we annotated parts 00 (for development) and 01 (for testing) of the Parallel Meaning Bank, version 3.0.0. We only used sentences whose annotation status was marked "gold". One trained annotator annotated the sentences with dependency trees following the Basic UD guidelines, but without labels, indicating only the head for each word. We then converted the PMB CCG derivations to dependency trees using the algorithm presented above, with all modules turned on, and computed the unlabeled attachment score when comparing to the manual annotation. The results, shown in Table 3, are consistently above 90%, suggesting that our conversion basically works, although some discrepancies remain.

We performed a manual error analysis to see what kinds of discrepancies were encountered. In a few cases, the discrepancies have nothing to do with our algorithm but are the result of plain annotation errors in the PMB or attachment ambiguity that the PMB's annotators and our annotator resolved differently. Unlike UD, the PMB has no strict rules for attaching punctuation, so it sometimes ends up modifying a different constituent from the one that the UD guidelines mandate. There are various relatively rare

---

[1]Our data and code is available at `https://github.com/texttheater/pmb2tsv`.

	Development				Testing			
	English	German	Italian	Dutch	English	German	Italian	Dutch
Statistics								
Sentences	383	100	73	37	208	35	27	13
Mean length	6.0	5.53	5.1	5.7	6.4	5.4	5.6	5.1
Scores								
UAS	.982	.993	.936	.921	.977	.937	.976	1
Error analysis								
PMB annotation error	1	1						
Attachment ambiguity	3				2	1		
Punctuation	4				1			
Tag question	2							
Embedded question					1			
Date					1			
Subordinating conjunction					1			
Possessive suffix					1	1		
Copula/auxiliary/modal				1	1		1	
Expletive nominal			2	1				
Question verb		3	1					
Inverted copula	1							
Pseudo-copula		1	1	2				
Non-local dependencies	4							

Table 3: Evaluation results and error analysis

categories and constructions that are not yet correctly identified by our rule inventory (sometimes due to arguably inconsistent annotation in the PMB), such as English tag questions, embedded questions, certain date expressions, certain subordinating conjunctions, certain instances of the German and English possessive suffix, certain copulas, auxiliaries, and modals, certain expletive nominals, certain verbs in questions, inverted copulas that have their subject on the right rather than the left, and "pseudo-copulas" where the PMB tags the verb like a copula in constructions like Dutch *gelijk hebben* ("to be right") or German *Hunger haben* ("to be hungry"). Finally, there are some dependencies that our algorithm cannot extract correctly because they are mediated non-locally via third categories in the PMB annotation. For example, here, the existential *is* mediates the dependency between *person* and *ginger* [PMB 00/0055]:

(8)   There   is   no   person   cutting   some   ginger
     $NP[thr]$ $((S[dcl]\backslash NP)/(S[ng]\backslash NP))/NP$ NP/N N $(S[ng]\backslash NP)/NP$ NP/N N

And here, the emphatic *how* mediates the dependency between *slow* and *are* [PMB 00/0778]:

(9)   How   slow   you   are
     $(S[dcl]/(S[dcl]/S[adj]\backslash NP))/S[adj]\backslash NP$ $S[adj]\backslash NP$ NP $(S[dcl]\backslash NP)/(S[adj]\backslash NP)$

5   Conclusions

We have presented a general and configurable algorithm to convert CCG derivations into dependency trees, together with a rule inventory for the Parallel Meaning Bank, achieving promising accuracy for conversion to unlabeled Basic UD on English, German, Italian, and Dutch. Compared to the method of Clark et al. (2002), the need for manually marking up all lexical category types in a CCG treebank is reduced because we only have to list the categories of modifiers and function words. However, if our approach was to be extended to dependency schemes with nonlocal dependencies, such as Enhanced UD (Schuster and Manning, 2016), or if labeled dependencies were desired, markup of content words would be required as well. And as our error analysis shows, at least in the PMB, there is a long tail of categories that cannot be discovered by looking at a small sample. Still, the modularity of our approach enables it to support different dependency treebank formats. The work has many possible applications, including feature extraction from CCG parses and cross-framework and cross-language parser evaluation.

Acknowledgments

The author would like to thank the anonymous reviewers for helpful feedback. This research was carried out within the TreeGraSP project, funded by a Consolidator Grant of the European Research Council (ERC).

References

Lasha Abzianidze, Johannes Bjerva, Kilian Evang, Hessel Haagsma, Rik van Noord, Pierre Ludmann, Duc-Duy Nguyen, and Johan Bos. 2017. The Parallel Meaning Bank: Towards a multilingual corpus of translations annotated with compositional meaning representations. In *Proceedings of the 15th Conference of the European Chapter of the Association for Computational Linguistics: Volume 2, Short Papers*, pages 242–247, Valencia, Spain, April. Association for Computational Linguistics.

Yonatan Bisk and Julia Hockenmaier. 2013. An HDP model for inducing Combinatory Categorial Grammars. *Transactions of the Association for Computational Linguistics*, 1:75–88.

Stephen Clark and James R. Curran. 2007. Wide-coverage efficient statistical parsing with CCG and log-linear models. *Computational Linguistics*, 33(4):493–552.

Stephen Clark, Julia Hockenmaier, and Mark Steedman. 2002. Building deep dependency structures using a wide-coverage CCG parser. In *Proceedings of the 40th Annual Meeting of the Association for Computational Linguistics*, pages 327–334, Philadelphia, Pennsylvania, USA, July. Association for Computational Linguistics.

Douwe Gelling, Trevor Cohn, Phil Blunsom, and João Graça. 2012. The PASCAL challenge on grammar induction. In *Proceedings of the NAACL-HLT Workshop on the Induction of Linguistic Structure*, pages 64–80, Montréal, Canada, June. Association for Computational Linguistics.

Kim Gerdes, Bruno Guillaume, Sylvain Kahane, and Guy Perrier. 2018. SUD or surface-syntactic universal dependencies: An annotation scheme near-isomorphic to UD. In *Proceedings of the Second Workshop on Universal Dependencies (UDW 2018)*, pages 66–74, Brussels, Belgium, November. Association for Computational Linguistics.

Julia Hockenmaier and Mark Steedman. 2007. CCGbank: A corpus of CCG derivations and dependency structures extracted from the Penn Treebank. *Computational Linguistics*, 33(3):355–396.

Alexander Koller and Marco Kuhlmann. 2009. Dependency trees and the strong generative capacity of CCG. In *Proceedings of the 12th Conference of the European Chapter of the ACL (EACL 2009)*, pages 460–468, Athens, Greece, March. Association for Computational Linguistics.

Mike Lewis and Mark Steedman. 2014. A* CCG parsing with a supertag-factored model. In *Proceedings of the 2014 Conference on Empirical Methods in Natural Language Processing (EMNLP)*, pages 990–1000, Doha, Qatar, October. Association for Computational Linguistics.

Joakim Nivre, Marie-Catherine de Marneffe, Filip Ginter, Yoav Goldberg, Jan Hajič, Christopher D. Manning, Ryan McDonald, Slav Petrov, Sampo Pyysalo, Natalia Silveira, Reut Tsarfaty, and Daniel Zeman. 2016. Universal Dependencies v1: A multilingual treebank collection. In *Proceedings of the Tenth International Conference on Language Resources and Evaluation (LREC 2016)*, pages 1659–1666, Portorož, Slovenia, May. European Language Resources Association (ELRA).

Sebastian Schuster and Christopher D. Manning. 2016. Enhanced English universal dependencies: An improved representation for natural language understanding tasks. In *Proceedings of the Tenth International Conference on Language Resources and Evaluation (LREC 2016)*, pages 2371–2378, Portorož, Slovenia, May. European Language Resources Association (ELRA).

Miloš Stanojević and Mark Steedman. 2019. CCG parsing algorithm with incremental tree rotation. In *Proceedings of the 2019 Conference of the North American Chapter of the Association for Computational Linguistics: Human Language Technologies, Volume 1 (Long and Short Papers)*, pages 228–239, Minneapolis, Minnesota, June. Association for Computational Linguistics.

Mark Steedman. 2001. *The Syntactic Process*. The MIT Press.

Masashi Yoshikawa, Hiroshi Noji, and Yuji Matsumoto. 2017. A* CCG parsing with a supertag and dependency factored model. In *Proceedings of the 55th Annual Meeting of the Association for Computational Linguistics (Volume 1: Long Papers)*, pages 277–287, Vancouver, Canada, July. Association for Computational Linguistics.

Yue Zhang and Stephen Clark. 2011. Shift-reduce CCG parsing. In *Proceedings of the 49th Annual Meeting of the Association for Computational Linguistics: Human Language Technologies*, pages 683–692, Portland, Oregon, USA, June. Association for Computational Linguistics.

Unifying the Treatment of Preposition-Determiner Contractions in German Universal Dependencies Treebanks

Stefan Grünewald[1,2]   **Annemarie Friedrich**[2]

[1]Institut für Maschinelle Sprachverarbeitung, University of Stuttgart
[2]Bosch Center for Artificial Intelligence, Renningen, Germany
`stefan.gruenewald|annemarie.friedrich@de.bosch.com`

Abstract

HDT-UD, the largest German UD treebank, as well as the German-LIT treebank, currently do not analyze preposition-determiner contractions such as *zum* (= *zu dem*, *"to the"*) as multi-word tokens, which is inconsistent both with UD guidelines as well as other German UD corpora (GSD and PUD). In this paper, we show that harmonizing corpora with regard to this highly frequent phenomenon using a lookup-table leads to a considerable increase in automatic parsing performance.

1 Introduction

Universal Dependencies (UD) are a cross-linguistic dependency grammar framework driven by a large-scale multi-lingual community effort (de Marneffe et al., 2014). In general, UD prioritizes relations between content words. The treatment of function words, being a rather language-specific issue, is to date sometimes inconsistent even across the treebanks of a single language. Function words including prepositions or negation words are often contracted with other words, which requires to decide whether to keep them as a fused unit or split them up during tokenization – a non-trivial problem.[1]

The German language allows to fuse certain combinations of preposition+determiner into a single token, resulting in what UD refers to as a *multiword token*, i.e., a single token that contains more than one *syntactic word*. Examples include *zum* (= *zu dem, "to the"*) and *ins* (= *in das, "into the"*). These constructions can even be regarded as lexicalized, i.e., as belonging to the inventory of the language's lexicon (Lehmann, 2002). Expanding such contractions into several tokens does not depend on the context, hence, treating them as multi-word tokens is rather straightforward. The only caveat is assigning the correct morphological features to the determiner, but these can easily be retrieved from the head noun.

The current UD annotation guidelines for German[2] suggest treating preposition-determiner contractions as multi-word tokens in the way outlined above, and their treatment is implemented accordingly in the German GSD treebank (292k tokens) as well as in German PUD (21k tokens). However, HDT-UD (Borges Völker et al., 2019), the largest German UD treebank (with 190k sentences and 3.4 million tokens currently the largest available UD treebank overall), as well as the small German-LIT treebank (40k tokens, Salomoni (2017)), do not expand these tokens. This may lead to inconsistency-based parsing errors in cross-treebank experiments or when training a parser on several treebanks.

In this paper, we analyze the extent of the problem, finding that in HDT-UD, 25% of all sentences contain such contractions. Our contributions are (i) the development of a simple lookup-based script for splitting German preposition-determiner contractions into several tokens, and (ii) a set of experiments showing that on the relevant sentences, the increased consistency leads to an increase in parsing accuracy by up to 0.8 points in terms of LAS F1. Hence, this paper constitutes a case study of the improvements we can expect from careful linguistic data analysis and corpus harmonization. We contribute our conversion script, as well as the fixed versions of the HDT-UD and German-LIT corpora, for the next UD release.

---

[1]See, e.g., `https://github.com/UniversalDependencies/docs/issues/641`
[2]`https://universaldependencies.org/de/index.html`

Proceedings of the Fourth Workshop on Universal Dependencies (UDW 2020), pages 94–98
Barcelona, Spain (Online), December 13, 2020

Contraction	Expansion	count	% sents
im	in dem	26236	12.8
am	an dem	7764	3.9
zum	zu dem	7584	3.9
zur	zu der	6149	3.1
vom	von dem	3404	1.8
beim	bei dem	2795	1.4
ins	in das	1422	0.7
fürs	für das	233	0.1
ans	an das	160	0.1
übers	über das	147	0.1
TOTAL		56150	25.0

(a) German-HDT-UD

Contraction	Expansion	count	% sents
im	in dem	89	4.2
zur	zu der	44	2.0
zum	zu dem	27	1.4
vom	von dem	17	0.9
am	an dem	17	0.9
ins	in das	8	0.4
aufs	auf das	7	0.3
beim	bei dem	5	0.3
fürs	für das	5	0.3
beym	bey dem	3	0.1
TOTAL		222	9.8

(b) German-LIT

Table 1: The 10 most common contractions in two German UD corpora, as well as the total count. (The computation of the TOTAL row considers the fact that one sentence may contain several contractions.)

2 Preposition–Determiner Contractions in German UD corpora

The German HDT-UD treebank (Borges Völker et al., 2019) has been automatically converted from the Hamburg Dependency Treebank (HDT, Foth et al. (2014)) using a tree transducer. The text data stems from the German technical website heise.de, which contains, among others, reports about new software and hardware as well as technology-related politics. HDT uses its own dependency annotation scheme (Foth, 2006), in which, in contrast to UD, relations are headed by function words. Preposition-determiner contractions are simply marked as prepositions and indicate their complement (i.e., what would be a preposition's head noun in UD) using the relation PN.

Table 1(a) reports corpus statistics for the occurrences of the most frequent preposition-determiner contractions in HDT-UD. Contractions occur in 25% of all sentences, showing that treating the phenomenon in a consistent way is non-negligible. Some contractions, including *im* (= *in dem*, "*in the*"), *am* (= *an dem*, "*at the*") and *zum* (= *zu dem*, "*to the*") are extremely common; others are more colloquial and rarer in written German (e.g., *übers* = *über das*, "*over the*").

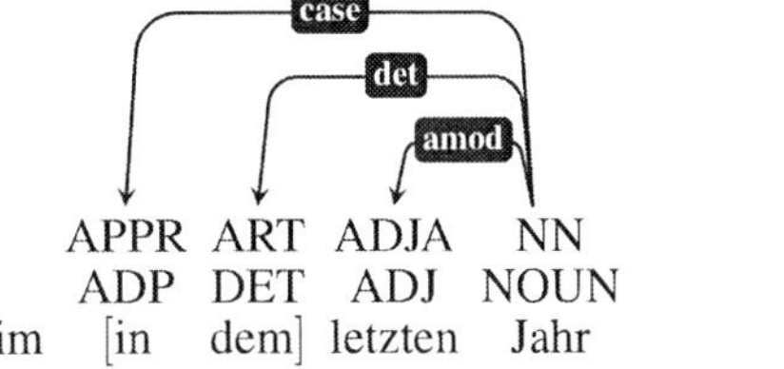

(a) Expanded contraction (according to guidelines).

(b) HDT-UD / German-LIT original version.

Figure 1: Annotation of contractions in the phrase *im letzten Jahr* (*"in the last year"*).

Figure 1 illustrates the two different ways of treating preposition-determiner contractions in German UD corpora. Version (a), introducing two trace-like tokens, is suggested by the official guidelines, and applied in GSD and German-PUD. The commonly used Stanza tokenizer (Qi et al., 2020) also employs this strategy. HDT-UD currently applies a single-token analysis (b). The contractions have their own language-specific XPOS tag APPRART ("preposition with article") taken from the STTS tagset (Schiller et al., 1995). Their UPOS tag in HDT is ADP, which further shows that the single-token analysis is inadequate: ADP stands for adpositions (a cover term for prepositions and postpositions), but the contractions also include a determiner in addition to a preposition. This information is lost in the single-token analysis, which attaches the contraction to its head via *case*, circumventing *det* altogether.

The same issue exists in the small German-LIT treebank (Salomoni, 2017), which consists of short fragments of 18th century literary essays about aesthetical issues by Schlegel and Novalis, written in the then-young Hochdeutsch (modern German). Corpus statistics for German-LIT are given in Table 1(b).

For each token with index i: if the token has the `APPRART` XPOS tag (and no exception applies*):

1. Increase the indices of all tokens after index i by 1.
2. Insert the contraction as a new multiword token with index $(i, i+1)$
3. Replace the contraction at i with two new tokens: a preposition and a determiner as specified by the lookup table.
4. Attach the preposition and determiner to the contractions's head via the *case* and *det* relations, respectively.
5. Copy the contraction's head's *Case* feature to the preposition and its *Case, Number, Gender* features to the determiner.

*Exceptions include tokens that are clearly incorrectly tagged and tokens attached via the *reparandum* relation (i.e., disfluencies).

```
1-2  Im        _    _     _ _
1    In        ADP  APPR  3 case
2    dem       DET  ART   4 det
3    letzten   ADJ  ADJA  3 amod
4    Jahr      NOUN NN     4 obl
5    stieg     VERB VVFIN  0 root
6    der       DET  ART    6 det
7    Umsatz    NOUN NN     4 nsubj
```

Example CoNLL-U file (output of algorithm). *"In the last year increased the sales"*

Figure 2: Algorithm for lookup-table based preposition-determiner expansion in German UD.

3 Expanding Contractions

Based on the above discussion, we propose a simple lookup-based method for expanding preposition-determiner contractions in German UD corpora into multi-word tokens in order to make the data consistent with the UD annotation guidelines. Figure 2 shows our algorithm, which operates on files of the CoNLL-U format.[3] Note that we do not make changes for the token *z.* from *z. B. = zum Beispiel = "for example,"* as well as in several other infrequent special cases resulting from annotation errors.

Since prepositions and determiners are closed word classes and the mapping from contractions to their expansions is unambiguous in German, we use a simple lookup table (see Table 1) for expansion. The full table was constructed by extracting all word forms labeled `APPRART` from the HDT-UD and LIT corpora and then using the authors' knowledge of German to assign the correct expansions. Morphological features of the syntactic words of the expansion may be ambiguous: for example, *zum* may be expanded into *zu dem*$_{Gender=Neut}$ or *zu dem*$_{Gender=Masc}$. However, we can easily derive the correct features by simply copying over the *Case, Number, Gender* features from the syntactic head of the contraction. (Note, however, that potential annotation errors are also propagated this way.)

We ensure the correctness of the output by manually inspecting some of the resulting annotated sentences as well as running the official UD validation script.[4]

4 Parser Evaluation

To evaluate how our changes to the corpora affect parsing accuracy, we train the state-of-the-art UDify parser (Kondratyuk and Straka, 2019) on the existing GSD corpus as well as the original and modified versions of the HDT-UD corpus, and report scores on various versions of the test sets. (LIT and PUD only provide test data.) We keep all hyperparameters the same as in the original setup, except that (a) we use the German BERT model by deepset[5] to initialize BERT weights; and (b) we only train on HDT-UD for 25 epochs due to the extremely large size of the corpus. We report results for gold tokens.

Table 2 shows parser performance on sentences containing contractions in the test sets of GSD, HDT-UD, and LIT (the latter two in both their original and modified versions, indicated by *+/-exp*). As can be seen, for the parser that is trained on the GSD corpus (in which contractions are split up), performance is higher on the modified versions of the HDT and LIT corpora than on the original versions, as would be expected due to the unified treatment of contractions. Interestingly, the same holds when training on the original version of HDT-UD. The reason for this is that the original corpus also contains many cases of non-contracted preposition-determiner combinations, enabling the parser to get expanded contractions right as well. Furthermore, scores increase on the fixed test sets because the expansion of contractions leads to more *det* relations, which are generally very easy to predict. However, training on the fixed data is still beneficial, as comparing the last two rows for each of the *+exp* test sets shows.

---

[3] `https://universaldependencies.org/format.html`
[4] `https://github.com/UniversalDependencies/tools/blob/master/validate.py`
[5] `https://deepset.ai/german-bert`

↓ train	test					
	GSD$_{+exp}$	PUD$_{+exp}$	HDT$_{-exp}$	HDT$_{+exp}$	LIT$_{-exp}$	LIT$_{+exp}$
GSD$_{+exp}$	85.78	85.34	85.70	**86.50**	79.76	**80.45**
HDT$_{-exp}$	79.15	81.32	95.57	**95.72**	76.33	**76.91**
HDT$_{+exp}$	79.23	81.41	95.45	**95.73**	76.34	**77.11**

Table 2: Parsing performance (**LAS F1**) on test set sentences that contain contractions. *+exp* indicates that contractions are analysed as multi-word tokens in the respective corpus, *-exp* indicates that they are analysed as single tokens.

An analysis by label type confirms that increases in accuracy are mainly caused by *case* and *det*. For example, when training on GSD, LAS F1 of *case* increases from 96.28 (HDT$_{-exp}$) to 96.60 (HDT$_{+exp}$); *det* increases from 96.74 (HDT$_{-exp}$) to 97.72 (HDT$_{+exp}$). We also observe modest improvements in parsing accuracy on a number of other dependency labels such as *obl*, *nmod*, and *ccomp*, indicating that surrounding syntactic constructions also benefit from the consistent handling of contractions.

Interestingly, our results also show that the parser trained on GSD, despite not having encountered contractions during training, still attaches the vast majority of contractions in HDT$_{orig}$/LIT$_{orig}$ correctly. We suspect that this may be owed to BERT's ability to generalize from simple prepositions to contractions because of their similar distribution in the pre-training data.

5   Related Work

Discussions within UD community. It is an on-going discussion within the UD community how to best achieve a standardized treatment of tokenization and word tokenization, e.g., how to treat multi-word tokens such as *gonna* (= *going to*) in English. A current proposal[6] suggests breaking up these tokens for formal English as was done in the original Penn TreeBank annotations, but allowing different solutions for informal language such as Twitter posts. We follow this suggestion in some sense as we also create multi-word tokens for highly frequent and lexicalized preposition-determiner contractions in German.

Within the context of Surface-Syntactic Universal Dependencies (SUD, Gerdes et al. (2018)), it has been proposed to treat propositions as heads, moving away from UD's focus on content words and applying distributional criteria for the units instead. In fact, in SUD, the question of how to deal with these contractions is even more pressing: Because the preposition part of the contraction would be the head of a noun, but the determiner part would be a dependent, it is not quite clear what the overall syntactic relation of the contraction to the noun should be if left as one syntactic word.

French amalgames. A similar issue arises in the word segmentation of French *amalgames* (contractions). Here, the situation is slightly more complicated due to the ambiguity of *du/des*, which may occur either as indefinite determiners as in *des enfants jouent* ("(some) kids play"), in partitive constructions such as *je bois du lait* (= *de le*, "I drink (some) milk"), or in possessive constructions such as *la lettre des filles* (*de les*, "the letter of the girls"). Currently, the major French treebanks annotate infinite determiner *des* as DET, while they split the other two cases into two tokens. However, a context-dependent treatment of tokenization bears technical difficulties for automatic processing; a discussion by the treebank maintainers suggests to always split these contractions and annotate the indefinite determiner case using a *fixed* relation between the two components.[7] To date, this does not seem to have been implemented.

6   Conclusion

In this paper, we have carefully analysed the treatment of preposition-determiner contractions in German UD corpora. Harmonizing representations lead to increases in LAS F1 of up to 0.8, indicating that a unified treatment of these frequent construction is essential. We here have presented a case study of how to unify word segmentation for the relatively simple case of German preposition-determiner contractions. Future work includes addressing similar phenomena in more difficult situations such as

---

[6]https://github.com/UniversalDependencies/docs/issues/641
[7]https://github.com/bguil/UD-French-discussion/issues/1

the context-dependent interpretation of French amalgames or, more generally, finding good guidelines for word segmentation and harmonizing corpora accordingly. The latter is especially tricky for informal genres where segmentation decisions seem to be a continuum.

References

Emanuel Borges Völker, Maximilian Wendt, Felix Hennig, and Arne Köhn. 2019. HDT-UD: A very large universal dependencies treebank for German. In *Proceedings of the Third Workshop on Universal Dependencies (UDW, SyntaxFest 2019)*, pages 46–57, Paris, France, August. Association for Computational Linguistics.

Marie-Catherine de Marneffe, Timothy Dozat, Natalia Silveira, Katri Haverinen, Filip Ginter, Joakim Nivre, and Christopher D. Manning. 2014. Universal Stanford dependencies: A cross-linguistic typology. In *Proceedings of the Ninth International Conference on Language Resources and Evaluation (LREC'14)*, pages 4585–4592, Reykjavik, Iceland, May. European Language Resources Association (ELRA).

Kilian A. Foth, Arne Köhn, Niels Beuck, and Wolfgang Menzel. 2014. Because size does matter: The hamburg dependency treebank. In *Proceedings of the Ninth International Conference on Language Resources and Evaluation (LREC'14)*, pages 2326–2333, Reykjavik, Iceland, May. European Language Resources Association (ELRA).

Foth, 2006. *Eine umfassende Constraint-Dependenz-Grammatik des Deutschen.*

Kim Gerdes, Bruno Guillaume, Sylvain Kahane, and Guy Perrier. 2018. SUD or surface-syntactic universal dependencies: An annotation scheme near-isomorphic to UD. In *Proceedings of the Second Workshop on Universal Dependencies (UDW 2018)*, pages 66–74, Brussels, Belgium, November. Association for Computational Linguistics.

Dan Kondratyuk and Milan Straka. 2019. 75 languages, 1 model: Parsing universal dependencies universally. In *Proceedings of the 2019 Conference on Empirical Methods in Natural Language Processing and the 9th International Joint Conference on Natural Language Processing (EMNLP-IJCNLP)*, pages 2779–2795, Hong Kong, China, November. Association for Computational Linguistics.

Christian Lehmann, 2002. *New reflections on grammaticalization and lexicalization*, volume 49, pages 1–18. 01.

Peng Qi, Yuhao Zhang, Yuhui Zhang, Jason Bolton, and Christopher D. Manning. 2020. Stanza: A Python natural language processing toolkit for many human languages. In *Proceedings of the 58th Annual Meeting of the Association for Computational Linguistics: System Demonstrations.*

Alessio Salomoni. 2017. Toward a treebank collecting german aesthetic writings of the late 18th century. In *Proceedings of the Fourth Italian Conference on Computational Linguistics (CLiC-it).*

Anne Schiller, Simone Teufel, and Christine Thielen. 1995. Guidelines für das tagging deutscher textcorpora mit stts. *Universität Stuttgart, Universität Tübingen, Germany.*

Annotation Issues in Universal Dependencies for Korean and Japanese

Ji Yoon Han[♠], Tae Hwan Oh[◇], Jin Lee[♠], Hansaem Kim[♠]
[♠]Interdisciplinary Graduate Program of Linguistics and Informatics,
Yonsei University, Seoul, South Korea
[◇]Department of Korean language and literature, Yonsei University, Seoul, South Korea
{clinamen35, ghks10604, sumomo, khss}@yonsei.ac.kr

Abstract

To investigate issues that arise in the process of developing a Universal Dependency (UD) treebank for Korean and Japanese, we begin by addressing the typological characteristics of Korean and Japanese. Both Korean and Japanese are agglutinative and head-final languages. And the principle of word segmentation for both languages is different from English, which makes it difficult to apply UD guidelines. Following the typological characteristics of the two languages and the issue of UD application, we review the application of UPOS and DEPREL schemes to the two languages. The annotation principles for `AUX`, `ADJ`, `DET`, `ADP` and `PART` are discussed for the UPOS scheme, and the annotation principles for `case`, `aux`, `iobj`, and `obl` are discussed for the DEPREL scheme.

1 Introduction

This article investigates issues arising in the process of building a Universal Dependency (UD) treebank for Korean and Japanese. The two languages possess similarities in typology. Korean and Japanese as a language have in common: SOV (subject-object-verb) word order and agglutination. In the design principles presented by the UD project, the principles do not conform to the characteristics of agglutinative languages. The following are part of design principles presented in the UD project:

1. UD needs to be satisfactory on linguistic analysis grounds for individual languages.

2. UD needs to be good for linguistic typology, i.e., providing a suitable basis for bringing out cross-linguistic parallelism across languages and language families.

For the Korean language, it is challenging to satisfy design principles 1 and 2. Berdicevskis et al. (2018) conducted a study on measuring cross-linguistic complexity using UD language resources. For a total of 37 languages, the study analyzes linguistic complexity utilizing a given measurement framework for morphological and syntactic complexity. In the provided measurement framework, morphological complexity has eight complexity variations that include TTR (Type-Token Ratio) and syntactic complexity has seven complexity variations that include CR_POSP (Diversity of POS bi-gram). The results indicate that measures of syntactic complexity might be on average less robust than those of morphological complexity. Unfortunately, the language analysis unit for Korean and Japanese were deemed too difficult and were excluded from this study.

In UD annotation scheme, the Part-of-Speech (POS) analysis results created a language specific part-of-speech layer (XPOS) field in addition to UPOS that exposes the characteristics within the individual languages. However, it is not easy nor ideal to apply the UD scheme created for an inflected language where the content and functional words are clearly separated by

Proceedings of the Fourth Workshop on Universal Dependencies (UDW 2020), pages 99–108
Barcelona, Spain (Online), December 13, 2020

word dividing whitespaces, directly onto an agglutinative language in which functional words are integrated with the content word to form a single unit such as a word or an eojeol. In this study, we examine the problem of how UD is applied to agglutinative languages and morphologically rich languages.

2 Typological characteristics of Korean and Japanese

Since UD was designed primarily for inflected languages, such as English, it is difficult to apply it directly onto the Korean language which is an agglutinative language. Characteristic to agglutinative languages, Korean is highly developed in postpositions and verbal endings. This is a major stumbling block to the application of UD to the Korean language. These problems are present not only in Korean but also in Japanese. Therefore, it is necessary to compare and analyze the application patterns of UD in Korean and Japanese. The following characteristics are mentioned as typological features of the Korean language, but also applies to the Japanese language:

1. Subject-Objective-Verb word order by default, but it is a relatively free word order language.
2. As an agglutinative language, Korean is abundant in postpositions and verbal endings. Functional morphemes determine grammatical relations - not by word order
3. Language in which the embedded clause precedes the main clause.

The Korean and Japanese languages are both agglutinative languages and also commonly follow a SOV word order.(Sohn, 2001) Furthermore, as the most distinctive feature of languages with a SOV word order, such as Korean and Japanese, the two languages are rich in postpositions and verbal endings. This preceding nature is one of the key differences compared to English and other languages where functional words with grammatical functions are placed in front of the content word.

In terms of the location of head directionality, Korean and Japanese place the head on the right-hand side from the existing parsing resources, which is characteristic to head-final languages (Kanayama et al., 2018). In English, which is the standard for Stanford Dependencies, places the head on the left-hand side. In other words, the location of the head in coordinate structures for English is different from languages such as Korean or Japanese. In Korean and Japanese, the head usually appears on the right-hand side, so if the coordinate or parallel elements are annotated, the root is assigned to the right-hand element according to the head-final principle. To prevent this confusion, establishment of principles addressing this issue is in dire need. Figure 1 is an example of the annotation of conj, the relation label between two elements connected by a coordinating conjunction.

Figure 1: annotation of conj; Sentences that translate to "Bill is sweet and honest."

In both Korean and Japanese, there is a form of postposition(called particle in Japanese) and verbal endings. These represent grammatical relations among the content words. In the correlating Japanese component, the categories "particle(case):" and "particle(phrase_final)" are included in the part-of-speech, while only "case postpositions" is included in the Korean part-of-speech. In the Korean component, case postpositions are generally accepted as words, but verbal endings are not considered within the category of a "word." This is because words are achieved only when combined with a verbal stem. Some of the endings in Korean correspond to the particle(case) in Japanese and some mapping to the particle(phrase_final). Compared to the other part-of-speech with relatively clear boundaries and clear lexical meanings, postposition and verbal ending are one cause of difficulties in assigning UD annotation labels to both languages.

The boundaries are not only vague, but also carry stronger grammatical meanings as opposed to lexical meanings.

3 The issue of UD application

3.1 Tokenization and word segmentation

Setting the basic unit of the annotation is the most rudimentary step in dependency relations analysis. UD guidelines define dependencies as occurring between syntactic words. However, the criteria for defining syntactic words are vaguely presented, making it difficult to clearly define syntactic words in each of the languages. For English, whitespace boundaries define the unit and usually also the word for POS annotation. Accordingly, the formal boundaries are consistent with the basic units tagged in UPOS and DEPREL. However, the basic unit for morphological analysis in Korean is not defined by whitespace boundaries. In fact, the whitespace boundaries in Korean defines a unit known as "eojeol," which is a combined form of content words and functional words. This is significant for both Korean and Japanese as the function of sequence within a sentence is represented using postpositions and verbal endings included within an eojeol. For example, in table 1, the following phrase "학교 생활을(to school life)" consists of three morphemes: "학교(school)," "생활(life)," and "을(to)." In this case, "학교 (school)" modifies "생활(life)." And "을(to)" is an objective case marker that indicates "school life" functions as an object in a sentence. As shown in this example, there exists a relationship between morphemes that delivers important grammatical information. If, for example, eojeol was the basic annotation unit, only the relationship between "학교(school)" and "생활(life)" would be represented through the annotations. If "을(to)" is annotated independently, a case tag will be assigned during the DEPREL process and indicate that "을(to)" refers to the case in the sentence. But this case information will be missing if annotation is conducted with eojeol as the basic unit. In the case of Japanese, this problem does not occur because all three levels separately annotate "を(to)". The most debated topic on the study of UD application for the Japanese language is on defining the basic unit of annotation. Unlike Korean, Japanese does not use whitespaces as a unit divider. Existing Japanese corpora are annotated with dependency structures, including the Kyoto University Text Corpus (Kurohashi and Nagao, 2003) and the Japanese Dependency Corpus (Mori and Sasada, 2014). These corpora use bunsetsu as the syntactic dependency annotation units for Japanese.

Korean Sentence 학교 생활을 즐겁게 할 수 있을지도 모르는 방법

XPOS (Sejong)	학교 hakgyo NNG	생활 saenghwal NNG	을 -ul JKO	즐겁 jeulgeop- VA	게 -key EC	하 ha- VV	ㄹ -l ETM	수 su NNB	있 iss- VX	을지 -eulji- EC	도 -do JX	모르 more- VV	는 -nun ETM	방법 bangbeop NNG
eojeol	학교	생활을		즐겁게		할		수	있을지도			모르는		방법

Japanese Sentence 学校生活を楽しくするかもしれない方法

	学校 gakkō	生活 seikatsu	を -o	楽しく tanoshiku	する -suru	か -ka	も -mo	しれ -shire	ない -nai	方法 hōhō
SUW										
LUW	学校生活		を	楽しく	する	かもしれない				方法
bunsetsu	学校生活を			楽しく	するかもしれない					方法

Table 1: Comparison of Korean and Japanese annotation units for the sentence, which translates to "the way you might be able to enjoy school life."

3.2 UPOS annotation

UD guideline uses UPOS tagset, a common morphological analysis scheme, for multilingual processing. Korean uses Sejong Scheme for morphological annotations and Japanese uses Unidic. Table 2 exhibits the mapping of each annotation scheme. This chapter focuses on some of its label: AUX, ADJ, DET, ADP, PART, CCONJ, and SCONJ. Balanced Corpus of Contemporary Written Japanese (BCCWJ) has been automatically tokenized and PoS-tagged by NLP analysers in a three-layered tokenization of Short Unit Word (SUW), Long Unit Word (LUW), and bunsetsu. SUWs are defined by the morphological properties and are minimal atomic units that can be combined in ways specific to particular classes of Japanese words. LUWs are defined by the syntactic properties and bunsetsu are word grouping units defined by the dependency structure (Omura and Asahara, 2018). BCCWJ_DepPara released in 2016 is the bunsetsu-level dependency structure annotations that relies on LUWs (Asahara and Matsumoto, 2016). In 2018, UD Japanese-BCCWJ adopted the SUW word unit. Unlike Japanese, Korean has the unit "eojeol" that is defined by the whitespace dividers. But lexical morphemes and functional morphemes make up one unit of eojeol. Therefore, Korean is also not excused from the conundrum of how to define the basic unit for annotation. Park et al. (2018) and Noh et al. (2018) defined eojeol as the basic unit of UD scheme. Park (2017) defines four different levels of segmentation granularity for Korean. The four levels are eojeol, punctuation, case markers, and verbal endings. The Sejong Treebank adopted eojeol as its basic unit (Hong, 2009). The Exobrain Corpus uses the same annotation system as the Sejong Treebank to express dependency and therefore also use eojeol as the basic annotation unit (Lim et al., 2015). however, there is still a need for discussion on determining the basic unit for syntax annotations and on how to best reflect linguistic characteristics.

UPOS	Sejong(kor)	Unidic(Jap)
VERB	VV+E ([NNG, NNP, MAG, XR])+XSV+E	verb noun(common.verbal suru)
ADJ	MM(attributive prenouns) VA+E VCN+E ([NNG, NNP, MAG, XR])+XSA+E ([N, MAG, SN])+VCP+E	adjective_i adnominal noun(adjectival)
DET	MM(except numeral & attributive prenouns)	adnominal
ADP	(JK, JX)	particle(case) particle(binding)
AUX	VX+E	verb(bound) adjective_i
PART	(EP, EC, EF, ET, XP, XS)	particle(phrase final) suffix(adjectival noun)
CCONJ	MAJ{및(mich), 또는(tto-neun)} JC	particle(case) particle(adverbial) conjunction
SCONJ	MAJ{All access adverbs except '및(mich), 또는(tto-neun)'}	particle(conjunctive) particle(nominal)

Table 2: part of the mapping table between UPOS, Sejong POS and UniDic POS

1) AUX

AUX seems somewhat applicable to Korean and Japanese, but the specific morphological categories are actually quite different. In Japanese, the Unidic annotation scheme corresponds to bound verb(auxiliary verbs, non-independent verbs) and adjective_i(non-independent adjectives). The Japanese non-independent verbs and non-independent adjectives function similar to that of Korean auxiliary verbs and are categorized into the same morphological categories.

However, the verbal ending in Korean is regarded as an auxiliary verb in Japanese and consequently all annotated as an AUX. Therefore, in the case of (a), た (-PAST) is labeled as an auxiliary verb in the past tense and accordingly annotated as AUX. In Korean, -았다/-었다(-PAST) is a verb ending that is equivalent to the Japanese auxiliary verb た (-PAST).In the Korean language, verbal ending is not allowed to construct eojeols independently and is not recognized as a part-of-speech. Likewise, only auxiliary verbs annotated as a VX in the Sejong annotation system are annotated as `AUX` in UD. In the case of (b), `AUX` is not singled out and assigned in Korean. This is because the Korean verbal ending -하다 *(do)* corresponds directly to the Japanese auxiliary verb する *(do)* and does not constitute a separate phrase. However, in (c) and (d), there is a Korean counterpart to the Japanese auxiliary verbs いる *(be)* and ない *(not)*. And for that reason, it is respectively annotated as `AUX` as an independent unit.

(a) kor

먹었다	
meogeossda	
eat+-PAST	
VERB	
食べ	た
tabe	*-ta*
eat	-PAST
VERB	AUX

(b) kor

공부하다	
gongbuhada	
study+do	
VERB	
勉強	する
benkyō	*-suru*
study	do
VERB	AUX

(c) kor

먹고	있다
meokgo	*itda*
eat+-ADP	-ing
VERB	AUX
食べて	いる
tabete	*-iru*
eat+-ADP	-ing
VERB	AUX

(d) kor

먹지	않다
meokji	*anta*
eat+-ADP	not
VERB	AUX
食べ	ない
tabe	*-nai*
eat	not
VERB	AUX

2) ADJ and DET

In English, a be verb is used to make an adjective a predicate. In Korean and Japanese, however, an adjective can be used alone as a predicate and can also be used as a modifier. In Japanese, `ADJ` includes adjective_i, adnominal, noun(adjectival). (e) is an example of adjective_i, and (f) is an example of adnominal. noun(adjectival) is noun, but it can function as adjective, such as in (g). In Japanese, the morpheme 健康だ *(healthy)* is converted to "健康な *(healthy)* + noun" when modifying a noun. In this case, 健康 *(health)* has a form of a noun, but annotated as an `ADJ` and な *(affix)* is annotated as an `AUX`.

Lastly, Japanese adnominals are similar to Korean prenoun. In Korean, only attributive prenouns are classified as an `ADJ`. Demonstrative prenouns are classified as a `DET`, and numeral prenouns are classified as a `NUM`. In Japanese, adnominals that convey a meaning of determining something, such as この *(this)*, その *(that)*, あんな *(that)* and どんな *(what)* are classified as a `DET`.

(e) kor

빨간	사과
ppalgan	*sagwa*
red	apple
ADJ	NOUN
あかい	りんご
akai	*ringo*
red	apple
ADJ	NOUN

(f) kor

큰	가방
keun	*gabang*
large	bag
ADJ	NOUN
大きな	かばん
ōkina	*kaban*
lare	bag
ADJ	NOUN

(g) kor

건강한		사람
geonganghan		*saram*
healthy		person
ADJ		NOUN
健康	な	人
kenkō	*-na*	*hito*
health	-ADP	person
ADJ	AUX	NOUN

3) ADP and PART

Since Korean and Japanese are agglutinative languages, the postposition or verbal ending is combined with a content word to show various grammatical relationships. Postpositions can also function as case indicators that describe the relationship that the noun it is dependent on has with other words or add meaning to the noun it is dependent on. For example, the Japanese phrase in (i), きれいですね *(pretty)* is broken down in the form of an "adjective_i

+ auxiliary_verb + particle(phrase_final". But in Korean, the corresponding counterpart is annotated simply as an adjective because the whitespace word boundaries define the basic unit.

Japanese has various types of postpositions(particles) - `ADP` includes particle(case) and particle(binding), `PART` includes particle(phrase_final). `PART` also includes the suffix(adjectival_noun) 的 *(affix)*. In Korean, when UPOS tags are allocated by the eojeol unit, postpositions and verbal endings are only annotated as `ADP` and `PART` when they are separated by a punctuation mark or an identifying symbol.

<table>
<tr><td rowspan="3">(h)</td><td rowspan="3">kor</td><td colspan="2" align="center">나는</td><td colspan="2" align="center">집에</td><td align="center">간다</td></tr>
<tr><td colspan="2" align="center">naneun</td><td colspan="2" align="center">jibe</td><td align="center">ganda</td></tr>
<tr><td colspan="2" align="center">I+-NOM</td><td colspan="2" align="center">home+-DAT</td><td align="center">go</td></tr>
<tr><td colspan="2" align="center">NOUN</td><td colspan="2" align="center">NOUN</td><td align="center">VERB</td></tr>
<tr><td rowspan="3">jap</td><td align="center">私</td><td align="center">は</td><td align="center">家</td><td align="center">に</td><td align="center">行く</td></tr>
<tr><td align="center">watashi</td><td align="center">-wa</td><td align="center">ie</td><td align="center">-ni</td><td align="center">iku</td></tr>
<tr><td align="center">I</td><td align="center">-NOM</td><td align="center">home</td><td align="center">-DAT</td><td align="center">go</td></tr>
<tr><td align="center">NOUN</td><td align="center">ADP</td><td align="center">NOUN</td><td align="center">ADP</td><td align="center">VERB</td></tr>
</table>

<table>
<tr><td rowspan="3">(i)</td><td rowspan="3">kor</td><td colspan="3" align="center">예쁘네요</td></tr>
<tr><td colspan="3" align="center">yeppeuneyo</td></tr>
<tr><td colspan="3" align="center">pretty</td></tr>
<tr><td colspan="3" align="center">ADJ</td></tr>
<tr><td rowspan="3">jap</td><td align="center">きれい</td><td align="center">です</td><td align="center">ね</td></tr>
<tr><td align="center">kirei-</td><td align="center">-desu-</td><td align="center">-ne</td></tr>
<tr><td align="center">pretty</td><td align="center"></td><td align="center"></td></tr>
<tr><td align="center">ADJ</td><td align="center">AUX</td><td align="center">PART</td></tr>
</table>

3.3 DEPREL annotation

1) case and aux

Japanese uses case-marking and predicate-argument structure information to allocate UD DEPREL annotations. When annotating a predicate-argument structure, it often utilizes case-marking information to allocate DEPREL annotations. For example, postposition は *(topic marker)* is a case-marker revealing a dependency relationship (`nsubj`) that also functions as a topic marker at the same time. This has a function similar to the postposition *(은/는 (topic marker))* in Korean. In Japanese, a short-unit is laid out as the basic unit for parsing, so the postposition is recognized as an independent unit and assigned the case annotation.

In Korean, on the other hand, since postposition is not a self-dependent component, it is always actualized by merging with another word such as a noun, a pronoun, or a numeral. Therefore, if words are used as the basic unit for parsing, the postposition is not recognized as an independent unit and cannot be processed separately from the preceding element. The only exception to this is if a postposition is separated from the dependent word using a punctuation mark or a symbol, then it is recognized as an independent unit. As such, postposition in Korean and Japanese has similar characteristics and appears at a high frequency.

As previously mentioned, aux is a label that corresponds to auxiliary verbs in Korean and modal verbs in Japanese. It supplements the meaning of verbs or adds meaning to the entire sentence. Ultimately, this is deeply correlated to the issue of determining the basic word unit that occurs in the process of language data processing. In Japanese, auxiliary_verbs are assigned the `AUX` label using UPOS and almost always correspond to aux in DEPREL. Since the UPOS label is already processed as a separate unit, it is more intuitive to receive a separate annotation in DEPREL. Additionally, the existence of forms that supplement the meaning of a predicate is a common phenomenon in agglutinating words, so we can anticipate high-frequency rates accordingly. Auxiliary verb(VX)s in Korean are also similar in function to auxiliary_verbs in Japanese. In other words, it plays the role of supplementing the lexical meaning or adding the grammatical meaning to the main verb. However, language data shows us that Korean auxiliary verbs are generally less independent than Japanese auxiliary verbs. Auxiliary verbs are often combined with the main verb because the actual meaning on its own is relatively not strong enough. Also important to note, in Japanese, aux also includes verb(bound)s that add grammatical meaning to verbs, which in most of them correspond to verbal endings rather than auxiliary verbs in Korean.

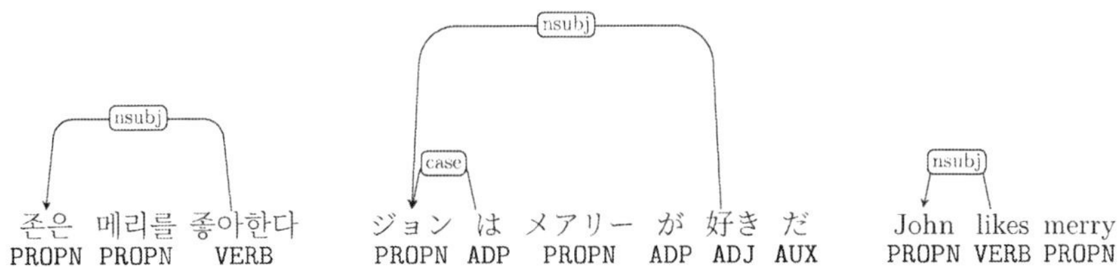

Figure 2: annotation of `case`; Sentences that translate to ".John likes merry."

2) `iobj` and `obl`

In addition to `case` and `aux`, `iobj` is a label for annotating indirect objects. The Korean and Japanese usage of this label differs significantly. An indirect object is a component that helps distinguish two objects in an argument. For example, in the sentence, "She gave me a book," the indirect object is "me" and the direct object is "a book." So in order to represent this dependency relationship, UD created a label known as `iobj` and suggested guidelines to assign it to indirect objects.

The problem is that in Korean and Japanese, excluding exceptional circumstances, there are very few cases in which two or more essential object arguments appear in a sentence. Instead, various postpositions are combined to show their relationship and role with the verb. For example, in Korean, indirect objects are realized as a noun phrase combined with an adverbial postposition (에/에게 *(to)*). These adverbial postpositions function as case-marking indicators that identify indirect objects, but also for some adjuncts like agent, comparison, and destination. Therefore, it is difficult to distinguish between adjunct and indirect objects in Korean. Since the distinction between an indirect object and an adjunct is not clear, the `iobj` label is not used in such arguments. Instead, the label `obl` assigned to adjuncts is used.

By contrast, according to the guidelines released by UD, the Japanese case-marker for indirect objects is presented as に *(to)*. However, there are some problems with this. First of all, in the IPA part-of-speech system, the most common part-of-speech system in Japanese, に *(to)* is classified as an adverbial postposition and it has various meanings similar to the Korean adverbial postposition (에/에게 *(to)*).

If the UD annotation scheme does not portray the characteristics of a specific language very well, it is best to selectively apply labels in a way that reflects the characteristics of the language rather than forcefully manipulating the label to use it all up. The recently published study by Omura and Asahara (2018) shows that the BCCWJ-DepPara corpus of the National Institute of the Japanese Language did not fully reflect the DEPREL labels.

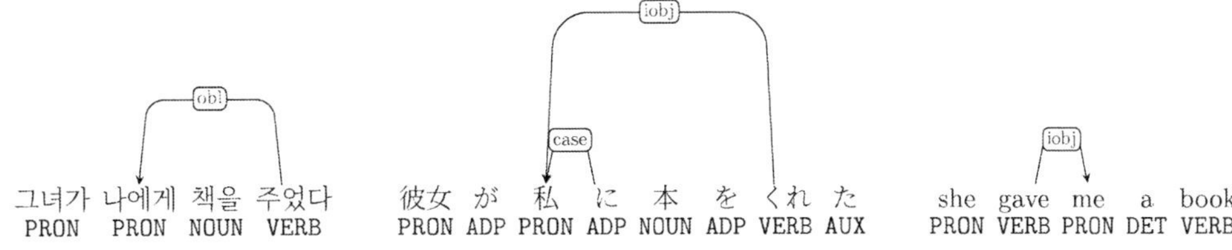

Figure 3: annotation of `iobj`; Sentences that translate to "She gave me a book."

4 Korean and Japanese UD corpora

There are five Korean treebanks that are registered on the UD project website: the Google Korean UD Treebank (McDonald et al., 2013), the Kaist UD Treebank (Choi et al., 1994), the Parallel Universal Dependencies Treebank (Zeman et al., 2017), the Penn Korean UD Treebank (Chun et al., 2018) and the Sejong UD Treebank (Choi and Palmer, 2011).

Five Japanese treebanks are also registered: the BCCWJ UD treebank (Maekawa et al., 2014), the Kyoto Text UD treebank (Tanaka et al., 2016), the Google Japanese UD Treebank (Zeman et al., 2017), the Parallel Universal Dependencies Treebank (Zeman et al., 2017) and the Modern Japanese UD Treebank (Omura and Asahara, 2017).

In this section, the Penn Korean UD Treebank and the BCCWJ UD Treebank, which were most recently revised, are compared in terms of UPOS and DEPREL label usage. The table 3 shows that the difference in UPOS is significant for the ADP label. It accounts for 20.1% of BCCWJ, but only 1.08% of PKT. Whereas AUX accounts for only 3.07% in PKT, but 11.58% in BCCWJ. And ADJ in the Korean PKT accounted for 5.33% of PKT and 2.16% in the Japanese BCCWJ. With the DEPREL scheme, the biggest gap between the two languages appeared in the total ratio of cases. case in PKT was not used, but accounted for 19.87% of the total in BCCWJ. Likewise, iobj was not used in PKT, but used in BCCWJ. aux also made up 3.08% of PKT and 10.36% in BCCWJ.

UPOS	PKTv2020	PC	BCCWJ	PC
ADJ	7,034	5.33%	27494	2.16%
ADP	1,425	1.08%	255976	20.10%
ADV	2,851	2.16%	18815	1.48%
AUX	4,060	3.07%	147400	11.58%
CCONJ	377	0.29%	16142	1.27%
DET	685	0.52%	5357	0.42%
INTJ	0	0.00%	915	0.07%
NOUN	58,367	44.20%	369172	28.99%
NUM	7,602	5.76%	58321	4.58%
PART	290	0.22%	7456	0.59%
PRON	1,142	0.86%	11557	0.91%
PROPN	12,769	9.67%	35938	2.82%
PUNCT	13,428	10.17%	107005	8.40%
SCONJ	533	0.40%	41512	3.26%
SYM	376	0.28%	60957	4.79%
VERB	21,102	15.98%	108692	8.54%
X	0	0.00%	578	0.05%
total	132,041	100.00%	1273287	100.00%

DEPREL	PKTv2020	PC	BCCWJ	PC
acl	11,210	8.49%	31794	2.50%
advcl	5,086	3.85%	30221	2.37%
advmod	3,125	2.37%	16940	1.33%
amod	1,593	1.21%	22253	1.75%
appos	1,173	0.89%	0	0.00%
aux	**4,061**	3.08%	**131946**	10.36%
case	0	0.00%	253009	19.87%
ccomp	1,989	1.51%	0	0.00%
cc	473	0.36%	16120	1.27%
compound	21,433	16.23%	170525	13.39%
conj	7,155	5.42%	0	0.00%
cop	0	0.00%	5661	0.44%
csubj	8,012	6.07%	0	0.00%
dep	10	0.01%	81623	6.41%
det	685	0.52%	5356	0.42%
fixed	589	0.45%	0	0.00%
flat	739	0.56%	0	0.00%
goeswith	2,199	1.67%	0	0.00%
discourse	0	0.00%	834	0.07%
dislocated	0	0.00%	379	0.03%
iobj	0	0.00%	15689	1.23%
mark	0	0.00%	41369	3.25%
nmod	5,501	4.17%	113787	8.94%
nsubj	4,114	3.12%	55117	4.33%
nummod	7,341	5.56%	53859	4.23%
obj	9,849	7.46%	33059	2.60%
obl	16,891	12.79%	29630	2.33%
orphan	9	0.01%	0	0.00%
punct	13,794	10.45%	106990	8.40%
reparandum	0	0.00%	17	0.00%
root	5,010	3.79%	57109	4.49%
total	132,041	100.00%	1273287	100.00%

Table 3: Universal dependency label comparison between PKT & BCCWJ

5 Conclusion

We reviewed the application of the UD scheme to the Korean and Japanese treebanks as we identified and discussed the areas that require awareness of when constructing a UD treebank for an agglutinative language. We identified issues that arise when determining the basic units and in applying UPOS and DEPREL schemes. For the UPOS scheme, issues related to applying AUX, ADJ, postposition, and verbal ending were addressed. For the DEPREL scheme, the application and usage of case, aux, and iobj labels are discussed. The above discussions will be essential in establishing standards for building or improving UD treebanks in agglutinative languages in the future.

This review of the current state of UD treebanks for agglutinative languages discloses a need for a UD treebank that better reflects the unique characteristics of the language for construction. PKT was revised to further reflect the unique characteristics of the Korean language by modifying UPOS and DEPREL in reference to the Korean XPOS (Oh et al., 2020). But still, the basic unit for analysis is a word unit, which does not capture all the syntactic functions of postpositions or verbal endings. The Japanese UD makes better use of its unique characteristics than the Korean UD in the sense that it uses its own units. However, as we can see from the application of `iobj` that there is still much room for improvement.

The UD scheme is evolving through continuous research and workshops. As a result, UD treebanks are also becoming more diverse. This study focused on Korean and Japanese to examine the characteristics of agglutinative languages, but the other languages such as Turkish did not explain together, which is left as future work. We hope that this article will contribute to the vitalization of discussions on agglutinative languages.

References

Masayuki Asahara and Yuji Matsumoto. 2016. Bccwj-deppara: A syntactic annotation treebank on the 'balanced corpus of contemporary written japanese'. In *Proceedings of the 12th Workshop on Asian Language Resources (ALR12)*, pages 49–58.

Aleksandrs Berdicevskis, Çağrı Çöltekin, Katharina Ehret, Kilu von Prince, Daniel Ross, Bill Thompson, Chunxiao Yan, Vera Demberg, Gary Lupyan, Taraka Rama, et al. 2018. Using universal dependencies in cross-linguistic complexity research. In *Proceedings of the Second Workshop on Universal Dependencies (UDW 2018)*, pages 8–17.

Jinho D. Choi and Martha Palmer. 2011. Statistical dependency parsing in korean: From corpus generation to automatic parsing. In *Proceedings of the Second Workshop on Statistical Parsing of Morphologically Rich Languages*, pages 1–11. Association for Computational Linguistics.

Key-Sun Choi, Young S Han, Young G Han, and Oh W Kwon. 1994. Kaist tree bank project for korean: Present and future development. In *Proceedings of the International Workshop on Sharable Natural Language Resources*, pages 7–14. Citeseer.

Jayeol Chun, Na-Rae Han, Jena D Hwang, and Jinho D Choi. 2018. Building universal dependency treebanks in korean. In *Proceedings of the Eleventh International Conference on Language Resources and Evaluation (LREC 2018)*.

Y Hong. 2009. 21st century sejong project results and tasks. In *In New Korean Life*.

Hiroshi Kanayama, Na-Rae Han, Masayuki Asahara, Jena D Hwang, Yusuke Miyao, Jinho D Choi, and Yuji Matsumoto. 2018. Coordinate structures in universal dependencies for head-final languages. In *Proceedings of the Second Workshop on Universal Dependencies (UDW 2018)*, pages 75–84.

Sadao Kurohashi and Makoto Nagao. 2003. Building a japanese parsed corpus. In *Treebanks*.

Joon-Ho Lim, Yongjin Bae, Hyunki Kim, Yunjeong Kim, and Kyu-Chul Lee. 2015. Korean Dependency Guidelines for Dependency Parsing and Exo-Brain Language Analysis Corpus. In *Proceedings of the 27tht Annual Conference on Human and Cognitive Language Technology*.

Ryan McDonald, Joakim Nivre, Yvonne Quirmbach-Brundage, Yoav Goldberg, Dipanjan Das, Kuzman Ganchev, Keith Hall, Slav Petrov, Hao Zhang, Oscar Täckström, et al. 2013. Universal dependency annotation for multilingual parsing. In *Proceedings of the 51st Annual Meeting of the Association for Computational Linguistics (Volume 2: Short Papers)*, pages 92–97.

Hideki Ogura Mori, Shinsuke and Tetsuro Sasada. 2014. A japanese word dependency corpus. In *Proceedings of the seventh International Conference on Language Resources and Evaluation (LREC 2014)*.

Younbin Noh, Jiyoon Han, Taehwan Oh, and Hansaem Kim. 2018. Enhancing universal dependencies for korean. In *Proceedings of the Second Workshop on Universal Dependencies (UDW 2018)*.

Taehwan Oh, Jiyoon Han, Hyonsu Choe, Seokwon Park, Han He, Jinho D. Choi, Na-Rae Han, Jena D. Hwang, and Hansaem Kim. 2020. Analysis of the penn korean universal dependency treebank (pkt-ud): Manual revision to build robust parsing model in korean. In *In Proceedings of the 16th International Conference on Parsing Technologies(IWPT 2020)*.

Yuta Takahashi Omura, Mai and Masayuki Asahara. 2017. Universal dependency for modern japanese. In *Proceedings of the 7th Conference of Japanese Association for Digital Humanities (JADH2017)*.

Mai Omura and Masayuki Asahara. 2018. Ud-japanese bccwj: Universal dependencies annotation for the balanced corpus of contemporary written japanese. In *Proceedings of the Second Workshop on Universal Dependencies (UDW 2018)*, pages 117–125.

Hyejin Park, Taehwan Oh, and Hansaem Kim. 2018. Universal pos tagset for korean. *The Korean Society for Language and Information*, 22(3):67–89.

Jungyeul Park. 2017. Segmentation granularity in dependency representations for korean. In *Proceedings of the Fourth International Conference on Dependency Linguistics (Depling 2017)*, pages 187–196.

Ho-Min Sohn. 2001. *The korean language.* Cambridge University Press.

Takaaki Tanaka, Yusuke Miyao, Masayuki Asahara, Sumire Uematsu, Hiroshi Kanayama, Shinsuke Mori, and Yuji Matsumoto. 2016. Universal dependencies for japanese. In *Proceedings of the Tenth International Conference on Language Resources and Evaluation (LREC'16)*, pages 1651–1658.

Daniel Zeman, Martin Popel, Milan Straka, Jan Hajič, Joakim Nivre, Filip Ginter, Juhani Luotolahti, Sampo Pyysalo, Slav Petrov, Martin Potthast, Francis Tyers, Elena Badmaeva, Memduh Gokirmak, Anna Nedoluzhko, Silvie Cinková, Jan Hajič jr., Jaroslava Hlaváčová, Václava Kettnerová, Zdeňka Urešová, Jenna Kanerva, Stina Ojala, Anna Missilä, Christopher D. Manning, Sebastian Schuster, Siva Reddy, Dima Taji, Nizar Habash, Herman Leung, Marie-Catherine de Marneffe, Manuela Sanguinetti, Maria Simi, Hiroshi Kanayama, Valeria de Paiva, Kira Droganova, Héctor Martínez Alonso, Çağrı Çöltekin, Umut Sulubacak, Hans Uszkoreit, Vivien Macketanz, Aljoscha Burchardt, Kim Harris, Katrin Marheinecke, Georg Rehm, Tolga Kayadelen, Mohammed Attia, Ali Elkahky, Zhuoran Yu, Emily Pitler, Saran Lertpradit, Michael Mandl, Jesse Kirchner, Hector Fernandez Alcalde, Jana Strnadová, Esha Banerjee, Ruli Manurung, Antonio Stella, Atsuko Shimada, Sookyoung Kwak, Gustavo Mendonça, Tatiana Lando, Rattima Nitisaroj, and Josie Li. 2017. CoNLL 2017 shared task: Multilingual parsing from raw text to universal dependencies. In *Proceedings of the CoNLL 2017 Shared Task: Multilingual Parsing from Raw Text to Universal Dependencies*, pages 1–19, Vancouver, Canada, August. Association for Computational Linguistics.

Exploring diachronic syntactic shifts with dependency length:
the case of scientific English

Tom S Juzek
Saarland University
Saarbrücken, Germany
`tom.juzek@`
`uni-saarland.de`

Marie Pauline Krielke
Saarland University
Saarbrücken, Germany
`mariepauline.krielke@`
`uni-saarland.de`

Elke Teich
Saarland University
Saarbrücken, Germany
`e.teich@`
`mx.uni-saarland.de`

Abstract

We report on an application of universal dependencies for the study of diachronic shifts in syntactic usage patterns. Our focus is on the evolution of Scientific English in the Late Modern English period (ca. 1700-1900). Our data set is the Royal Society Corpus (RSC), comprising the full set of publications of the Royal Society of London between 1665 and 1996. Our starting assumption is that over time, Scientific English develops specific syntactic choice preferences that increase efficiency in (expert-to-expert) communication. The specific hypothesis we pursue in this paper is that changing syntactic choice preferences lead to greater dependency locality/dependency length minimization, which is associated with positive effects for the efficiency of human as well as computational linguistic processing. As a basis for our measurements, we parsed the RSC using Stanford CoreNLP. Overall, we observe a decrease in dependency length, with long dependency structures becoming less frequent and short dependency structures becoming more frequent over time, thus marking an overall push towards greater communicative efficiency.

1 Introduction

It is obvious that language use changes dynamically due to external pressures, e.g. new vocabulary emerging continuously, but what is less reflected upon is how despite these pressures language remains communicatively intact. There is accumulating evidence of the regulatory function of grammar in the process of changing language use, helping retain efficiency in communication. Specifically, grammatical variation in word order, taxis and syntactic embedding is an important means to control linguistic complexity and is thus instrumental in levelling out processing effort (see e.g. Hawkins (1994); Hawkins (2004); Hawkins (2014)).

One approach to capture syntactic complexity with a view to cognitive processing is dependency locality theory (Gibson, 2000). This theory says that languages try to minimize syntactic dependencies in order to manage processing effort by reducing the time in which linguistic elements are held in working memory, e.g. by modulating word order (cf. Hahn et al. (2020)). For instance, Temperley (2007) shows for English that syntactic choices exhibit a preference for structures with shorter dependencies on the basis of the WSJ and Brown corpora and Futrell et al. (2015) provide cross-linguistic evidence of dependency length minimization. Recently, there is an increasing interest in dependency length minimization as a diachronic optimization process affecting the language system in general (e.g. Tily (2010); Gulordava and Merlo (2015)) or specific sublanguages/registers in particular (e.g. Lei and Wen (2020)).

In our research, we are taking a diachronic perspective looking for traces of optimization of syntactic complexity by dependency length minimization in the development of Scientific English from the mid 17th century onward. Our overarching hypothesis is that the changes in grammatical choice preferences can, at least partially, be explained by dependency length minimization. Such changes include for instance the shift from paratactic clause complexes to single clauses with complex NPs; see examples (1) and (2) below, both taken from the Royal Society Corpus (Fischer et al., 2020).

Proceedings of the Fourth Workshop on Universal Dependencies (UDW 2020), pages 109–119
Barcelona, Spain (Online), December 13, 2020

(1)   *...I found not only one hollowness, but as often as I cut the Nerve asunder, the hollowness still continued therein, and I found not only one cavity...* (1674)

(2)   *In contrast to the complete and temporary visual motion blindness which occurs during stimulation of V5, a less-prominent interference with the perception of visual motion occurs at 70–80 ms after the onset of the visual stimulus when TMS is applied to V1.* (1992)

The two examples illustrate two kinds of syntactic organization associated with orality and informal prose (example 1) and writtenness and informativeness (example 2). Example (1) is a historical example illustrating a paratactic clause complex, marked by the coordinating conjunctions *but* and *and*; example (2) is a contemporary example that is syntactically characterized by a simple structure at clause level (*X occurs (at Y)*). Its complexity is in the nominal phrases, which exhibit complex premodification with multiple adjectives as well as compounds (*temporary visual motion blindness*), postmodification with relative clauses (*... motion blindness* WHICH *occurs during stimulation of V5*) and prepositional phrases (*less-prominent interference* WITH *the perception* OF *visual motion*).

In this light, assuming that shorter dependencies result in more efficient code, our overarching research question is whether this is borne out diachronically for Scientific English: If the structures that become typical (more frequent) of Scientific English over time are associated with greater dependency locality, then we may conclude that the sublanguage of Scientific English develops a more efficient code. Specifically, we expect dependency length minimization to arise through a shift from cross-clausal, tactic relations to a preference of single-clause structures with (complex) nominal phrases.

The remainder of the paper is organized as follows. Section 2 discusses more related work. Section 3 provides details on the data set (Royal Society Corpus), Universal Dependency parsing and the measure of dependency length. In Section 4 we present our results, including a discussion of the kinds of syntactic structures involved in dependency length minimization. Section 5 concludes the paper with a summary and sketch of follow-up studies.

2   Related work

There is a good deal of research on Scientific English from a synchronic as well as diachronic perspective. From a diachronic perspective, important descriptive work is found in Halliday (1988) and Halliday and Martin (1993) and corpus-based analyses are pursued e.g. by Biber and Gray (2011); Biber and Gray (2016). Existing works converge on the observation of a basic linguistic shift to heavy noun phrases and simpler clause structure resulting in higher lexical density and simpler sentence structures, such as single relational or passive clauses (cf. also Atkinson (1999), Banks (2008)). More recently, Degaetano-Ortlieb and Teich (2019) forward the hypothesis that Scientific English, as it evolves, develops towards an optimal code for communication. Using information-theoretic measures (relative entropy, average surprisal), they find that over time Scientific English becomes more distinct from "general language", due to a drift towards nominal style and distinctive syntactic usage at clause level. These insights from previous work build our starting point.

The operationalization of syntactic complexity we draw upon is dependency length, assuming along with others that shorter dependency length makes grammars more efficient, both computationally as well as in human language processing (Hahn et al., 2020). Dependency locality theory (Gibson, 1998; Gibson, 2000) claims that dependencies between words should be as short as possible rendering sentence processing more efficient through a lower cost in working memory in incremental comprehension and production (Gibson et al., 2019). Vice versa, experimental studies have shown that long dependencies lead to comprehension difficulty (Grodner and Gibson, 2005; Bartek et al., 2011). Large-scale corpus studies show this to be true across languages (Liu et al., 2017; Futrell et al., 2015) with only small cross-linguistic differences (e.g. Gildea and Temperley (2010) comparing English and German). Several other corpus studies find dependency locality driving clause level word order (Liu, 2008; Gildea and Temperley, 2010; Wasow, 2002; Rijkhoff, 1990). Gulordava et al. (2015) show that dependency locality is involved in noun phrase structuring and Wasow (2002) illustrates its relevance for word order in the postverbal region. For a recent, comprehensive review of research on dependency length see also Temperley and Gildea (2018). Particularly relevant in our context are studies of English that inspect a range of syntactic phenomena, such as Rajkumar et al. (2016), Temperley (2007) or Levshina (2019). Also, studies that highlight dependency length minimization from a diachronic perspective, such as Gulordava et al. (2015) or Lei and Wen (2020) are directly relevant. Here, we pursue similar goals as Levshina (2019), taking note of the specific syntactic phenomena marked by relatively short dependency lengths that occur with high frequencies and thus contribute a lot to average dependency length minimization and overall efficiency as well as those with relatively large dependency lengths that are highly frequent and therefore have a negative impact on efficiency. Correspondingly, low frequency phenomena with short/large dependency lengths will not have a big (positive or negative) impact overall.

3   Data and Methods

3.1   Corpora

Royal Society Corpus. The Royal Society Corpus (RSC) is a diachronic corpus of Scientific English covering the period from 1665 until 1996 drawn from the *Philosophical Transactions* and *Proceedings* of the Royal Society of London (Fischer et al., 2020). In total, the corpus contains 295,895,749 tokens in 47,837 texts. The corpus comes tokenized, lemmatized and PoS-tagged. Here, we use RSC version 4.0, which covers the first 200 years of publications of the Royal Society (1665-1869; ca. 32 million tokens), roughly corresponding to the late Modern period.[1]

Penn Parsed Corpus of Modern British English. For comparative purposes, we employ the Penn Parsed Corpus of Modern British English (PPCMBE). PPCMBE consists of prose texts from 1700 to 1914 and contains about 1 million tokens (Kroch et al., 2010) covering a (unbalanced) mix of genres and registers[2] While much smaller than the RSC, it roughly spans the same time period. We use PPCMBE to be able to check whether the observed tendencies in dependency length development are specific to scientific language or also hold for language use more broadly in the given time period.

We start from the assumption that in the course of becoming a language for experts, scientific writing is under more pressure to develop an efficient code for communication than many other domains or genres, e.g. literary texts or travel reports. On the other hand, in the given time period, literacy becomes more wide spread and general writing standards develop that will reflect an overall communicative optimization for written language (McIntosh, 1998).

3.2   Universal Dependencies parsing

For the analysis of dependency lengths, we employ the framework of Universal Dependencies (UD), which expresses syntactic relations through dependencies: each element depends on another element, its head (Nivre et al., 2019). In UD, in contrast to most other dependency frameworks, the head is taken to be the semantically salient element and the dependent modifies the head. The top-level head is the root of a sequence, which is typically the main verb of the matrix clause. For instance, in the sentence *The great sailor is waiving*, *the* and *great* modify and depend on *sailor*, while *sailor* and *is* modify and depend on *waiving*, which is the root of the sentence. Figure 1, created with spaCy's visualizer[3], illustrates a dependency analysis of this example. The UD framework aims to be universal, i.e. suitable for all of the world's languages, and there are a great number of resources and tools available.[4] Importantly, UD parsing labels nodes with syntactic functions such as *nominal subject, adverbial modifier*, etc. This is crucial for exploring the functions that are associated with dependency length minimization over time (see Section 4).

We use the Stanford Parser (Klein and Manning, 2003) with out-of-the-box settings to parse our corpora. To reduce end-of-sentence errors, we collected and escaped additional abbreviations in the RSC. An evaluation of 1500 head tags taken from randomly sampled sentences gives an accuracy rate of 91.1%

---

[1] https://fedora.clarin-d.uni-saarland.de/rsc_v4/URLRSC4.0
[2] https://www.ling.upenn.edu/ppche/ppche-release-2016/PPCMBE2-RELEASE-1/
[3] https://spacy.io/
[4] See https://universaldependencies.org/tools.html for details.

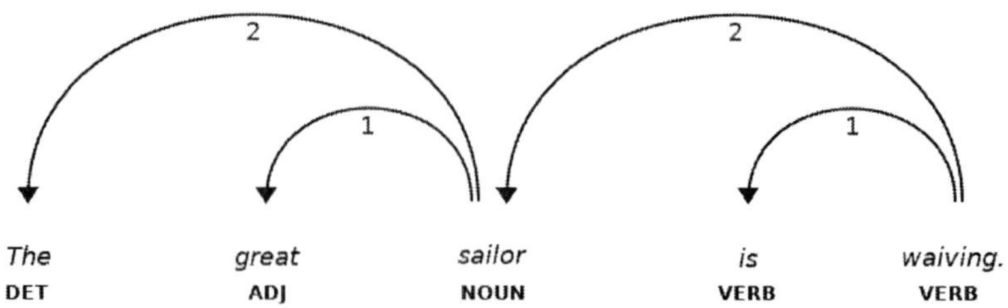

Figure 1: Visualising a simple sequence in the Universal Dependencies framework. The edges represent a dependency relation pointing from head to dependent; the numbers denote dependency distances between tokens/nodes. The distance is measured in number of tokens, starting at 1.

for data from 1665 to 1699 and 91.5% for 1850 to 1869. We also analysed parsing accuracy by sentence length. An analysis of 1500 tokens shows that accuracy for sentences with 13 tokens comes out at 91.4%, at 91.6% for sentences with 26 tokens (the median sentence length in the RSC), and at 92.6% for sentences with 52 tokens. Sentences with less than three tokens were excluded, as they typically lack a verb and thus a root. Punctuation was included for parsing but excluded for the analyses below, by excluding tokens with the dependency tag *punct*. We put both the RSC and PPCMBE through the same pipeline, to ensure comparability.

3.3 Dependency measure

We measure the dependency length of sentences summing all the words' distances to their heads averaged by sentence length. The measure is taken from Futrell et al. (2015) and Gibson et al. (2019) and builds on work by Liu (2008). The sum of distances is measured in word/token distance between a head and its dependent, with a minimal distance of 1. The formula is as follows.

$$\sum d_{s(n)} = |t_1.id - t_2.hd| + |t_2.id - t_2.hd| + ... + |t_n.id - t_n.hd| \tag{3}$$

For any sentence s of length n, the distances for all tokens t_1 to t_n are summed up, where a distance is calculated between a token's position, *t.id*, and its head *t.hd*. For illustration, consider the example in Figure 1. The dependency distances between two tokens/nodes are marked by the numerals below a dependency edge. For instance, the distance from *the* to its head *sailor* is 2; the sum of distances for the sentence is 6 (2+1+2+1). We average the summed distances per sentence length, which gives us the *averaged summed distances* per sentence length.

The value of the measure comes from the fact that it can be interpreted as a proxy of (cumulative) processing difficulty/complexity of a sequence, where long distance structures are regarded as more complex than structures with shorter distances. The analysis of particle verbs illustrate this point: In *Mary picked the guy that we met the other day up*, the particle *up* has a long distance to its head *picked* and the sequence is relatively hard to process. This contrasts to *Mary picked up the guy that we met the other day*, where the dependency between the particle and its head is short – which reduces cognitive load.

4 Analyses and results

We here present the results of the overall diachronic tendency regarding dependency lengths (Section 4.1), followed by a micro-analysis of the types of syntactic structure that contribute to dependency length minimization (Section 4.2).

4.1 Results for dependency length

Figure 2 illustrates the results for the averaged sums of dependency length by sentence length and 50-year periods. For ease of interpretation, the measure is normalised by sentence length. For the RSC, we observe a tendency towards lower dependency length over time, pointing to greater efficiency over-all. Comparing the first larger period (1665-1699) with the latest (1850-1869), the difference is highly significant with $p \leq 0.01$. The trend for PPCMBE is not significant ($p > 0.05$). Recall that PPCMBE, while containing scientific texts as well, is a mixed-register corpus. On average, dependency lengths are slightly higher in the RSC, Figure 2 (left), in comparison to PPCMBE, Figure 2 (right), the difference being significant at $p \leq 0.01$.

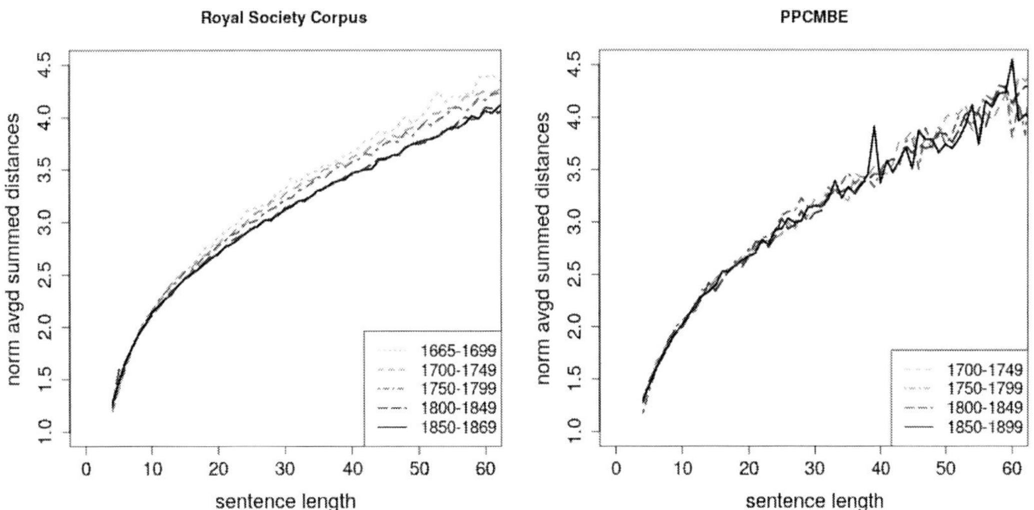

Figure 2: Averaged summed dependency lengths (y-axis) per sentence length (x-axis) over time for the RSC (left) and for the PPCMBE (right). The lengths are normalised by sentence length.

4.2 Types of syntactic functions marked by dependency length

In addition to the general trends, we are interested in the syntactic phenomena involved in dependency length minimization in scientific language. For this, we focus on sentences of 26 tokens in length (the median sentence length in the RSC) assuming that this length is representative of the majority of the data contained in our corpus. For comparison we replicate our analyses on parses of another, randomly chosen and non-extreme sentence length of 52 tokens. Considering the average sum of dependency lengths per 50 years (see Figure 3), we see a decreasing general trend for both sentence lengths. Sentences with 26 tokens decrease in their sum of dependencies from 81.6 in the first period (1650-1700) to 77.1 in the period between 1800-1850, then slightly rising again to 77.2. Sentences with 52 tokens fall from 249 to 239.

To find out what this dependency length reduction is owed to, we look at average dependency length of each syntactic function defined by the UD annotation guidelines[5] with a frequency of at least 1000 per million tokens, altogether 31 different functions. Consider Figure 4 showing all functions[6] and their average dependency length, ranging between 1 (for multi word expressions and phrasal verb particles) and 10.8 (for parataxis). We analyse the relative frequency of each function in 1850 compared to 1650 in relation to their average dependency length, finding that functions with dependency length > 5 decrease in frequency (see Figure 4: dark bars show decreasing frequency, light grey bars increasing frequency). Functions responsible for long dependencies are conjuncts (Example 4), adverbial clauses (Example 5), clausal complements (Example 6) relative clauses (Example 7) and parataxis (Example 8), which is plausible, since they involve cross-clausal dependencies (a dependency between the sentence root and the main verb of the subordinate clause). Conjuncts, however are a special case, since they can represent

---

[5] https://universaldependencies.org/guidelines.html
[6] We exclude the functions punct and ROOT.

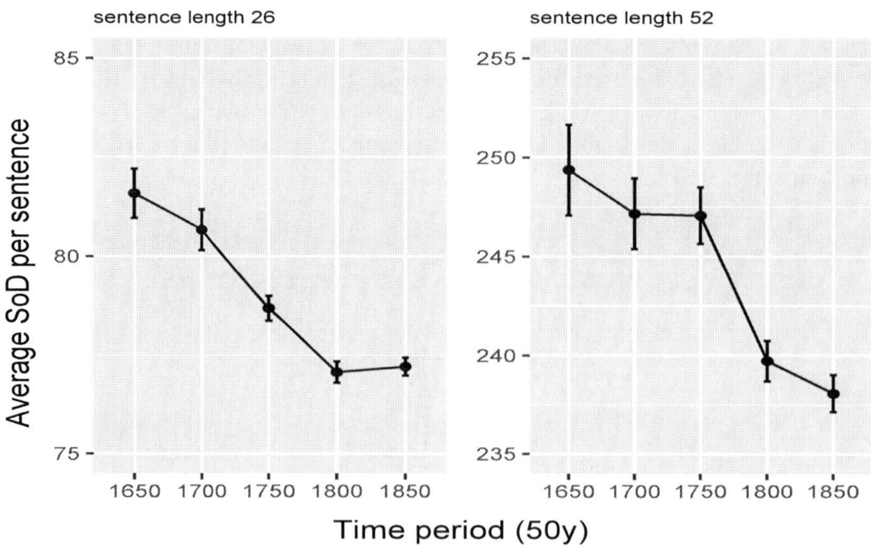

Figure 3: Average sum of distances per sentence of 26 (left) and 52 (right) tokens length by 50 years.

coordinate structures between lexical, phrasal or clausal categories. An equivalent development is shown for sentence length 52 with appositions (as one more nominal function) becoming more frequent over time (see Figure 7 in the appendix).

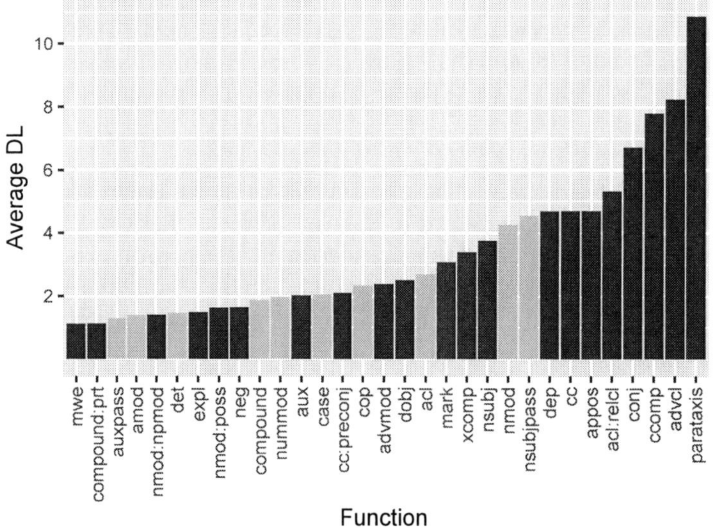

Figure 4: Syntactic functions and their average dependency length. Black denotes decreasing frequency of a function over time, light grey marks increasing frequency.

(4)   *When they have done, they **lick** (ROOT) their fingers, and as often as they have a hot dish, they **wash** (conj) their hands afresh. (1699)*

(5)   *I shall **give** (ROOT) you an Abstract of the Accounts I received in Answer to these Letters, after I have **described** (advcl) our Observations at Edinburgh. (1737)*

(6)   *I **think** (ROOT) it may be inferred, therefore, that when other vegetable and animal substances are similarly treated they will also **yield** (ccomp) analogous results. (1850)*

(7)   *Indeed, we find many **Plants** (head) mentioned by the same Author, which either are not **known*** (acl:relcl) *to us at this present, or neglected.* (1671)

(8)   *Thus this poor creature **lived** (ROOT) without any other considerable complaint above thirty years, the most remarkable circumstance, I **think*** (parataxis), *in her case.* (1714)

Looking at the diachronic development of these long distance functions (Figure 5 left), the longest dependencies are formed by parataxis. Overall, dependency length does not vary significantly over time ($p > 0.9$). The relative frequencies (see Figure 5 right), however, show that all long functions decrease significantly ($p < 0.05$). The same is observed for the longer sentences (see Figure 8 left in the appendix). Over time, the highly frequent conjuncts decrease remarkably. The less frequent functions (adverbial and relative clauses, parataxis and clausal complements) instead, decrease to a smaller extent making conjuncts the principal suspects to contribute to a shorter dependency length on average in the later time periods.

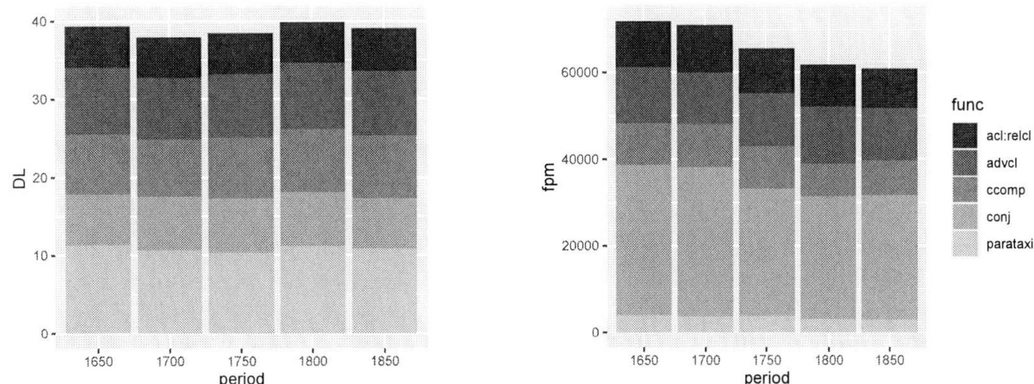

Figure 5: Development of **average dependency lengths** (left) and **fpm** (right) of long distance functions by 50 years.

Looking at the syntactic functions with the shortest dependencies (dependency length between 1 and 2) confirms the intuition that these are relationships with very fixed intra-clausal and intra-phrasal dependency relations (e.g. determiners). They are not flexible in their syntactic placement and can therefore hardly undergo dependency length minimization. We split these functions into nominal (see Figure 6 left) and verbal (see Figure 6 right) modifiers for further inspection, to see whether they indicate the assumed development from an oral/verbal to a written/nominal style, tracking their relative frequencies over time. We exclude multi word expressions since they are known to be tricky relations and not strictly classifiable into either of the groups above. The short nominal modifiers show significant variation over time ($p < 0.05$). Determiners being by far the most frequent function, indeed increase in frequency over time. This corroborates the results of Degaetano-Ortlieb and Teich (2019), ranking the definite determiner as the most distinctive feature over time in the RSC and a clear pointer to nominal style. Adjectival, numeric modifiers and compounds become more frequent over time as well, supporting the expected increasing tendency towards complex premodified noun phrases and again pointing to an expansion of the noun phrase overall. Possessive modifiers as well as the extremely infrequent noun phrases as adverbial modifiers (nmod:npmod, < 2000 per 1 million tokens), however, decrease over time in frequency. In Figure 8 (appendix) we show that the same is true for sentences with 52 tokens with the differences being significant as well. Relative frequency of verbal modifiers decreases in all cases but for passive auxiliaries, indicating the complementary tendency of a dispreference for verbal structures and a preference for a simple clause level structure, as illustrated in Example (2). The comparison between parses of sentences with length 26 and 52 has shown that the observed trends do not only hold for one single sentence length but seem to represent a trend for sentences of relatively common sentence lengths.

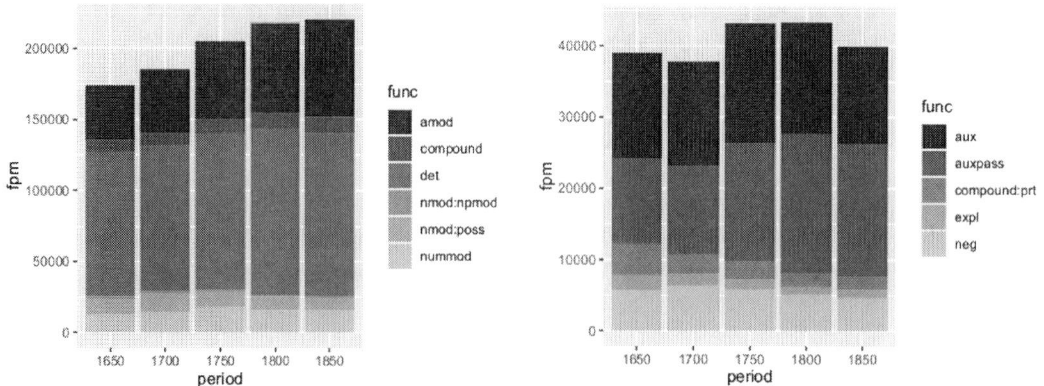

Figure 6: FPM of **nominal** short dependency functions (left) and of **verbal** short dependency functions (right) by 50 years.

5   Summary and conclusions

Using the framework of Universal Dependencies and Dependency Locality Theory, we studied the diachronic development of dependency lengths in a diachronic corpus of Scientific English in the Late Modern period. Our starting assumption was that Scientific English develops a more efficient code over time reflected in a statistical preference of syntactic structures with shorter dependency lengths over time. We found that overall, the average sum of dependencies per sentence goes down over time, if only slightly, and the relative frequency of longer dependencies decreases and particular shorter dependencies become more frequent, especially nominal premodification. This confirms the observed trend towards a nominal, informational style (cf. Section 1). Comparing the trends in sentences of 26 tokens length with sentences of the double length we found that the above mentioned trends seem to generalize across different sentence lengths. In future work we plan to extend this comparison to further (more extreme) sentence lengths to see whether the trends are stable.

Regarding the utility of the UD framework for the present purpose of analysis, the crucial aspect was the labeling with functions, which we found to be descriptively adequate overall with the exception of parataxis and coordination which are notorious problems in dependency parsing (cf. Ahrenberg (2019)). This impacted negatively on our analysis, since we could not interpret the values for the parataxis function.

In our ongoing research, we apply other measures of syntactic complexity, including *dependency depth*, to capture shifts in complexity in terms of syntactic embedding. Recall that we observe nominal phrases becoming more complex over time by multiple pre- and postmodification. This cannot be captured with dependency length alone. Also, we are looking to complement dependency-based analyses of complexity with information-theoretic measures, such as surprisal. For instance, we have estimated the average surprisal of nouns and verbs on a subsample of the RSC and found that while the information content of nouns vs. verbs stays fairly stable over time, nouns have higher surprisal (>9 bits) than verbs (<8 bits) on average. If nouns are generally higher in informativity than other lexical words, then we have additional evidence that "nominal style" can be explained on the grounds of efficient communication.

Acknowledgments

This work is supported by the Deutsche Forschungsgemeinschaft (DFG, German Research Foundation) - Project-ID 232722074 - SFB 1102. We thank the anonymous reviewers for their detailed comments and suggestions for improving the paper.

References

Lars Ahrenberg. 2019. Towards an adequate account of parataxis in universal dependencies. In *Proceedings of the Universal Dependencies Workshop 2019*, Paris.

Dwight Atkinson. 1999. *Scientific discourse in sociohistorical context: The Philosophical Transactions of the Royal Society of London, 1675-1975*. Erlbaum, New York.

David Banks. 2008. *The development of scientific writing. Linguistic features and historical context*. Equinox, London, Oakville.

Brian Bartek, Richard L. Lewis, Shravan Vasishth, and Mason R. Smith. 2011. In search of on-line locality effects in sentence comprehension. *Journal of Experimental Psychology: Learning, Memory, and Cognition*, 37(5):1178.

Douglas Biber and Bethany Gray. 2011. The historical shift of scientific academic prose in English towards less explicit styles of expression. *Researching specialized languages*, 47:11.

Douglas Biber and Bethany Gray. 2016. *Grammatical complexity in academic English: Linguistic change in writing*. Studies in English Language. Cambridge University Press.

Stefania Degaetano-Ortlieb and Elke Teich. 2019. Toward an optimal code for communication: The case of scientific English. *Corpus Linguistics and Linguistic Theory (open access)*, pages 1–33.

Stefan Fischer, Katrin Menzel, Jörg Knappen, and Elke Teich. 2020. The Royal Society Corpus 6.0 providing 300+ years of scientific writing for humanistic study. In *Proceedings of the Conference on Language Resources and Evaluation (LREC)*. ELRA.

Richard Futrell, Kyle Mahowald, and Edward Gibson. 2015. Large-scale evidence of dependency length minimization in 37 languages. *Proceedings of the National Academy of Sciences*, 112(33):10336–10341.

Edward Gibson, Richard Futrell, Steven Piantadosi, Isabelle Dautriche, Kyle Mahowald, Leon Bergen, and Roger Levy. 2019. How efficiency shapes human language. *Trends in Cognitive Sciences*, 23(5):389–407.

Edward Gibson. 1998. Linguistic complexity: Locality of syntactic dependencies. *Cognition*, 68(1):1–76.

Edward Gibson. 2000. The dependency locality theory: A distance-based theory of linguistic complexity. *Image, language, brain*, 2000:95–126.

Daniel Gildea and David Temperley. 2010. Do grammars minimize dependency length? *Cognitive Science*, 34(2):286–310.

Daniel Grodner and Edward Gibson. 2005. Consequences of the serial nature of linguistic input for sentenial complexity. *Cognitive science*, 29(2):261–290.

Kristina Gulordava and Paola Merlo. 2015. Diachronic trends in word order freedom and dependency length in dependency-annotated corpora of Latin and Ancient Greek. In *Proceedings of the Third International Conference on Dependency Linguistics (Depling 2015)*, pages 121–130, Uppsala, Sweden. Uppsala University.

Kristina Gulordava, Paola Merlo, and Benoit Crabbé. 2015. Dependency length minimisation effects in short spans: a large-scale analysis of adjective placement in complex noun phrases. In *Proceedings of the 53rd Annual Meeting of the Association for Computational Linguistics and the 7th International Joint Conference on Natural Language Processing (Volume 2: Short Papers)*, pages 477–482.

Michael Hahn, Dan Jurafsky, and Richard Futrell. 2020. Universals of word order reflect optimization of grammars for efficient communication. *Proceedings of the National Academy of Sciences*, 117(5):2347–2353.

Michael A. K. Halliday and James R. Martin. 1993. *Writing science: Literacy and discursive power*. Falmer Press, London.

Michael A. K. Halliday. 1988. On the language of physical science. In Mohsen Ghadessy, editor, *Registers of written English: Situational factors and linguistic features*, pages 162–177. Pinter, London.

John A. Hawkins. 1994. *A performance theory of order and constituency*. Cambridge University Press.

John A. Hawkins. 2004. *Efficiency and complexity in grammars*. Oxford University Press.

John A. Hawkins. 2014. *Cross-linguistic variation and efficiency*. OUP Oxford.

Dan Klein and Christopher D. Manning. 2003. Accurate unlexicalized parsing. In *Proceedings of the 41st Annual Meeting on Association for Computational Linguistics - Volume 1*, ACL '03, pages 423–430, Stroudsburg, PA, USA. Association for Computational Linguistics.

Anthony Kroch, Beatrice Santorini, and Ariel Diertani. 2010. Penn Parsed Corpus of Modern British English.

Lei Lei and Ju Wen. 2020. Is dependency distance experiencing a process of minimization? a diachronic study based on the state of the union addresses. *Lingua*, 239:102762.

Natalia Levshina. 2019. Universal dependencies in a galaxy far, far away... what makes Yoda's English truly alien. In *Proceedings of the Third Workshop on Universal Dependencies (UDW, SyntaxFest 2019)*, pages 35–45, Paris, France, August. Association for Computational Linguistics.

Haitao Liu, Chunshan Xu, and Junying Liang. 2017. Dependency distance: A new perspective on syntactic patterns in natural languages. *Physics of life reviews*, 21:171–193.

Haitao Liu. 2008. Dependency distance as a metric of language comprehension difficulty. *Journal of Cognitive Science*, 9(2):159–191.

Carey McIntosh. 1998. *The evolution of English prose, 1700-1800: style, politeness and print culture*. Cambridge University Press.

Joakim Nivre, Mitchell Abrams, and Željko Agić. 2019. Universal Dependencies 2.4. *LINDAT/CLARIAH-CZ digital library at the Institute of Formal and Applied Linguistics (ÚFAL), Faculty of Mathematics and Physics, Charles University.*

Rajakrishnan Rajkumar, Marten Van Schijndel, Michael White, and William Schuler. 2016. Investigating locality effects and surprisal in written English syntactic choice phenomena. *Cognition*, 155:204–232.

Jan Rijkhoff. 1990. Explaining word order in the noun phrase. *Linguistics*, 28(1):5–42.

David Temperley and Daniel Gildea. 2018. Minimizing syntactic dependency lengths: typological/cognitive universal? *Annual Review of Linguistics*, 4:67–80.

David Temperley. 2007. Minimization of dependency length in written English. *Cognition*, 105(2):300–333.

Harry Tily. 2010. *The role of processing complexity in word order variation and change*. Ph.D. thesis, Stanford University.

Thomas Wasow. 2002. *Postverbal behavior*. CSLI Stanford, CA.

A   Appendix

A.1   Comparison with Sentence Length 52

In the following we replicate the figures provided in Section 4.2 for parses of sentences with a 52 tokens length.

A.1.1   Average DL and frequency trend

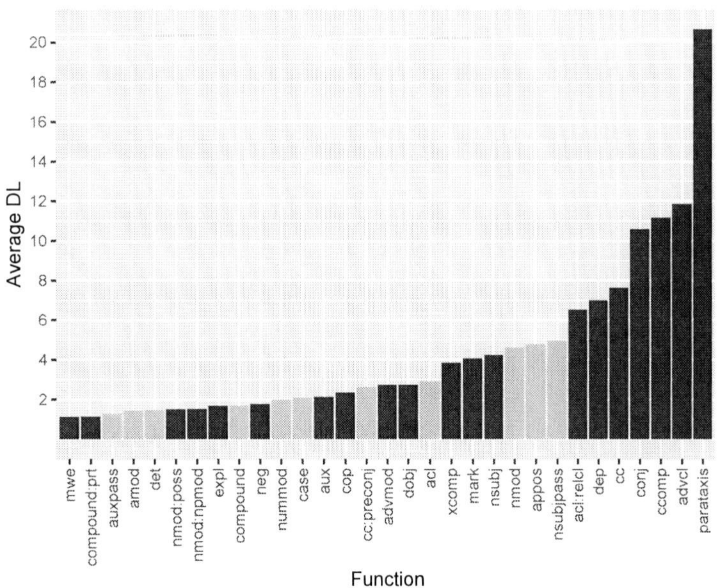

Figure 7: Syntactic functions and their average dependency length (SL 52). Black denotes decreasing frequency of a function over time, light grey marks increasing frequency.

A.1.2   Frequency of Long Distance Functions v. Short Distance Nominal Functions

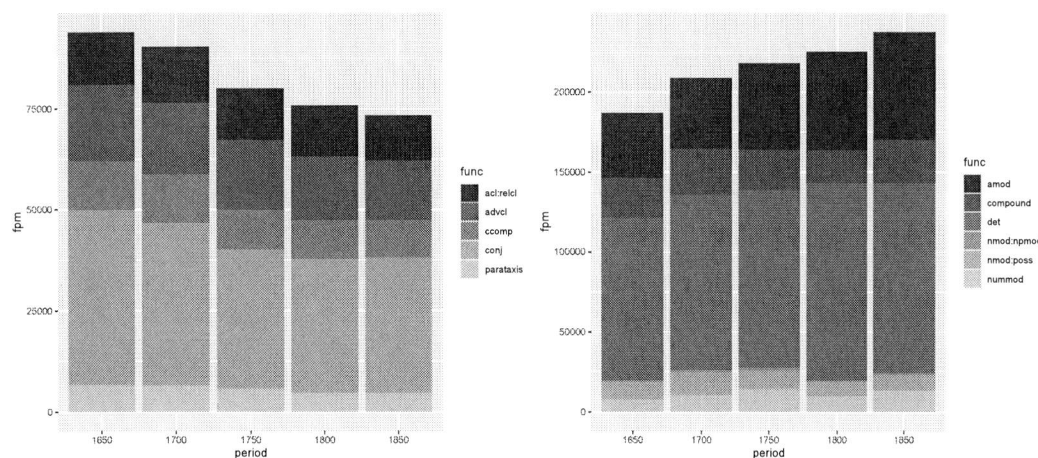

Figure 8: FPM of **long** distance functions (left) and **short nominal** functions (right) (SL 52) by 50 years.

UDon2: a library for manipulating Universal Dependencies trees

Dmytro Kalpakchi and Johan Boye
Division of Speech, Music and Hearing
KTH Royal Institute of Technology
Stockholm, Sweden
`dmytroka@kth.se, jboye@kth.se`

Abstract

UDon2 is an open-source library for manipulating dependency trees represented in the CoNLL-U format. The library is compatible with the Universal Dependencies. UDon2 is aimed at developers of downstream Natural Language Processing applications that require manipulating dependency trees on the sentence level (to complement other available tools geared towards working with treebanks).

1   Introduction

Universal Dependencies (UD) is a framework unifying ways of annotating grammar for different human languages (Nivre et al., 2020). To date, the UD community has produced more than 150 treebanks in 90 languages and a number of UD-compatible tools for processing data. Most of the available tools focus on working with treebanks, e.g. annotating textual data, validating existing treebanks or making simple edits. However, many downstream Natural Language Processing (NLP) applications require researchers to manipulate individual dependency trees. For instance, finding all subordinate clauses in the sentence might help in performing text simplification, finding all objects connected to a verb in the passive form might be useful for creating a list of candidate referents for co-reference resolution, and being able to remove certain subtrees might assist in generating reading-comprehension questions.

Some of those tasks are easy to achieve with some simple scripting, but such ad-hoc solutions become difficult to maintain over time. Furthermore, they tend to lack speed and hinder large-scale experimentation, since they are typically written in high-level programming languages in presence of time pressure. To aid the community in solving these tasks, we present UDon2 - a library for manipulating UD dependency trees optimized for querying. UDon2 has a user-friendly API allowing to perform routine tasks with only a couple of lines of code. For instance, finding all nominal objects in singular requires only a code snippet below.

```python
import udon2
nodes = udon2.ConllReader.read_file("example.conll")
sing = [obj for node in nodes for obj in node.select_by("deprel", "obj")
        if obj.has("feats", "Number", "Sing")]
```

UDon2 is an open-source library written in C++ with Python bindings, combining the speed of C++ and the flexibility and ease-of-use of Python. UDon2 is hosted on Github (the source code is available at `https://github.com/udon2/udon2`), and everyone is welcome to contribute.

2   Example use cases

UDon2 operates on dependency trees for individual sentences. Preparing a raw text for downstream applications requires segmenting it into sentences and then parsing every sentence to get its dependency tree stored in CoNLL-U format. The result of reading a CoNLL-U file is an instance of the `Node` class

---

Proceedings of the Fourth Workshop on Universal Dependencies (UDW 2020), pages 120–125
Barcelona, Spain (Online), December 13, 2020

representing a 'root' pseudonode of the dependency tree. The dependent of the 'root' pseudonode will be later referred to as *a root word*. In the section below, we present possible use cases along with the manipulations available for a generic `Node` instance n, and exemplify using the dependency tree in Figure 1 with its root word *study* being denoted as r.

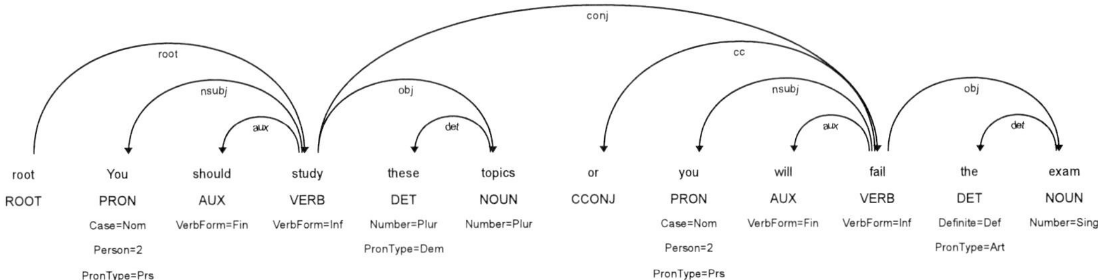

Figure 1: A dependency tree for the sentence "You should study these topics or you will fail the exam", obtained using the ewt-model of Stanza package (Qi et al., 2020) and visualized using UDon2.

2.1 Accessing basic properties

Each node n has a number of accessors and mutators for its word index, universal part-of-speech (POS) tag, language-specific POS tag, lemma, form, dependency relation with its head node, universal morphological features (FEATS) or any other annotation (MISC). Each accessor can be called as n.`<prop>` substituting `<prop>` for `id`, `upos`, `xpos`, `lemma`, `form`, `deprel`, `feats` and `misc` respectively. The last two will be referred to as key-value properties. Each mutator can be called as n.`<prop>` = `val` with the same values of `<prop>`. The parent node of n can be accessed by calling n.`parent`, and the children of n can be accessed by calling n.`children`. While mutator for a parent is available (by calling n.`parent` = n1), no direct mutator for children is. Instead, calling n.`add_child` or n.`remove_child` is required to modify the list of children.

Let T_n denote a subtree rooted at n. Calling n.`get_subtree_text()` will return a textual representation of T_n. For instance, calling r.`get_subtree_text()` will return the whole sentence.

Comments and enhanced dependency relations are currently not supported, since those are typically not provided by existing dependency parsers.

2.2 Multiword and empty nodes

Multiword tokens are supported and can be accessed by calling n.`multi_word`. If n belongs to any multiword token, an instance of `udon2.MultiWordNode` will be returned, otherwise the accessor will return None. Mutators for multi-word nodes are currently not available. Getting a textual representation of a subtree (by calling n.`get_subtree_text()`) accounts for the multiword nodes. Empty nodes[1] are currently ignored while reading CoNLL-U files.

2.3 Querying

Querying a dependency tree for a specific type of node is useful, for instance, for finding all relative clauses of a sentence, or finding the subject of a sentence. UDon2 allows issuing a variety of queries for selecting the nodes in T_n:

- having a property with a specified value, by calling n.`select_by(<prop>, <val>)`. Here, `<prop>` could be substituted for the same values as in the previous section, except key-value properties. `<val>` should be substituted for the desired value of the respective property. For instance, r.`select_by("upos", "VERB")` will return a list of `Nodes` corresponding to the verbs *study* and *fail*;

---

[1] `https://universaldependencies.org/format.html#words-tokens-and-empty-nodes`

- having specified key-value properties in the universal feature format[2] `<key-val-str>`, by
  calling `n.select_having(<prop>, <key-val-str>)`, where `<prop>` is one of `feats`
  or `misc`. For instance, the nodes for words *You* and *you* will be returned after calling
  `r.select_having("feats", "Case=Nom|Person=2|PronType=Prs"))`;

- being *direct* children of `n` and having a specified non key-value property, by calling
  `n.get_by(<prop>, <val>)`.

- having a specified chain of dependency relations, by calling `n.select_by_deprel_chain` or
  `n.get_by_deprel_chain` (if the requirement of being a *direct* child is added). For instance,
  `r.select_by_deprel_chain("obj.det")` will return a list of `Nodes` corresponding to the
  determiners *these* and *the*, whereas `r.get_by_deprel_chain("obj.det")` will return only
  the `Node` corresponding to the determiner *these*;

- being identical to another node `n'`, by calling `n.select_identical(n')`;

- being identical to another node `n'` except for properties `props`, by calling
  `n.select_identical_except(n', props)` with `props` being a comma-separated
  string of property names (later referred to as *a prop-string*), e.g. `pos, rel`;

A number of simpler indicator queries to check whether a specified property is present are also available and described in our online documentation[3].

2.4 Pruning

Suppose we want, as a step in text simplification, to split all coordinate clauses in a sentence into separate sentences. This requires identifying the nodes corresponding to the roots of coordinate clauses, by using the querying functionality from the previous section. Each clause should then be converted to a separate dependency tree, and all coordinate conjunctions should be removed. UDon2 makes this possible via its `n.prune(<rel>)` and `n.make_root()` functions, where `rel` corresponds to the chain of dependency relations pointing at the node to be pruned. To exemplify the pruning operation, `r.prune("conj")` will result in a subtree corresponding to the sentence "You should study these topics". `r.make_root()` function will create a root pseudonode and assign it to be a parent of `r`.

If the same tree is going to be used multiple times, destructive pruning might not be a viable option. In order to avoid copying trees, which might be a time-intensive (currently not implemented) operation, UDon2 allows ignoring individual nodes or subtrees by calling `n.ignore(<label>)` (`n.ignore_subtree(<label>)`), which assigns an ignore label `label` to n (all nodes in a subtree induced by n). All ignored nodes (no matter the label) will be excluded for all the queries presented in the previous section and during calling `n.get_subtree_text()`.

Reverting to the original state, possible by calling `n.reset(<label>)` (`n.reset_subtree(<label>)`), will unignore only nodes with a matching ignore label. The `<label>` argument defaults to 0 for all mentioned methods. If all nodes should be reset (no matter the label), `n.hard_reset()` or `n.hard_reset_subtree()` should be used.

2.5 Visualization

UDon2 is capable of visualizing the dependency tree and storing it as an SVG file. An example of such visualization is shown in Figure 1 and the code for visualizing a tree with a root `node` is presented below.

```
1 from udon2.visual import render_dep_tree
2 render_dep_tree(node, "tree.svg") # node is an instance of udon2.Node
```

Providing support for other image formats is an ongoing work.

---

[2] `https://universaldependencies.org/u/overview/morphology.html#features`
[3] `https://udon2.github.io`

2.6 Transformations and convolution tree kernels

It is non-trivial to represent dependency trees as features to use in machine learning contexts. One option was proposed by Moschitti (2006) in the form of convolution partial tree kernels that can be used with Support Vector Machines (Cortes and Vapnik, 1995). In a nutshell, a partial tree kernel calculates the number of common tree structures (not only full subtrees) between two trees. Unfortunately, tree kernels cannot handle trees with labeled edges, which is why Moschitti (2006) applied kernels to dependency tree containing only lexicals. An alternative solution, proposed by Croce et al. (2011) and implemented in UDon2, is to re-format dependency trees to include the edge labels as separate nodes. Three possible formats were proposed, depending on the order of inclusion:

- POS-tag Centered Tree (PCT) - each grammatical relation is added as the father of the POS-tag and a lexical as a child (transformation is possible by calling `udon2.transform.to_pct(node)`);

- Grammatical Relation Centered Tree (GRCT) - each POS-tag is a child of a grammatical relation and a father of a lexical (transformation is possible by calling `udon2.transform.to_grct(node)`);

- Lexical Centered Tree (LCT) - both a POS-tag and a grammatical relation are children of a lexical (transformation is possible by calling `udon2.transform.to_lct()`).

In UDon2, a partial tree kernel can be calculated in any of the aforementioned formats by substituting a string `tree_format` with any of `PCT`, `GRCT` or `LCT` in the code snippet below.

```
from udon2.kernels import ConvPartialTreeKernel
# ptk_lambda and ptk_mu are decay factors as defined by Moschitti (2006)
kernel = ConvPartialTreeKernel(tree_format, ptk_lambda, ptk_mu)
# prints a number of common tree fragments between trees rooted at root1 and root2
print(kernel(root1, root2)) # root1 and root2 are udon2.Node instances
```

3 Related work

Currently available UD processing tools for Python are geared towards working with treebanks and making batch manipulations and edits. UDPipe (Straka and Straková, 2017) is a library written in C++ with bindings to other programming languages. UDPipe provides a trainable pipeline which performs sentence segmentation, tokenization, POS-tagging, lemmatization and dependency parsing. The library provides no built-in support for manipulations on dependency trees. A similar functionality is also provided by the Stanza package (Qi et al., 2020).

DepEdit (Peng and Zeldes, 2018) is a configurable tool for manipulating dependency trees in the CoNLL-U format. The manipulations are specified in the configuration file using regular expressions for selecting nodes of interest, and a custom syntax for specifying relations between the nodes, and actions to perform on the matched nodes. The tool is geared towards performing batch operations and thus operations like querying to get a list of matching nodes for performing further manipulations, getting a text of the subtree induced by the node or implementing convolution tree kernels are impossible to achieve, to the best of our knowledge.

Udapi (Popel et al., 2017) is one such framework providing the ability to parse dependency trees, visualize them, convert between different representation formats (CoNLL-U, SDParse and VISL-cg), applying batch queries and edits to treebanks, and validate the format and contents of treebanks. Udapi is available as a command line tool, and has APIs for Java, Python and Perl. One of the reviewers has brought to our attention that Udapi is capable of performing directly (or gives a possibility to implement) the same transformations as UDon2.

Two smaller packages, pyconll[4] and conllu[5], provide an interface to the CoNLL-U annotation scheme without the possibility of visualization, but with a possibility to reimplement the same transformations as in UDon2.

---

[4] https://pyconll.github.io/
[5] https://github.com/EmilStenstrom/conllu/

In order to compare the last three mentioned packages, we provide the benchmark results for UDon2 and Udapi in Table 1 on the same CoNLL-U file[6] as in (Popel et al., 2017) ran on the same machine having Intel(R) Core(TM) i7-8750H CPU @ 2.20GHz on Ubuntu (x86_64) and Windows 10 (win32).

Package	OS	Memory	Load	Save	Read	Write	Text	Relchain
pyconll	Ubuntu	1683.1	12.88*	6.32	0.34	0.23	NA	0.47
	Windows	876.4	10.97	6.23	0.38	0.23	NA	0.54
conllu	Ubuntu	1208.7	16.83	4.28	0.19	0.1	NA	0.25
	Windows	707.2	19.11*	5.23*	0.22	0.09	NA	0.3
Udapi-Python	Ubuntu	756.0	19.88*	6.86	0.19	0.14	0.94	0.16
	Windows	421.6	19.09*	8.51*	0.2	0.11	1.01	0.15
UDon2	Ubuntu	772.0	3.27	3.34	0.75	0.42	0.24	0.14
	Windows	439.7	4.44	5.53	0.83	0.42	0.41	0.15

Table 1: Speed and memory comparison on `cs-ud-train-l.conllu` from UDv1.2 (68 MiB, 41k sentences, 800k words). Memory is in MiB and all other benchmarks provide average time in seconds after 30 runs on the computer with Intel(R) Core(TM) i7-8750H CPU @ 2.20GHz. **Load** refers to loading from CoNLL-U file, **Save** - to storing to the CoNLL-U file, **Read** - getting a form and a lemma for every node of every tree, **Write** - changing a deprel for every node of every tree, **Text** - computing a textual representation of a subtree induced by every root node of every tree, **Relchain** - finding nodes at the end of a relchain for every tree. The values with star indicate experiments with a standard deviation of more than 1 second.

4 Discussion and conclusions

Most of the current UD-compatible tools are focused on treebank developers, whereas UDon2 aims at helping researchers explore the use of dependency trees for downstream applications, and hence is optimized mostly for querying and interacting with CoNLL-U files. To the best of our knowledge, UDon2 is the first package providing the possibility to both perform manipulations on dependency trees, perform advanced transformations (such as GRCT, PCT or LCT), and compute convolution tree kernels.

UDon2 provides a superior performance on the majority of the benchmarks, except for Read and Write. The reason is that these two benchmarks require using Python's for-loops for C++ objects, requiring a lot of type conversions between Python and C++. UDon2 tries to avoid this by offering various query methods for common tasks, where looping is done in C++ as well (e.g. Text, Relchain, Load and Save benchmarks), which brings evident performance gains. Optimizing UDon2 for working better with Python's loops is an ongoing work and contributions are welcome. We hope that UDon2 is going to aid researchers in experimenting with dependency trees, and that it will be expanded with the help of the UD community.

Acknowledgements

This work was supported by Vinnova (Sweden's Innovation Agency) within project 2019-02997. We are also sincerely grateful to both reviewers for the incredibly useful comments (especially Reviewer 1 for the most thorough review we have ever seen). We would also like to thank Martin Popel for helpful discussions on the matter of benchmarking.

References

Corinna Cortes and Vladimir Vapnik. 1995. Support-vector networks. *Machine learning*, 20(3):273–297.

---

[6]`https://github.com/UniversalDependencies/UD_Czech-PDT/raw/r1.2/cs-ud-train-l.conllu`

Danilo Croce, Alessandro Moschitti, and Roberto Basili. 2011. Structured lexical similarity via convolution kernels on dependency trees. In *Proceedings of the 2011 Conference on Empirical Methods in Natural Language Processing*, pages 1034–1046.

Alessandro Moschitti. 2006. Efficient convolution kernels for dependency and constituent syntactic trees. In *European Conference on Machine Learning*, pages 318–329. Springer.

Joakim Nivre, Marie-Catherine de Marneffe, Filip Ginter, Jan Hajič, Christopher D Manning, Sampo Pyysalo, Sebastian Schuster, Francis Tyers, and Daniel Zeman. 2020. Universal dependencies v2: An evergrowing multilingual treebank collection. *arXiv preprint arXiv:2004.10643*.

Siyao Peng and Amir Zeldes. 2018. All roads lead to ud: Converting stanford and penn parses to english universal dependencies with multilayer annotations. In *Proceedings of the Joint Workshop on Linguistic Annotation, Multiword Expressions and Constructions (LAW-MWE-CxG-2018)*, pages 167–177.

Martin Popel, Zdeněk Žabokrtský, and Martin Vojtek. 2017. Udapi: Universal api for universal dependencies. In *Proceedings of the NoDaLiDa 2017 Workshop on Universal Dependencies (UDW 2017)*, pages 96–101.

Peng Qi, Yuhao Zhang, Yuhui Zhang, Jason Bolton, and Christopher D Manning. 2020. Stanza: A python natural language processing toolkit for many human languages. *arXiv preprint arXiv:2003.07082*.

Milan Straka and Jana Straková. 2017. Tokenizing, pos tagging, lemmatizing and parsing ud 2.0 with udpipe. In *Proceedings of the CoNLL 2017 Shared Task: Multilingual Parsing from Raw Text to Universal Dependencies*, pages 88–99, Vancouver, Canada, August. Association for Computational Linguistics.

Annotating MWEs in the Irish UD Treebank

Sarah McGuinness, Jason Phelan, Abigail Walsh and **Teresa Lynn**
ADAPT Centre, School of Computing, Dublin City University, Ireland
`sarah.mcguinness26@mail.dcu.ie`
`jason.phelan09@gmail.com`
`{abigail.walsh,teresa.lynn}@adaptcentre.ie`

Abstract

This paper reports on the analysis and annotation of Multiword Expressions in the Irish Universal Dependency Treebank. We provide a linguistic discussion around decisions on how to appropriately label Irish MWEs using the `compound`, `flat` and `fixed` dependency relation labels within the framework of the Universal Dependencies annotation guidelines. We discuss some nuances of the Irish language that pose challenges for assigning these UD labels and provide this report in support of the Irish UD annotation guidelines. With this we hope to ensure consistency in annotation across the dataset and provide a basis for future MWE annotation for Irish.

1   Introduction

The aim of the Universal Dependencies (UD) project (Nivre et al., 2016) is to facilitate and improve cross-lingual learning and multilingual parsing through the creation of a harmonised set of annotation guidelines for treebanks across multiple languages. As the project and guidelines evolve, new language treebanks are being added at each 6 monthly release. The Irish UD Treebank (IUDT) (Lynn et al., 2017) has been part of the UD project since the v.1 release in 2015, following a conversion from the original Irish Dependency Treebank (IDT)[1] (Lynn, 2016).[2] Until recently, however, there was little opportunity to fully explore the treatment of Multiword Expressions (MWEs) in either the original IDT annotation scheme or the converted UD scheme. This is mainly due to two factors: (i) both treebanks were the product of a PhD dissertation with limited scope, and (ii) prior research (both theoretical and applied) on MWEs in Irish was limited and generally insufficient in terms of Natural Language Processing (NLP) relevance or application (see Section 2). These factors are commonplace as challenges that face low-resource languages such as Irish.

MWEs are reported to make up a large part of natural language, as much as forty percent of our mental lexicon (Jackendoff, 1997; Fellbaum, 1998). As Constant et al. (2017) observe, providing an exact definition of MWEs can be controversial and there are varying interpretations and analyses to be found. These variations may well be due to the differing motivations for the need for definition (theoretical, applied, etc.). Our approach has been informed by the work of Sag et al. (2002), Baldwin and Kim (2010) and Ramisch (2015), whose works lie within the field of NLP. We define MWEs to be a string of two or more tokens, which form a unit at a semantic, syntactic or lexical level.

Research into MWEs, particularly with respect to NLP, has grown substantially since it has become increasingly apparent that they present a bottleneck for automatic processing of human language (Sag et

---

[1] `https://github.com/tlynn747/IrishDependencyTreebank`

[2] The data for the v2.6 Irish Universal Dependency Treebank is based on a gold standard POS-tagged sample of the National Corpus of Ireland developed by Uí Dhonnchadha (2009).

Proceedings of the Fourth Workshop on Universal Dependencies (UDW 2020), pages 126–139
Barcelona, Spain (Online), December 13, 2020

al., 2002). In fact, both the ICT COST Action PARSEME (IC1207)[3] and the establishment of the MWE Workshop series[4] were motivated by the need to establish how best to represent and encode MWEs for the benefit of improving NLP across languages.

Syntactic parsing is one particular area that can see improvement in accuracy when additional information is known with respect to the use of Multiword Expressions in a language (Nivre and Nilsson, 2004; Seretan, 2011; Green et al., 2013; Candito and Constant, 2014; Savary et al., 2015). Essentially, a parsing system is expected to perform better when it is aware that a string of words should be treated as one syntactic unit instead of individual tokens (e.g. *They tried to **hold up** a bank* vs *the container can **hold** up to 10 gallons*). Given the small size of the Irish UD treebank,[5] it makes sense that both improving the quality of the trees with additional information (such as accurately labelled MWEs) and increasing the size of the dataset should be treated with similar levels of importance.

This paper reports on the labelling of MWEs in the v2.6 release of the Irish UD treebank. A summary of our contribution is as follows: (1) We contribute to the quality of the v2.6 IUDT release by fully reviewing and updating MWE annotation. (2) We propose an approach to analysing and labelling Irish compounds, fixed expressions and flat proper noun strings within the UD framework. (3) In particular, we highlight the issues arising in differentiating between `compound` and nominal modifier (`nmod`) dependents while reporting on a small survey to address this, and hope that this may be helpful to other treebank developers who face similar challenges.

While the UD guidelines aim to capture linguistic universals, there will always be language specific features to consider when meeting the trade-off between cross-lingual consistency and a sufficient representation of that language. Given that this field of research is still relatively under-explored in Irish, some annotation choices may still be controversial to those in the field of Irish linguistics outside the UD framework, but nonetheless this starting point will be useful for any future studies in this area.

2   Related Work

As highlighted by Losnegaard (2016) and Parra Escartín (2018), for a long time, most MWE research was traditionally based on major languages such as English. In terms of linguistic data annotation, analysis of MWEs had only been carried out in a limited number of dependency treebanks (e.g. Czech (Bejček and Straňák, 2010), Hungarian (Vincze et al., 2013) and Turkish (Eryiğit et al., 2015)). In a step to address this, the ICT COST Action PARSEME[6] set out to draw up guidelines for classifying and categorising MWEs across multiple languages. The main goal was to provide a framework for processing MWEs in order to improve performance in the areas of machine translation and parsing (Savary et al., 2015; Savary et al., 2017; Ramisch et al., 2018; Losnegaard et al., 2016).[7]

Complementary work (Rosén et al., 2015; Rosén et al., 2016) proposed general guidelines for annotating MWEs in both constituency and dependency treebanks across 15 languages with the help of a focused survey. Through this, it was observed that it should be possible to search for various types of MWEs based on their characteristics (e.g. compositional vs non-compositional).

In terms of syntactic parsing, Candito and Constant (2014) observe that while MWE information is intuitively supposed to help parsing, it is difficult to prove this in a realistic setting. Difficulties arise when MWEs are automatically identified – an approach which can result in error propagation (Constant et al., 2012). It was also noted that the use of external lexicons did not seem to suffice in MWE processing, and that the use of data-driven external information would potentially help with this. This was supported by Schneider (2014) and the various experiments carried out by Constant et al. (2019) in assessing different approaches to MWE identification and parsing. Constant and Nivre (2016) developed a transition-based system which performed joint syntactic analysis and MWE identification, with promising results based

---

[3]`https://typo.uni-konstanz.de/parseme/`
[4]`https://www.aclweb.org/anthology/venues/mwe/`
[5]The v2.6 UD release has 2,924 trees and roughly 64,000 tokens.
[6]`https://parsemefr.lis-lab.fr`
[7]The PARSEME guidelines for annotating Verbal MWEs now cover 27 languages `https://parsemefr.lis-lab.fr/parseme-st-guidelines/1.1/`

on English and French. Overall, the need for MWE-aware treebanks to appropriately train statistical parsers has therefore become more evident.

With respect to UD treebank annotation, the language agnostic guidelines for MWEs deal mainly with compounds, fixed expressions and strings such as proper nouns. The following labels are proposed in the UD v2 guidelines:[8] `compound`; `fixed`; and `flat`. However, as interpretation of MWEs seems to vary across treebank development teams, a working group has been formed in the UD project to seek to harmonise the treatment of MWEs across treebanks.[9] Some treebank groups have also reported on their specific approaches to dealing with MWEs in their data (e.g. Croatian (Sojat and Filko, 2016), English (Schuster and Manning, 2016), Spanish (Martínez Alonso and Zeman, 2016), Turkish (Sulubacak and Eryiğit, 2018) and Farsi (Qasemizadeh, 2014)). More recently, Kahane (2018) provided an alternative proposal for treating idioms and fixed expressions through examining current French and English analyses in UD treebanks.

The following research contributes to our understanding of MWEs in Irish. Stenson (1981) discusses idiomatic constructions including verb-object constructions, verb-particle constructions and idiomatic constructions using the copula. In terms of theoretical studies, Bloch-Trojnar (2009) and Bayda (2015) have both carried out some research on light verb constructions, Ní Loingsigh (2016) on idioms, and Ó Domhnalláin and Ó Baoill (1975) on verbal constructions with prepositions. The Christian Brothers (1999) offer a limited summary of compounds in Irish, but without a specific discussion of MWEs. Uí Dhonnchadha (2009) provides a summary on treatment of phrasal verbs in her work on part-of-speech tagging and a constraint grammar for Irish. The output format of this POS-tagger resulted in some compounds, fixed expressions and proper noun strings being captured in earlier versions of the IUDT (Lynn and Foster, 2016) – the annotation of which were reviewed in this study. In terms of categorisation, a definition of a taxonomy of MWEs in Irish is in its early stages of development (Walsh et al., 2019). This work also discusses phrasal verbs in more detail through the lens of verb particle constructions and inherently adpositional verbs.

Our main sources of reference on Irish grammar in our work are Studies in Irish Syntax (Stenson, 1981), The Christian Brothers' Irish Grammar (Christian-Brothers, 1999) and also online dictionaries such as An Bunachar Náisiúnta Téarmaíochta don Ghaeilge (The National Terminology Database for Irish),[10] The New English-Irish Dictionary,[11] and also the Foclóir Gaeilge-Béarla and An Foclóir Beag which are available at the Teanglann website.[12] A valency dictionary for Irish verbs has also been developed and made available on the Pota Focal website (Foclóir Briathra Gaeilge), providing additional insight into the labelling of verb particles.[13]

3 Categories of MWEs in the IUDT

The Irish Universal Dependency Treebank (IUDT) v2.5 (and earlier releases) contained many inconsistencies with respect to MWE annotations. This was mainly as a result of (i) automatic conversion from the IDT annotation scheme (ii) changes in the UD guidelines and (iii) a lack of broad coverage research into Irish MWEs. In this section we highlight the various UD labels for MWE categories (`compounds`, `fixed`, and `flat` (Nivre et al., 2020)) and how we have applied them to Irish in the v2.6 release. These categories are generally tailored towards those MWE types that demonstrate *syntactic idiosyncrasy*, i.e. they do not conform to the normal syntactic behaviour of the language. As such, many categories dealt with elsewhere (e.g. the verbal MWEs recognised in the PARSEME Shared Task) are not specifically addressed here. Our discovery/labelling approach involved flagging potential MWEs during treebank expansion annotation for the v2.6 release. Based on patterns we observed, we then actively searched for candidates for review in the v2.5 version. Compound labelling proved most challenging and therefore constitutes much of the discussion below.

---

[8] `https://universaldependencies.org`
[9] `https://universaldependencies.org/workgroups/mwe.html`
[10] `https://www.tearma.ie/`
[11] `https://www.focloir.ie/`
[12] `https://www.teanglann.ie/ga/`
[13] `http://www.potafocal.com/fbg/`

3.1 Compounds

It is difficult to define what is meant by the term 'compound', as, much like with MWEs themselves, different definitions abound (Marchand, 1960; Lieber and Štekauer, 2011; Fábregas and Scalise, 2012; Altakhaineh, 2016). Bauer (2001) offers the following definition: "We can now define a compound as a lexical unit made up of two or more elements, each of which can function as a lexeme independent of the other(s) in other contexts, and which shows some phonological and/grammatical isolation from normal syntactic usage" (p. 695). However, unlike MWEs in general, a compound can either be written as a single combined word or a construction composed of multiple tokens.

Nivre et al. (2020) specifies that the compound relation should be used "for any kind of lexical compounds: noun compounds such as *phone book*, but also verb and adjective compounds, such as the serial verbs that occur in many languages, or a Japanese light verb construction such as *benkyō suru* ('to study')."

Compounds can pose problems for NLP analysis and their prevalence in written text along with their productive nature makes them an important consideration in computational processing (Ó Seaghdha, 2008; Nakov, 2013). However, compounds are often highly ambiguous and a large degree of "world knowledge" seems necessary to understand them, e.g. a cheese knife is a knife used to cut cheese, and not a knife made of cheese (Ó Séaghdha, 2007). We discuss the relevance of semantic compositionality further in Section 3.1.2.

3.1.1 Observation of variability across treebanks

The adoption of the `compound` relation and its subtypes varies across UD treebanks and this challenge is reflected in the extensive discussions on compounds on the UD MWE discussion forum.[14] In fact, there have been suggestions that only languages with a regular system of compounding should consider using the label. Based on our annotators' linguistic backgrounds, we examined several treebanks and observed that the `compound` label is used relatively conservatively and inconsistently across UD treebanks, even within language groups:

French: The French documentation page notes that the compound label is seldom used.[15] This could be due to French syntax requiring prepositions to break up most seemingly compound nouns e.g. *tarte aux pommes* 'apple tart'.[16] However, the `compound` relation is often used (instead of `fixed` or `goeswith`) for hyphenated words that have been split during tokenisation: e.g. *procès-verbal* 'official report', *outre-mer* 'overseas'.[17] The label also appears to be used in rare cases in the French ParTUT treebank; *états membres* 'member states', *vote sanction* 'protest vote' and sometimes in cases that could be considered as nominal modifiers (nmod): *vendredi soir* 'Friday evening', in the French Spoken treebank. The leftmost noun is the head (right branching) in all cases. The `compound:prt` label is not used in any of the French treebanks.

Chinese: Chinese has several subtypes that reflect how compounding occurs naturally within the language, i.e. the `compound` label, used for noun-noun compounds such as 长途汽车'long-haul coach' and five subtypes which include; `compound:vv` used for verb-verb compounds, e.g. 找到'to [try to] find', as well as for verb-adjective compounds which are usually idiomatic, e.g. 他喊湿件恤衫'He cried his shirt wet'; `compound:dir` verb-verb or verb-preposition compounds where one component is directional, e.g. 爬下来'to climb down'; `compound:ext` used for the structural particle "得" in descriptive complements and complements of extent, e.g. 你门汉语说得很棒！'Your Chinese is very good !'; and `compound:vo` which is used for verb-object compounds, e.g. 打电话'to make a phone call'.

Spanish: Examples of the `compound` label use in the AnCora treebank include *por ciento* 'per cent'; date strings: *el siglo XXI* 'the 21st century', *el año 2000* 'the year 2000', *el 6 de junio* 'the 6th of June';

---

[14] https://universaldependencies.org/workgroups/mwe.html
[15] https://universaldependencies.org/fr/dep/compound.html
[16] Example from French GSD treebank
[17] Examples from the UD-French-Spoken corpus.

light verb constructions: *tener en cuenta* 'to take into account', *dar derecho a* 'to authorize/to allow', *tener lugar* 'to take place', *poner fin (a)* 'to put an end (to)'; and verbal idiomatic constructions: *hacer hincapié* 'to emphasize the point'. The `compound` label is used in the GSD treebank for noun-noun compounds (e.g. *artista pop* 'pop star') and set phrases *hemisferio norte* 'northern hemisphere', *marca registrada* 'registered trademark' and *inmigrantes pos-apartheid* 'post-apartheid immigrants'. The label is also used for fixed adverbials *tal vez* 'perhaps', and for text in foreign languages (instead of `flat:foreign`) e.g. *nuevas mujeres (Xīn nǚxìng, 1934)*. The use of the compound label therefore appears to be inconsistent across the sampled Spanish treebanks.

While the Spanish PUD treebank has no instances of the `compound` label it is the only Spanish treebank that uses the `compound:prt` label. It is applied to the reflexive pronoun *se* and all its forms, e.g. *Se ha recalcado* '(It) has been emphasised'.

English: The `compound` label is used in all the English Treebanks (GUM, GUMReddit, PUD, LinES, EWT, English-ESL) apart from the English-Pronouns Treebank. The rightmost noun is the head (left branching) in all cases. Noun phrases are marked as compounds in some treebanks (e.g. *wheel chair* (EWT) and *bank account* (PUD)). Adjectival compounds are labelled in some treebanks (e.g. *thought-provoking* (EWT), *Oscar-winning* (PUD) and *Dutch speaking* (GUM), *self-driven* (EWT)). The `compound` label is also used for numbers in some treebanks (e.g. *two hundred* (EWT), *3 million* (PUD)). Some named entities are also labelled as `compound` (e.g. *United States* (PUD) and *Auckland Castle* (GUM)). The `compound:prt` label is used for some phrasal verbs in PUD & EWT (e.g. *sign up, point out*).

3.1.2 Labelling compounds in the Irish UD treebank

Compounds in Irish are briefly dealt with by the Christian Brothers (1999). According to their analysis (p.277), Irish compounds are formed in two ways:

(i) when a prefix or suffix is added to a word to form a single-token compound (e.g *idirdhealaigh* 'to differentiate', *idir-* 'inter' + *dealaigh* 'to detach/to separate').

(ii) two words appear together to form a compound (adjectival, verbal and nominal) – which is of most interest to our work here. These can occur as (a) a single token (e.g. *cúl* 'back' + *caint* 'talk' → *cúlchaint* 'gossip') or (b) multiword compounds *mac léinn* ('student', lit. son of learning), *mac tíre* ('wolf', lit. son of land). We are only concerned with annotation of the second type (b) here. This type of compound is less frequent in Irish than the single-token type and would therefore suggest a conservative use of the label in the treebank.

In the Irish UD treebank, we apply two UD compound labels: the standard dependency relation label `compound` and the subtype label `compound:prt`. It should be noted that due to Irish word order, the head noun of a noun phrase is usually the first noun, hence the compounding attachment is right-branching. The following reports on the criteria used for determining compound constructions in the Irish UD treebank, while aligning as closely as possible to the UD documentation and conventions.

Compound label The `compound` label is used exclusively for labelling noun-noun compound constructions in the IUDT. Applying the `compound` label proved challenging in the Irish data. Initial annotation discussions revealed different interpretations as to what would be deemed a compound noun in Irish. Often a disagreement arose with respect to two nouns appearing together that some believed to be nominal modifiers (nmod e.g. *fonn díoltais* 'revengefulness') as opposed to compounds.

As a first step to identifying Irish compound nouns, a number of tests, inspired by the PARSEME guidelines,[18] were used as a preliminary attempt at determining whether an Irish nominal multiword unit should be marked as compound or nmod. However, while helpful to some degree, it transpired that no test on its own was sufficient to decide this.

Test 1: The absence of a definite article We theorised that the absence of a definite article between nouns could indicate a nominal compound. There is no indefinite article in Irish. Therefore, the article

---

[18] `https://gitlab.lis-lab.fr/PARSEME-FR/PARSEME-FR-public/-/wikis/Criteres`

is absent in noun-noun compound constructions where the dependent noun is indefinite (e.g. *deireadh seachtaine* 'weekend' (lit. end of week)), which we label as `compound`. The same construction with a definite noun dependent would usually be labelled as a nominal modifier `nmod` (*deireadh **na** seachtaine*: 'end of **the** week'). Other examples of this phenomenon include *caitheamh aimsire* 'pastime' vs *caitheamh **na** haimsire* 'passing of **the** time' and *tiarna talún* ('landlord') vs *tiarna **na** talún* ('lord of **the** land').

This test cannot be reliable in all cases where the definite article is absent, however, as the article is also dropped in other instances (1) the possessive genitive case; *pá iriseora* 'a journalist's pay' (lit. pay of a journalist); (2) when a noun is followed by another qualified noun *pá iriseoir **an** nuachtáin* 'the newspaper's journalist's pay' (lit. pay of **the** journalist of **the** newspaper). We would consider both (1) and (2) to be nominal modifiers `nmod`.

Furthermore, there are other exceptions that affect the reliability of this test and these are usually idiomatic or institutionalised phrases; *Mí na meala* 'honeymoon' (lit. month of the honey); *cothrom na Féinne* 'fair treatment' (lit. balance of the warriors).

Test 2: Presence of a cranberry word If a noun-noun construction contains a *cranberry* word (i.e. a word that does not occur outside of that specific construction) (Aronoff, 1976), it is a strong indicator that the construction should be labelled as `compound`. For example, *déag* 'teen' only occurs as part of a numeral phrase (*cúig déag* 'fifteen' (lit. 'five teen')). While cranberry words can occur in other types of phrases (e.g. adverbial, *go deo* 'forever', which is annotated as `fixed`, see Section 3.2), *déag* remains the only cranberry word identified in a nominal construction in the Irish UD treebank and accounts for a small percentage of compounds in our data.[19]

Test 3: Determining if the meaning of either noun is sufficiently changed Nakov (2013) notes non-compositionality as semantic criteria for compounds and that this criterion asks that compounds be at least partially non-compositional. However, he also notes that compositionality is a matter of degree. In a compound construction, the meaning of the whole must be significantly different from the meaning of the individual tokens in the noun phrase. Compositionality, therefore, appeared to be a good basis for assessing compound candidates and finding agreement amongst annotators: `Fully compositional`: the meaning as a whole can be easily interpreted from the meaning of each of the parts of the multiword construction (e.g. *turas scoile* 'school trip'); `Semi-compositional`: the meaning of the whole expression can be partially understood from the meaning of the individual parts e.g. *lucht leanúna* 'followers' (lit. group of following) or *feadóg stáin* 'tin whistle' (that can be made of wood); `Non-compositional`: the meaning of the unit or expression as a whole is not discernible from the meaning of the individual parts. e.g. *mac tíre* 'wolf' (lit. son of land).

We carried out an anonymous poll to categorise 30 contentious nominal multiword units in terms of compositionality. Six participants with varying levels of fluency and knowledge of Irish syntax reviewed the candidates, and selected one of the three compositionality measures for each one. Based on agreement levels, it was established that this compositional categorisation approach was useful for compound categorisation. Table 1 shows that agreement on whether constructions were fully-compositional compounds rather than semi- or non-compositional compounds was easier to achieve than differentiating between semi- and non-compositional compounds.[20] This is significant for differentiating between `compound` and `nmod`. The overall compositionality scores for each candidate were averaged across the 6 annotators. If the average score for fully-compositional was higher than 0.5, the `nmod` label was applied. Otherwise, (i.e. the average score for either a semi-compositional or non-compositional label was greater than or equal to 0.5), the `compound` label was applied. Figure 1 shows the dependency annotation of an Irish semi-compositional compound.

---

[19]There are 20 occurrences of *déag* 'teen' in v2.6 of the IUDT.

[20]A possible reason for disagreement in cases with a clear majority is a potential confusion on the part of a survey participant of the terms fully and non-compositional, e.g. *mac tíre* is clearly idiomatic and should be regarded as non-compositional.

Compound candidate	Literal meaning	Translation	F.C.	S.C.	N.C.
deireadh seachtaine	'end of week'	weekend	2	3	1
mí na meala	'month of the honey'	honeymoon	1	1	4
mac tíre	'son of land'	wolf	1		5
mac léinn	'son of learning'	student	1	1	4
lucht féachana	'people of watching'	audience	3	3	
caitheamh aimsire	'spending of time'	past time	2	4	
cothrom na Féinne	'balance of the Fianna'	fair treatment		3	3
tús áite	'start place'	priority	1	5	
feadóg stáin	'whistle of tin'	tin whistle	1	5	
foinse saibhris	'source of wealth'	source of wealth	5		1
fonn díoltais	'vengeful mood'	vengeful mood	4	1	1
cumas an pháiste	'the ability of the child'	the ability of the child	5		1

Table 1: Poll results on 6 annotators' opinions on compositionality of some controversial compound candidates. F.C. Fully Compositional; S.C Semi-compositional; N.C. Non-compositional Blue text indicates categorisation as `compound`.

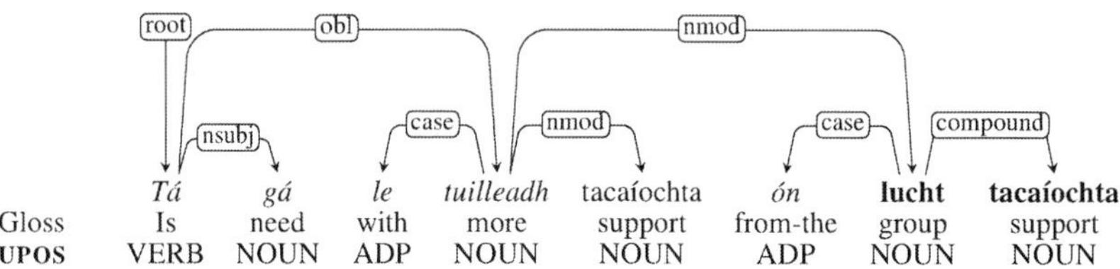

'There is a need for more support from the supporters'

Figure 1: Dependency annotation of semi-compositional compound

Compound:prt label   We apply the `compound:prt` label to verb particles as per the UD guidelines.
[21] Verb particle constructions consist of a verb and a dependent particle, where the particle significantly changes the meaning of the verb. In Irish, this particle is usually a directional adverb, although certain prepositions can also function as particles (e.g. *faoi* 'under/beneath', *as* 'off/out'). As both the particle and the verb are necessary for understanding of the construction as a whole, we consider these constructions as MWEs. Table 2 provides examples of Irish verb particles and Figure 2 shows an example in terms of dependency tree annotation.

	Gloss	Literal meaning
tabhair suas	'to give up'	(give + up)
tabhair faoi	'to undertake'	(give + under)
éirigh as	'to retire'	(rise + from)
éirigh amach	'to revolt'	(rise + out)
leag amach	'to outline'	(lay + out)
leag síos	'to lay out'	(lay + down)
bain amach	'to get/to reach'	(extract + out)
dul as	'escape'	(go + from)

Table 2: Examples of Irish verb particles labelled as `compound:prt`

---

[21]`https://universaldependencies.org/docs/en/dep/compound-prt.html`

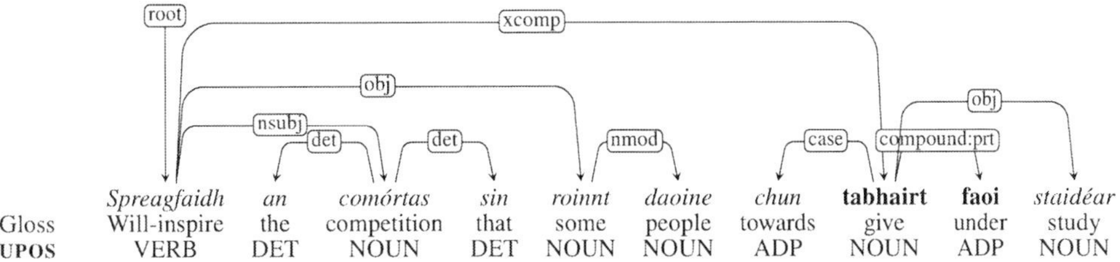

Figure 2: Dependency annotation of verb particle

3.2 Fixed

Fixed expressions are a class of fully lexicalised immutable expressions that are generally non-compositional in nature (Sag et al., 2002). Flexibility is a widely used characteristic for determining fixed expressions, which refers to the potential for components of the expression to inflect for gender, number, etc. Examples of fixed expressions in English include set phrases (*of course*), function words (*as if*) and/or short adverbials (*at least*). Within the UD annotation scheme, the `fixed`[22] dependency label is used for "certain fixed grammaticized expressions that behave like function words or short adverbials" and it is assumed that "these expressions do not have any internal syntactic structure (except from a historical perspective)".[23] The dependents within the fixed construction each attach to the leftmost token (the head), as per Figure 3.

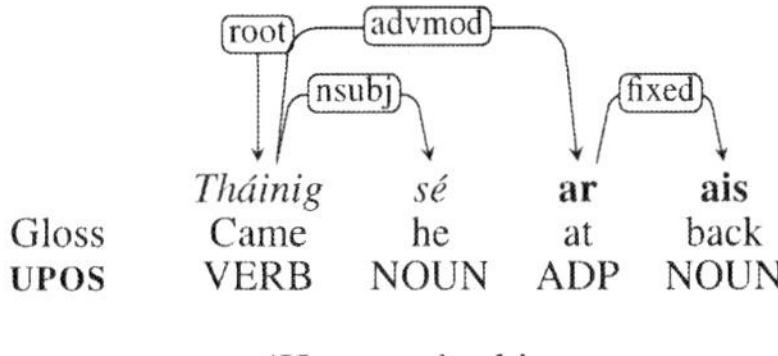

Figure 3: Dependency annotation of fixed multiword adverbial modifier

With regards to the application of the `fixed` label in the Irish treebank, it can be said that Irish fixed MWEs have the following characteristics:

Fixed grammaticized expressions   Such fixed expressions perform a specific grammatical role (e.g. adverbial modifiers such as *go deo* 'forever', *mar sin* 'so', *ar ais* 'back'; or nominal modifiers like *a thuilleadh* 'more' and *go leor* 'enough').

Neither semi-fixed, flexible or productive   It is generally considered that the flexibility of the tokens within the MWE determine whether or not they are fixed. For example, we currently treat *chomh maith* 'as well' as a fixed adverbial. The preposition *le* 'with' often follows this expression. However, *le* may inflect for gender and person (as a pronominal preposition, e.g. *liom* 'with me') and given that such multi-token units are not currently split, it is therefore too flexible to be considered part of the fixed expression. Likewise, no tokens can be inserted within the fixed expression (e.g. **faoi an bhun*).

No discernible internal syntactic structure   In spite of the term used, we annotate compound prepositions as `fixed` and not as `compound`, given that they are often a combination of preposition and noun, yet their joint functional role is that of preposition (e.g. *in aice* 'near'; *tar éis* 'after'; *i gcoinne* 'against';

---

[22]Formerly the mwe label in UD v1 guidelines `https://universaldependencies.org/docsv1/`
[23]`https://universaldependencies.org/u/dep/fixed.html`

de réir 'according to'). They also select for a prepositional object (e.g. *in aice na tine* 'beside the fire'; *de réir na comhairle sin* 'according to that advice').[24]

MWEs labelled as `fixed` in the Irish treebank are outlined in Table 3 and grouped according to their syntactic role.

Fixed MWE	Gloss	Fixed MWE	Gloss
Adverbial Modifier		**Prepositional (case)**	
go deo	'forever'	*in aice*	'beside'
mar sin	'so'	*tar éis*	'after'
ar ais	'back'	*ar fud*	'throughout/ all over'
chomh maith	'as well'	*le haghaidh*	'for'
fad is	'as long as'	*le linn*	'during'
a mhéid	'to the extent that'	*faoi bhun*	'below'
Determiners		*go dtí*	'towards/to'
seo caite	'last'	*de bharr*	'because of/ due to'
seo chugainn	'next'	*i rith*	'during'
Nominal Modifier		*i gceann*	'at the end of'
ar bith	'at all'	**Open Complement (xcomp:pred)**	
Subject/Object		*in ann*	'able to'
a thuilleadh†	'more'	**Subordinating Conjunction**	
go leor†	'a lot'	*le go*	'so that'

Table 3: Types of Irish MWEs labelled with the UD `fixed` dependency label. † indicates that these MWES can also function as adverbials.

3.3 Flat

According to the UD guidelines, the `flat` dependency relation is used for exocentric (or headless) semi-fixed MWEs, such as personal names and dates strings. The assumption is that these expressions do not have any internal syntactic structure and that the structural annotation is in principle arbitrary. Therefore, flat MWEs are annotated with a flat structure, where all subsequent tokens in the expression are attached to the first token using the `flat` label.

The `flat` relation and its subtypes `flat:foreign` and `flat:name` (see below) are all therefore used for headless semi-fixed MWEs. MWEs that come under this category vary widely across languages but a "regular compositional syntactic structure" is assumed when using the flat label.[25] Examples from the Irish UD treebank include days of the week (*Dé Luain*, 'Monday') and dates (*Deireadh Fómhair* 'October'; *(I) mí Iúil 1995* '(In) July 1995'; *(roimh) 1 Feabhra 1997* '(before) February 1 1997'). The internal components of these MWEs are attached to the left-most token of the noun phrase using the flat label.

The UD guidelines state that "For organization names with clear syntactic modification structure, the dependencies should also reflect the syntactic modification structure using regular syntactic relations, as in: 'Lord of the Rings'". However, it should be noted that we diverged from this temporarily in an exercise in capturing Named Entity (NE) information during the MWE review. We currently use the `flat` relation in v2.6 for named entities and proper noun strings regardless of whether or not their internal syntactic structure is discernible. Some examples include: organisations such as *Choiste Turasóireachta na Gaillimhe* 'Galway Tourism Board' and *Roinn na Gaeltachta* 'Department of the Gaeltacht'; titles such as *Ard-Cheannasaí* 'High Commander' and *Mharascal Machaire* 'Field Marshal', titles of published works such as *Leatrom na Cinniúna* 'The Injustice of Destiny', placenames such as *Baile Átha an*

---

[24]It should be noted that prior to conversion to UD style, fixed expressions in the IDT were treated as one token joined together by an underscore in the data (e.g. *in_aice*) as per the output of the standard Finite-State Irish POS-tagger (Dhonnchadha, 2002).

[25]`https://universaldependencies.org/u/dep/flat.html`

Rí 'Athenry' and other named entities such as *Bunscoil Mhic Reachtain* 'McCracken Primary School'.[26]

flat:name   The use of this label is reserved for personal name strings whereby the first nominal token is labelled as the head and its subsequent tokens in the string are annotated as `flat:name` (e.g. *Pádraig Mac Piarais* 'Patrick Pearse'). The various name particles used in Irish (*Ó, Ua, Mac, Mag, Uí, Ní, Mhic, Nic, Nig*) are also assigned the `flat:name` label, as are professional titles (e.g. *An tUasal* 'Mr', *Dochtúir* 'Doctor', *T.D. (Teachta Dála)* 'Member of the Irish Parliament')). Therefore, in the personal name *Liam Ó Briain*, both the particle *Ó* and the proper noun *Briain* are both attached to *Liam* with the dependency relation `flat:name`.

flat:foreign   This label replaces the `foreign` label that was used in v1 of the UD guidelines.[27] It is used for words in other languages that appear in a linear sequence, including cases where foreign text is incorporated into a sentence, e.g. *go raibh sé cut off with a shilling* 'that he was cut off with a shilling'. The treatment of proper noun strings such as personal names and titles in other languages that occur in the data (e.g. Monsieur Dupont, 'Nor Meekly Serve My Time') raised a question amongst annotators (i.e. `flat` vs `flat:foreign`). The approach taken was that personal names, regardless of their origin (e.g. Bertie Ahern, *an tUasal* Durkan, Mr Mulligan, Robert de Niro, *an tUas* Morten Kjaerum) are to be labelled with the `flat:name` relation (see above). Titles in a foreign language (e.g. 'The Pope's Green Island', 'Entering Jerusalem', 'Tristan Und Isolde') should be treated as `flat:foreign`. Multiword expressions in other languages are also labelled as `flat:foreign`, e.g. *vice versa*.

Another interesting question relates to the POS-tagging of foreign words in the treebank. In previous IUDT releases, English tokens were POS-tagged according to English morpho-syntax (e.g. NOUN, PROPN, etc). However, according to current UD guidelines, the X tag should be used for foreign words. Nevertheless, in future releases it is hoped that English tokens will be re-annotated with their appropriate POS tag to allow for more concise code-switching studies, as per recent recommendations by Sanguinetti et al. (2020).[28]

4   Conclusion

In this article we have reported on a review and update of MWE annotations in the Irish UD Treebank for the v2.6 UD release. We have provided our analysis and motivations for applying the `compound`, `fixed` and `flat` labels to Irish MWEs, and discussed the various challenges involved therein. In the v2.6 treebank of size 64,745 tokens, the `compound` label was applied 160 times (141 `compound`, 19 `compound:prt`), `fixed` was applied 950 times, and `flat` was applied 2252 times (1399 `flat`, 695 `flat:name`, 150 `flat:foreign`).

While our approach is mostly in line with the UD annotation guidelines, we note that our use of the `flat` label is too broad as it also incorporates Named Entities (NE) in general. The opportunity for manual review of the treebank data allowed for previously unknown NE data to be captured easily. In the future, we want to remove the `flat` label in these cases and capture NE information in the MISC column instead. Finally, a note on inflected prepositions (see Section 3.2). Currently we do not split pronominal prepositions into ADP + PRON. If however, future versions of the treebank undergo changes with respect to splitting multi-token units (e.g. *leis* 'with it' → *le* + *é*), the uninflected preposition token could be considered part of a fixed expression (e.g. *chomh maith le*).

Acknowledgements

This work is funded by the Irish Government Department of Culture, Heritage and the Gaeltacht under the GaelTech Project, and also supported by Science Foundation Ireland in the ADAPT Centre (Grant 13/RC/2106) at Dublin City University. We would like to thank Jennifer Foster, Lauren Cassidy, Mícheál John Ó Meachair and Carla Parra Escartín for their input to our linguistic discussions.

---

[26] Plans to review this approach are underway, with the consideration of using the MISC column instead to capture NE information, as per the English-GUM treebank.

[27] `https://universaldependencies.org/docsv1/u/dep/foreign.html`

[28] In their work on treebanks for user-generated content, they propose appropriate POS-tagging of foreign text along with an indication (LangID=EN in the MISC column) that code-switching has taken place, when the language is known to annotators.

References

Abdel Rahman Altakhaineh. 2016. What is a compound? the main criteria for compoundhood. *Explorations in English Language and Linguistics*, 4, 10.

Mark Aronoff. 1976. *Word Formation in Generative Grammar*. MIT Press, Cambridge, Massachusetts and London, England.

Timothy Baldwin and Su Nam Kim. 2010. Multiword Expressions. *Handbook of Natural Language Processing, Second Edition*, pages 267–292, 01.

Laurie Bauer. 2001. *Compounding*. Language Typology and Language Universals, volume 1. Walter de Gruyter, Berlin.

Victor Bayda. 2015. Irish constructions with bain. *Yn llawen iawn, yn llawn iaith: Proceedings of the 6th International Colloquium of Societas Celto-Slavica. Vol. 7 of Studia Celto-Slavica. Johnston, D., Parina, E. and Fomin, M. (eds)*, 7:213–228, 01.

Eduard Bejček and Pavel Straňák. 2010. Annotation of multiword expressions in the Prague dependency treebank. *Language Resources and Evaluation*, 44:7–21, 04.

Maria Bloch-Trojnar. 2009. On the Nominal Status of VNs in Light Verb Constructions in Modern Irish. In *PASE Papers 2008. Vol. 1: Studies in Language and Methodology of Teaching Foreign Languages*, page 25–33, Wrocław: Oficyna Wydawnicza ATUT.

Marie Candito and Mathieu Constant. 2014. Strategies for Contiguous Multiword Expression Analysis and Dependency Parsing. In *ACL 14 - The 52nd Annual Meeting of the Association for Computational Linguistics*, Baltimore, United States, June. ACL.

Christian-Brothers. 1999. *Graiméar Gaeilge na mBráithre Críostaí*. An Gúm, Baile Átha Cliath.

Matthieu Constant and Joakim Nivre. 2016. A Transition-Based System for Joint Lexical and Syntactic Analysis. In *Proceedings of the 54th Annual Meeting of the Association for Computational Linguistics*, volume 1, pages 161–171, 01.

Matthieu Constant, Anthony Sigogne, and Patrick Watrin. 2012. Discriminative Strategies to Integrate Multiword Expression Recognition and Parsing. In *Proceedings of the 50th Annual Meeting of the Association for Computational Linguistics (Volume 1: Long Papers)*, pages 204–212, Jeju Island, Korea, July. Association for Computational Linguistics.

Mathieu Constant, Gülşen Eryiğit, Johanna Monti, Lonneke van der Plas, Carlos Ramisch, Michael Rosner, and Amalia Todirascu. 2017. Survey: Multiword Expression Processing: A Survey. *Computational Linguistics*, 43(4):837–892, December.

Matthieu Constant, Gülşen Eryiğit, Carlos Ramisch, Mike Rosner, and Gerold Schneider, 2019. *Statistical MWE-aware parsing*, pages 147–182. Berlin: Language Science Press, 01.

Elaine Uí Dhonnchadha. 2002. Two-level Finite-State Morphology for Irish. In *Proceedings of the Third International Conference on Language Resources and Evaluation (LREC'02)*, pages 2299–2306, Gran Canaria, Spain. European Language Resources Association (ELRA).

Elaine Uí Dhonnchadha. 2009. *Part-of-Speech Tagging and Partial Parsing for Irish using Finite-State Transducers and Constraint Grammar*. Ph.D. thesis, Dublin City University.

Gülşen Eryiğit, Kübra Adali, Dilara Torunoğlu-Selamet, Umut Sulubacak, and Tuğba Pamay. 2015. Annotation and extraction of multiword expressions in Turkish treebanks. In *Proceedings of the 11th Workshop on Multiword Expressions*, pages 70–76, Denver, Colorado, June. Association for Computational Linguistics.

Antonio Fábregas and Sergio Scalise. 2012. *Morphology: From Data to Theories*. Edinburgh Advanced Textbooks in Linguistics. Edinburgh University Press.

Christiane Fellbaum. 1998. A Semantic Network of English: The Mother of All WordNets. *Computers and the Humanities*, 32(2/3):209–220.

Spence Green, Marie-Catherine de Marneffe, and Christopher D. Manning. 2013. Parsing Models for Identifying Multiword Expressions. *Computational Linguistics*, 39(1):195–227.

Ray Jackendoff. 1997. *The Architecture of the Language Faculty*. Linguistic Inquiry monographs volume 28. MIT Press.

Sylvain Kahane, Martine Courtin, and Kim Gerdes. 2018. Multi-word annotation in syntactic treebanks: Propositions for Universal Dependencies. In *Proceedings of the 16th International Workshop on Treebanks and Linguistic Theories (TLT16)*, pages 181–189, Prague, Czech Republic, 01.

Rochelle Lieber and Pavol Štekauer. 2011. Introduction: Status and definition of compounding. In *The Oxford Handbook of Compounding*, pages 3–18, Oxford: Oxford University Press.

Gyri Smørdal Losnegaard, Federico Sangati, Carla Parra Escartín, Agata Savary, Sascha Bargmann, and Johanna Monti. 2016. PARSEME survey on MWE resources. In *Proceedings of the Tenth International Conference on Language Resources and Evaluation (LREC'16)*, pages 2299–2306, Portorož, Slovenia, May. European Language Resources Association (ELRA).

Teresa Lynn and Jennifer Foster. 2016. Universal Dependencies for Irish. In *Proceedings of the Second Celtic Language Technology Workshop*, Paris, France.

Teresa Lynn, Jennifer Foster, and Mark Dras. 2017. Morphological features of the Irish Universal Dependency Treebank. In *TLT 2017 : Proceedings of the 15th International Workshop on Treebanks and Linguistic Theories*, volume 1779, pages 111–122, Bloomington, U.S.

Teresa Lynn. 2016. *Irish Dependency Treebanking and Parsing*. Ph.D. thesis, Dublin City University and Macquarie University, Sydney.

Hans Marchand. 1960. *The Categories and Types of Present-day English Word-formation: A Synchronic-diachronic Approach*. Wiesbaden: Otto Harrassowitz.

Héctor Martínez Alonso and Daniel Zeman. 2016. Universal Dependencies for the AnCora treebanks. *Procesamiento del Lenguaje Natural*, 57:91–98, 09.

Preslav Nakov. 2013. On the interpretation of noun compounds: Syntax, semantics, and entailment. *Natural Language Engineering*, 19(3), 07.

Katie Ní Loingsigh. 2016. *Tiomsú agus Rangú i mBunachar Sonraí ar Chnuasach Nathanna Gaeilge as Saothar Pheadair Uí Laoghaire*. Ph.D. thesis, Dublin City University.

Joakim Nivre and Jens Nilsson. 2004. Multiword units in syntactic parsing. In *Workshop on Methodologies and Evaluation of Multiword Units in Real-World Applications*, 01.

Joakim Nivre, Marie-Catherine de Marneffe, Filip Ginter, Yoav Goldberg, Jan Hajič, Christopher D. Manning, Ryan McDonald, Slav Petrov, Sampo Pyysalo, Natalia Silveira, Reut Tsarfaty, and Daniel Zeman. 2016. Universal dependencies v1: A multilingual treebank collection. In *Proceedings of the Tenth International Conference on Language Resources and Evaluation (LREC'16)*, pages 1659–1666, Portorož, Slovenia, May. European Language Resources Association (ELRA).

Joakim Nivre, Marie-Catherine de Marneffe, Filip Ginter, Jan Hajič, Christopher D. Manning, Sampo Pyysalo, Sebastian Schuster, Francis Tyers, and Daniel Zeman. 2020. Universal Dependencies v2: An evergrowing multilingual treebank collection. In *Proceedings of The 12th Language Resources and Evaluation Conference*, pages 4034–4043, Marseille, France, May. European Language Resources Association.

Diarmuid Ó Séaghdha. 2007. Annotating and Learning Compound Noun Semantics. In *Proceedings of the ACL 2007 Student Research Workshop*, pages 73–78, Prague, Czech Republic, June. Association for Computational Linguistics.

Diarmuid Ó Seaghdha. 2008. *Learning Compound Noun Semantics*. Ph.D. thesis, University of Cambridge.

Carla Parra Escartín, Almudena Nevado, and Eoghan Martínez. 2018. Spanish multiword expressions: Looking for a taxonomy. In *Multiword expressions: Insights from a multi-lingual perspective*, pages 271–323. Berlin: Language Science Press, 05.

Behrang Qasemizadeh. 2014. Annotation of Multiword Expressions in the Farsi Section of the Universal Dependencies Project. Second PARSEME General Meeting Posters, March.

Carlos Ramisch, Silvio Ricardo Cordeiro, Agata Savary, Veronika Vincze, Verginica Barbu Mititelu, Archna Bhatia, Maja Buljan, Marie Candito, Polona Gantar, Voula Giouli, Tunga Güngör, Abdelati Hawwari, Uxoa Iñurrieta, Jolanta Kovalevskaitė, Simon Krek, Timm Lichte, Chaya Liebeskind, Johanna Monti, Carla Parra Escartín, Behrang QasemiZadeh, Renata Ramisch, Nathan Schneider, Ivelina Stoyanova, Ashwini Vaidya, and Abigail Walsh. 2018. Edition 1.1 of the PARSEME Shared Task on Automatic Identification of Verbal Multiword Expressions. In *Proceedings of the Joint Workshop on Linguistic Annotation, Multiword Expressions and Constructions (LAW-MWE-CxG-2018)*, pages 222–240. ACL.

Carlos Ramisch. 2015. *Multiword Expressions Acquisition: A Generic and Open Framework*, volume XIV of *Theory and Applications of Natural Language Processing*. Springer.

Victoria Rosén, Koenraad De Smedt, Gyri Smørdal Losnegaard, Eduard Bejček, Agata Savary, and Petya Osenova. 2016. MWEs in Treebanks: From Survey to Guidelines. In *Proceedings of the Tenth International Conference on Language Resources and Evaluation (LREC'16)*, pages 2323–2330, Portorož, Slovenia, May. European Language Resources Association (ELRA).

Victoria Rosén, Gyri Smørdal Losnegaard, De Smedt Koenraad, Eduard Bejček, Agata Savary, Adam Przepiórkowski, Manfred Sailer, and Mitetelu Verginica. 2015. A survey of multiword expressions in treebanks. In *Proceedings of the 14th International Workshop on Treebanks and Linguistic Theories*, page 179–193, Warsaw.

Ivan Sag, Timothy Baldwin, Francis Bond, Ann Copestake, and Dan Flickinger. 2002. Multiword Expressions: A Pain in the Neck for NLP. pages 1–15, 02.

Manuela Sanguinetti, Cristina Bosco, Lauren Cassidy, Özlem Çetinoglu, Alessandra Teresa Cignarella, Teresa Lynn, Ines Rehbein, Josef Ruppenhofer, Djamé Seddah, and Amir Zeldes. 2020. Treebanking User-Generated Content: A Proposal for a Unified Representation in Universal Dependencies. In Nicoletta Calzolari, Frédéric Béchet, Philippe Blache, Khalid Choukri, Christopher Cieri, Thierry Declerck, Sara Goggi, Hitoshi Isahara, Bente Maegaard, Joseph Mariani, Hélène Mazo, Asunción Moreno, Jan Odijk, and Stelios Piperidis, editors, *Proceedings of The 12th Language Resources and Evaluation Conference,LREC*, pages 5240–5250, Marseille, France, May. European Language Resources Association.

Agata Savary, Manfred Sailer, Yannick Parmentier, Michael Rosner, Victoria Rosén, Adam Przepiórkowski, Cvetana Krstev, Veronika Vincze, Beata Wójtowicz, Gyri Smørdal Losnegaard, Carla Parra Escartín, Jakub Waszczuk, Mathieu Constant, Petya Osenova, and Federico Sangati. 2015. PARSEME – PARSing and Multiword Expressions within a European multilingual network. In *7th Language & Technology Conference: Human Language Technologies as a Challenge for Computer Science and Linguistics (LTC 2015)*, Poznań, Poland, November.

Agata Savary, Carlos Ramisch, Silvio Cordeiro, Federico Sangati, Veronika Vincze, Behrang QasemiZadeh, Marie Candito, Fabienne Cap, Voula Giouli, Ivelina Stoyanova, and Antoine Doucet. 2017. The PARSEME Shared Task on Automatic Identification of Verbal Multiword Expressions. In *Proceedings of the 13th Workshop on Multiword Expressions (MWE 2017)*, pages 31–47, Valencia, Spain, April. Association for Computational Linguistics.

Gerold Schneider. 2014. Improving PP attachment in a hybrid dependency parser using semantic, distributional, and lexical resources. In *Second PARSEME Meeting*, Athens, Greece.

Sebastian Schuster and Christopher D. Manning. 2016. Enhanced English Universal Dependencies: An Improved Representation for Natural Language Understanding Tasks. In *Proceedings of the Tenth International Conference on Language Resources and Evaluation (LREC'16)*, page 2371–2378, Portorož, Slovenia, 05. European Language Resources Association (ELRA).

Violeta Seretan. 2011. *Syntax-Based Collocation Extraction*. Text, Speech and Language Technology volume 44. Springer Netherlands.

Kresimir Sojat and Matea Filko. 2016. Verbal Multiword Expressions in Croatian. In *Proceedings of the Second International Conference Computational Linguistics in Bulgaria (CLIB 2016)*, pages 78–85, 09.

Nancy Stenson. 1981. *Studies in Irish syntax*. Ars linguistica. Tübingen: Gunter Narr Verlag.

Umut Sulubacak and GülşenT Eryiğit. 2018. Implementing Universal dependency, morphology, and multiword expression annotation standards for Turkish language processing. *Turkish Journal of Electrical Engineering and Computer Sciences*, 26:1662–1672, 05.

Veronika Vincze, János Zsibrita, and T. IstvánNagy. 2013. Dependency parsing for identifying Hungarian light verb constructions. In *Proceedings of the International Joint Conference on Natural Language Processing*, page 207–215, Nagoya, Japan, 10.

Abigail Walsh, Teresa Lynn, and Jennifer Foster. 2019. Ilfhocail: A lexicon of Irish MWEs. In *Proceedings of the Joint Workshop on Multiword Expressions and WordNet (MWE-WN 2019)*, pages 162–168, Florence, Italy, August. Association for Computational Linguistics.

Tomás Ó Domhnalláin and Dónall Ó Baoill. 1975. *Réamhfhocail le briathra na Gaeilge*. Tuarascáil taighde. Institiúid Teangeolaíochta Éireann.

I've got a construction looks funny – representing and recovering non-standard constructions in UD

Josef Ruppenhofer
Leibniz-Institut für Deutsche Sprache
R5, 6-13
68161 Mannheim
ruppenhofer@ids-mannheim.de

Ines Rehbein
Data and Web Science Group
Universität Mannheim
68159 Mannheim
ines@informatik.uni-mannheim.de

Abstract

The UD framework defines guidelines for a crosslingual syntactic analysis in the framework of dependency grammar, with the aim of providing a consistent treatment across languages that not only supports multilingual NLP applications but also facilitates typological studies. Until now, the UD framework has mostly focussed on bilexical grammatical relations. In the paper, we propose to add a constructional perspective and discuss several examples of spoken-language constructions that occur in multiple languages and challenge the current use of basic and enhanced UD relations. The examples include cases where the surface relations are deceptive, and syntactic amalgams that either involve unconnected subtrees or structures with multiply-headed dependents.We argue that a unified treatment of constructions across languages will increase the consistency of the UD annotations and thus the quality of the treebanks for linguistic analysis.

1 Introduction

The Universal Dependencies (UD) initiative is a project that aims for crosslinguistically consistent annotation of morphosyntax (de Marneffe and Nivre, 2019). The sharing of representations across languages is intended to support multilingual NLP applications on the one hand and to facilitate the linguistic study of similarities and differences from a typological perspective.

While the UD framework also covers the annotation of parts of speech and of morphological features, the annotation of syntactic dependencies is at its core. UD currently uses 37 labels for broadly attested grammatical relations. In addition to these basic UD dependencies, UD allows for an enhanced representation that "aims to make implicit relations between content words more explicit by adding relations and augmenting relation names" (Schuster and Manning, 2016). The most prominent examples of added relations in enhanced representations are links that help propagate relations over conjunctions. While the basic dependency structure is assumed to form a (possibly non-projective) tree, enhanced UD representations often no longer are trees. The subtyping of relations serves to capture more fine-grained language-specific constructions (de Marneffe et al., 2014). For instance, in English, subjects of passive clauses bear the relation `nsubj:pass`.

In this paper, we discuss several constructions that are found in spoken language and data from social media, which are not trivial to analyze. The first set of constructions involves cases where a head and dependent are related in a hybrid way, exhibiting for instance properties of both coordination and subordination, or of coordination and predication. The second group of constructions involves syntactic amalgams where arguably the assumption that a basic UD analysis should form a tree is not met. We

Proceedings of the Fourth Workshop on Universal Dependencies (UDW 2020), pages 140–151
Barcelona, Spain (Online), December 13, 2020

discuss possible trade-offs with respect to how basic and enhanced UD relations might be used in these cases to give linguistically adequate analyses. Note that, our unmarked examples come from Twitter. The others come from the ukWaC corpus (Baroni et al., 2009), UD treebanks, or the linguistic literature.

2   Constructions with hybrid properties

We first discuss constructions that superficially look as if a head and dependent are connected by a certain relation but where the construction also, or even mainly, exhibits properties of another type of relation.

2.1   Conditional coordinations

The first group of constructions involves superficial coordinations that are understood as conditionals, with the first conjunct being subordinated to the second conjunct (Culicover and Jackendoff, 1997; Culicover and Jackendoff, 2005). Some more common forms involve coordination of two declaratives (1), of an NP and a declarative (2), and of an imperative and a declarative (3). Constructions like this are found in German, French, Dutch and Russian (Fortuin and Boogaart, 2009), and probably in further languages.

(1)   You say another word and I'll start hating you.

(2)   One more word outta you and you're gettin kissed boy

(3)   Say that again and imma fight you

In what follows, we focus on the simple declarative type in English, as illustrated in (1). As discussed by Culicover and Jackendoff (2005), while on the one hand the construction looks like syntactic coordination, it does not behave like it in every aspect but also has features of subordination. First, reversing the two conjuncts leads to a loss of the relevant meaning, which is somewhat unexpected for a simple coordination (4). Second, we cannot add coordinates with the intention of expanding the condition/protasis: (5) cannot be used to convey that 'If you drink another can of beer and Bill eats more pretzels, then I'm leaving'. At most, we can add coordinates if they are interpreted as part of the conclusion/apodosis (6).

(4)   I'll start hating you and you say another word.

(5)   # You say another word, Bill agrees with you and I'll start hating you.

(6)   You say another word, I'll start hating you and Bill will stop talking to you.

Third, while regular coordination is compatible with gapping (7), conditional coordination is not (8). In this respect, it is similar to an explicit *if*-conditional, which also does not allow gapping (9).

(7)   Big Louie stole another car radio and Little Louie the hubcaps. (from Culicover and Jackendoff (2005))

(8)   #Big Louie steals one more car radio and Little Louie the hubcaps.

(9)   #If Big Louie steals one more car radio, then Little Louie the hubcaps.

However, a treatment in terms of subordination is not clear-cut either. While English subordinate clauses, including *if*-clauses, can precede or follow the main clause, the first conjunct of a subordinating conditional coordination cannot be moved (10–11), whether we assign *and* to the left or the right conjunct.

(10)   # And I'll start hating you, you say another word.

(11)   # I'll start hating you, you say another word and.

Certainly, *and* would make a very odd subordinator: all other English subordinators are clause-initial. The fact that pauses in the conditional coordination construction precede, rather than follow *and* also suggests that it should be integrated with the right conjunct rather than the left, whatever the analysis. As a semantic peculiarity, we note that these conditionals are restricted to root conditional meanings. Speech act uses, for instances, are not possible unlike with *if*-conditionals (cf. 12–13).

(12)   #You're hungry and there's pizza in the fridge. (constructed)

(13)   If you're hungry, there's pizza in the fridge. (constructed)

Figure 1: Conditional coordination

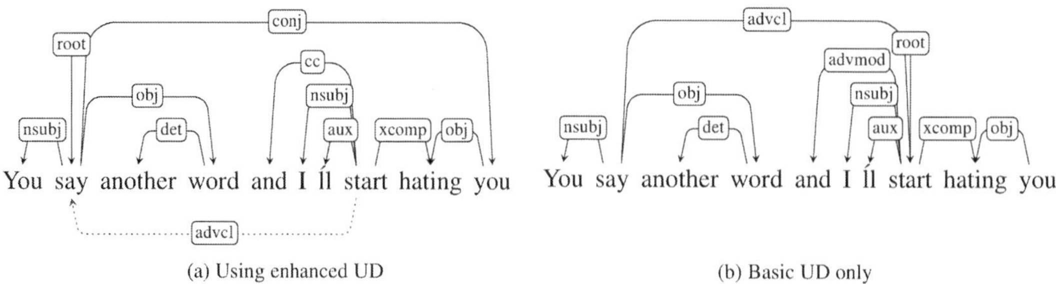

(a) Using enhanced UD   (b) Basic UD only

What are the options for representing instances of this construction in UD? One option that preserves Culicover and Jackendoff's diagnosis that the construction involves a mismatch between syntax and semantics might be to proceed as follows. In terms of basic UD, we treat the structure as involving coordination while adding an `advcl` relation in the enhanced representation, as shown in Figure 1, to capture the subordination characteristics. However, as one of our reviewers argues, "the encoding of the fact that it's a different construction [from ordinary coordination] cannot be done at the enhanced level" and "[i]f you identify new constructions, you must introduce new labels to name them". We take this argument seriously but also want to point out that current UD annotations do not seem to differentiate fully all the constructions that one might want to recognize. For instance subject-auxiliary inversion constructions in English are not recoverable from specific relation labels. Likewise, instances of, for instance, the Group Identity NP construction such as *the rich/poor*, *the young/old*, etc. are not recoverable from specific labels. For instance, in example (14) below from UD-EWT (Silveira et al., 2014) *rich* is an adjective by POS and the NP-status of the subtree it heads is seen only from the fact that it is determined by *the* and governed as an `nmod` by *many*. But these relations also apply to NPs with regular nouns as heads.[1]

(14)   . . . too many of **the rich** made their money not by succeeding in business, but . . .

Now, if we want to forego the use of enhanced relations but still point to the hybrid properties of the construction, we could introduce a new relation subtype `conj:advcl` for the relation between the conjuncts and still treat *and* as related to its head via `cc`. However, insofar as we understand current usage, subtype labels have not been used to indicate hybrids. E.g. while there is for instance a label `csubj:cop`, this label is used for a clause that acts as the subject of another, copular clause; it does not refer to something that is at the same time a `csubj` and a `cop`. To avoid the problem of how a subtyped relation name is likely to be interpreted, we could simply introduce a new relation name such as `conjcond`. But this relation may be sparse and hard to learn for statistical parsers. Yet another option is to treat this construction as involving subordination of the first conjunct as an `advcl` in the basic UD analysis, with *and* being tied to the main clause by a relation other than *cc*. In analogy to the treatment of *then* in *if-then* conditionals, *and* could be treated as an ADV that depends on the main clause head as an `advmod`. What is odd about this analysis is that it involves an obligatorily marked main clause and an obligatory unmarked subordinate clause. At least, *and* would not be the only conjunction that changes function in a pseudo-coordination construction. *But* similarly figures in constructions that are interpreted as (concessive) conditionals with readings such as 'despite P, Q' or 'even if P, Q', as shown by (15).

(15)   Say what you want about this label , but with Delight they really have picked a winner (ukWaC)

And further, whatever analysis we choose also applies to conditional coordinations involving *or* (cf. (16)), which correspond to explicit *unless*-conditionals.

(16)   Give me the money or I'll bite.

---

[1]Unlike UD, construction grammar and HPSG can represent the fact that certain phrases/subtrees have unexpected external semantics or syntax through features on phrasal mother signs. For constructional treatments of the Group Identity NP construction see Fried (2015) and Fillmore et al. (2012), where the construction is called Adjective-as-nominal.

For consistency's sake we also suggest extending the same treatment to cases of paratactic conditionals such as (17)–(18).

(17)   You do that again, I'm gonna smack you where the sun don't shine.

(18)   One more word outta you I'll take the servers down all day

Finally, we want to note that conditional coordinations are not the only 'weird' constructions involving *and*. Other pseudo-coordination constructions with a hortative-mandative semantics have verbs like *try* and *remember* or *be*+Adjective combinations such as *be sure* in the left conjunct (Flach, 2017).

(19)   If you 're a woman , then try and find the cheapest policy - whoever it 's marketed at . (ukWaC)

2.2   German non-finite predication construction (NFPK)

The example in (20) is an instance of a German construction that, while apparently a coordination, semantico-pragmatically serves to express the speakers' incredulity about a hypothetical state of affairs mentioned in prior discourse. The German and related constructions in other languages are known under various names that reflect either their form, function or distribution, among them: Oxymoron construction (Deppermann, 2007), Bare predication construction in polar echoes (Huddleston and Pullum, 2002), Echo exclamation (Quirk et al., 1985) Mad Magazine sentences (Akmajian, 1984) and Incredulity Reponse Construction (Lambrecht, 1990). We will use the descriptive name Non finite predication construction (NFPK) proposed by Bücker (2012). Alongside the variant featuring *und* (NFPK$_{und}$), there is a version of the construction where *und* is lacking (NFPK$_{bare}$) (21). Functionally similar constructions exist in English and Spanish. They are structurally different, though also grammatically special (Etxepare and Grohmann, 2005). For instance, the English construction is similar to the German NFPK$_{bare}$ variant but the English construction involves an object-form subject (cf. the gloss of (20).) whereas the German construction has a subject in the nominative case typical of subjects even though there is no finite verb.

(20)   Der   und ein Vorbild   , - lachhaft   ! ...
       that_one and a   role_model , - ridiculous !
       'Him (be) a role model, . ridiculous! ...'

(21)   Frau Merkel ehrlich zu sich   selbst sein ???
       Mrs. Merkel honest to 3.REFL self   be   ???
       'Mrs Merkel be honest with herself???'

Example (20) is a case of the NFPK construction that is also identified as such by the presence of an optional coda (above: *lachhaft* 'ridiculous') that explicitly expresses the speaker's disbelief/incredulity. Many instances of the NPFK construction with *und* also involve coordination of unalikes (cf. 22–23).

(22)   Der   und gewonnen ?
       that_one and won   ?
       'He is supposed to have won?'

(23)   Der   und im Himmel ? Wohl eher ein paar   Stockwerke tiefer .
       that_one and in heaven ? Likely rather a   couple floors   lower .
       'Him in heaven? More likely a few floors lower down.'

Assuming a predication relation between the two conjuncts is supported by the fact that reflexives in the right conjunct can be bound by governors in the left (24), unlike in regular coordinations (25).

(24)   A: Der   Sänger postete ein   Bild von   sich mit stylischer Brille ...B: Der   und ein Bild
       the singer posted a   picture of   3.REFL with with stylish   glasses ...B: that_one and a   picture
       von sich/#ihm   ?
       of   3.REFL/#him ?

       A: The singer posted a picture of himself with stylish glasses ...B: Him take a picture of himself/#him?

(25) A: Was hast du gesehen ? B: Queen Elisabeth und ein Bild von ihr/#sich.   (constructed)
     a: What have you seen   ? B: Queen Elizabeth and a picture of her/#3.REFL
     'A: What did you see? B: Queen Elizabeth and a picture of her/#herself.'

As in English, the predicate, even when involving a verbal phrase as in (22), cannot normally bear tense or modal markings.

However, note that with nominal right conjuncts, the right conjunct need not always be a predicate nominal as in (20). In (26), the two nominals in the conjuncts are not related as subject and predicate. Rather, both are to be understood as dependents of a zero predicate that is inferable from prior discourse.

(26) Der   und ein klares ethisches Profil ?
     that_one and a   clear ethical   profile ?
     'Him have a clear ethical profile?'

The NFPK$_{und}$ variant presents a mismatch between form and semantics. An early analysis of this variant nevertheless treats it as a case of real coordination where the predicate (and sentence) that governs it is omitted (Behaghel, 1928). The two conjuncts are thus treated as metalinguistically mentioned rather than used, as in the English cases (27–28) where incongruity is explicitly stated or alluded to.

(27) The words Obama/Biden, and "scandal-free" should NEVER appear in the same sentence again. EVER.

(28) How often have you heard the terms ' entrepreneur ' and ' social conscience ' in the same sentence ? (ukWaC)

This analysis does not generalize well to the NFPK$_{bare}$ variant (21). A second type of ellipsis analysis assumes that NFPK$_{bare}$ features the elision of a finite verb form from what would otherwise be a regular finite sentence. This does not generalize to the NFPK$_{und}$ variant: adding a finite verb to instances of that variant does not produce grammatical sentences. Further, the NFPK$_{bare}$ version has constraints on the ordering of pronouns in particular that do not obtain in sentences where a finite verb has been inserted, which argues against NFPK being simply the result of finite verb elision (Bücker, 2012).

If we reject a simple ellipsis analysis, we have the same options as for the conditional coordination. Sticking close to the surface, we may propose annotating a coordination structure in the basic UD representation and making the subject-predicate relation, when present, explicit in the enhanced annotation, as shown in Figure 2a. Otherwise, we annotate an `orphan` relationship for cases like (26). A downside of this proposal is that we connect two words in the enhanced representation that are already related in the basic representation, with the roles of head and dependent being switched now. On the other hand, this would be in keeping with our enhanced UD analysis for the conditional coordination construction.

Avoiding the use of the enhanced representation, an alternative treatment directly uses the `nsubj` relation in the basic UD annotation for all cases where the second conjunct is understood as a predicate and the first conjunct as its subject (Fig. 2b). This would treat cases like (26) differently in the basic annotation since these cases would involve an `orphan` relationship. Further, the apparent conjunction, where present, would need to be changed both in terms of POS and syntactic dependency. We might, for instance, treat *und* somewhat arbitrarily as an ADV related by `advmod` to the head of the right conjunct.

2.3 Presentational relative clause construction (PRC)

The presentational relative construction (PRC) involves the combination of a semantically weak main clause and a relative clause which, rather than the main clause, contains the assertion of the utterance (Lambrecht, 1988; Duffield et al., 2010). The PRC is, therefore, normally more aptly paraphrased by a single sentence (29a) than by a sequence of sentences (29b).

(29) You have some folks who deny she LOST when she suspended her campaign.

     a. Some folks deny she LOST when she suspended her campaign.

     b. #You have some folks. They deny she LOST when she suspended her campaign.

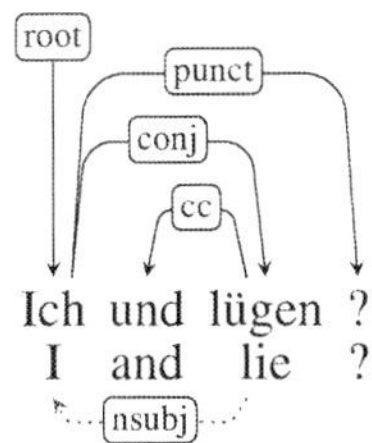
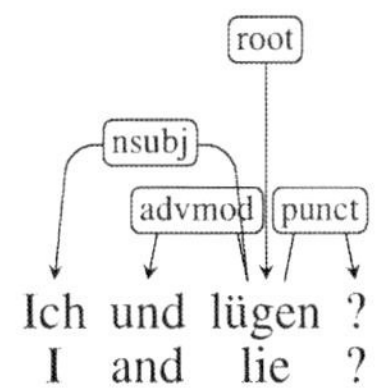

Figure 2: NFPK construction

(a) Subject and predicate, using enhanced UD

(b) Subject and predicate, basic UD only

Formally, PRCs mostly feature subject gaps in the relative clause.[2] By contrast, restrictive and non-restrictive relative clauses with a relative pronoun or a complementizer have no such restriction (30–31).

(30)   OMG I want the car that shots from the headlights.

(31)   My 68 month old has a toy truck that he rides up and down the street in.

(32)   Whole family voting including my father who has never voted.

(33)   In full survival mode, I forgot to water my lemon tree, which I love.

Restrictive relative clauses without a relative pronoun or complementizer do not allow subject gaps (34).

(34)   #I chose the dress _ made me want to dance.

As argued by Lambrecht (1988), the PRC allows the speaker to avoid violating an information-packaging constraint that Lambrecht (1994) refers to as the Principle of Separation of Reference and Role (PSRR): "Do not introduce a referent and talk about it in the same clause". While the main clause serves to introduce the referent, the relative clause makes an assertion. In accord with the assertive pragmatic function of the relatives in PRCs, these relative clauses can be conjoined with assertive main clauses, unlike restrictive or appositive main clauses (cf. (35)).

(35)   Once upon a time there was an old cockroach who lived in a paper bag and <u>he</u> was very poor. (from Lambrecht (1988))

The assertive status of the relative clause is underscored by the fact that its proposition can be challenged by the lie-test (36), which is not the case for restrictive or appositive relative clauses (37).

(36)   A: have you tried simultaneous Twitter comments during lecture? I know colleagues who have done this.
       B: That's a lie!
       a. Nobody's doing this.
       b. #You don't know colleagues.

(37)   A: I'm looking for a gift for my son. He wants a car that he can build.
       B: That's a lie.
       a. He doesn't want a car.
       b. # He can't build it.

Presentational relative clauses are also not the same as the relative clauses in cleft-sentences. Contrast the effect of the lie-test in response to a cleft (38) with that in response to the PRC (36)

(38)   A: It's colleagues of mine who have done this.
       B: That's a lie!

---

[2]Lambrecht (1988) assumes PRCs are restricted to involve subject gaps in the relative clause but Duffield et al. (2010) report instances with object gaps in the relative clause.

a. It's not them (but Pat who did it).

b. #Nobody has done this.

The Italian PoSTWITA treebank (Sanguinetti et al., 2018) contains an instance of what we call PRC that is simply annotated as a relative clause.[3] The treebank for spoken French (Lacheret et al., 2014) handles PRC instances the same way. But given their special properties, presentational relative clauses should be treated differently from restrictive and appositive relative clauses. A simple option involving only basic UD would be to only subtype the `acl`-relation further and introduce `acl:presrel`.

Figure 3: Presentational Relative Construction

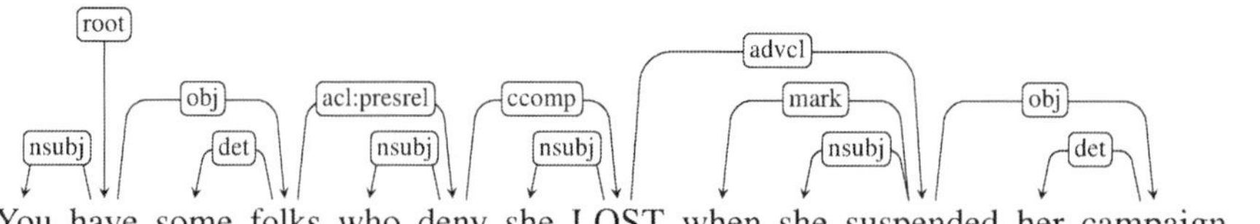

The annotation strategy for the English PRC can also be carried over to Italian, French and German. Note that German presentational relative clauses, unlike restrictive and appositive relative clauses, exhibit the verb-second word order that is characteristic of matrix clauses (39).

(39) Ich hatte mal   nen Freund, der hatte was   im Auge und ging damit   in die Notaufnahme.
      I   had some_time a   friend, who had something in eye   and went therewith in the ER.
      'I had a friend once who got something into his eye and went to the ER about it.'

There likely are quite a few more similar constructions in other languages. We know of (i) complement clauses in Danish, Icelandic, Swedish, Norwegian and German as well as (ii) marked subordinate clauses in German that have unexpected main clause (verb-second) word order and which are said to have main clause properties (Günthner, 1996; Gärtner and Michaelis, 2010; Antomo and Steinbach, 2010; Reis, 2013; Wiklund, 2009; Bentzen, 2014). For French, there is discussion of constructions involving *reverse subordination* (Benzitoun, 2013).

3   Syntactic amalgams

We now turn to two constructions where arguably a basic UD analysis mirroring the analyses proposed in the theoretical literature from the construction grammar tradition would not result in simple trees and which for that reason need some special treatment.

3.1   Presentational amalgam construction (PAC)

Examples (40)–(41) exemplify what Lambrecht (1988) calls the presentational amalgam construction (PAC), which is common in spoken language but also found in social media. The construction consists of a sequence [[NP1 V NP2] [VP]], which apparently combines an existential *there*-clause or a clause with *have (got)* with a final VP. The postverbal NP in the initial presentational clause is usually indefinite.

(40)   There's a guy says he's gonna run a marathon every time Wigan win this season!

(41)   I've got a friend of mine, does this all the time, especially during PE.

The instances of PAC thus are like instances of PRC (cf. section 2.3) but without a relative pronoun or complementizer. Like PRC, PAC allows only subject gaps. Also, instances of PAC behave like instances of PRC with respect to the lie-test (cf. §2.3): challenges do affect the final VP.

---

[3]Cruschina (2018) calls the instances of the construction presentational ci-sentences (PCS).

Figure 4: Presentational amalgam construction

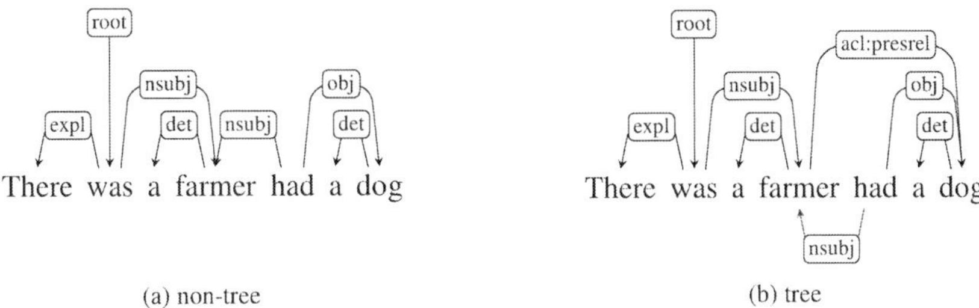

(a) non-tree   (b) tree

(42) A: there was a guy stole a yacht down south.
      B: That's a lie. He only borrowed it.

On the analysis of Lambrecht (1988), PAC features an NP, namely NP2, that is simultaneously a dependent in the existential clause and the subject of a clause it forms with the final VP (cf. Figure 4a). Part of the motivation for this treatment is semantic. The presentational part of some instances such as (41), repeated below in (43), is by itself an odd proposition because of the redundancy.

(43) ??I've got a friend of mine.

But, as Lambrecht argues, NP2 is specifically produced with an eye towards its role as subject of the final VP. From that vantage point, an NP2 like that in (41) is not odd when considered within the PAC construction. This is so because the purpose of PAC is to solve the same communicative problem that the presentational relative construction addresses. PAC sentences are alternatives to simple sentences such as (44), which is a modified version of (40). Sentences like (44) are dispreferred in spoken language because they involve predicating something about a newly introduced referent in the same clause, while speakers normally like to first separately introduce a referent before predicating about it.

(44) A guy says he's gonna run a marathon every time Wigan win this season!

However, unlike with PRC, in the case of PAC there is full fusion between the presentational clause and the clause containing the main assertion. If we accept Lambrecht's analysis, then we have the undesirable situation that the same content word is a dependent of two different heads (Fig. (4a)). We could avoid this, by shifting the subject relation to the enhanced representation. The question is then how to connect the final VP to the initial existential clause. Our suggestion is to use a subtype of `acl` that we call `acl:presrelbare` to connect the VP to the head of NP2 (4b) . Because this subtype of `acl` always lacks a relativizer or pronoun, we cannot reuse the `acl:presrel` subtype introduced for PRC.

3.2 Double *is* construction (ISIS)

Consider examples (45–47). All three feature sequences where two instances of *is* immediately or very closely follow each other.

(45) He's certainly not as dominant in that role as he is, uh, is his, in his normal role.

(46) @RetroAperture @BeardedGenius what he is is stupid.

(47) But the thing is is that I'm naturally thin... (ISIS)

Example (45) involves a disfluent repetition where UD's `reparandum` relation would be used. Sentence (46) involves a specifying pseudo-cleft construction where a so-called fused relative (*what he is*) (Huddleston and Pullum, 2002) serves as the subject of the second instance of *is*, which takes the final phrase as `ccomp`. Sentence (47) is an example of the double *is* or ISIS construction.[4] As argued by Coppock et al. (2006), ISIS sentences do not involve disfluent repetition, although they might appear to do so. With ISIS, the copula *be* is typically repeated after certain nouns, such as *issue* and *point*, indicating that ISIS is a subtype of the specificational construction (Mikkelsen, 2005). Further, ISIS is often

---

[4]Another designation of the construction is copula doubling.

147

found before short, easy-to-process clauses where disfluencies are unexpected. And in fact human raters in Coppock et al. (2006)'s study found the ISIS instances involving declarative clauses highly fluent.

The formal construction grammar analysis of ISIS by Brenier and Michaelis (2005) treats this construction as a syntactic amalgam, a phrasal construction with two daughters: (i) the so-called setup clause including the subject NP and the first form of *be* and (ii) the second *is* and the following clause. This phrase-based analysis does not translate into a connected dependency tree (Figure 5a). To produce such a tree, we need to employ some sort of dependency relation to connect the two instances of the copular verb. This is not easy to decide, however, since common headedness criteria are inconclusive. Copulas do not normally depend on copulas. Both parts of the construction are non-optional. However, since semantically the second phrase seems to complement the first, we treat the head of the first as `root`.

(48)   The real question <u>was is</u> are we getting a reasonable return on our investment. (from Brenier & Michaelis 2005)

The subject NP would be connected to it as an `nsubj`; the second copula would be connected to the first copular instance by a `ccomp` relation; and the finite clause in turn would be connected to the second copular instance by another `ccomp` (Figure 5b). This treatment would preserve the analysis of Brenier and Michaelis (2005) with the exception that the setup clause and the final *is*+clause are here connected by a dependency rather than both simply being daughters of the same phrase.

Figure 5: Double *is* construction

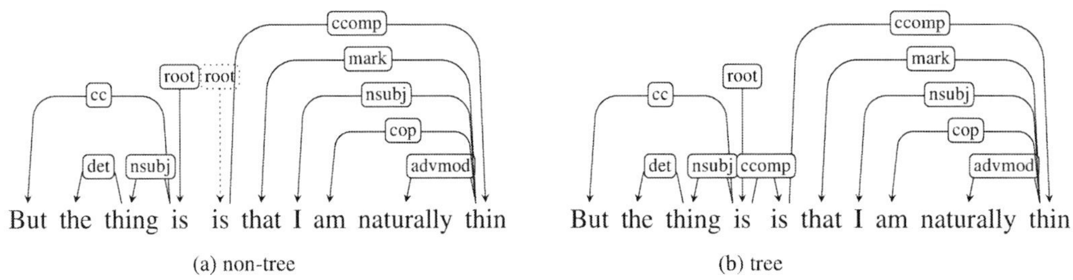

(a) non-tree   (b) tree

4   Conclusion

We have presented several constructions that are associated with social media or spoken language and that have special properties that do not readily fit the current use of basic and enhanced UD relations. The first set of constructions involved pseudo-coordinations whose surface structure is mismatched with their semantics. The second set of constructions featured cases of syntactic amalgams that either involved unconnected subtrees (double *is*) or structures with multiply-headed dependents (PAC).

While one can disagree both with the analyses of these constructions in the theoretical literature and with our ideas for dealing with them in UD, we are confident that as UD treebanks expand to more languages, domains, genres and registers, further constructions with similar challenges will be encountered. To allow for consistent and expressive analyses, we think the UD community would benefit from discussing which mechanisms to use for which kinds of constructions. We have explored the use of enhanced UD annotations, keeping the relation inventory the same, and as an alternative introducing new dependency relations and relation subtypes, which may lead to sparsely attested relation types. One option we have not explored but which the GUM corpus uses is a kind of constructional annotation (specifically, of sentence types) in the metadata (Zeldes and Simonson, 2016). This would, however, not localize which words are part of the construction. Other ways to track constructions may be conceivable.

Whatever the annotation mechanisms used, we think that adding linguistic analyses for such constructions to the UD guidelines might help to improve annotation consistency across languages, and thus the quality of the treebanks. Existing UD treebanks already feature some well-represented constructions that are treated inconsistently between treebanks and/or languages along the lines we discussed. For instance, the two clauses of the paratactic correlative construction (*the X-er, the Y-er*) are related by `conj` in German treebanks (HDT (Borges Völker et al., 2019), TüBa (Çöltekin et al., 2017), GSD (McDonald et al., 2013)), while English treebanks (EWT, GUM (Zeldes, 2017)) mostly use `advcl`.

References

Adrian Akmajian. 1984. Sentence types and the form-function fit. *Natural Language & Linguistic Theory*, 2(1):1–23.

Mailin Antomo and Markus Steinbach. 2010. Desintegration und Interpretation: Weil-V2-Sätze an der Schnittstelle zwischen Syntax, Semantik und Pragmatik. *Zeitschrift für Sprachwissenschaft*, 29(1):1–37.

Marco Baroni, Silvia Bernardini, Adriano Ferraresi, and Eros Zanchetta. 2009. The wacky wide web: a collection of very large linguistically processed web-crawled corpora. *Language Resources and Evaluation*, 43(3):209–226, September.

Otto Behaghel. 1928. *Deutsche Syntax: eine geschichtliche Darstellung*, volume 3. Carl Winters's Universitäts-buchhandlung, Heidelberg.

Kristine Bentzen. 2014. Embedded verb second (v2). *Nordic Atlas of Language Structures Journal*, 1(1).

Christophe Benzitoun. 2013. Faut-il remettre les pendules de la subordination temporelle à l'heure ? Description de deux fonctionnements de quand et avant que/de. *Cahiers Chronos*, 26:419–435.

Emanuel Borges Völker, Maximilian Wendt, Felix Hennig, and Arne Köhn. 2019. HDT-UD: A very large universal dependencies treebank for German. In *Proceedings of the Third Workshop on Universal Dependencies (UDW, SyntaxFest 2019)*, pages 46–57, Paris, France, August. Association for Computational Linguistics.

Jason M Brenier and Laura A Michaelis. 2005. Optimization via syntactic amalgam: Syntax-prosody mismatch and copula doubling. *Corpus Linguistics and Linguistic Theory*, 1(1):45–88.

Jörg Bücker. 2012. *Sprachhandeln und Sprachwissen [Linguistic Action and Linguistic Knowledge]*. De Gruyter, Berlin, Boston.

Çağrı Çöltekin, Ben Campbell, Erhard Hinrichs, and Heike Telljohann. 2017. Converting the TüBa-d/z treebank of German to universal dependencies. In *Proceedings of the NoDaLiDa 2017 Workshop on Universal Dependencies (UDW 2017)*, pages 27–37, Gothenburg, Sweden, May. Association for Computational Linguistics.

Elizabeth Coppock, Jason Brenier, Laura Staum, and Laura Michaelis. 2006. Isis: It's not disfluent, but how do we know that? In *Proceedings of the 32nd Annual Meeting of the Berkeley Linguistics Society. Berkeley, CA*.

Silvio Cruschina. 2018. Setting the boundaries: Presentational ci-sentences in Italian. *Belgian Journal of Linguistics*, 32(1):53–85.

Peter Culicover and Ray Jackendoff. 1997. Semantic Subordination Despite Syntactic Coordination. *Linguistic Inquiry*, 28:195–217, 06.

Peter Culicover and Ray Jackendoff. 2005. *Simpler Syntax*. Oxford linguistics. Oxford University Press.

Marie-Catherine de Marneffe and Joakim Nivre. 2019. Dependency grammar. *Annual Review of Linguistics*, 5(1):197–218.

Marie-Catherine de Marneffe, Timothy Dozat, Natalia Silveira, Katri Haverinen, Filip Ginter, Joakim Nivre, and Christopher D. Manning. 2014. Universal Stanford dependencies: A cross-linguistic typology. In *Proceedings of the Ninth International Conference on Language Resources and Evaluation (LREC'14)*, pages 4585–4592, Reykjavik, Iceland, May. European Language Resources Association (ELRA).

Arnulf Deppermann. 2007. *Grammatik und Semantik aus gesprächsanalytischer Sicht [Grammar and Semantics from a Conversation Analytic Perspective]*. De Gruyter, Berlin, Boston.

Cecily Jill Duffield, Jena D Hwang, and Laura A Michaelis. 2010. Identifying assertions in text and discourse: The presentational relative clause construction. In *Proceedings of the NAACL HLT Workshop on Extracting and Using Constructions in Computational Linguistics*, pages 17–24.

Ricardo Etxepare and Kleanthes K Grohmann. 2005. Towards a grammar of adult root infinitives. In *Proceedings of the 24th West Coast Conference on Formal Linguistics*, pages 129–137.

Charles Fillmore, Russell Lee-Goldman, and Russell Rhomieux. 2012. The framenet constructicon. In *Sign-Based Construction Grammar*.

Susanne Flach. 2017. Idiomatic singleton or prototype? a productivity analysis of be-adj-and-v. *Yearbook of the German Cognitive Linguistics Association*, 5(1):129 – 142.

Egbert Fortuin and Ronny Boogaart. 2009. Imperative as conditional: From constructional to compositional semantics. *Cognitive Linguistics*, 20, 01.

Mirjam Fried. 2015. Construction grammar. In T. Kiss and A. Alexiadou, editors, *Syntax - Theory and Analysis. Volume 2*, Handbücher zur Sprach- und Kommunikationswissenschaft / Handbooks of Linguistics and Communication Science (HSK), pages 974–1003. De Gruyter.

Hans-Martin Gärtner and Jens Michaelis. 2010. On modeling the distribution of declarative V2-clauses: The case of disjunction. *Judgements and propositions*, pages 11–25.

Susanne Günthner. 1996. From subordination to coordination? Verb-second position in German causal and concessive constructions. *Pragmatics*, 6(3):323–356.

Rodney D. Huddleston and Geoffrey K. Pullum. 2002. *The Cambridge Grammar of the English Language*. Cambridge University Press.

Anne Lacheret, Sylvain Kahane, Julie Beliao, Anne Dister, Kim Gerdes, Jean-Philippe Goldman, Nicolas Obin, Paola Pietrandrea, and Atanas Tchobanov. 2014. Rhapsodie: a prosodic-syntactic treebank for spoken french. In Nicoletta Calzolari, Khalid Choukri, Thierry Declerck, Hrafn Loftsson, Bente Maegaard, Joseph Mariani, Asunción Moreno, Jan Odijk, and Stelios Piperidis, editors, *Proceedings of the Ninth International Conference on Language Resources and Evaluation, LREC 2014, Reykjavik, Iceland, May 26-31, 2014*, pages 295–301. European Language Resources Association (ELRA).

Knud Lambrecht. 1988. There was a farmer had a dog: Syntactic amalgams revisited. In *Annual Meeting of the Berkeley Linguistics Society*, volume 14, pages 319–339.

Knud Lambrecht. 1990. "What, me worry?"–'Mad Magazine Sentences' Revisited. In *Annual Meeting of the Berkeley Linguistics Society*, volume 16, pages 215–228.

Knud Lambrecht. 1994. *Information Structure and Sentence Form: Topic, Focus, and the Mental Representations of Discourse Referents*. Cambridge Studies in Linguistics. Cambridge University Press.

Ryan McDonald, Joakim Nivre, Yvonne Quirmbach-Brundage, Yoav Goldberg, Dipanjan Das, Kuzman Ganchev, Keith Hall, Slav Petrov, Hao Zhang, Oscar Täckström, Claudia Bedini, Núria Bertomeu Castelló, and Jungmee Lee. 2013. Universal Dependency annotation for multilingual parsing. In *Proceedings of the 51st Annual Meeting of the Association for Computational Linguistics (Volume 2: Short Papers)*, pages 92–97, Sofia, Bulgaria, August. Association for Computational Linguistics.

Line Mikkelsen. 2005. *Copular clauses: Specification, predication and equation*, volume 85. John Benjamins Publishing.

Randolph Quirk, Sidney Greenbaum, Geoffrey Leech, and Jan Svartvik. 1985. *A Comprehensive Grammar of the English Language*. Longman, London.

Marga Reis. 2013. „Weil-V2 "-Sätze und (k) ein Ende? Anmerkungen zur Analyse von Antomo & Steinbach (2010). *Zeitschrift für Sprachwissenschaft*, 32(2):221–262.

Manuela Sanguinetti, Cristina Bosco, Alberto Lavelli, Alessandro Mazzei, Oronzo Antonelli, and Fabio Tamburini. 2018. PoSTWITA-UD: an Italian Twitter Treebank in Universal Dependencies. In Nicoletta Calzolari (Conference chair), Khalid Choukri, Christopher Cieri, Thierry Declerck, Sara Goggi, Koiti Hasida, Hitoshi Isahara, Bente Maegaard, Joseph Mariani, Hélène Mazo, Asuncion Moreno, Jan Odijk, Stelios Piperidis, and Takenobu Tokunaga, editors, *Proceedings of the Eleventh International Conference on Language Resources and Evaluation (LREC 2018)*, Miyazaki, Japan, May 7-12, 2018. European Language Resources Association (ELRA).

Sebastian Schuster and Christopher D. Manning. 2016. Enhanced English Universal Dependencies: An Improved Representation for Natural Language Understanding Tasks. In *Proceedings of the 10th Language Resource and Evaluation Conference (LREC 2016)*, pages 2371–2378. ELRA.

Natalia Silveira, Timothy Dozat, Marie-Catherine de Marneffe, Samuel Bowman, Miriam Connor, John Bauer, and Christopher D. Manning. 2014. A gold standard dependency corpus for English. In *Proceedings of the Ninth International Conference on Language Resources and Evaluation (LREC-2014)*.

Anna-Lena Wiklund. 2009. In search of the force of dependent V2: A note on Swedish. *Working papers in Scandinavian syntax*, 83:27–36.

Amir Zeldes and Dan Simonson. 2016. Different flavors of GUM: Evaluating genre and sentence type effects on multilayer corpus annotation quality. In *Proceedings of the 10th Linguistic Annotation Workshop held in conjunction with ACL 2016 (LAW-X 2016)*, pages 68–78, Berlin, Germany, August. Association for Computational Linguistics.

Amir Zeldes. 2017. The GUM corpus: Creating multilayer resources in the classroom. *Language Resources and Evaluation*, 51(3):581–612.

Universal Dependencies for Manx Gaelic

Kevin P. Scannell
Department of Computer Science
Saint Louis University
St. Louis, Missouri, USA
`kscanne@gmail.com`

Abstract

Manx Gaelic is one of the three Q-Celtic languages, along with Irish and Scottish Gaelic. We present a new dependency treebank for Manx consisting of 291 sentences and about 6000 tokens, annotated according to the Universal Dependency (UD) guidelines. To the best of our knowledge, this is the first annotated corpus of any kind for Manx. Our annotations generally follow the conventions established by the existing UD treebanks for Irish and Scottish Gaelic, although we highlight some areas where the grammar of Manx diverges, requiring new analyses. We use 10-fold cross validation to evaluate the accuracy of dependency parsers trained on the corpus, and compare these results with delexicalized models transferred from Irish and Scottish Gaelic.

1 Introduction

Manx Gaelic, spoken primarily on the Isle of Man, is one of the three Q-Celtic (or Goidelic) languages, along with Irish and Scottish Gaelic. Although the language fell out of widespread use during the 19th and 20th centuries, it has seen a vibrant revitalization movement in recent years. The number of speakers is now growing, thanks in part to a Manx-language primary school on the island. The language also has a strong online presence relative to the size of the community.

Several Manx dictionaries were published in the 19th and 20th centuries, and a number of these have been digitized in recent years and published online.[1] The full text of the Bible, originally published in the 18th century, is also available and provides an easily-accessible source of parallel text.[2] In terms of spoken language, the Irish Folklore Commission recorded fluent speakers on the Isle of Man in 1948, and those recordings are now available digitally as well.[3]

Outside of these corpus resources, very little advanced language technology exists for Manx. The lack of a lemmatizer and part-of-speech tagger makes it more difficult for language learners and linguistic researchers to search corpora of Manx texts. These difficulties are compounded by spelling variations in the traditional texts as well as the system of initial mutations. With these challenges in mind, we set out to lay the foundation for Manx language technology by developing a lemmatizer, tagger, and dependency parser. The Universal Dependencies framework (Nivre et al., 2016; Nivre et al., 2020) was ideal for our purposes, offering a unified annotation scheme which opens up the possibility of cross-lingual analysis, as well as a rich ecosystem of computational tools.

In §2, we present our new treebank for Manx, annotated according to the Universal Dependencies (v2) guidelines and released under an open source license. There are now UD treebanks for five of the six Celtic languages, with Manx joining Irish (Lynn and Foster, 2016; Lynn et al., 2017), Breton (Tyers and Ravishankar, 2018), Scottish Gaelic (Batchelor, 2019), and Welsh (Heinecke and Tyers, 2019) — only Cornish remains to be done. The Manx treebank is relatively small, consisting of 291 sentences and about 6000 tokens, and was annotated entirely by hand. Because of the close linguistic relationship between Manx and its sister languages of Irish and Scottish Gaelic, we were able to refer to the existing

---

[1] See `https://sites.google.com/view/gailck-hasht/fockleyryn`.
[2] See `http://bible.learnmanx.com/`.
[3] See `https://www.imuseum.im/search/collections/archive/mnh-museum-676861.html`.

Proceedings of the Fourth Workshop on Universal Dependencies (UDW 2020), pages 152–157
Barcelona, Spain (Online), December 13, 2020

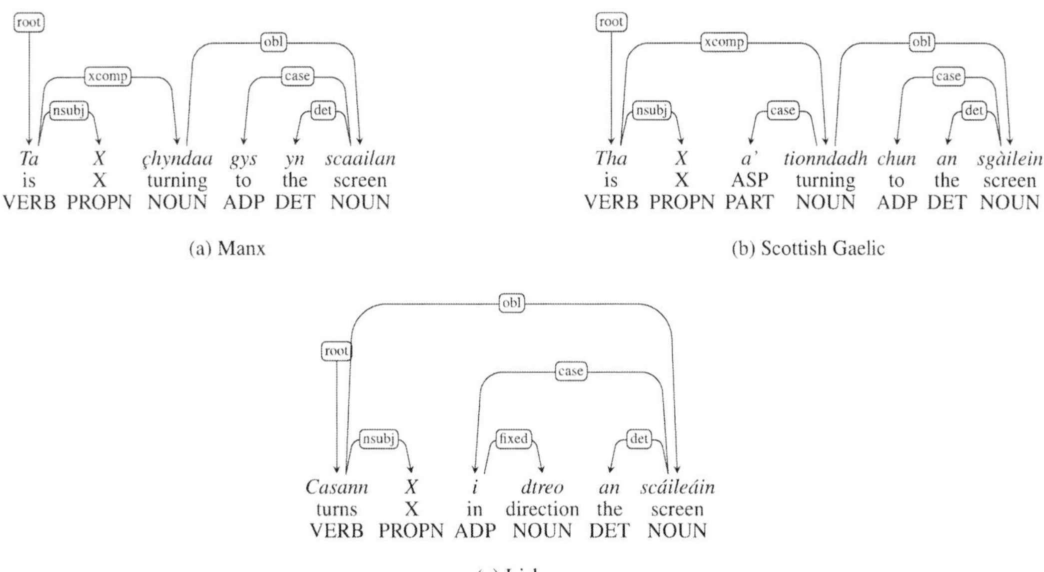

(a) Manx   (b) Scottish Gaelic

(c) Irish

Figure 1: A trilingual example; "X turns to the screen"

UD treebanks for these languages while constructing the corpus. That said, the grammar of Manx does differ in a few important ways, and we discuss some of these divergent analyses in §3.

In §4, we evaluate the accuracy of several dependency parsing models on the Manx corpus. First, we trained UDPipe models using the corpus itself via 10-fold cross validation, achieving labeled accuracy scores of 65.20 on plain text input, and 76.29 when the parser was given access to the gold POS tags. We then evaluated the performance of delexicalized models trained on the Irish and Scottish Gaelic treebanks on the Manx corpus but were unable to achieve comparable results despite the close linguistic relationships. Other approaches to cross-lingual parsing such as annotation projection might give better results in the future, but these would depend on the development of machine translation engines and large parallel corpora between the Gaelic languages.

2 Corpus Development and Annotation

The grammar of Manx is very close to both Irish and Scottish Gaelic, sharing features such as VSO word order, initial consonant mutations, inflected prepositions, and extensive use of the verbal noun. In places where Irish and Scottish Gaelic diverge, Manx is typically more closely allied with Scottish Gaelic, e.g. in the use of a periphrastic construction involving the verbal noun to express the present tense; see Figure 1. For reasons of space we make no attempt to survey the grammar here, referring the interested reader to Draskau (2008) for a general overview. In terms of Universal Dependencies *per se*, we refer to Lynn and Foster (2016) and Batchelor (2019), as well as the detailed guidelines for those languages on the Universal Dependencies web site.[4]

The sentences in the treebank were taken from a web-crawled corpus of Manx consisting of more than eight million words of text. This corpus contains virtually all non-trivial Manx language texts on the open web, and therefore the treebank presented here is as close as possible to a "random sample" of Manx on the web. As such, the Bible is heavily represented, but there are also many sentences from modern sources: the Manx Wikipedia, news stories from Manx Radio, blog posts, etc.[5]

The web corpus was segmented by sentences and shuffled; then, 300 random sentences were chosen for annotation (nine of these require further analysis and did not make it into the initial release of the

---

[4]https://universaldependencies.org/

[5]This design choice is not without controversy; there are significant differences between the traditional language and the Manx of the modern revival. By including samples of both in the corpus, we hope to develop tools that will be effective in processing both varieties.

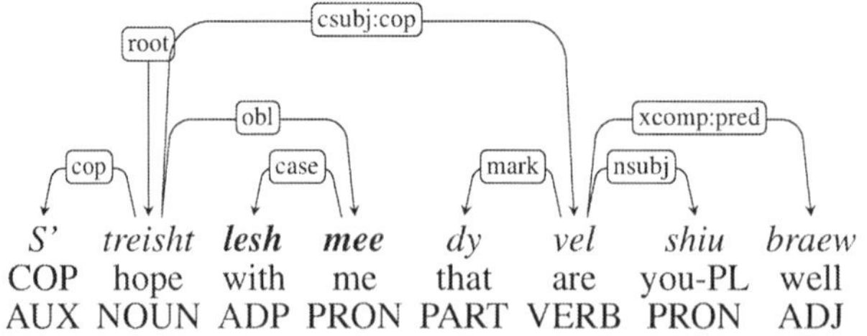

S'treisht **lhiam** dy vel shiu braew "I hope that you are well"

Figure 2: Example of a decomposed inflected preposition

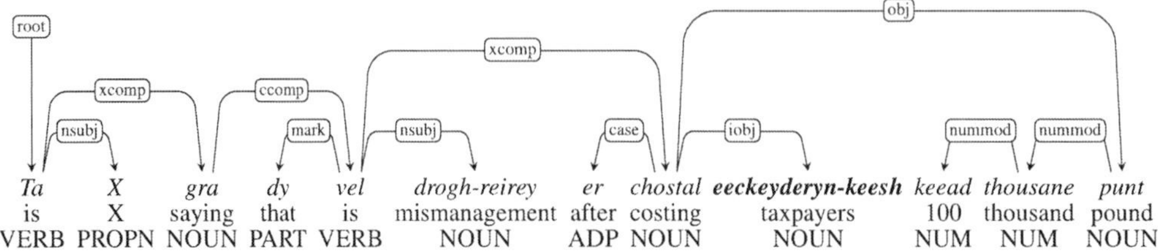

"X says that mismanagement has cost taxpayers one hundred thousand pounds"

Figure 3: Example of an indirect object in Manx. In Irish and Scottish Gaelic, where there are no indirect objects, verbs meaning "to cost" would express this argument via an oblique PP.

treebank). The UD part-of-speech tags and dependency annotations were added manually by the present author. We have not added detailed morphological information, although we plan to do this in future releases. Since there are only about 6000 tokens in the final corpus, we have released the data as a single file (without splitting into train/dev/test sets), per the recommendation of the UD maintainers.

3   Comparison with Irish and Scottish Gaelic

In this section we highlight some differences between the Manx treebank and the Irish and Scottish Gaelic treebanks.

All of the Celtic languages have so-called "inflected prepositions," e.g. Manx *lhiam* "with me" (Ir. *liom*, Sc.G *leam*), Manx *lhiat* "with you" (Ir. and Sc.G. *leat*), etc. These are treated as single tokens in the Irish and Scottish treebanks, while we have instead followed the Breton (Tyers and Ravishankar, 2018) and Welsh (Heinecke and Tyers, 2019) treebanks by decomposing these into their constituent preposition and pronoun. Figure 2 shows the parse for sentence `aa_239` from the treebank: *S'treisht lhiam dy vel shiu braew* ("I hope that you are well"), in which the word *lhiam* has been decomposed into *lesh* "with" plus *mee* "me". Treating inflected prepositions in this way helps address ambiguities in some third person singular cases (e.g. *lesh* is also the inflected form meaning "with him"), and we hope it also makes it easier to learn syntactic generalizations since these prepositions behave like standard prepositional phrases.

Indirect objects do not occur in Irish or Scottish Gaelic, and, to the best of our knowledge, do not appear in traditional Manx texts either. There are examples of indirect objects in revived Manx, however, presumably under the influence of English. See Figure 3, which is a simplified version of sentence `aa_093` in the treebank.

Verbal nouns play an important role in all of the Celtic languages but particularly so in Manx. We follow the lead of Irish, Scottish Gaelic, and Welsh by tagging verbal nouns as NOUN and treating them syntactically as xcomp of the surrounding verb (in contrast with the Breton treebank which treats them as full-fledged verbs). Objects can come before or after the verbal noun in all three Gaelic languages, although there is a greater tendency for them to follow the verbal noun in Manx. An unusual feature of

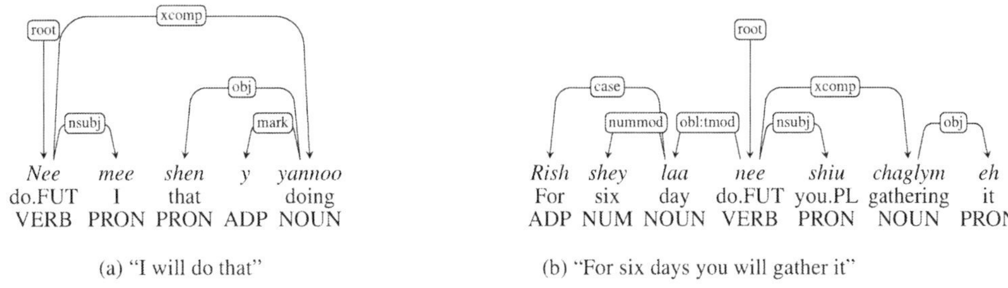

(a) "I will do that"   (b) "For six days you will gather it"

Figure 4: Examples of verbal nouns as xcomp of *jean*

Manx is the frequency with which verbal nouns are used together with the verb *jean* ("do", Ir. *déan*, Sc.G. *dèan*) to express past or future tense, where the other Gaelic languages would commonly use an inflected form of the verb itself. One sees this construction even with the verbal noun *jannoo* corresponding to *jean* itself, as in the first example in Figure 4. One consequence of this is a much higher overall frequency for the lemmas *jean* and *jannoo* in the Manx treebank (occurring once out of every 64 tokens on average) than for the corresponding lemmas in Irish or Scottish Gaelic (occurring once per 197 and 224 tokens, respectively).

4   Parsing Experiments

All of the experiments in this section make use of the latest version[6] of UDPipe (Straka and Straková, 2017) with the default settings (hidden layer size of 200 and the projective parsing algorithm).

We began by evaluating the UDPipe lemmatizer, POS tagger, and parser via 10-fold cross validation on the Manx treebank itself. In each iteration, 261 sentences were used for training and 30 sentences were used for testing; the same splits were preserved across the experiments. In the first set of experiments we evaluated on plain text input, which is to say we made no use of the gold standard tokens, lemmas, or POS tags. The F_1 scores and standard deviations over the ten splits are presented in Table 1, with the parser accuracy reported as both unlabeled (UAS) and labeled (LAS) attachment scores. The results are comparable to the corresponding scores for Irish and Scottish Gaelic, despite the much smaller size of our corpus. Since those treebanks are large enough to have a standard train/test split, we used those in place of 10-fold cross validation, obtaining UAS of 77.91 and LAS of 68.91 for Irish, and UAS of 71.55, LAS of 63.86 for Scottish Gaelic (again making no use of gold-standard inputs).

Model	Lemma	POS	UAS	LAS
Manx 10-fold cross validation	87.43	89.06	72.83	65.20
Manx 10-fold standard deviation	1.55	1.13	2.74	2.96

Table 1: Manx lemmatization, part-of-speech tagging, and dependency parsing evaluated on plain text input

In the second set of experiments, we again evaluated the parser via 10-fold cross validation, but this time we gave the tagger access to the gold-standard tokenization for making its predictions, and gave the parser access to the gold tokens, lemmas, and POS tags for making its predictions. Doing this allows a fairer comparison with the results of the delexicalized cross-lingual parsing experiments below. The F_1 scores and standard deviations are presented in the first two rows of Table 2. We ran the analogous experiments for Irish and Scottish Gaelic, again using the standard train/test splits, obtaining UAS of 80.57 and LAS of 73.71 for Irish, and UAS of 81.60, LAS of 76.90 for Scottish Gaelic.

Given the close relationship between the three Gaelic languages, we thought it worth exploring the possibility of cross-lingual parsing, particularly in this context of a severely under-resourced language

---

[6]The version on the master branch on GitHub as of 1 August 2020: `https://github.com/ufal/udpipe/commit/a2e2ffa24fc8d9c487073dfa17472699f8c59134`.

and its better-resourced neighbors. To this end, we trained delexicalized parsers on the Irish and Scottish Gaelic UD treebanks and evaluated those models directly on the Manx treebank by providing the gold-standard Manx POS tags as the input. The results are presented in the third and fourth rows of Table 2. The scores were poor in comparison with the monolingual 10-fold cross-validation, and indeed worse than comparable results for language pairs that one might expect to be more difficult; see, for example, (Agić et al., 2014; Aepli and Clematide, 2018), and notably (Tiedemann, 2015) which includes results for a delexicalized Irish model transferred to several other European languages.

Model	Lemma	POS	UAS	LAS
Manx 10-fold cross validation	90.40	92.19	82.61	76.29
Manx 10-fold standard deviation	1.22	1.11	1.82	2.30
Irish delexicalized	-	-	40.43	31.59
Scottish delexicalized	-	-	28.71	19.66

Table 2: Evaluation scores for Manx lemmatization, part-of-speech tagging, and dependency parsing using gold-standard inputs

5   Conclusion and Future Work

In §2 and §3, we presented a new corpus for Manx Gaelic annotated according to version 2 of the Universal Dependencies guidelines, and gave several examples where the grammar of Manx differed from Irish and Scottish Gaelic.

In the previous section, we evaluated a lemmatizer, tagger, and dependency parser trained on the Manx corpus, and obtained encouraging results. We also trained delexicalized cross-lingual models on the Irish and Scottish Gaelic treebanks, but their performance on Manx was relatively poor. These results, together with the relative ease with which we were able to annotate almost 300 sentences,[7] seem to argue in favor of under-resourced language groups investing energy primarily into monolingual treebank development. It remains to be seen whether the parsing scores can be improved by augmenting the Manx training data with trees obtained by other means, e.g. annotation projection (Yarowsky et al., 2001; Tyers et al., 2018), making use of some existing parallel texts between Irish and Manx. Unfortunately, there are no machine translation engines from Irish or Scottish Gaelic into Manx, so cross-lingual methods like those described by Tiedemann et al. (2014) are not available to us.

We also plan to continue adding to the treebank. All of the sentences in the initial release were annotated manually, but given the strong results above we should be able to accelerate development by post-editing the output of the UDPipe parser. We will also add morphological information to bring our treebank in line with the structure of the Irish and Scottish Gaelic versions.

Finally, we hope to develop a small trilingual parallel treebank with Irish and Scottish Gaelic consisting of sentences from the respective translations of *Alice in Wonderland* (the only substantial text available in all three languages, the Bible excluded), and through that work further harmonize the annotation guidelines across the Gaelic language family.

Acknowledgements

I created the treebank while visiting Acadamh na hOllscolaíochta Gaeilge in Carna, Co. na Gaillimhe as a Fulbright Scholar. All of the work was done during the COVID-19 lockdown in Ireland.

I am grateful to the staff at the Acadamh in Carna for their hospitality during my visit, to the Fulbright Program for the financial support which made it possible, and to Saint Louis University for a much-needed sabbatical leave.

Thanks to the anonymous reviewers for helpful comments and suggestions.

Finally, thanks to Teresa Lynn and Colin Batchelor for their invaluable work on the Irish and Scottish Gaelic treebanks, without which the present work would not have been possible.

---

[7] About three weeks for one annotator working full-time.

References

Noëmi Aepli and Simon Clematide. 2018. Parsing approaches for Swiss German. In *SwissText 2018*.

Željko Agić, Jörg Tiedemann, Kaja Dobrovoljc, Simon Krek, Danijela Merkler, and Sara Može. 2014. Cross-lingual dependency parsing of related languages with rich morphosyntactic tagsets. In *EMNLP 2014 Workshop on Language Technology for Closely Related Languages and Language Variants*.

Colin Batchelor. 2019. Universal dependencies for Scottish Gaelic: syntax. In *Proceedings of the Celtic Language Technology Workshop*, pages 7–15, Dublin.

Jennifer Draskau. 2008. *Practical Manx*. Liverpool University Press.

Johannes Heinecke and Francis M. Tyers. 2019. Development of a Universal Dependencies treebank for Welsh. In *Proceedings of the Celtic Language Technology Workshop*, pages 21–31, Dublin. European Association for Machine Translation.

Teresa Lynn and Jennifer Foster. 2016. Universal Dependencies for Irish. In *Proceedings of the 2nd Celtic Language Technology Workshop*, Paris.

Teresa Lynn, Jennifer Foster, and Mark Dras. 2017. Morphological features of the Irish Universal Dependency treebank. In *Proceedings of the 15th International Workshop on Treebanks and Linguistic Theories (TLT15)*, Bloomington, Indiana.

Joakim Nivre, Marie-Catherine de Marneffe, Filip Ginter, Yoav Goldberg, Jan Hajič, Christopher D. Manning, Ryan McDonald, Slav Petrov, Sampo Pyysalo, Natalia Silveira, et al. 2016. Universal Dependencies v1: A multilingual treebank collection. In *Proceedings of the Tenth International Conference on Language Resources and Evaluation (LREC'16)*, pages 1659–1666.

Joakim Nivre, Marie-Catherine de Marneffe, Filip Ginter, Jan Hajič, Christopher D. Manning, Sampo Pyysalo, Sebastian Schuster, Francis Tyers, and Daniel Zeman. 2020. Universal Dependencies v2: An evergrowing multilingual treebank collection. *arXiv preprint arXiv:2004.10643*.

Milan Straka and Jana Straková. 2017. Tokenizing, POS tagging, lemmatizing and parsing UD 2.0 with UDPipe. In *Proceedings of the CoNLL 2017 Shared Task: Multilingual Parsing from Raw Text to Universal Dependencies*, pages 88–99.

Jörg Tiedemann, Željko Agić, and Joakim Nivre. 2014. Treebank translation for cross-lingual parser induction. In *Eighteenth Conference on Computational Natural Language Learning (CoNLL 2014)*.

Jörg Tiedemann. 2015. Cross-lingual dependency parsing with Universal Dependencies and predicted PoS labels. In *Proceedings of the Third International Conference on Dependency Linguistics (Depling 2015)*, pages 340–349.

Francis M. Tyers and Vinit Ravishankar. 2018. A prototype dependency treebank for Breton. In *Actes de la conférence Traitement Automatique de la Langue-Naturelle, TALN*, volume 1, pages 197–204.

Francis Tyers, Mariya Sheyanova, Aleksandra Martynova, Pavel Stepachev, and Konstantin Vinogorodskiy. 2018. Multi-source synthetic treebank creation for improved cross-lingual dependency parsing. In *Proceedings of the Second Workshop on Universal Dependencies (UDW 2018)*, pages 144–150, Brussels, Belgium, November. Association for Computational Linguistics.

David Yarowsky, Grace Ngai, and Richard Wicentowski. 2001. Inducing multilingual text analysis tools via robust projection across aligned corpora. In *Proceedings of the first international conference on Human language technology research*, pages 1–8.

Variation in Universal Dependencies annotation: A token-based typological case study on adpossessive constructions

Kaius Sinnemäki
General linguistics
P.O. Box 24 (Unioninkatu 40)
00014 University of Helsinki
FINLAND
kaius.sinnemaki@helsinki.fi

Viljami Haakana
General linguistics
P.O. Box 24 (Unioninkatu 40)
00014 University of Helsinki
FINLAND
viljami.haakana@helsinki.fi

Abstract

In this paper we present a method for identifying and analyzing adnominal possessive constructions in 66 Universal Dependencies treebanks. We classify adpossessive constructions in terms of their morphological type (locus of marking) and present a workflow for detecting and analyzing them typologically. Based on a preliminary evaluation, the algorithm works fairly reliably in adpossessive constructions that are morphologically marked. However, it performs rather poorly in adpossessive constructions that are not marked morphologically, so-called zero-marked constructions, because of difficulties in identifying these constructions with the current annotation. We also discuss different types of variation in annotation in different treebanks for the same language and for treebanks of closely related languages. The research focuses on one well-circumscribed and universal construction in the hope of generating more interest in using UD for cross-linguistic comparison and for contributing towards developing yet more consistent annotation of constructions in the UD annotation scheme.

1 Introduction

Universal Dependencies (UD) and other multilingual language corpora have in many ways boosted cross-linguistic corpus research to a completely new level, enabling novel developments, for instance, in the so-called token-based typology (Levshina, 2019). One of the aims of UD is to provide universal annotations for various syntactic relations (called universal dependency relations in UD), parts-of-speech, and grammatical categories (features in UD), which then enable productive cross-linguistic comparison. However, the currently available universal dependency relations are what from a typological perspective could be described as higher-level functions, such as subject, object, nominal modifiers, and adjectival modifiers. In addition, the dependency relations are not consistently based on universal construction types, as observed and recommended by Croft et al. (2017), but often on language-specific strategies. For instance, nominal modifiers encompass constructions that have a wide range of functions in the world's languages, including possession, but it is not easy to compare them in the UD treebanks owing to variation in annotation across treebanks. Such variation has been noted earlier as well, in relation to research on linguistic complexity (Berdicevskis et al., 2018).

In this paper we focus on one well-defined and universal construction, namely adnominal possessives (also called adpossessive constructions or possessive noun phrases). Adpossessive constructions are syntactically noun phrases whose head is a noun and that may have a noun or a pronoun as a dependent modifier. Semantically the relation between the head and the dependent in these constructions expresses typically ownership (alienable possession), such as *my car*, part-whole relationships (including inalienable possession), such as *my hand*, and kinship relationships, such as *my daughter*. Syntactic adpossessive constructions can also be used for various other functions depending on each language (Koptjevskaja-Tamm, 2003; Haspelmath, 2017; Ortmann, 2018). In adpossessive constructions the syntactic **dependent** is semantically the possessor and the syntactic **head** is semantically the possessee. For

Proceedings of the Fourth Workshop on Universal Dependencies (UDW 2020), pages 158–167
Barcelona, Spain (Online), December 13, 2020

example, in the construction *my daughter* the syntactic head is the possessee *daughter* and the dependent is the possessor *my*.

We aim to research how these constructions can be identified in the UD treebanks. Our analyses are based on a sample of 63 treebanks from 44 languages that have a large corpus in the UD. The selected languages represent ten language families from Eurasia, Africa, and the Pacific (see Table 1). The treebanks were part of a shared task in the Interactive Workshop on Measuring Language Complexity (IWMLC), organized in September 2019 at the Freiburg Institute for Advanced Studies (FRIAS) in Freiburg, Germany. The treebanks were pre-selected by the workshop organizers and the analyses were based on Universal Dependencies (UD) 2.3 corpora (Nivre et al., 2018). Our work for identifying adpossessive constructions started in relation to that workshop, but the full results are published here for the first time. Our analyses, algorithms, and the full dataset are published as supplements in the hope of encouraging and enabling further development of universal annotations in the UD treebanks.[1]

Family	N	%
Afro-Asiatic	2	4.5
Austro-Asiatic	1	2.3
Austronesian	1	2.3
Basque	1	2.3
Indo-European	31	70.5
Japanese	1	2.3
Korean	1	2.3
Sino-Tibetan	1	2.3
Turkic	2	4.5
Uralic	3	6.8

Table 1: Distribution of sample languages.

In the following section, we discuss the process of identifying adpossessive constructions from the UD treebanks. In Section 3 we discuss several examples of variation in the UD annotation, followed by a short discussion and conclusions in Section 4.

2 Identifying and classifying adpossessive constructions

2.1 Preliminaries

In token-based typological research, constructions can ideally be identified using a small set of criteria across treebanks. For instance, the dependency relation `nsubj` identifies nominal subjects consistently in all UD treebanks. Further division into subjects of intransitive and transitive predicates is less straightforward to do but possible by identifying those clauses in which the predicate has a dependent with the dependency relation `obj`.

As for adpossessive constructions, the treebanks may optionally use the dependency relation `nmod:poss` (or `det:poss`). These relations are subtypes, which are not universally defined and their usage thus varies depending on language-specific criteria. In many treebanks, `nmod:poss` is used for distinguishing non-adpositional possessives from adpositional possessives. For instance, in the DDT treebank for Danish (see the example in Table 2), the subtype `nmod:poss` is used for non-adpositional possessives. In adpositional possessives, such as in the Danish *af* construction (Table 3), the dependency relation of the possessor is coded as `nmod`. Danish thus uses two types of adpossessive constructions and in the latter type it is necessary to identify the construction using information about the adposition, because the subtype `nmod:poss` is not used. Such practice results in a wider range of annotations compared to, for instance, the identification of the nominal subject and object. Note that in some treebanks, such as the CRB treebank for Bambara (not in our sample), the relation `nmod:poss` is used for

---

[1] The supplements are available at <https://version.helsinki.fi/gramadapt/udw2020-adpossessive-constructions>. Note that since our purpose is to identify adpossessive constructions, the algorithms are aimed for that purpose and not, for instance, for fixing UD annotations.

both adpositional and non-adpositional possessives. This would be recommendable for other treebanks as well, because adpositional possessives can be distinguished from non-adpositional possessives in any case by using the possessive adposition as a separate criterion.

N	Wordform	Lemma	UPOS	Features	Head	Dependency
23	i	i	ADP	AdpType=Prep	25	case
24	Camillas	Camilla	PROPN	Case=Gen	25	nmod:poss
25	sofa	sofa	NOUN	Definite=Ind|Gender=Com|Number=Sing	22	nmod

Table 2: An adpossessive construction in the Danish treebank DDT (sent_id = dev-268; excluding some columns).

N	Wordform	Lemma	UPOS	Features	Head	Dependency
16	i	i	ADP	AdpType=Prep	17	case
17	form	form	NOUN	Definite=Ind|Gender=Com|Number=Sing	7	obl
18	af	af	ADP	AdpType=Prep	19	case
19	udgifter	udgift	NOUN	Definite=Ind|Gender=Com|Number=Plur	17	nmod

Table 3: An adpositional adpossessive construction in the Danish treebank DDT (sent_id = dev-100; excluding some columns).

2.2 Locus of marking

As implied by the discussion of the Danish *af* construction, it may not be possible to identify adpossessive constructions without information about how the dependency relation between the head and the dependent in these constructions is marked morphologically. In cross-linguistic research the morphological typology of this relation is called locus of marking (Nichols, 1992). Locus of marking refers to the position of morphological marking of syntactic relations (or dependencies) in a construction. There are four logical loci for morphological marking, illustrated here for adpossessive constructions: it occurs either on the head of the construction (the possessed in possessive NP) as in (1a), the dependent of the construction (the possessor) as in (1b), on both (called double marking) as in (1c), or on neither (called zero marking) as in (1d).[2]

(1)   a. Head marking (Indonesian, Austronesian; (Sneddon, 1996, 146))

        ibu-nya   Suparjo
        mother-3SG.POSS Suparjo

        'Suparjo's mother'

    b. Dependent marking (Swedish, Germanic, Indo-European)

        min   bok
        1SG.POSS book

        'My book' (Swedish)

    c. Double marking (Finnish, Finnic, Uralic)

        häne-n   pyörä-nsä
        3SG-GEN bike-3POSS

        'his bike'

    d. Zero-marking (Indonesian, Austronesian; (Sneddon, 1996, 144))

        rumah Tomo
        house Tomo

        'Tomo's house'

---

[2]We exclude a fifth type called floating marking, which is cross-linguistically rare.

Locus of marking may vary across constructions even within the same language and certainly across languages. This means that one language may have several different types of adpossessive constructions depending on the particular language-specific strategies of marking the dependency relation (e.g., genitive case, adpositions, and possessive suffixes) as well as on their locus of marking. In the absence of systematic and universal annotation for adpossessive constructions, their identification process is essentially driven by identifying treebank-specific morphological strategies and their loci from the corpora (Croft et al., 2017). That process is very similar to the regular work that typologists practice in crosslinguistic comparison.

2.3 Workflow

Typological research starts by defining the object of research, called comparative concepts by Haspelmath (2010), in such a way that similar constructions can be identified and compared in the sample languages. Constructions and patterns in particular languages are then analyzed in relation to the comparative concept and classified to different types. This is what we did for identifying adpossessive constructions in the UD treebanks. We define adpossessive constructions by using both morphosyntactic and semantic criteria. Semantically adpossessive constructions express a possessive relationship, such as ownership, kinship relation, or part-whole relationship; morphosyntactically they are noun phrases (sometimes single nouns) whose syntactic head noun functions as a possessee and that may also be modified by a noun or a bound form that functions as a possessor (Koptjevskaja-Tamm, 2003; Haspelmath, 2017).[3] When identifying adpossessive constructions in the UD treebanks, our workflow was roughly as described schematically in Figure 1.

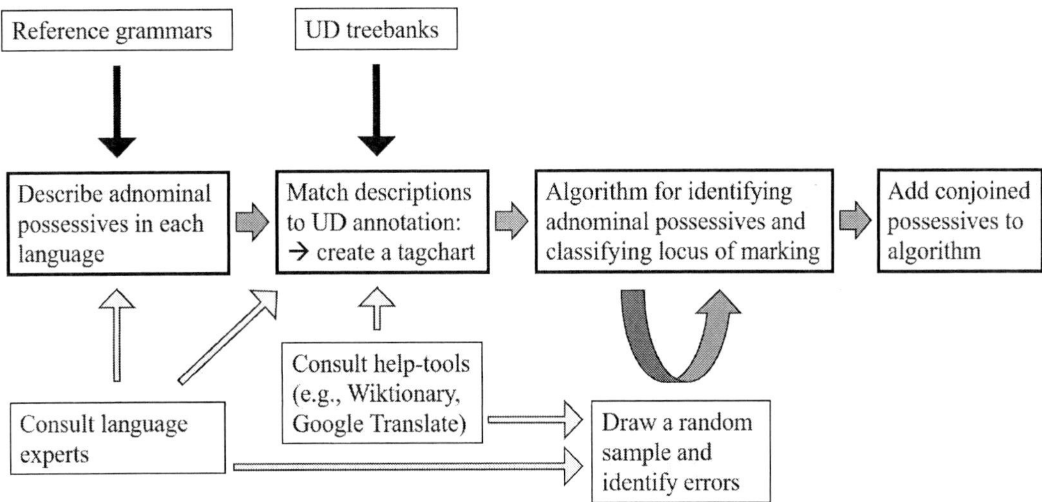

Figure 1: Workflow for identifying adpossessive constructions.

First, we used reference grammars, such as Schmidt (1999) on Urdu, to describe how adpossessive constructions are marked in the sample languages. The reference sources that we used are listed at the end of Supplement S1. Next we matched these descriptions to the annotation of adnominal possessives in the UD treebanks. For the majority of treebanks (45 out of 63) it was possible to create a tagchart of the treebank-specific annotations for identifying adnominal possessives in their various forms. Table 3 lists the 22 UD tags used in the tagchart. In addition to these tags, dozens of individual constructions were identified by comparing the lemmas and surface forms to one another. For the first two steps in the workflow we consulted language experts as well as online tools, such as Wiktionary and Google Translate, to help us determine how adpossessive constructions are annotated in the UD. Third, we wrote Python

---

[3]Note that we use a somewhat broader definition of possessive relationship than e.g. Koptjevskaja-Tamm (2003) and Haspelmath (2017), who delimit possessive relationship only to ownership, kinship relation, and part-whole relationship.

algorithms to detect each individual adpossessive construction in the 63 treebanks. For 18 treebanks we created separate algorithms because they were impossible to analyze by merely listing a set of required annotations in a tagchart. Supplement S2 contains the tagchart, the Python algorithms, and some other files involved in the computational analysis. Fourth, we randomly selected a few dozen sentences containing adnominal possessives from each treebank, detected errors in the analysis, doublechekced that the identified constructions expressed a possessive relationship, and updated the algorithm accordingly. Emphasis was on updating and correcting the algorithm rather than producing evaluative data on its performance. Fifth, we classified locus of marking for each individual adpossessive construction. This step was done largely in parallel with step three. As the last step, the algorithm was updated to include conjoined possessors where possible. The output of this process is a dataset (Supplement S3) that contains information about each individual adpossessive construction that we identified and classified. The analyzed UD treebanks (the `CoNLL-U` files) are available at the website of the IWMLC workshop.[4] Our analyses follow the principles of late aggregation in the spirit of Levshina (2019) and Zakharko et al. (2017), which enables researching language-internal variation at the level of each individual dependency relation without needlessly aggregating the data in different ways.

We delimited the analysis of adpossessive constructions in a few important ways. First, we focus on constructions in which the possessed is a full noun, that is, either a common noun (POS tag `NOUN` or a proper noun (POS-tags `PROPN`). Second, we focus on constructions in which the possessor is a personal possessive pronoun (e.g., feature `PronType=Prs`), a common noun, a proper noun, or a possessive adjective (as in many Slavic languages). However, we generally exclude demonstrative and other pronouns as possessors. Third, we define head/dependent marking as any morphological marking on the head or the dependent, be it via affixes, tones, morphophonological alternations, clitics, or independent function words (Bickel and Nichols, 2007). In the UD annotation the morphological marking is identifiable from the feature annotation and from the use of separate function words, such as particles and adpositions, for modifying the possessor. Relevant annotations include features such as `Case=Gen` and `Poss=Yes` for identifying dependent marking and layered features, such as `psor` for identifying head marking (see Table 4). In addition, we used information about particles and adpositions that mark the possessor as the dependent of the adpossessive construction (see Table 1).

Type of annotation	Tags
Parts-of-speech tags	ADJ, ADP, DET, NOUN, PART, PRON, PROPN
Feature annotations	Case, Number, Person, Poss, PronType, psor, Reflex
Dependency relations	amod, case, case:gen, det, det:poss, nmod, nmod:att, nmod:poss, nmod:gobj, nmod:gsubj

Table 4: UD annotations used in the identification and classification of adpossessive constructions.

2.4 Zero marked adpossessives

Adpossessive constructions with zero marking were probably the most difficult ones to identify and we expect most of the unresolved issues to concern this type. The most important reason for this was that in many languages it was necessary to use annotation about morphological marking to identify adpossessive constructions to begin with. As a result, zero-marked constructions were sometimes practically impossible to detect reliably. For instance, in adpossessive constructions in Vietnamese the dependency relation is marked with a possessive preposition (Thompson, 1965). However, this preposition is optional in some contexts, leading to zero marked adpossessive constructions. Yet it was difficult to identify adpossessive constructions reliably without recourse to the possessive preposition, because that would have meant classifying all noun-noun juxtapositions as adnominal possessives, which seemed to result in many false positives. For this reason, in the Vietnamese treebank we could sift only dependent marked adpossessive constructions (with noun possessors) but not zero marked ones.

For research in token-based typology zero-marked adnominal possessives are, however, theoretically very interesting at least for two reasons. For one, in many languages the dependency relation in in-

---

[4]The selected UD treebanks can be accessed at <`http://www.christianbentz.de/MLC2019/UDtrack.zip`>.

alienable possessives is morphologically zero marked but in alienable possessives it tends to be overtly marked. While there is ongoing debate about the reasons for this typological distribution, frequency and predictability may be among the strongest factors causing it (Haspelmath, 2017). In addition, from the perspective of linguistic efficiency it would be natural to hypothesize that zero marking would be preferred only when the head and the dependent are adjacent to one another and that the probability of morphological marking would increase as a function of dependency length (Gibson et al., 2019). These issues are exactly what multilingual annotated corpora, such as UD, are excellent tools for, but only to the extent they provide the sufficient means for reliably identifying the relevant constructions across treebanks. This is something that seems currently problematic especially for zero marked adpossessive constructions.[5]

3   Results

Our algorithm identified altogether 724 694 adpossessive constructions in the data. The distribution of different morphological types across sample languages are presented in Figure 2 as percent shares. Dependent marking is clearly a dominating pattern overall. It occurs in all but four languages, occurs with at least 65% share in 39 languages, and is the only type in 18 languages. This strong domination of dependent marking is an areal feature. Head and dependent marking in adpossessive constructions are fairly evenly distributed in the world's languages, but dependent marking dominates in Eurasia and Africa and head marking in the Americas (Nichols and Bickel, 2013). In our data head marking is a relatively minor type, occurring only in six languages, but where it occurs it is a dominating pattern (in five languages with 65% share or more). These figures for head and dependent marking clearly reflect the fact that languages of Eurasia are overrepresented in the sample. Double marking is a rare and minor type occurring in only three languages (Finnish, Turkish, and Uyghur) and only as a minor type in each of them (with less than 20% shares in each). Zero marking, on the other hand, is a common pattern, occurring in 23 sample languages (52% of languages); however, it is only a minor pattern in most of these languages, being fairly common only in Indonesian and Estonian. In addition, zero marking seems to occur in languages that have also dependent marking, but in this sample this is clearly a side-effect of dependent marking dominating in adpossessive constructions overall.

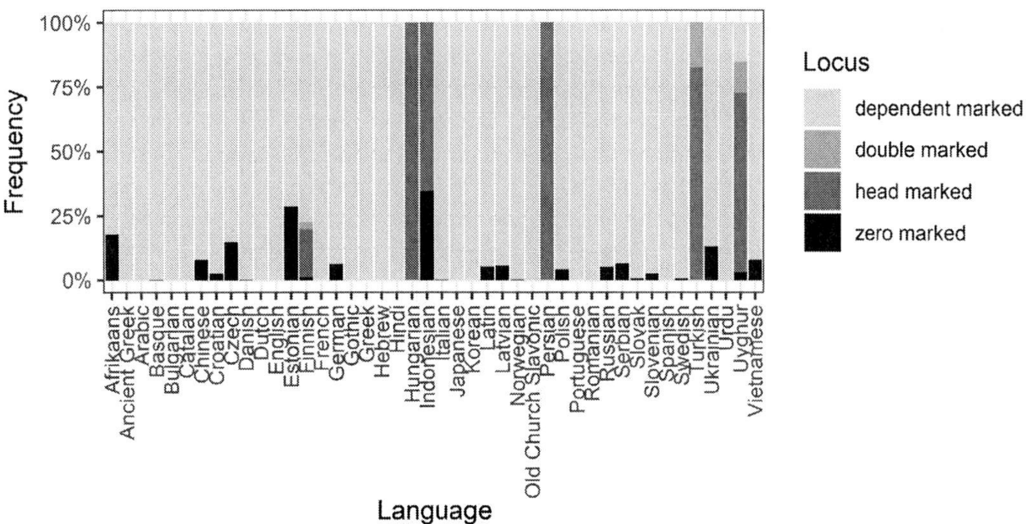

Figure 2: Distribution of morphological types in adpossessive constructions.

<hr>

[5]Our dataset contains information also about length of dependency between the head and the dependent as well as their word order, as these were straightforward to compute and will increase the usefulness of the dataset in future research. Within the limited scope of this paper it is not possible to report on any results concerning these additional features.

Overall the process for identifying adpossessive constructions in the sampled treebanks required us to define up to 1,000 tags (on average 14 per treebank), including POS tags, specific features, dependency relations, and lemmas for pronouns and adpositions in several cases. Figure 3 presents a boxplot of how many tags were needed to identify adpossessive constructions in the treebanks, grouped into language families.[6] This figure represents only those languages included in the tagchart. The boxplot suggests that languages in most families required roughly 10-15 tags, in a few languages around 20 tags, and in the Turkic family more than 30 tags. This variation may reflect real diversity in adpossessive constructions in these language families, but it may at least in part reflect also the variation in the annotation of adpossessive constructions in the treebanks, suggesting potential places of concern in terms of annotation consistency.

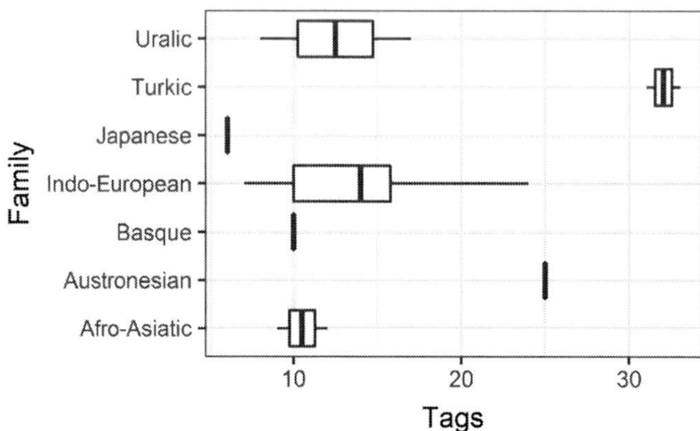

Figure 3: Number of tags needed in each language family for identifying adpossessive constructions.

It was not possible to estimate automatically the performance of the algorithm, including the range and incidence of false positives and negatives. The main reason for this is that there is no gold standard available, which precludes comparing our results against such benchmark. Whether such a benchmark will be reached in the future is an open question. However, to achieve at least a very preliminary and crude idea of the algorithm's performance, we manually analyzed a few dozen adpossessive constructions in four languages from four different language families. The results of this evaluation are presented in Table 5. Recall and precision of the algorithm were quite high in Afrikaans, Finnish, and Turkish (both ¿ 0.9). In these languages there were no false positives and only a handful of false negatives. In Indonesian, precision was 0.92, but recall was only 0.34, mostly due to a high number of false negatives. The algorithm for Indonesian currently fails to detect zero marked adpossessive constructions adequately: all false positives and negatives are of this type. This is no wonder, since a range of different functions (apparently at least `det`, `obj`, and `compound`) seem to be used for zero-marked possessors in the Indonesian GSD treebank, and it is not very clear to us whether any of these functions are systematically used for this construction. Overall, it seems that morphologically overtly marked adpossessive constructions can already be fairly reliably identified despite language-specific variation. More effort is needed to identify zero-marked adpossessive constructions in an equally reliable way.

Language	Recall	Precision	False positives	False negatives	Adpossessive constructions	Sentences
Afrikaans	0.96	0.92	0	2	52	30
Finnish	0.97	1.00	0	1	32	40
Indonesian	0.34	0.92	3	23	35	53
Turkish	0.94	1.00	0	2	33	30

Table 5: Evaluation of algorithm performance.

[6]The package `ggplot2` (Wickham, 2016) was used for graphics and statistics in the R environment (R Core Team, 2020).

The detailed linguistic analysis involved in identifying adpossessive constructions from the UD treebanks led to noting some unexpected variation in annotations, some of which we describe here. One issue concerns the differential treatment of clitics. For instance, in the English treebanks, the possessive clitic *'s* is analyzed as a separate token on its own. In Korean, the possessor is marked with the possessive clitic *-uy*, but in the Korean treebanks this clitic is analyzed neither as a separate token nor is its morphological category annotated in the features. We identified this clitic as the last element of the lemma, and analyzed all adpossessive constructions as dependent marked. In the Korean GSD treebank this clitic is marked in the language-specific POS as JKG and in the Korean Kaist treebank in the language-specific POS as jcm, so its identification could have been done in different ways. Another issue concerned Persian, in which the possessive relation is marked on the head via the so-called ezafe construction. However, ezafe is usually not at all marked in written language, and therefore it is not visible in the Persian Seraji treebank at all. We thus assumed that all identified adpossessive constructions had also the ezafe and they were accordingly classified as head marked.

Sometimes different treebanks for the same language varied a lot in their logic for annotation. As an example, in the ITTB treebank for Latin the POS of possessive pronouns is ADJ, its features contain Poss=Yes, and its dependency relation is amod or nmod. In the PROIEL treebank for Latin, on the other hand, the POS of possessive pronouns is PRON, its identifying features contain Case=Gen and PronType=Prs, and its dependency relation is det. Possessive pronouns in the Latin treebanks are thus identified with different tags on all three major criteria that we used (POS, features, dependencies).

There was variation also between treebanks for closely related languages. As an example, Slavic languages have two distinct adpossessive constructions, the possessive genitive and the possessive adjective constructions. In the majority of the sampled Slavic treebanks, the POS of the possessor is ADJ, its features contain Poss=Yes, and its dependency relation is amod. However, in the SNK treebank for Slovak, possessive adjectives cannot be identified and distinguished from other adjectives, because they are not tagged with the feature Poss=Yes. In other words, all possessive adjectives were unnoticed by our algorithm for Slovak.

Syncretism is another cause of variation in the treebanks. Because it was important for us to try detecting zero marking, for instance, via detecting absence of case distinctions, syncretism caused some issues with analyzing locus of marking. Table 6 presents an illustrative example from the German GSD treebank. Like many German nouns, the word *Region* does not inflect for case at all. However, according to the feature annotation *Region* is in the genitive case and thus using the feature Case=Gen as an identifying tag would have resulted in analyzing *Region* as dependent marked. On the other hand, because the article inflects for case, analyzing this construction as dependent marked would have been correct in any case. The example illustrates the fact that the annotated features do not necessarily reflect the surface structures but more abstract structures. One solution to syncretism would be to synthesize UD with Unimorph, which does address syncretism (McCarthy et al., 2017).

N	wordform	lemma	UPOS	features	head	dependency
8	der	der	DET	Case=Gen|Definite=Def|Gender=Fem|Number=Sing|PronType=Art	9	det
9	Region	Region	NOUN	Case=Gen|Gender=Fem|Number=Sing	7	nmod

Table 6: Example of an adpossessive construction in the German GSD treebank (sent_id = dev-s15); excluding unnecessary columns.

When determining whether the construction was zero marked we often compared the lemma of the possessor's form directly with its surface form. If the two forms were identical, we analyzed the adpossessive construction zero marked, otherwise as dependent (or double marked). However, because the difference between the lemma and the surface form may depend on many other features besides e.g. case marking, we limited the lemma comparisons to contexts in which the other features were identical. In other words we excluded comparing genitive plural and nominative singular when they were identical and different from nominative plural, for instance, and compared the case-inflected forms only in the singular.

The UD annotations sometimes have tags that do not reflect the word form in itself. These examples are probably very rare, but still worth mentioning. Consider the first two words of the sentence `b204.33` in the Finnish TDT treebank: *Meidän suhde* 'our relationship'. In Standard Finnish the head of this adpossessive construction has a possessive suffix, resulting in the word form *suhteemme* instead of the base form *suhde* which occurs in colloquial usage. However, the features for this word contained `Number[psor]=Plur` and `Person[psor]=1`, which represent the standard form with the possessive suffix. Such examples from colloquial usage are probably so difficult and inefficient to detect systematically that their existence in the treebanks have to be accepted.

4 Discussion and conclusion

Our analyses suggest that there are different types of variations in how adpossessive constructions are annotated across UD treebanks. To some extent this is expected because languages sometimes have several different morphosyntactic ways for expressing adnominal possession and across languages this diversity is multiplied. On the other hand, adnominal possession is a prominent and universal syntactic construction in the languages of the world, and reducing unnecessary variation in annotation would enable more efficient identification of these constructions by linguists and language technologists.

Given the variation in annotation it is natural that our method for identifying adpossessive constructions contained both false positives and false negatives, as even the limited evaluation suggested. False negatives were rare and they seem structurally quite similar with adpossessive constructions albeit expressing some other function which is difficult to delineate from adpossessive constructions based on the current annotation. False negatives, on the other hand, result largely from errors in the algorithm, from our insufficient knowledge of the languages and treebanks, and from problems with the current annotation of the treebanks, as discussed in relation to zero marking in Indonesian and Vietnamese. A further challenge, for instance, in Vietnamese, is possessive classifiers (Hui, 2005), but since we did not have sufficient knowledge about this type of construction, we did not even try detecting them. Overall, since in many languages morphological annotation had to be used for identifying adpossessive constructions, it is possible that in quite many languages potential zero-marked adpossessive constructions went unnoticed.

The success and usefulness of UD and other multilingual language corpora rest largely on their annotation schemes. In this paper we have reported on a typological case study of identifying and analyzing adpossessive constructions in 63 UD treebanks. This construction represent much variation in annotation even in different treebanks of the same language and in treebanks of closely related languages. In line with earlier research (Berdicevskis et al., 2018), our results suggest that there are some limitations to the extent which UD can currently be used for cross-linguistic research, especially concerning zero-marked constructions; however, the results also indicate that for morphologically marked adpossessive constructions, UD can currently be used quite reliably for token-based typological research.

Acknowledgements

We are grateful to the following people for help with linguistic analyses: Çağrı Çöltekin (Turkish), Sonja Dahlgren (Ancient Greek), Andrei Dumitrescu (Romanian), Yoonmi Oh (Korean), Marja Vierros (Ancient Greek), and Max Wahlström (Old Church Slavonic). All remaining errors are our own. We thank Miikka Silfverberg for help with UD-related technical issues and Jarmo Niemelä for help with technical issues related to ortographies using LaTeX. Some earlier parts of this research were presented at the Interactive Workshop Measuring Language Complexity (IWMLC), in Freiburg in September 2019 and at the Helsinki Area and Language Studies seminar in Helsinki in February 2020; we are grateful for the organizers of these workshops for having invited us, and for the participants for useful comments. This project has received funding from the European Research Council (ERC) under the European Union's Horizon 2020 research and innovation programme (grant agreement No 805371).

References

Aleksandrs Berdicevskis, Çağrı Çöltekin, Katharina Ehret, Kilu von Prince, Daniel Ross, Bill Thompson, Chunxiao Yan, Vera Demberg, Gary Lupyan, Taraka Rama, and Christian Bentz. 2018. Using Universal Dependencies in cross-linguistic complexity research. In *Proceedings of the Second Workshop on Universal Dependencies (UDW 2018)*, pages 8–17, Brussels, Belgium.

Balthasar Bickel and Johanna Nichols. 2007. Inflectional morphology. In Timothy Shopen (ed.) *Language Typology and Syntactic Description 3*, pages 169–240, Cambridge University Press, Cambridge.

William Croft, Dawn Nordquist, Katherine Looney, and Michael Regan. 2017. Linguistic Typology meets Universal Dependencies. In *Proceedings of the 15th International Workshop on Treebanks and Linguistic Theories (TLT15)*, pages 63–75, Bloomington, IN, USA.

Edward Gibson, Richard Futrell, Steven P. Piantadosi, Isabelle Dautriche, Kyle Mahowald, Leon Bergen, and Roger Levy. 2019. How efficiency shapes human language. *Trends in Cognitive Sciences*, 23(5):389–407.

Martin Haspelmath. 2010. Comparative concepts and descriptive categories in crosslinguistic studies. *Language*, 86(3):663–687.

Martin Haspelmath. 2017. Explaining alienability contrasts in adpossessive constructions: Predictability vs. iconicity. *Zeitschrift für Sprachwissenschaft*, 36(2):193–231.

Sim Sook Hui. 2005. The Semantics and Grammar of Vietnamese Classifiers. MA Thesis, National University of Singapore.

Maria Koptjevskaja-Tamm. 2003. Possessive noun phrases in the languages of Europe. In Frans Planck (ed.) *Noun phrase structure in the languages of Europe*, pages 621–722, Mouton de Gruyter, Berlin.

Natalia Levshina. 2019. Token-based typology and word order entropy: A study based on Universal Dependencies. *Linguistic Typology*, 23(3):533–572.

Arya D. McCarthy, Miikka Silfverberg, Ryan Cotterell, Mans Hulden, and David Yarowsky. 2018. Marrying Universal Dependencies and Universal Morphology. In *Proceedings of the Second Workshop on Universal Dependencies (UDW 2018)*, pages 91–101, Brussels, Belgium.

Johanna Nichols. 1992. *Linguistic Diversity in Space and Time*. University of Chicago Press, Chicago, IL.

Johanna Nichols and Balthasar Bickel. 2013. Locus of marking in possessive noun phrases. In Matthew S. Dryer and Martin Haspelmath (eds.) *The World Atlas of Language Structures Online*. Max Planck Institute for Evolutionary Anthropology, Leipzig. Available online at http://wals.info/chapter/24.

Joakim Nivre, Mitchell Abrams, Željko Agić, et al. 2018. Universal Dependencies 2.3. LINDAT/CLARIAH-CZ digital library at the Institute of Formal and Applied Linguistics (ÚFAL), Faculty of Mathematics and Physics, Charles University. http://hdl.handle.net/11234/1-2895.

Albert Ortmann. 2018. Connecting the typology and semantics of nominal possession: alienability splits and the morphology–semantics interface. *Morphology*, 28(1):99–144.

R Core Team. 2020. R: A language and environment for statistical computing. R foundation for statistical computing, Vienna, Austria. Available at https://www.R-project.org.

Ruth Laila Schmidt. 1999. *Urdu: An Essential Grammar*. Routledge, London.

James N. Sneddon. 1996. *Indonesian: A Comprehensive Grammar*. Routledge, London.

Laurence C. Thompson. 1965. *A Vietnamese Grammar*. University of Washington Press, Seattle, WA.

Taras Zakharko, Alena Witzlack-Makerevich, Johanna Nichols, and Balthasar Bickel. 2017. Late aggregation as a design principle for typological databases. ALT Workshop on Design Principles of Typological Databases, 15 December 2017.

Hadley Wickham. 2016. *ggplot2: Elegant Graphics for Data Analysis*. Springer-Verlag, New York, NY.

PALMYRA 2.0: A Configurable Multilingual Platform Independent Tool for Morphology and Syntax Annotation

Dima Taji and **Nizar Habash**

Computational Approaches to Modeling Language (CAMeL) Lab

New York University Abu Dhabi, UAE

`{dima.taji,nizar.habash}@nyu.edu`

Abstract

We present PALMYRA 2.0, a graphical dependency-tree visualization and editing software. PALMYRA 2.0 is designed to be highly configurable to any dependency parsing representation, and to enable the annotation of a multitude of linguistic features. It uses an intuitive interface that relies on drag-and-drop utilities as well as pop-up menus and keyboard shortcuts that can be easily specified.

1 Introduction

The development of treebanks is central to research on automatic syntactic and morphological analysis. Treebanks can vary based on the syntactic representations they are in, and the languages they encode. There is a large number of syntactic representations that vary in terms of linguistic theories underlying them, and in terms of their file formats. The Universal Dependency (UD) representation (Nivre et al., 2016) aims to be applicable in all languages. UD is currently one of the most popular representations being available in 90 languages, but many other treebanks are designed for a limited number of languages. The Penn Treebank (PTB) (Marcus et al., 1993) is the most used representation for constituency treebanks, and it is available in a number of different languages including English (Marcus et al., 1993), Arabic (Maamouri et al., 2003), and Chinese (Xue et al., 2005). The Prague Dependency Treebank (PDT) (Böhmová et al., 2003) is another representation used to annotate treebanks in Czech (Böhmová et al., 2003) as well as Arabic (Hajič et al., 2004).

The annotation of syntactic trees with morphological features, especially for morphologically rich languages, is often done in a cascading manner: text is annotated first for morphology then for syntax. This method of annotation can have errors cascading from one level of annotation to the other. Having the annotation done in tandem, or at least having the morphological features displayed and editable when annotating syntax, will allow annotators to look at the annotations in a different light, bringing to their attention different readings that may have been missed otherwise.

The richness of a language's morphology is not necessarily related to the richness of its treebank representation. Arabic, for example, is a very morphologically rich language, and it has different treebanks, with different representations. The Penn Arabic Treebank (PATB) (Maamouri et al., 2003) uses a constituency representation that is rich in morphological features. The Columbia Arabic Treebank (CATiB) (Habash and Roth, 2009), on the other hand, is a dependency representation with poor morphology. The designers of CATiB claimed that the simplified morphology was intended among other choices to speed annotation up. This motivated us to create a tool that is configurable and can work for multiple languages and morphosyntactic representations.

The existence of these varying treebanks and different approaches to annotation naturally raise the need for a tool that can be used with the different representation schemes and languages. We sum up our desiderata for such a tool as follows:

- A tool that is platform independent and requires no special installation.
- A tool that is lightweight and can be used offline.

Proceedings of the Fourth Workshop on Universal Dependencies (UDW 2020), pages 168–177

Barcelona, Spain (Online), December 13, 2020

- A tool that is open-source.
- A tool that is intuitive to use and requires minimal training.
- A tool that allows the text of the trees to be easily displayed and searched.
- A tool that can be used at any point in the annotation process.
- A tool that supports morphologically rich languages.
- A tool that is usable with various syntactic representations.
- A tool that is usable with various linguistic features.

In our previous work describing the creation of PALMYRA (Javed et al., 2018) (henceforth, PALMYRA 1.0), we addressed platform independence by building a web-based dependency syntax annotation tool that did not require any installation. PALMYRA 1.0 uses an intuitive drag-and-drop interface, and has the options of annotating using both buttons and shortcut keys. PALMYRA 1.0's most important feature is the ease of fixing tokenization errors caused by morphological analyzers or syntactic parsers, by allowing users to easily split and merge nodes in the displayed trees.

In the new iteration of PALMYRA (henceforth, PALMYRA 2.0),[1] we extend the tool's ability to be used with varying syntactic representations and linguistics features through the introduction of an adaptable configuration file. PALMYRA 2.0 can be configured to support annotations that go beyond POS tags and syntactic relations, and extend to other linguistic features such as morphological features.

When building PALMYRA 2.0 we only focused on syntactic dependency representations, but we imagine many of its design elements can be expanded to constituency trees.

We discuss some related work in Section 2. We then present our design specifications (Section 3), user interface (Section 4), and the configuration setup (Section 5).

2 Related Work

Many annotation tools have been created in the context of all the work done on syntactic parsing and morphological analysis. Most tools are designed for one type of annotation only, and have limited configurations. In this section, we review previous work that was done on developing tools for linguistic annotation, specifically syntactic annotation as well as joint syntax and morphology annotation. While the tools we present here all have great features, some features that we consider key for ease of annotation are also lacking.

Morphological Annotation Tools A few tools exist to carry out morphological annotations. CorA (Bollmann et al., 2014) is an annotation tool for 'non-standard' language texts in German that has options for normalization, lemmatization, and morphological tagging. DIWAN (Al-Shargi and Rambow, 2015) and MADARi (Obeid et al., 2018) are morphological annotation interfaces designed specifically for Arabic text. Wasim (Alosaimy and Atwell, 2018) is a web-based tool for morphological annotation of inflectional languages that has some support for editing tokenization. None of these tools can be used to annotate for features that are beyond the ones they are initially designed for.

Syntactic Annotation Tools The best known tool for dependency treebank creation is TrEd (Pajas, 2008), which is a graph visualization and manipulation program written in Perl. Although it can be configured to automate frequently repeated operations, TrEd does not have a simple option for word tokenization, and can be difficult to install and learn. EasyTree (Little and Tratz, 2016) is a light-weight tool designed to annotate dependency trees in browsers. It does not maintain sentence order of nodes, and it has no functionality for editing word tokenization. However, EasyTree is very intuitive to use, and it is the base on which PALMYRA is built. EasyTree's successor, CrowdTree (Tratz and Phan, 2018), is designed to support human-in-the-loop methods as well as crowdsourcing, using a TrEd-inspired interface. It has a backend servlet that can train a parsing model during the annotation process, which helps produce automatic annotations for the annotators to start from. However, CrowdTree does not support the annotation of any other linguistic features, or word tokenization.

---

[1] We use the term PALMYRA to refer to the tool generically; and only specify the version number when discussing version-specific features.

Joint Morphology and Syntax Annotation Tools   BRAT (Stenetorp et al., 2012) is a web-based annotation tool that focuses on collaborative annotation. One of the features of BRAT is that it is not limited to one kind of annotation. It can be used to annotate syntax, event extraction, named entity detection, and coreference resolution, to mention a few. However, BRAT requires users to login to be able to annotate their text online, and it does not allow for web-based configuration of tag sets, and it does not support word tokenization. Another web-based tool is WebAnno (de Castilho et al., 2016) which allows the annotation of various layers of linguistic annotations, including semantic and syntactic annotations. But similar to BRAT, WebAnno does not support word tokenization. Finally, ConlluEditor (Heinecke, 2019) is an editor designed with UD in mind, allowing for the editing of syntactic information, as well as morphological features. It supports word tokenization editing, and displays multi-word tokens, empty nodes, and enhanced dependencies. However, ConlluEditor requires installation and a server setup.

3   Design Specifications

In this section, we discuss the key decisions that we followed in designing PALMYRA 2.0. We are aware that there are various specification that are desirable by different annotators, such as user management, automatic parsing, and inter-annotator agreement reports. However, there is a tradeoff between having those features and having a lightweight and fast tool that can run offline, which we prioritized.

Design and Implementation   PALMYRA is a platform independent open-source software[2] that is written entirely in JavaScript, HTML, and CSS. This makes it usable with modern browsers without the need of any installation or setup.[3]

Input File   The most commonly used format for dependency parsing currently is the CoNLL-U format, a revised version of CoNLL-X (Buchholz and Marsi, 2006), that was made popular for its use in UD (Nivre et al., 2016). Because we want PALMYRA 2.0 to be usable by people annotating in different dependency representations, we decided to adopt this well established format for our files. Furthermore, PALMYRA 2.0 can be used to display any languages that can be encoded in Unicode.

Entries in CoNLL-U files have ten columns that correspond to the following fields: ID, form, lemma, POS, XPOS, features, parent, relation, enhanced dependency, and miscellaneous. The POS field is what is used to populate the tree with POS tags. The XPOS field, if specified in the configuration files, can be edited alongside the morphological features.

Figure 1 shows two trees from different representations, in the same CoNLL-U file format. We decided to go with an example in Arabic, a morphologically rich language, for two reasons. First, we want to illustrate the usability of PALMYRA 2.0 with different representations, in this case CATiB (Figure 1 (a)) and UD (Figure 1 (b)). And secondly, we want to demonstrate a use case that requires word tokenization and rich morphological features as part of creating syntactic trees: in Figure 1, see tokens 1, 8 and 11 which are proclitics, and the many features in column 6.

In the current version of PALMYRA 2.0, the CoNLL-U enhanced dependency field and the miscellaneous field are not used in the visualization of the tree, and are not editable through the interface. However, if they appear in the input file, they will be saved by the tool and written in the output file. Multi-token words and hidden nodes are not supported in the current version. Comments in the CoNLL-U format are stored and written to the output file. However, we currently do not allow editing them. We plan to do these extensions in the future.

Output Files   PALMYRA 2.0's main output is in the same CoNLL-U format as the input files. It also give the option of downloading the trees as PNG images.

Configuration File   PALMYRA 2.0 uses JSON format for its configuration file. The configuration file is discussed in details in Section 5.

---

[2] PALMYRA's code is available at `https://github.com/CAMeL-Lab/palmyra`.
[3] Try PALMYRA online at `https://camel-lab.github.io/palmyra`.

Gloss	ID	Token	Lemma	POS	XPOS	Features	Parent	Relation	Depd	Misc
and	1	+وَ	وَ	PRT	_	gloss=and	2	MOD	_	_
was	2	كَانَ	كَان	VRB	_	gloss=be;was;were|asp=p|vox=a|mod=i|per=3|gen=m|num=s	0	--	_	_
people	3	أَهْلُ	أَهْل	NOM	_	gloss=family;people|gen=m|num=p|stt=c|cas=n|rat=r	2	SBJ	_	_
the-Earth	4	الأَرْضِ	أَرْض	NOM	_	gloss=earth;land|gen=f|num=s|stt=d|cas=g|rat=i	3	IDF	_	_
all	5	جَمِيعاً	جَمِيع	NOM	_	gloss=all|gen=m|num=p|stt=i|cas=a	3	MOD	_	_
speak	6	يَتَكَلَّمُونَ	تَكَلَّم	VRB	_	gloss=speak;talk|asp=i|vox=a|mod=i|per=3|gen=m|num=p	2	PRD	_	_
primarily	7	أَوَّلاً	أَوَّل	NOM	_	gloss=primarily|gen=m|num=s|stt=i|cas=a	6	MOD	_	_
with	8	+بِ	بِ	PRT	_	gloss=with;by	6	MOD	_	_
tongue	9	لِسَانٍ	لِسَان	NOM	_	gloss=tongue|gen=m|num=s|stt=i|cas=g|rat=i	8	OBJ	_	_
one	10	وَاحِدٍ	وَاحِد	NOM	_	gloss=one|gen=m|num=s|stt=i|cas=g	9	MOD	_	_
and	11	+وَ	وَ	PRT	_	gloss=and	9	MOD	_	_
language	12	لُغَةٍ	لُغَة	NOM	_	gloss=language|gen=f|num=s|stt=i|cas=g|rat=i	11	OBJ	_	_
one	13	وَاحِدَةٍ	وَاحِد	NOM	_	gloss=one|gen=f|num=s|stt=i|cas=g	12	MOD	_	_
.	14	.	.	PNX	_	....	2	MOD	_	_

(a) CATiB Tree in CoNLL-U Format

Gloss	ID	Token	Lemma	POS	XPOS	Features	Parent	Relation	Depd	Misc
and	1	+وَ	وَ	CCONJ	conj	....	6	cc	_	_
was	2	كَانَ	كَان	AUX	verb	Aspect=Perf|Gender=Masc|Num=Sing|Mood=Ind	6	cop	_	_
people	3	أَهْلُ	أَهْل	NOUN	noun	Gen=Masc|Num=Sing|Case=Nom|Definite=Cons	6	nsubj	_	_
the-Earth	4	الأَرْضِ	أَرْض	NOUN	noun	Gen=Fem|Num=Sing|Case=Gen|Definite=Def	3	nmod	_	_
all	5	جَمِيعاً	جَمِيع	ADJ	noun_quant	Case=Acc|Definite=Ind	3	amod	_	_
speak	6	يَتَكَلَّمُونَ	تَكَلَّم	VERB	verb	Aspect=Imp|Gender=Masc|Num=Plur|Mood=Ind	0	root	_	_
primarily	7	أَوَّلاً	أَوَّل	ADJ	adj	Case=Acc|Definite=Ind	6	amod	_	_
with	8	+بِ	بِ	PART	prep	_	9	case	_	_
tongue	9	لِسَانٍ	لِسَان	NOUN	noun	Gen=Masc|Num=Sing|Case=Gen|Definite=Ind	6	obj	_	_
one	10	وَاحِدٍ	وَاحِد	NUM	noun_num	Gen=Masc|Num=Sing|Case=Gen|Definite=Ind	9	nummod	_	_
and	11	+وَ	وَ	PART	conj	_	9	cc	_	_
language	12	لُغَةٍ	لُغَة	NOUN	noun	Gen=Fem|Num=Sing|Case=Gen|Definite=Ind	9	conj	_	_
one	13	وَاحِدَةٍ	وَاحِد	NUM	noun_num	Gen=Fem|Num=Sing|Case=Gen|Definite=Ind	12	nummod	_	_
.	14	.	.	PUNCT	punct	....	6	punct	_	_

(b) UD Tree in CoNLL-U Format

Figure 1: Two CoNLL-U trees representions of the same sentence وَكَانَ أَهْلُ الأَرْضِ جَمِيعاً يَتَكَلَّمُونَ أَوَّلاً بِلِسَانٍ وَاحِدٍ وَلُغَةٍ وَاحِدَةٍ. *wakAna Âhlu AlÂarĎi jamiyς Aā yatakal~amuwna Âw~alAā bilisAnĩ wAHidĩ walugaĥĩ wAhidaĥĩ* 'And the whole earth was of one language, and of one speech.': (a) CATiB representation, with features in a format similar to MADAMIRA (Pasha et al., 2014), and (b) UD representation, with UD morphological features. The first column on the left of the figure is added to display the English glosses of the Arabic tokens for ease of reading.

171

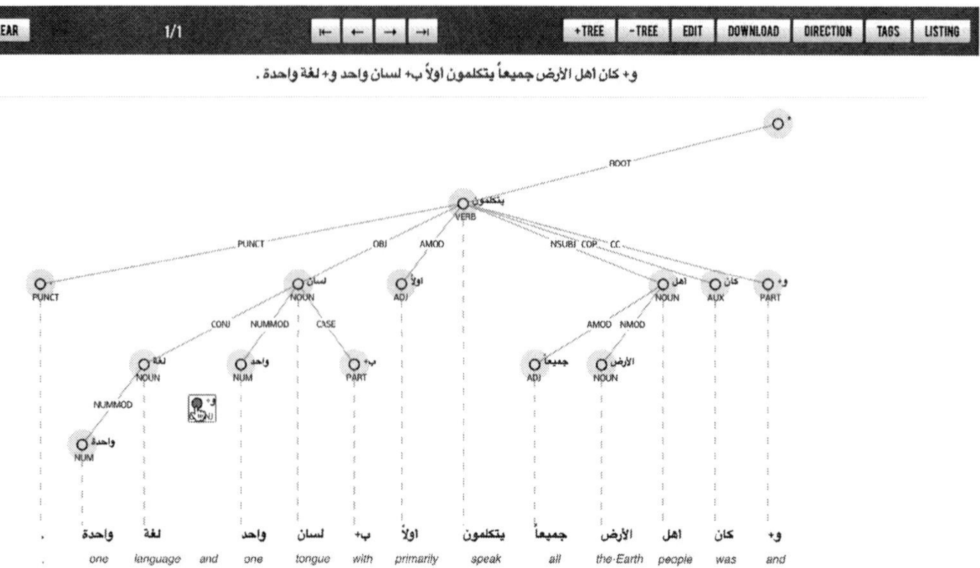

Figure 2: PALMYRA 2.0 interface while editing a tree using the drag-and-drop functionality. The tree shown in this example is the visualization of the UD tree shown in Figure 1 (b). The translation in blue at the bottom of the image is added for clarification purposes, and should be read from right to left.

4   PALMYRA 2.0's User Interface

In this section, we present the details of the interface. This section has some information that was first presented in PALMYRA 1.0 (Javed et al., 2018), however, some repetition is required to illustrate the work we built on top of it.

Dependency Tree Display   Figure 2 presents a dependency tree being edited. The sentence's tokens are projected at the bottom, and the tree nodes are aligned directly above them. The POS tag for each word is shown directly below it, and the relation is displayed half-way on the edge connecting the node to its parents. The display direction can be changed to be left-to-right or right-to-left using the DIRECTION button. It can also be automatically configured, as we will show in Section 5.

The screenshot in Figure 2 is taken midway through dragging and dropping a node. The 'drop zone' of each node is indicated by a red halo around it. When a node is attached to a new parent, the order of the words in the sentence, and in the tree, remains the same. PALMYRA also has tree zoom-in and zoom-out options.

Tree Navigation and Editing   Users who prefer to use the keyboard to edit the trees can do that with ease. Once a node is selected, users can use arrows to move from one node to the other. The selected node is always highlighted to provide visual feedback to the user.

Editing POS tags and relation labels can be done by either using configurable keyboard shortcuts, or using sub-menus that provide button lists of all available annotation options. The tagging sub-menus are invoked by clicking on the TAGS button. The sub-menu button lists are populated dynamically from the configuration file, and can be grouped in whichever way the user feels relevant to their annotations task. Figure 4 (a) shows an example of these sub-menus for UD annotation. Switching between annotating POS tags and relation labels is done using the Tab key.

Additions, Deletions, and Mergers   In PALMYRA 2.0, the addition and deletion of nodes is done using the Edit mode, which can be initiated by clicking on the EDIT button. In this mode, icons are displayed on the tree to indicate addition, deletion, and left and right mergers. Figure 3 displays the tree in sentence token editing mode. The clickable red "x" sign and green "+" sign are used to delete and insert nodes, respectively. The default POS tag and relation of the new node are configurable. Merging neighboring

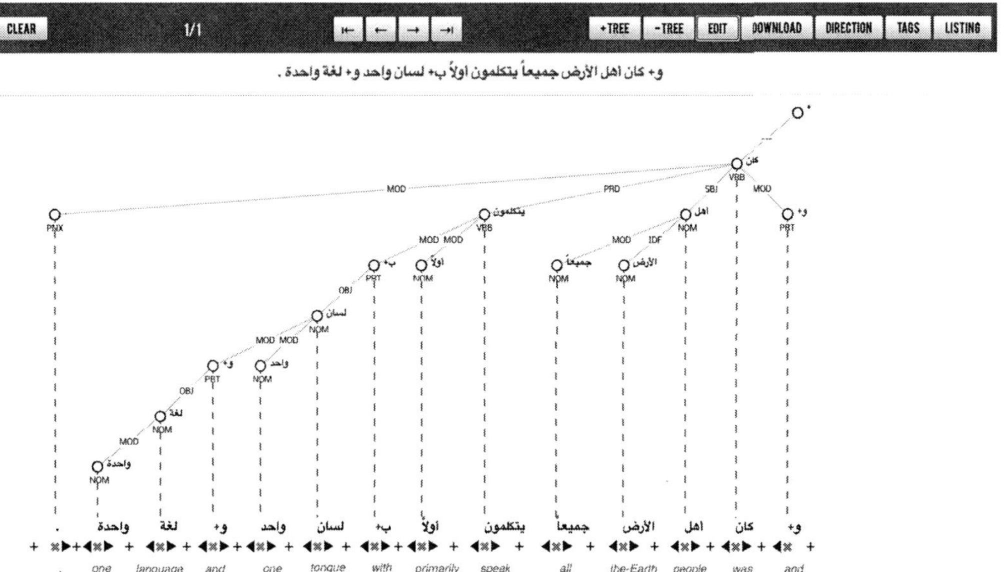

Figure 3: PALMYRA 2.0 interface in sentence token editing mode. The tree shown in this example is the visualization of the CATiB tree shown in Figure 1 (a). The translation in blue at the bottom of the image is added for clarification purposes, and should be read from right to left.

words is done through the clickable left and right arrows. The node under which the arrow is clicked is deleted, and its "name", i.e. the word itself, is added to the "name" of the respective neighbor node. The children of the merged node are assigned to the node it was merged with.

The user can also use the button +TREE to add a new tree to the end of the the file. The tree starts as a root node only, and the user can add new nodes using the word insertion functionality described above. The -TREE button deletes the tree that is currently in focus.

Word and Feature Editing Clicking on one of the words projected at the bottom of the tree allows the users to edit that word and its features. This includes the token, which users can edit to fix typographical errors, or add spaces to split the token into multiple tokens. Additionally, PALMYRA 2.0 gives the option of editing lemmas, and the features that appear in the sixth column of the CoNLL-U file.

Figure 4 shows the menu that pops up when a word is clicked. Users can use the configuration file to allow or disallow some features from being annotated with specific POSs. Figure 4 (b) shows the menu with a verb selected, where the features *state*, *case*, and *rationality* are disabled, and Figure 4 (c) shows the same menu when a noun is selected where *person*, *voice*, *aspect*, and *mood* are disabled.

Text Listing PALMYRA 2.0 can show a listing of the sentences that are in the file that is being displayed. Figure 5 presents the box that appears when clicking on the LISTING button, showing all the sentences that are in the uploaded file. Because PALMYRA 2.0 is a light tool, our approach is to exploit the existing search utility in web browsers to our advantage. The text in this box is searchable with the search utility, and the users can easily navigate to the sentence they desire by clicking on it in this box. If a specific key is specified in the configuration file, the text displayed in the listing box will come from the text in the comments with that key. If the key is not in the configuration, or if a tree does not have a comment with that key value, the text displayed in the listing box will be the concatenation of the sentence's tokens.

5 Configuration

PALMYRA 2.0's configuration file is a JSON file. The configuration file allows users to specify options related to the following features:

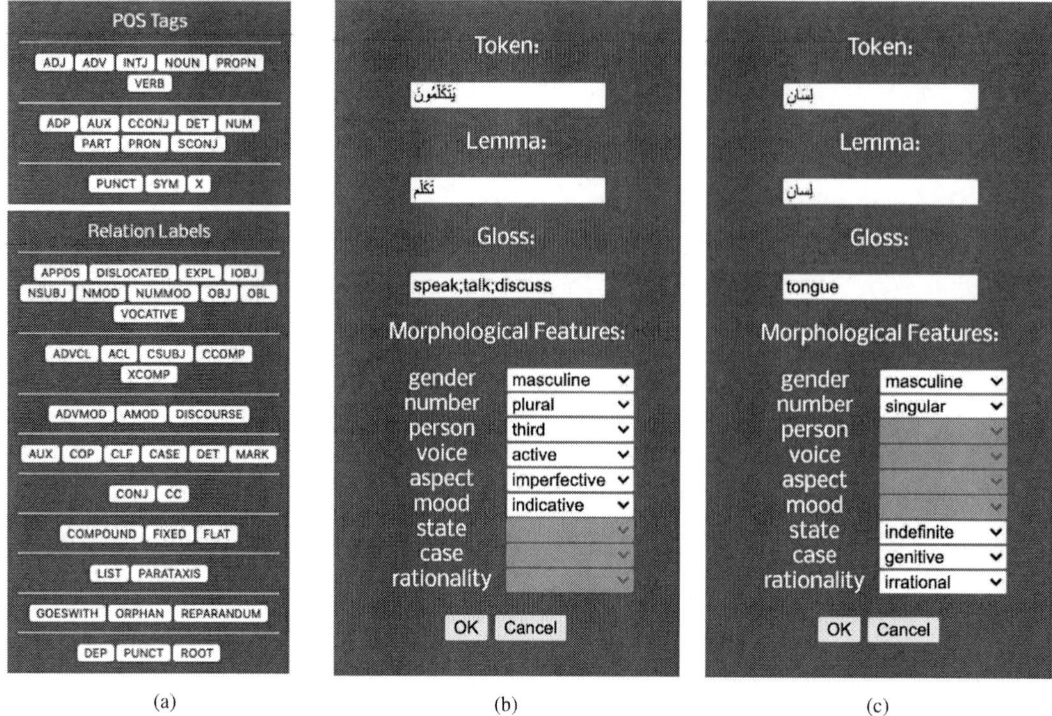

Figure 4: (a) Selection menus for POS tags (top) and relation labels (bottom); (b) and (c) Word and feature editing interfaces, showing the difference between editing a verb (b) and editing a noun (c).

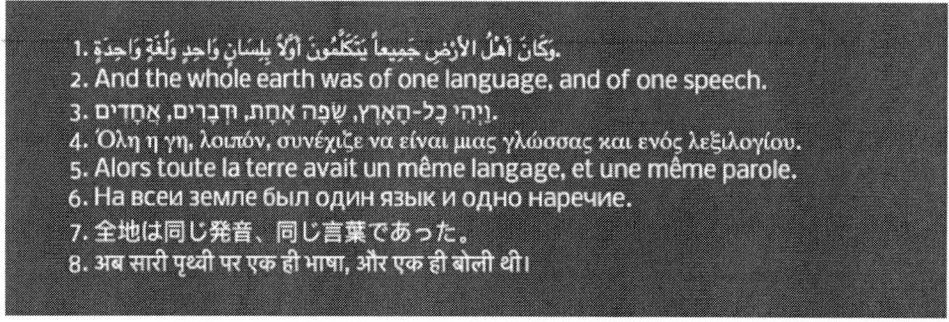

Figure 5: The listing of the sentences that are in the file being displayed. All are translations in different languages of the same sentences.

Orientation   PALMYRA 2.0 can display dependency trees in right-to-left and left-to-right orientations. The user can set their preferred orientation through the configuration file.

Text Listing   The text displayed in the listing box by default comes from treating the tokens in the tree as independent words. PALMYRA 2.0 can be configured to populate the listing box from a specific comment in the CoNLL-U file.

Display Features   The features that are displayed by default on syntax trees are the tokens' POS tags, and their relations to their parents. The possible POS tags and relation labels that can be used for annotation are defined in the configuration file. Figure 6 (a) and (b) show a partial definition of POS tags and relations, respectively, in a UD configuration file. The *label* defines the name of the label that will be displayed on the tree. The *key* defines the shortcut that is used to select that label. Clicking on a shortcut key multiple time will circulate among all the tags that have the same key value, in the order in

<table>
<tr><td>

```
"pos":{
 "values":[
  {"label":"adj",
        "key":"a", "group":"1"},
  {"label":"adv",
        "key":"a", "group":"1"},
  {"label":"cconj",
        "key":"c","group":"2"},
  ... ]}
```

</td><td>

```
"features":[
 {"name":"case",
  "type":"list",
  "values":["nominative","accusative",
            "genitive"]},
 {"name":"gender",
  "type":"list",
  "values":["feminine","masculine"]},
 {"name":"gloss",
  "type":"lexical"},
  ... ]
```

</td></tr>
<tr><td align="center">(a)</td><td align="center">(c)</td></tr>
<tr><td>

```
"relation":{
 "values":[
  {"label":"det",
        "key":"d", "group":"4"},
  {"label":"dep",
        "key":"d","group":"9"},
  ... ]}
```

</td><td>

```
"default_features":[
 {"pos":"NOM",
  "features":[
    {"name":"case","value":"nominative"},
    {"name":"gender","value":"masculine"},
    ... ]},
 {"pos":"VRB",
  "features":[
    {"name":"case","value":"N/A"},
    {"name":"gender","value":"masculine"},
    ... ]},
 ...]
```

</td></tr>
<tr><td align="center">(b)</td><td align="center">(d)</td></tr>
</table>

Figure 6: Excerpts of the configuration file showing partial definition of (a) the POS tags and (b) the relation labels that will be displayed on the tree, as well as (c) the features and values that can be annotated and (d) the associated default feature values.

which they appear in the configuration file. This applies to both POS tags and relation labels. The *group* is used to group specific keys together in the pop-up menu. Figure 4 (a) shows the pop-up menu for the basic UD POS tags and relation labels, with specific tags and labels grouped together.

Linguistic Annotations CoNLL-U files use the sixth column for representing token features. PALMYRA 2.0's configuration file allows users to specify which features they are interested in annotating. Each feature can be one of two types: list or lexical. A lexical feature is edited using a text box, with no limitation on its value. A list feature can be edited through a drop-down list that is predefined in the configuration file. Figure 6 (c) shows a partial definition of three features; *case* and *gender*, both of which are list features that can take a limited set of specific values, and *gloss* which is a lexical feature. Figure 4 shows the linguistic features' pop-up menu that is populated from the full configuration file.

Default Values Users can define default feature values that are connected to specific POS tags. Figure 6 (d) shows a partial definition of default features. A *NOM* POS tag per this configuration will have a default *case* value of 'nominative', unless it is annotated otherwise in the input file. A *VRB* POS tag, on the other hand, cannot have a *case* feature value, so it is declared to be 'N/A'. Figure 4 shows the difference between the linguistic pop-up menus for a verb (b) and a noun (c).

Configuration file examples and examples of corresponding dependency tree files are provided in the PALMYRA website (see footnote 3).

6   Conclusion and Future Work

In this paper, we described PALMYRA 2.0, a platform independent graphical software for dependency tree visualization and editing. The features of PALMYRA 2.0 allow it to be easily configured to work with any syntactic dependency representation. They also allow for editing linguistic features through simple drop-down menus and text fields. Being built entirely using standard web technologies, PALMYRA 2.0 runs on all major web browsers.

PALMYRA 2.0's configuration file allows it to be used for annotating features that do not commonly appear in syntactic dependency treebanks. The flexibility of not limiting the linguistic annotations to one kind of features makes the repurposing of this tool to annotate, for example, sentiment datasets, or NER gazetteers, a functionality that can be easily integrated into the tool.

We plan to continue maintaining and enhancing PALMYRA 2.0's capabilities, such as supporting multi-token words, hidden node representations, and enhanced dependencies annotation. We also plan on adding support for additional linguistic annotations, and sentence splitting. Inter-annotator agreement, user management, and automatic parsing are also features we are looking to add to PALMYRA to increase its usability in large annotation projects, particularly since we will be using PALMYRA 2.0 heavily as part of a large-scale treebanking annotation project in the near future.

Acknowledgments

This project is funded by a New York University Abu Dhabi Research Enhancement Fund. We would like to thank Jamila El-Gizuli, Ossama Obeid, Arfath Pasha for helpful conversations and interface design and implementation advice. We thank the anonymous reviewers for their feedback and comments.

References

Faisal Al-Shargi and Owen Rambow. 2015. Diwan: A dialectal word annotation tool for Arabic. In *Proceedings of the Workshop for Arabic Natural Language Processing (WANLP)*, pages 49–58, Beijing, China.

Abdulrahman Alosaimy and Eric Atwell. 2018. Web-based annotation tool for inflectional language resources. In *Proceedings of the Eleventh International Conference on Language Resources and Evaluation (LREC 2018)*.

Alena Böhmová, Jan Hajič, Eva Hajičová, and Barbora Hladká, 2003. *The Prague Dependency Treebank*, pages 103–127. Springer Netherlands, Dordrecht.

Marcel Bollmann, Florian Petran, Stefanie Dipper, and Julia Krasselt. 2014. Cora: A web-based annotation tool for historical and other non-standard language data. In *Proceedings of the 8th Workshop on Language Technology for Cultural Heritage, Social Sciences, and Humanities (LaTeCH)*, pages 86–90.

Sabine Buchholz and Erwin Marsi. 2006. Conll-x shared task on multilingual dependency parsing. In *Proceedings of the Conference on Computational Natural Language Learning (CoNLL)*, pages 149–164, New York City, New York.

Richard Eckart de Castilho, Eva Mujdricza-Maydt, Seid Muhie Yimam, Silvana Hartmann, Iryna Gurevych, Anette Frank, and Chris Biemann. 2016. A web-based tool for the integrated annotation of semantic and syntactic structures. In *Proceedings of the Workshop on Language Technology Resources and Tools for Digital Humanities (LT4DH)*, pages 76–84.

Nizar Habash and Ryan Roth. 2009. CATiB: The Columbia Arabic Treebank. In *Proceedings of the Joint Conference of the Association for Computational Linguistics and the International Joint Conference on Natural Language Processing (ACL-IJCNLP)*, pages 221–224, Suntec, Singapore.

Jan Hajič, Otakar Smrž, Petr Zemánek, Jan Šnaidauf, and Emanuel Beška. 2004. Prague Arabic Dependency Treebank: Development in Data and Tools. In *Proceedings of the International Conference on Arabic Language Resources and Tools*, pages 110–117, Cairo, Egypt. ELDA.

Johannes Heinecke. 2019. Conllueditor: a fully graphical editor for universal dependencies treebank files. In *Proceedings of the Third Workshop on Universal Dependencies (UDW, SyntaxFest 2019)*, pages 87–93.

Talha Javed, Nizar Habash, and Dima Taji. 2018. Palmyra: A Platform Independent Dependency Annotation Tool for Morphologically Rich Languages. In *Proceedings of the Language Resources and Evaluation Conference (LREC)*, Miyazaki, Japan.

Alexa Little and Stephen Tratz. 2016. Easytree: A graphical tool for dependency tree annotation. In *Proceedings of the Language Resources and Evaluation Conference (LREC)*, Portorož, Slovenia.

Mohamed Maamouri, Ann Bies, Hubert Jin, and Tim Buckwalter. 2003. Arabic treebank: Part 1 v 2.0. Linguistic Data Consortium (LDC2003T06).

Mitchell P. Marcus, Beatrice Santorini, and Mary Ann Marcinkiewicz. 1993. Building a large annotated corpus of English: The Penn treebank. *Computational Linguistics*, 19(2):313–330.

Joakim Nivre, Marie-Catherine de Marneffe, Filip Ginter, Yoav Goldberg, Jan Hajic, Christopher D. Manning, Ryan McDonald, Slav Petrov, Sampo Pyysalo, Natalia Silveira, Reut Tsarfaty, and Daniel Zeman. 2016. Universal dependencies v1: A multilingual treebank collection. In *Proceedings of the Language Resources and Evaluation Conference (LREC)*, Portorož, Slovenia.

Ossama Obeid, Salam Khalifa, Nizar Habash, Houda Bouamor, Wajdi Zaghouani, and Kemal Oflazer. 2018. MADARi: A Web Interface for Joint Arabic Morphological Annotation and Spelling Correction. In *Proceedings of the Language Resources and Evaluation Conference (LREC)*, Miyazaki, Japan.

Petr Pajas. 2008. Tred: Tree editor. http://ufal.mff.cuni.cz/ pajas/tred.

Arfath Pasha, Mohamed Al-Badrashiny, Mona Diab, Ahmed El Kholy, Ramy Eskander, Nizar Habash, Manoj Pooleery, Owen Rambow, and Ryan Roth. 2014. Madamira: A fast, comprehensive tool for morphological analysis and disambiguation of Arabic. In *Proceedings of the Language Resources and Evaluation Conference (LREC)*, pages 1094–1101, Reykjavik, Iceland.

Pontus Stenetorp, Sampo Pyysalo, Goran Topić, Tomoko Ohta, Sophia Ananiadou, and Jun'ichi Tsujii. 2012. Brat: A web-based tool for nlp-assisted text annotation. In *Proceedings of the Conference of the European Chapter of the Association for Computational Linguistics (EACL)*, pages 102–107, Avignon, France.

Stephen Tratz and Nhien Phan. 2018. A web-based system for crowd-in-the-loop dependency treebanking. In *Proceedings of the Eleventh International Conference on Language Resources and Evaluation (LREC 2018)*.

Naiwen Xue, Fei Xia, Fu-Dong Chiou, and Marta Palmer. 2005. The Penn Chinese Treebank: Phrase structure annotation of a large corpus. *Natural Language Engineering*, 11(02):207–238.

Universal Dependencies for Albanian

Marsida Toska and **Joakim Nivre**
Uppsala University
Department of Linguistics and Philology
Uppsala, Sweden
marsida.toska.1494@student.uu.se
joakim.nivre@lingfil.uu.se

Daniel Zeman
Charles University
Faculty of Mathematics and Physics
Prague, Czechia
zeman@ufal.mff.cuni.cz

Abstract

In this paper, we introduce the first Universal Dependencies (UD) treebank for standard Albanian, consisting of 60 sentences collected from the Albanian Wikipedia, annotated with lemmas, universal part-of-speech tags, morphological features and syntactic dependencies. In addition to presenting the treebank itself, we discuss a selection of linguistic constructions in Albanian whose analysis in UD is not self-evident, including core arguments and the status of indirect objects, pronominal clitics, genitive constructions, prearticulated adjectives, and modal verbs.

1 Introduction

Albanian is an Indo-European language and also part of the Balkan Sprachbund.[1] It is spoken primarily in Albania and secondarily in neighbouring Balkan countries by Albanian minorities but also elsewhere in Europe and outside by the Albanian diaspora. Its vocabulary, but even more so its grammar, exhibits a lot of similarities and parallelisms with the languages of the Balkan Sprachbund, while it also features linguistic constructions that could be characterized as idiosyncratic.

Computational and other online resources that could facilitate NLP research and comparative studies of Albanian are scarce. A large part-of-speech tagged corpus for the language was created only recently by Kote et al. (2019), but there is still no corresponding treebank with full syntactic annotation, which means that it is hard to develop language technology applications that require both tagging and parsing. It is in this context that we have developed the first Universal Dependencies (UD) treebank for Albanian, called UD Albanian-TSA.[2] Although still very limited in size, it constitutes a first step towards developing a large-scale treebank within the UD scheme, enabling NLP research as well as comparative studies involving other languages, and there is also research showing that even a few annotated sentences can contribute to good parsing results (Meechan-Maddon and Nivre, 2019).

In the following sections we introduce some of the key features of the Albanian language (Section 2), provide a brief summary of related work with regard to NLP for Albanian (Section 3), and describe the steps taken to develop the treebank (Section 4). We then discuss in some detail a selection of linguistic constructions in Albanian that pose challenges for the UD annotation framework and that are interesting from a cross-linguistic perspective (Section 5).

2 The Albanian Language

Albanian belongs to the Indo-European family of languages, but it constitutes its own branch within the family. It is spoken by around 7.5 million people, of which, due to the Albanian diaspora, less than 3 million are estimated to reside in Albania (Hoxha and Baxhaku, 2019). There are two main Albanian dialects, the Tosk and the Gheg, with the former being the one Standard Albanian is based on. Its alphabet relies on the Latin one and comprises 36 letters, 9 of which are digraphs (dh, gj, ll, nj,

---

[1]Lindstedt (2000) explains that the Balkan Sprachbund comprises Albanian, Greek, Balkan Slavic, Balkan Romance and Balkan Romani languages.

[2]TSA is short for Treebank for Standard Albanian.

Proceedings of the Fourth Workshop on Universal Dependencies (UDW 2020), pages 178–188
Barcelona, Spain (Online), December 13, 2020

rr, sh, th, xh, zh) while 2 have diacritics (ë, ç) (Karanikolas, 2009). The dominant word order is SVO, but the rich morphology often allows relatively free word order. Breu (2010) lists the following salient characteristics of the Albanian language, which also apply, with some variation, to most languages of the Balkan Sprachbund:

- Lack of infinitive
- Analytical comparison system:

    (1)   më   i   miri
           PART ART.M good.M
           'the best'

- Future construction with "will/want":

    (2)   do   të vij
           will to come.1SG.PRES
           'I will come'

- Object redoubling in dative and accusative (clitic doubling):

    (3)   i-a   dhash   libr-in   shok-ut
           him.CL.DAT-it.CL.ACC gave.1SG.PAST book-the.ACC friend-the.DAT
           'I gave the book to the friend'

- Suffixed definite article:

    (4)   libr-in
           book-the
           'the book'

- Complex verb system (3 tenses, 6 moods, etc.), e.g., admirative mood:[3]

    (5)   qenke   i   shpejtë
           be.2SG.PRES.ADM ART fast
           'You are surprisingly/unexpectedly fast'

3   NLP for Albanian

In recent years, the development of NLP resources for Albanian has been increasing. Most research has focused on the morphological analysis and the creation of part-of-speech tagging models. Trommer and Kallulli (2004) first introduced a morphological analyzer that made use of off-line components, while later on Piton and Lagji (2008), performing a morphological study of Albanian, developed electronic dictionaries of inflected forms as well as transducers using NooJ. In the area of part-of-speech tagging, Kabashi and Proisl (2018) proposed a part-of-speech tagset after noticing there did not exist one of moderate size, mapping it also to the UD tagset (Nivre et al., 2016; Nivre et al., 2020). They built on their own previous work (Kabashi and Proisl, 2016) and that of other researchers, such as that of Hasanaj (2009), who had developed a statistical part-of-speech tagging model with accuracy around 70%, and Kadriu (2013) who had presented a part-of-speech tagging model using the NLTK toolkit.

In 2019, the authors[4] of the Albanian National Corpus[5] (Morozova and Rusakov, 2014) (ANC) developed and made publicly available in the official website of the ANC a lemmatizer, tagger and morphological analyzer for Albanian. However, they use their own part-of-speech tagset and do not rely on the UD annotation scheme, and there is no disambiguation of either lemmatization, tagging or morphological analysis. ANC itself contains around 20 million tokens and is therefore the largest resource currently available for Albanian.

Also recently, Kote et al. (2019) presented an Albanian corpus with part-of-speech tags and morphological features containing around 118,000 tokens. Additionally, the team trained a neural morphological

---

[3]The admirative mood in Albanian incorporates a number of modality nuances such as admiration, surprise etc.
[4]Maria Morozova, Alexander Rusakov, Timofey Arkhangelsky
[5]http://albanian.web-corpora.net/

tagger and lemmatizer which achieved promising results, the best of which being 92.74% in part-of-speech tagging. The annotation of the corpus was based on the UD guidelines and underwent a manual review.

4 Treebank Development

In this section, we describe the development of UD Albanian-TSA. Given the lack of preprocessing tools and resources for Albanian compatible with the UD framework,[6] most tasks undertaken in the creation of the treebank were performed manually. However, some steps, such as word segmentation, lemmatization, tagging and morphological analysis were semi-automated through scripts that we developed or tools that were available from other researchers, as described in more detail below. In the end, the entire treebank underwent manual checking and correction, so as to resolve cases of ambiguity, eliminate errors and ensure overall consistency, and was also tested with the UD validation script.

4.1 Data Selection

Although our initial intention was to work with data from the ANC, which contains a wide compilation of texts from different genres, we eventually collected our data from random entries of the Albanian Wikipedia because of the free license. The selection of the sentences was manual and guided by the aim to include as many linguistically diverse structures as possible. Our data set consists of 60 sentences in total corresponding to 922 tokens.

4.2 Word Segmentation and Lemmatization

The segmentation of sentences into words was performed based on white-space delimiters and punctuation. This means, for instance, that the adjective *i zi* (black), which is a so-called prearticulated adjective, was split into the preposed article *i* and the main word *zi*, despite the latter being ungrammatical and not falling within a word class on its own.[7]

For lemmatization, we used the lemmatizer developed by the Albanian National Corpus team.[8] However, since this lemmatizer does not disambiguate between identical tokens with different lemmas, manual disambiguation was required. For example, the token *vinte* (3rd person singular past tense verb), depending on the context, could be lemmatized as either *vij* (to come) or *vë* (to put).

4.3 Morphological Features

The morphological analysis of the tokens was to a great extent manual, except for cases where it was possible to automate the process through scripts. The classes that were assigned morphological features are the following: verbs, nouns, adjectives, pronouns and determiners.

For verbs, we included features such as aspect, mood, number, person, tense and voice, unless these occurred in form of participles or gerunds, in which case only the feature `VerbForm` was used. For nouns, we decided to include the following features: case, definiteness, gender and number. In addition, the feature `NounType=Het` was added for nouns displaying different gender in singular and plural (also known as "two-gender nouns" or "dual nouns").[9] The features case, gender and number were also adopted for pronouns; in addition, the type of pronoun is specified by the feature `PronType`. For adjectives, we narrowed down the number of features to two, namely gender and number, unless further features were explicitly marked, such as `AdjType` (if the adjective was grammatically a perfect passive participle). The last class to get features was that of determiners, for which only the gender was specified.

---

[6]The corpus and tools developed by Kote et al. (2019) unfortunately appeared only after our work had been finished.

[7]The syntactic analysis of prearticulated adjectives is discussed in detail in Section 5.4.

[8]`https://bitbucket.org/timarkh/uniparser-albanian-grammar/src/master/`

[9]Beqiraj (2014) states that in Albanian, two-gender nouns are masculine in the singular (originally classified as neuter) and change to feminine in the plural, usually by adding the suffix -e or -ra. He also mentions that this phenomenon appears (although less frequently and systematically) in other Indo-European languages as well, such as French, e.g., l'amour (singular masculine, "the love") vs. les amours (plural feminine, "the loves").

4.4 Part-of-Speech Tagging

In order to speed up the process of assigning UD part-of-speech tags to words, we created scripts that tagged closed-class words such as particles, adpositions, determiners, coordinating and subordinating conjunctions, numerals, punctuation marks, interjections and symbols. As for verbs, adjectives and adverbs, these were tagged by combining lexicon- and rule-based methods, whereas all the remaining words were tagged as nouns by default. Finally, all words underwent manual disambiguation and correction.

Our tagging approach coincides to a great extent with that of the new corpus developed concurrently by Kote et al. (2019). There are however a few discrepancies:

1. Verbs expressing modality such as *mund* (can), *duhet* (must), *dua/do* (want) are treated differently. Kote et al. (2019) adopt the AUX tag, thereby grouping them together with semantically similar verbs in many other languages including English. We instead use the VERB tag, because we want to maintain uniformity in the syntactic annotation of verbal structures introduced with the particle *të* (verbal forms in the subjunctive mood), to be discussed in more detail in Section 5.5.

2. The mediopassive clitic *u*, appearing in the analytical formation of the mediopassive past tense and the gerund form (in which case it is preceded by the particle *duke*) is tagged PART by Kote et al. (2019) and AUX by us. Our choice is motivated by the fact that it is associated here with the category of voice and/or tense, and that the tag AUX in UD v2 is not restricted to verbal auxiliaries.

3. The copula verb *jam* (to be) is tagged VERB by Kote et al. (2019) and AUX by us, while both corpora use AUX when *jam* is used as a temporal auxiliary. The discrepancy here seems to be due to a difference between UD v1, where copula verbs were tagged VERB, and UD v2, where AUX is the prescribed tag.

In addition to these systematic differences, we have observed that the corpus of Kote et al. (2019) shows some variation in the tagging of ambiguous word forms. For example, the word *të* (to/of) appears both with PART and DET when occurring in verb groups, while our treebank only uses PART in this position.[10] Similarly, the word *që* (that) appears with CCONJ, SCONJ and PRON when introducing relative clauses, while our treebank only uses PRON in this position. Most of these differences should be relatively easy to harmonize.

4.5 Syntactic Annotation

The syntactic annotation was performed manually using the annotation tool UD Annotatrix (Tyers et al., 2017), a browser-based tool customized for manual annotation of dependency trees in UD. Applying the UD guidelines to Albanian turned out to be relatively straightforward for the majority of syntactic constructions. In the next section, we discuss some phenomena that gave rise to questions that may be of more general interest to the community.

5 Challenging Constructions

5.1 Core Arguments

One of the fundamental questions when annotating a new language in UD is to determine criteria for distinguishing core arguments from oblique modifiers, including deciding whether there are more than two core arguments. In Albanian, subjects and objects are marked by nominative and accusative case, respectively. In addition, the verb agrees with the subject in person and number; the subject is usually dropped if it is a pronoun. In addition to subjects (nsubj) and direct objects (obj), we also recognize as core arguments indirect objects (iobj) marked by dative case. The argument for treating dative verbal dependents as core is that they behave like (accusative) objects in two important respects. First, they trigger clitic doubling, as discussed in Section 5.2. Secondly, they can permute freely with direct objects when occurring after the verb. Example (6) shows a sentence with three core arguments.

---

[10] Both corpora consistently use DET when it occurs in noun phrases.

(6) Anna   i-a   dërgoi Mariës   letrën
     Anna.NOM her.DAT.CL-it.ACC.CL sent   Maria.DAT letter.DEF.ACC
     'Anna sent Maria the letter'

5.2 Clitic Doubling

Clitic doubling, the phenomenon where pronominal clitics appear in a sentence along with the noun phrase they refer to – despite being complementary – is widespread in Albanian. It can occur with objects either in the dative or the accusative case. However, while clitic doubling is obligatory for dative objects, it is variable with accusative objects, depending on the focal and topical aspect of the sentence.[11]

In the current treebank, there are two different cases of clitic doubling which are illustrated in examples (7) and (8). In (7), the clitic *E*, which is positioned before the verb, is present along with the nominal it refers to, *qenësinë*. Its presence implies that the focus of the sentence does not lie in the NP itself, otherwise focality would require absence of clitic doubling for the accusative in Albanian (Kapia, 2012). The dedicated solution that UD has for clitic doubling is to treat the full nominal as a core argument and attach the clitic to the verb with the relation `expl` (expletive).

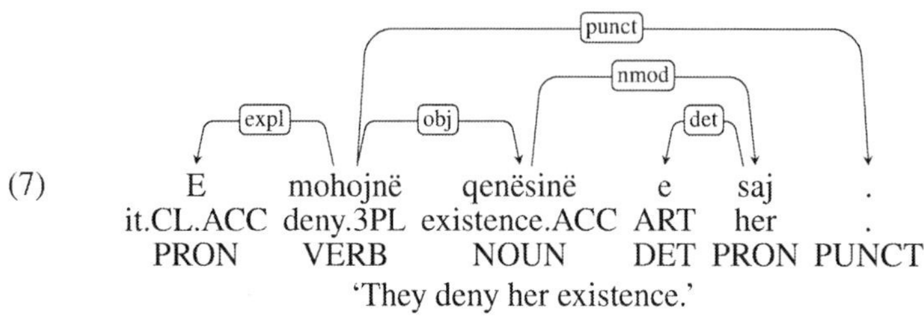

(7)   E   mohojnë   qenësinë   e   saj   .
         it.CL.ACC deny.3PL existence.ACC ART   her   .
         PRON   VERB   NOUN   DET   PRON PUNCT
                  'They deny her existence.'

Similarly, example (8) features clitic doubling with a dative object, with which clitic doubling always occurs independently of the information structure. Here the same annotation principle was followed, where the nominal is treated as a core argument (here `iobj`), whereas the clitic *u* is an expletive (`expl`). This scheme generally applies when a lexical nominal and its pronominal copy appear together in a sentence.

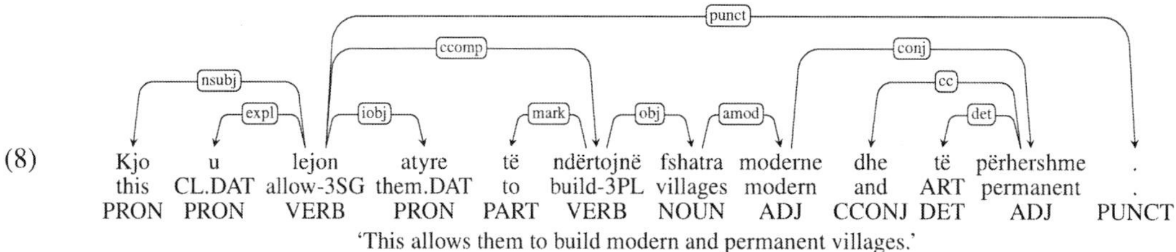

(8)   Kjo   u   lejon   atyre   të   ndërtojnë fshatra moderne dhe   të   përhershme .
         this   CL.DAT   allow-3SG them.DAT to   build-3PL villages modern and   ART   permanent   .
         PRON   PRON   VERB   PRON   PART VERB   NOUN   ADJ   CCONJ DET   ADJ   PUNCT
                  'This allows them to build modern and permanent villages.'

It is worth noting here that, although UD does not treat such clitics (co-appearing with their lexical nominal) as arguments, the dative clitics in Albanian (here *u*) appearing with dative objects are grammatically indispensable as opposed to the nominal (here *atyre*). For example, while the lexical nominal *atyre* could be elided with no grammatical or semantic consequences, as in example (9), the same is not true of *u*, which cannot be omitted without loss of grammaticality, as shown in (10).

(9)   Kjo u lejon të...
         this CL.DAT allows to...
         'This allows them to...'

(10)   *Kjo lejon atyre të...
         this allows them.DAT to...
         'This allows them to...'

---

[11]Kapia (2012) and Kallulli (2008) provide more information about the specifics of clitic doubling in Albanian, how focality and topichood affect the presence of a clitic, and how definiteness is also a requirement for clitic doubling in the accusative.

The fact that the clitic is obligatory while the noun phrase or full pronoun is optional might suggest treating the clitic as the core argument and instead use the relation *dislocated* for the co-referential nominal. However, according to our interpretation of the UD guidelines, the dislocation analysis should be used only when the co-occurrence of the pronoun and the nominal is optional. In Albanian though, the full nominal cannot occur without the pronominal clitic (at least in the dative) and the latter is tantamount to an agreement inflection on the verb. The possible omission of the full nominal can therefore be regarded as equivalent to pro-drop. Nevertheless, since the clitic is assigned a syntactic relation (unlike a morphological agreement inflection), we might consider changing the annotation from `expl` to `obj/iobj` when the full nominal is omitted. This is in fact what the UD guidelines recommend[12] and what is currently done also in Bulgarian, another language of the Balkan Sprachbund, as shown in example (11):

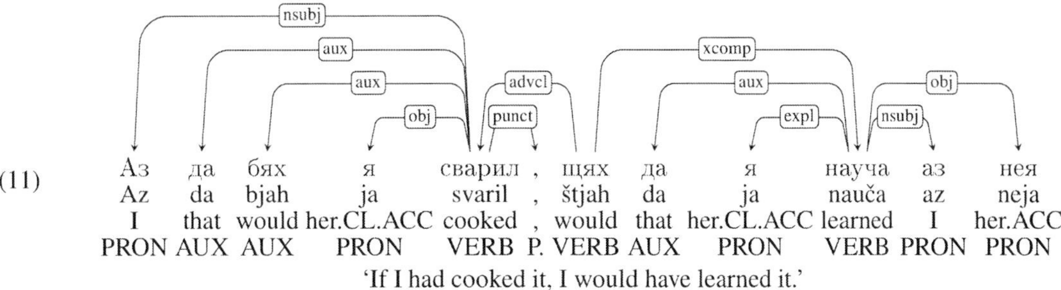

(11)

Аз	да	бях	я	сварил	,	щях	да	я	науча	аз	нея
Az	da	bjah	ja	svaril	,	štjah	da	ja	nauča	az	neja
I	that	would	her.CL.ACC	cooked	,	would	that	her.CL.ACC	learned	I	her.ACC
PRON	AUX	AUX	PRON	VERB	P.	VERB	AUX	PRON	VERB	PRON	PRON

'If I had cooked it, I would have learned it.'

Similarly, a dative clitic is also analyzed as expletive in Romanian when accompanied with a full nominal (12), while it becomes a core argument when the full nominal is missing (13).

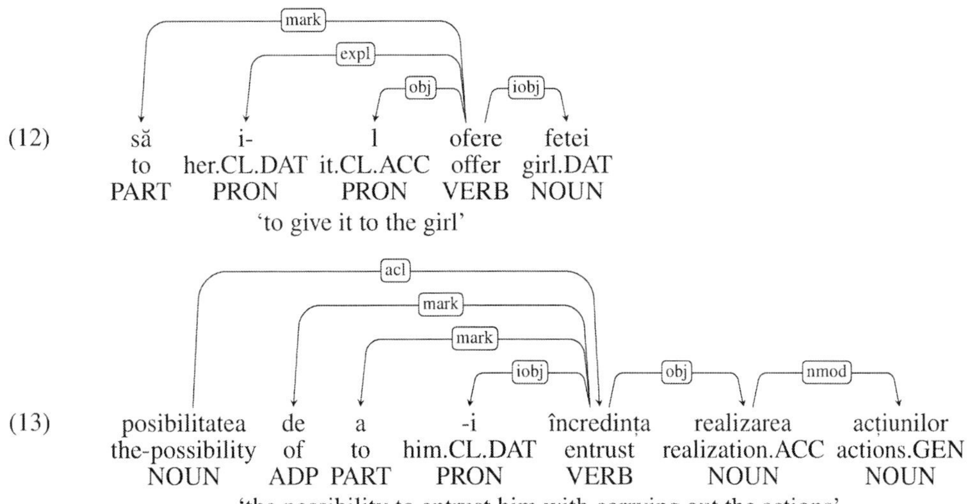

(12)

să	i-	l	ofere	fetei
to	her.CL.DAT	it.CL.ACC	offer	girl.DAT
PART	PRON	PRON	VERB	NOUN

'to give it to the girl'

(13)

posibilitatea	de	a	-i	încredinţa	realizarea	acţiunilor
the-possibility	of	to	him.CL.DAT	entrust	realization.ACC	actions.GEN
NOUN	ADP	PART	PRON	VERB	NOUN	NOUN

'the possibility to entrust him with carrying out the actions'

5.3 Genitive Case-Marking

The genitive case is special in Albanian as its formation requires the use of an article/case marker before the noun[13] with which it forms a constituent. Other languages form the genitive seemingly in the same way: compare the Greek example (14) with Albanian (15).

(14)

το	βιβλίο	της	κοπέλας
to	vivlío	tis	kopélas
the.ART.NOM.N	book.NOM.N	of.ART.GEN.F	girl.GEN.F

'the girl's book'

---

[12] https://universaldependencies.org/u/dep/expl.html

[13] Breu (2010) states that the purpose of this article, or "linking particle", as he refers to it, is to morphologically disambiguate the genitive from the dative due to syncretism.

(15) libr-i   i   vajz-ës
     book.M-the.NOM of.ART.M girl.F-the.GEN
     'the girl's book'

However, the difference lies in the fact that, in Albanian, the article, here *i*, although syntactically dependent on the possessor, agrees in gender, definiteness and number with the possessum (which is the preceding noun) (Catasso, 2011). For instance, in the example *libri i vajzës*, *i* is masculine, just like the possessum *libri*, despite the possessor *vajzës* being feminine. Nevertheless, the clitic is syntactically dependent on the possessor noun, as is clearly seen in predicative uses of the genitive, where the clitic is separated from the possessum but not from the possessor (Çanta, 2017).

(16) libr-i   është i   vajz-ës
     book.M-the.NOM is   ART.M girl.F-the.GEN
     'the book is the girl's'

Another question is what kind of modifier the clitic is. One might want to treat it as a case marker, in analogy with the English preposition *of*. However, Albanian *i/e* is considered an article by most linguists; it is also marked for gender, number and case, which aligns with determiners in other Indo-European languages, such as Greek του *(tou)* or German *des*. Therefore, our syntactic annotation treats the clitic as a determiner of the possessor noun, as shown below.

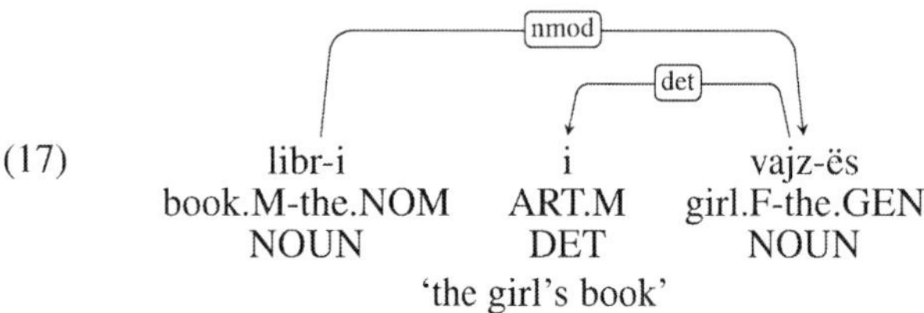

(17)
     libr-i   i   vajz-ës
     book.M-the.NOM   ART.M   girl.F-the.GEN
     NOUN   DET   NOUN
     'the girl's book'

Example (18) shows that a similar phenomenon in genitive constructions can be found in Romanian, where the so-called possessive article also agrees with the possessum rather than the possessor. We therefore believe that the construction should be annotated in the same way in both languages.

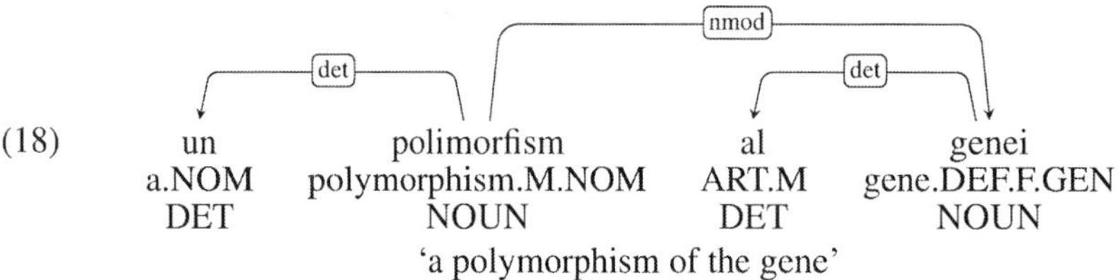

(18)
     un   polimorfism   al   genei
     a.NOM   polymorphism.M.NOM   ART.M   gene.DEF.F.GEN
     DET   NOUN   DET   NOUN
     'a polymorphism of the gene'

Finally, it is worth noting that some researchers claim that this multifunctional and controversial article in Albanian have features in common with ezafe (the linking particle) in Persian and other languages (Franco et al., 2015).

5.4 Prearticulation

The peculiar article/particle/clitic *i/e*, except for its presence in the formation of the genitive, is also present in other expressions such as the days of the week (*e martë*, Tuesday) and nominalized adjectives (*të vdekurit*, the dead; *të* is the plural form of *i/e*). However, its most systematic use is in the formation of prearticulated adjectives[14] and pronouns, although there are plain ones as well.

We considered several possible ways of analyzing prearticulated adjectives. One option is to treat them as single words with spaces, but the UD guidelines recommend using this option very restrictively and it would make word segmentation more challenging. Another option is to analyze them as compounds,

---

[14]Hendriks (1982) does not agree with this term due to the primary function of articles to connect, which according to him is not fulfilled in the case of these adjectives, as their role is contained in the formation of the adjective itself. Therefore, he prefers to refer to them as particle-adjectives.

using the `compound` relation, but this was rejected based on the observation that the article is inflected for gender, number and case along with the main adjective and does not add to its meaning, but rather displays an established grammatical phenomenon. Finally, although it is not common for UD to have a determiner depend on a nominal other than a noun (except for cases of ellipsis), the label `det` seemed to us as the most suitable solution for the annotation of such constructions in Standard Albanian.

Nevertheless, even though this annotation is identical to that deployed for the genitive, it should be noted that these are different constructions since prearticulated adjectives are preceded by that article/particle in all cases and the omission of it makes them either ungrammatical or in certain cases leads to changes in part of speech (e.g., *i mirë* good vs. *mirë* well), as opposed to nouns that are preceded by this article only in genitive (e.g., *mendime*, thoughts vs. *i/e mendimeve*, of the thoughts). Examples (19) and (20) illustrate how the noun *mendimeve* appears prearticulated only when in genitive, as opposed to its modifying adjective *të*[15] *bukura*, which is prearticulated by default, independently of the case.

(19)   mendime   të   bukura
           thoughts.NOM.F.PL ART.PL beautiful.NOM.F.PL
           'beautiful thoughts'

(20)   kultivimi   i   mendimeve   të   bukura
           cultivation.NOM.M.PL ART.M thoughts.GEN.F.PL ART.PL beautiful.GEN.F.PL
           'the cultivation of beautiful thoughts'

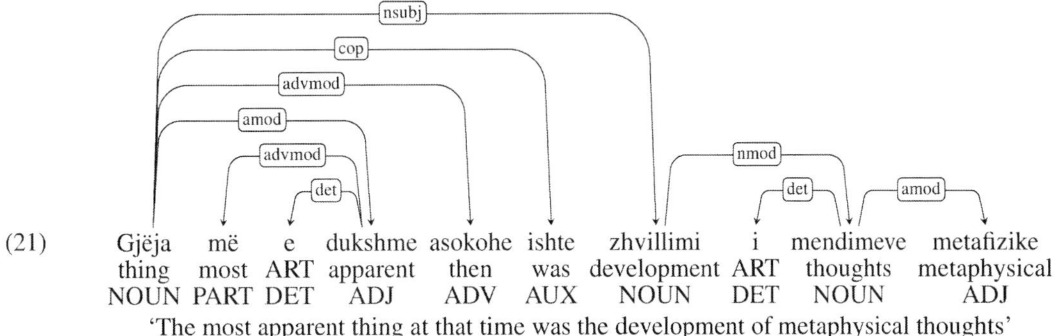

(21)   Gjëja   më   e   dukshme asokohe ishte   zhvillimi   i   mendimeve   metafizike
        thing   most ART apparent then   was development ART   thoughts metaphysical
        NOUN PART DET   ADJ   ADV   AUX   NOUN   DET   NOUN   ADJ
        'The most apparent thing at that time was the development of metaphysical thoughts'

As seen in example (21), there are two types of adjectives, *e dukshme* (apparent), which is a prearticulated adjective, and *metafizike* (metaphysical), which is a plain one. There is also a genitive construction present, *i mendimeve* (of the thoughts) which as seen, functions as a nominal modifier to another noun, while itself it is modified by an adjective.

5.5 Modal Verbs

Common auxiliary verbs in Albanian are the copula *jam* (to be) and the verb *kam* (to have), which is used in the formation of the perfect aspect, e.g., *kam shkruajtur* (I have written). These have been assigned the part-of-speech tag AUX and the dependency label `aux` when acting as temporal auxiliaries, as in (22). When used as a main verb, *kam* has instead been tagged as VERB.

(22)   kanë   arritur
       have.3PL arrived
         AUX   VERB
       'they have arrived'

However, verbs expressing modality, such as *mund* (can), *duhet* (must) and *do* (will/want), the uninflected form of *dua* (want), have on the contrary been tagged as VERB, despite being semantically equivalent to

---

[15]Here, *të* is the declined form of *i* or *e*. Therefore, in masculine nominative singular, the adjective would be *i bukur*.

modal auxiliaries in some other languages.[16] This treatment is motivated by the subjunctive construction with the particle *të* that the modal verbs govern, e.g., *mund të shkoj* (I may go), *duhet të shkoj* (I must go), and *do të shkoj* (I will go). Consequently, in such constructions the verb in the subjunctive mood depends on the modal verb with the relation xcomp, while taking *të* as a *mark* dependent, as shown in (23). A smilar analysis of modal verbs is employed in UD for, e.g., the Slavic languages. There is even a parallelism with the analysis of English *ought*, which combines with a *to*-infinitive, and is analyzed with the same syntactic structure that we propose for the Albanian modal verbs.

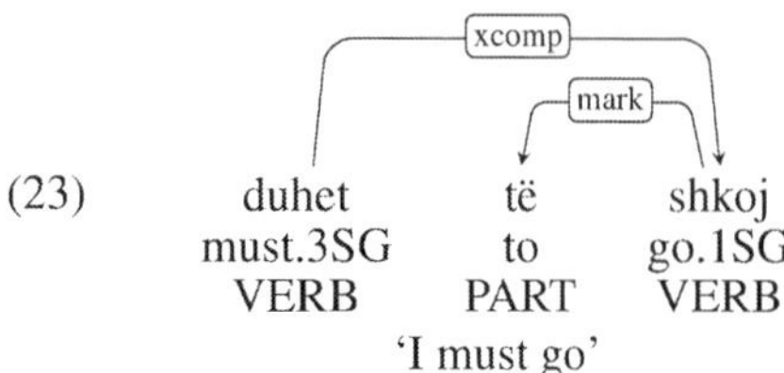

(23)   duhet   të   shkoj
       must.3SG   to   go.1SG
       VERB   PART   VERB
              'I must go'

This analysis is parallel to constructions of modal-like verbs with verbal complements, e.g., *shpresoj të kthehem* (I hope to return) and therefore ensures a uniform analysis for all subjunctive constructions introduced by *të*. However, we note that similar constructions are not annotated consistently in all UD treebanks. For example, in Modern Greek (Prokopidis and Papageorgiou, 2017), the analysis of a construction with πρέπει *prépei* (must), which also takes the form of a subjunctive with a particle (να *na*), treats the second verb as the head and assigns the relation aux to both the modal verb and the particle.

On the other hand, a drawback of the analysis that we propose for Albanian is that it calls for a different treatment of *duhet* in impersonal constructions, where *duhet* takes a past participle instead of a verb in subjunctive as a complement.[17] An example of this is illustrated in (24).

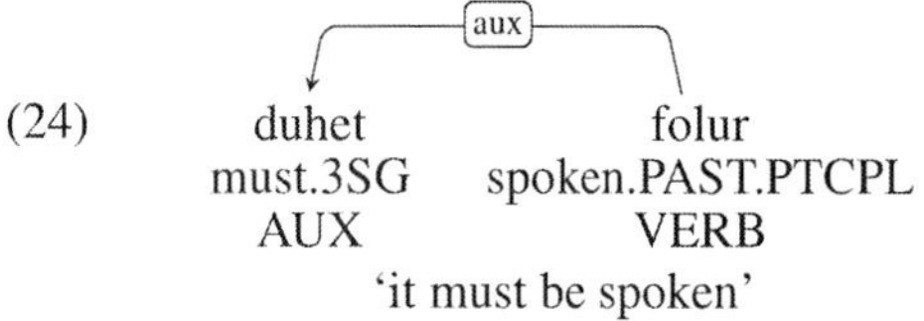

(24)   duhet   folur
       must.3SG   spoken.PAST.PTCPL
       AUX   VERB
            'it must be spoken'

The reason behind this different treatment of *duhet* lies in the consistent analysis we aimed to maintain across VP constructions built with a past participle, as in Example (22).

6   Conclusion

Albanian is a morphologically rich language with several grammatical particularities which can prove challenging when trying to find analogies to other languages. In this paper, we presented the first UD treebank for Standard Albanian, which features some of the most characteristic constructions of Albanian. We gave an overview of the formal aspects of the language and analyzed in more detail a few dependency structures that are rather rare or even unique in UD and call for special solutions. Although its current size is not sufficient for the training of tools such as parsers, which in turn could be used for the development of more sophisticated NLP applications, we envision that this starter treebank will encourage further work in the area and will be enlarged in the future.

References

Xhafer Beqiraj. 2014. *Problems of gender accord of two-gender noun determiners.* GRIN Verlag.

---

[16]Breu (2010) refers to these verbs in Albanian as semi-auxiliary verbs and provides a detailed analysis of all the modals and their usage in this language.

[17]The modal *duhet* (3SG.PRES) is technically the mediopassive form of *dua* (want) and as a regular verb means *he/she/it is needed/wanted*. However, when bearing the modal nuance of obligation, it is always used in the 3rd person singular present tense regardless of the subject. It assumes the meaning of *must* and governs either subjunctive verbs, in the active voice, or past participles, in impersonal constructions.

Walter Breu. 2010. Mood in Albanian. In *Mood in the Languages of Europe.*

Agnesa Çanta. 2017. The category of case in English and Albanian nominal system: A contrastive analysis. *International Journal of English Linguistics*, 7:226, 01.

Nicholas Catasso. 2011. Genitive-dative syncretism in the Balkan sprachbund: An invitation to discussion. *SKASE Journal of Theoretical Linguistics*, 8:70–93, 01.

Ludovico Franco, M. Rita Manzini, and Leonardo M. Savoia. 2015. Linkers and agreement. *The Linguistic Review*, 32(2):277–332.

Besmir Hasanaj. 2009. *A Part of Speech Tagging Model for Albanian.* Lambert Academic Publishing, Saarbrücken, Germany.

Peter Hendriks. 1982. On distinguishing articles in Albanian. *Studies in Slavic and General Linguistics*, 2:95–108.

Klesti Hoxha and Artur Baxhaku. 2019. Albanian language identification in text documents. *CoRR*, abs/1901.04216.

Besim Kabashi and Thomas Proisl. 2016. A proposal for a part-of-speech tagset for the Albanian language. In *Proceedings of the Tenth International Conference on Language Resources and Evaluation (LREC'16)*, pages 4305–4310, Portorož, Slovenia, May. European Language Resources Association (ELRA).

Besim Kabashi and Thomas Proisl. 2018. Albanian part-of-speech tagging: Gold standard and evaluation. In *Proceedings of the Eleventh International Conference on Language Resources and Evaluation (LREC 2018)*, Miyazaki, Japan, May. European Language Resources Association (ELRA).

Arbana Kadriu. 2013. NLTK tagger for Albanian using iterative approach. *Proceedings of the ITI 2013 35th International Conference on Information Technology Interfaces*, pages 283–288.

Dalina Kallulli. 2008. Clitic doubling, agreement and information structure: The case of Albanian. In *Clitic Doubling in the Balkan Languages*, page 227–255.

Enkeleida Kapia. 2012. Clitic doubling and information structure in Albanian. *Linguistics*, 50(5):901 – 927.

Nikitas N. Karanikolas. 2009. Bootstrapping the albanian information retrieval. *2009 Fourth Balkan Conference in Informatics*, pages 231–235.

Nelda Kote, Marenglen Biba, Jenna Kanerva, Samuel Rönnqvist, and Filip Ginter. 2019. Morphological tagging and lemmatization of Albanian: A manually annotated corpus and neural models. *CoRR*, abs/1912.00991.

Jouko Lindstedt. 2000. Linguistic balkanization: Contact-induced change by mutual reinforcement. *Studies in Slavic and General Linguistics*, 28, 01.

Ailsa Meechan-Maddon and Joakim Nivre. 2019. How to parse low-resource languages: Cross-lingual parsing, target language annotation, or both? In *Proceedings of the Fifth International Conference on Dependency Linguistics (Depling, SyntaxFest 2019)*, pages 112–120, Paris, France, August. Association for Computational Linguistics.

Maria Morozova and Alexander Rusakov. 2014. Albanian national corpus: Composition, text processing and corpus-oriented grammar development. *Akten der 5. Deutsch-albanischen kulturwissenschaftlichen Tagung*, pages 270–304.

Joakim Nivre, Marie-Catherine de Marneffe, Filip Ginter, Yoav Goldberg, Jan Hajič, Christopher D. Manning, Ryan McDonald, Slav Petrov, Sampo Pyysalo, Natalia Silveira, Reut Tsarfaty, and Daniel Zeman. 2016. Universal Dependencies v1: A multilingual treebank collection. In *Proceedings of the Tenth International Conference on Language Resources and Evaluation (LREC'16)*, pages 1659–1666, Portorož, Slovenia, May. European Language Resources Association (ELRA).

Joakim Nivre, Marie-Catherine de Marneffe, Filip Ginter, Jan Hajič, Christopher D. Manning, Sampo Pyysalo, Sebastian Schuster, Francis Tyers, and Daniel Zeman. 2020. Universal Dependencies v2: An evergrowing multilingual treebank collection. In *Proceedings of the Twelfth International Conference on Language Resources and Evaluation (LREC'20)*. European Language Resources Association (ELRA).

Odile Piton and Klara Lagji. 2008. Morphological study of Albanian words, and processing with NooJ. In *Proceedings of the 2007 International NooJ Conference*, pages 189–205. Cambridge Scholars Publishing.

Prokopis Prokopidis and Harris Papageorgiou. 2017. Universal dependencies for greek. In *Proceedings of the NoDaLiDa 2017 Workshop on Universal Dependencies (UDW 2017)*, pages 102–106.

Jochen Trommer and Dalina Kallulli. 2004. A morphological analyzer for standard Albanian. In *Proceedings of the Fourth International Conference on Language Resources and Evaluation (LREC'04)*, Lisbon, Portugal, May. European Language Resources Association (ELRA).

Francis M. Tyers, Mariya Sheyanova, and Jonathan North Washington. 2017. UD Annotatrix: An annotation tool for Universal Dependencies. In *Proceedings of the 16th International Workshop on Treebanks and Linguistic Theories*, pages 10–17, Prague, Czech Republic.

First Steps towards Universal Dependencies for Laz

Utku Türk[‡], Kaan Bayar[‡], Ayşegül Dilara Özercan[‡],
Görkem Yiğit Öztürk[‡], Şaziye Betül Özateş[*]
[‡]Department of Linguistics
[*]Department of Computer Engineering
Boğaziçi University
Bebek, 34342 İstanbul, Turkey
`utku.turk,kaan.bayar,aysegul.ozercan`
`gorkem.ozturk,saziye.bilgin@boun.edu.tr`

Abstract

This paper presents the first treebank for the Laz language, which is also the first Universal Dependencies Treebank for a South Caucasian language. This treebank aims to create a syntactically and morphologically annotated resource for further research. We also aim to document an endangered language in a systematic fashion within an inherently cross-linguistic framework: the Universal Dependencies Project (UD). As of now, our treebank consists of 576 sentences and 2,306 tokens annotated in light with the UD guidelines. We evaluated the treebank on the dependency parsing task using a pretrained multilingual parsing model, and the results are comparable with other low-resourced treebanks with no training set. We aim to expand our treebank in the near future to include 1,500 sentences. The bigger goal for our project is to create a set of treebanks for minority languages in Anatolia.

1 Introduction

In recent years, many understudied languages have been in the spotlight of NLP studies. Within the Universal Dependencies Framework (Nivre et al., 2016), languages like Wolof (Dione, 2019), Mbyá Guaraní (Thomas, 2019), Eryza (Rueter and Tyers, 2018), Bhojpuri (Ojha and Zeman, 2020), and many others have been introduced to NLP studies. Laz is also another understudied language on which there are no NLP resources, with the exception of a recent morphological analyzer (Önal and Tyers, 2019).

Laz is spoken in the Southeastern part of the Black Sea among a declining population which is estimated to consist of somewhere between 250,000 and 500,000 people (Haznedar, 2018). It is a highly agglutinative language which makes use of prefixes and suffixes, and it is reported to have 16 different slots for verb inflection (Öztürk and Pöchtrager, 2011). Laz is also reported to have extensive dialectal variation (Öztürk and Pöchtrager, 2011). In this work, when we use the word Laz, we specifically mean the Atina-Pazar dialect of Laz.

Through this work, we hope to contribute to the revitalization efforts of the Laz language by providing a gold standard dependency treebank. We provide the first publicly available human-annotated morphosyntactic Laz treebank. We utilize the already existing Universal Dependency framework to represent UPOS tags, morphological features, and syntactic dependency relations. We also provide parsing results with no training data using UDify (Kondratyuk and Straka, 2019). Thus, we provide attachment scores (UAS and LAS) which are comparable with other low resource languages within the UD framework.

2 BOUN Laz Treebank

2.1 Data and Treebank Statistics

The data used in this treebank consist of linguistic examples from academic works which describe the Laz language. These works include theses, articles, proceedings, and presentation handouts.[1] In our

---

[1]The full list of resources is as follows: Emgin (2009), Demirok (2018), Demirok et al. (2019), Demirok (2014), Demirok (2020), Demirok (2013), Öztürk (2016), Öztürk and Taylan (2013), Öztürk (2019)

Proceedings of the Fourth Workshop on Universal Dependencies (UDW 2020), pages 189–194
Barcelona, Spain (Online), December 13, 2020

future work, we want to include reference grammars, user-generated data, and folk stories. As of now, we present 576 sentences and 2,306 tokens which have glosses in the source files they are taken, but not syntactically annotated before. We annotated every sentence and every token manually following UD guidelines. This process includes annotating morphological features, syntactic dependency relations and POS tags. In our treebank, we also included a gloss and English translation for every sentence. Additionally, we used easily parsable sentence IDs which follow the `source-genre_number` template. When we include sentences extracted from fictions, we will also provide paragraph ID for sentences.

Caucasian languages have always presented a challenge to mainstream notion in linguistics research. The challenge mainly stem from their highly allomorphic and fusional morphology (Blix, 2020; Demirok, 2020). We believe that the addition of these languages would pose new questions for the typological adequacy of the UD framework. These issues include the representation of complex subordinating conjunctions and the need for finer analysis in the morphological representation.

2.2 Annotation Process

The treebank was annotated with a team of 4 linguists, comprised of 3 annotators and one reviewer. The annotators were responsible for their own batch of sentences. After the annotation, these sentences were sent to the reviewer to be checked. All changes made in this review process were discussed by the entire annotator group. The decision agreed upon was then applied uniformly to the treebank and recorded as part of the guidelines we prepared.

3 Linguistic Analysis of Laz Dependency Treebank

As we stated earlier, we followed UD v2 guidelines to annotate our Laz treebank. There were some challenging data that needed to be implemented to UD framework. We mention three of them in this section with the linguistic discussion behind our decision.

3.1 Complementizer 'YA'

One challenge in annotating Laz linguistic data is coding sentences that include the complementizer 'ya'. Interestingly, embedded YA sentences may be existentially closed, meaning that they do not need any verb to be reported as in (1) (Demirok et al., 2019).[2]

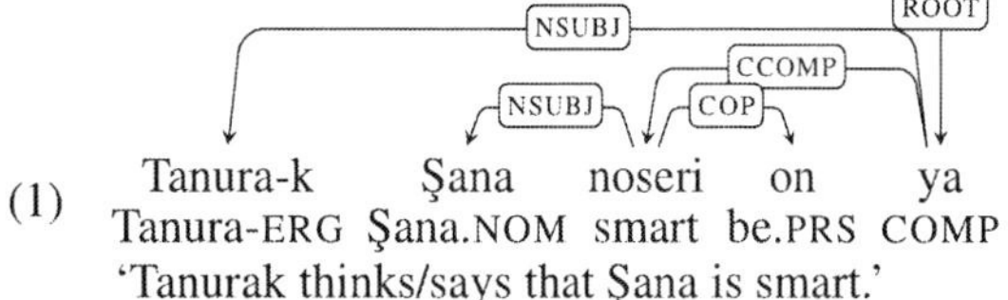

(1)
Tanura-k   Şana   noseri   on   ya
Tanura-ERG Şana.NOM smart   be.PRS COMP
'Tanurak thinks/says that Şana is smart.'   (Adapted from Demirok et al. (2019))

The problem with such sentences is that they lack an attitude verb even though they contain a context-sensitive meaning of reporting. Since UD guidelines only allow empty nodes for elision and conjunction, we were not able to implement a solution which involves speculating a hidden verb (Droganova and Zeman, 2019). A syntax and semantics oriented explanation of this phenomenon pushes for a complex YA analysis in which the YA complementizer encompasses the attitude verb, *say* in this case. This analysis is supported with other examples such as (2). The adverbials *slowly* and *yesterday* modifies the omitted main verb *say* instead of the embedded verb *swim*.

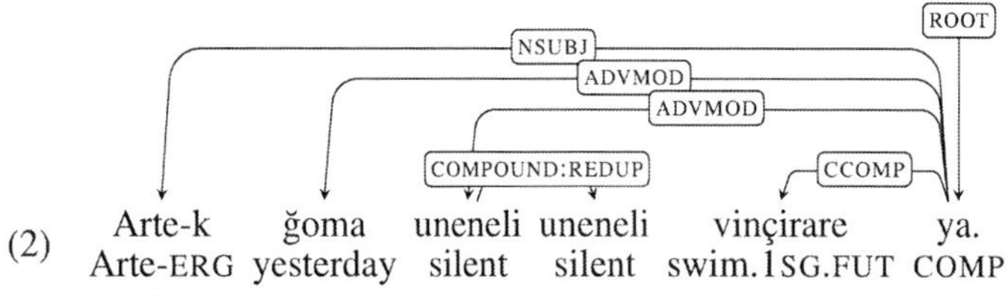

(2)
Arte-k   ğoma   uneneli   uneneli   vinçirare   ya.
Arte-ERG yesterday silent   silent   swim.1SG.FUT COMP

---

[2] 1 = first person, 2 = second person, 3 = third person, A = agent, AUG = augmentative, AUX = auxiliary, CAUS = causative, COMP = complementizer, COND = conditional, ERG = ergative, FUT = future, IMPF = imperfective, INTR = intransitive, NOM = nominative, OBL = oblique, P = patient, PL = plural, PRF = perfect, PRS = present, PST = past, PV = preverb, SBJV = subjunctive, SG = singular, TR = transitive, TS = thematic suffix.

'Yesterday, Arte silently said that he would swim.'

Following the discussion in the UD repository,[3] we marked the complementizer YA as the root of the sentence. One other possibility is to treat the ergative case as the marker for *'in somebody's opinion'*. With *'in my opinion'* reading, the sentence (1) is grammatical and means "According to Tanura, Şana is smart." However, sentence (2) would not be grammatical and we would still need YA-as-a-root solution. Thus, we did not use *'in somebody's opinion'* reading in our annotations even though this is a possible reading.

3.2 Morphological Person Marking

Another challenging aspect is the morphological annotation of person and number agreement. The verbal agreement paradigm in Laz makes use of both suffixes and prefixes. Verbs may host agreement markers not only for subjects, but also objects, indirect objects, and non-core arguments such as benefactors. However, these markers are partially co-indexable and follow the hierarchy given in (3) (Öztürk and Pöchtrager, 2011).

(3)   OBL.1SG/2SG > P.1SG/2SG > A.1SG > OBL.3SG = P.3SG = A.2SG/3SG

Instead of representing the agreement paradigm in terms of theta-roles, we utilized the already proposed morphological features in the UD version of the Basque Dependency Treebank (Aranzabe et al., 2015). They mark the morphological case of the controller of the agreement as a language specific suffix to the features `Number` and `Person`. We adopted the same approach and used the following features: `Number[erg]={Sing,Plur}`, `Number[nom]={Sing,Plur}`, `Number[dat]={Sing,Plur}`, `Person[erg]={1,2,3}`, `Person[nom]={1,2,3}`, and `Person[dat]={1,2,3}`. This enables us to cover another language specific feature of Laz. The subject of an intransitive verb is marked with either the ergative or the accusative case according to the type of the verb (unergative or unaccusative) (Öztürk and Pöchtrager, 2011). By using this method for the agreement paradigm, we also mark the intransitive verb types indirectly. Unergative verbs which only have agent argument will be represented with `[erg]` layer and unaccusative ones with the `[nom]` layer.

3.3 Affirmative Preverbs

The verb in Laz has a highly complex structure which can host 16 different slots for inflection (Öztürk and Pöchtrager, 2011).[4] Four of these slots are used by preverbal affixes. One such type of a preverbal affix is the affirmative preverb. The affirmative preverbs (*ko-, do-, menda-, o-*) conveys either habitual reading or certainty reading.

For the annotation process, it presents two challenges. The first challenge is related to its syncretic functions. Without any context information, it is impossible to differentiate between the habitual reading and the certainty reading. For this treebank, we followed the glosses presented in the linguistic works.

The second challenge stems from its certainty reading. It signals that the speaker knows that the event has *certainly* happened or will happen (Öztürk and Pöchtrager, 2011). The only morphological feature related with this reading is the `Evident` feature within the UD framework. However, affirmative preverbs do not convey the source information. For example, the sentence (4) may be uttered even when the speaker does not witness Ali's coming.

(4)   *Ali   ko-mo-xt'-u.*
      Ali.NOM PV$_{aff}$-PV$_{spat}$-come-PST.3SG

    'Ali certainly came.'   (Öztürk and Pöchtrager, 2011)

One possibility is adding a new value to the feature as `Polarity=Aff`. However, the rest of the values within the polarity feature is not directly related to the phenomenon in Laz. Additionally, the

---

[3]`https://github.com/UniversalDependencies/docs/issues/734`
[4]Morphological slots of the verb are as follow: PV$_{aff}$-PV$_{spat}$-Person-Valency-Root-AUG-CAUS.INTR-CAUS-TR-CAUS.PRF-TS-IMPF-SBJV-Person-COND-PL-AUX

name *affirmative* comes from its complementary distribution with the negative marker, which is pointed out to be irrelevant by Öztürk and Pöchtrager (2011). Affirmative reading is still possible without the preverb. Instead, we introduced a new value *certain* to the feature aspect as `Aspect=Crt`. The feature aspect is also used with its other reading as `Aspect=Hab`.

4 Parsing with a Multilingual Parser

Since the size of the treebank is insufficient to train a dependency parser for the Laz language, we instead observed the parsing success of a multilingual parser on our treebank without using any resources on the Laz language in the training phase. We chose to use UDify for this task. UDify is a state-of-the-art multilingual multi-task model that can predict annotations for any treebank annotated in UD style. The UDify model is fine-tuned on multilingual BERT pretrained embeddings (Devlin et al., 2019) and can syntactically annotate sentences in any language without requiring any language-specific components. We want to benefit from an automatic annotator in the hope that it will ease the manual annotation task of additional Laz text.

We used a pretrained multilingual UDify model to parse our treebank. Since the Laz language does not have any NLP resources other than this treebank, such as pretrained word embeddings or a publicly available corpus,[5] the language is completely unknown to the UDify model. Moreover, none of the language resources that were used in training of the UDify and BERT models belong to South Caucasian language family, which includes the Laz language.

Treebank	Token count	UAS	LAS
Our Laz Treebank	2K	44.15	29.05
Akkadian-PISANDUB[6]	1K	27.65	4.54
Amharic-ATT (Seyoum et al., 2018)	5K	17.38	3.49
Cantonese-HK (Wong et al., 2017)	6K	46.82	32.01
Erzya-JR (Rueter and Tyers, 2018)	15K	31.90	16.38
Komi Zyrian-IKDP (Partanen et al., 2018)	1K	36.01	22.12
Komi Zyrian-Lattice (Partanen et al., 2018)	2K	28.85	12.99
Naija-NSC[7]	12K	45.75	32.16
Sanskrit-UFAL[8]	1K	40.21	18.56
Warlpiri-UFAL[9]	< 1K	21.66	7.96
Yoruba-YTB (Ishola and Zeman, 2020)	2K	37.62	19.09

Table 1: Test results for our treebank and some of the low-resourced treebanks in (Kondratyuk and Straka, 2019). The UDify and BERT models have no training data for any of these treebanks. The token counts given in the second column are from the UD v2.3 versions of the treebanks.

In their paper, Kondratyuk and Straka (2019) stated the success of their UDify model on every available treebank in the Universal Dependencies v2.3 corpus. Like the Laz language, there are other languages that are unknown to UDify in this corpus, although some of them have close relatives in the training data. In Table 1, we give the UAS and LAS scores of the model on our treebank as well as the scores of the treebanks used in (Kondratyuk and Straka, 2019) that were not used in the training phase of the UDify model for comparison. All of the treebanks in Table 1 have 15K or less tokens.

In Table 1, we observe that, the highest two attachment scores are achieved on Naija-NSC and Cantonese-HK, which is somewhat expected because Naija is an English-based creole language and

---

[5]Only existing corpus is mentioned in the work of Önal and Tyers (2019); however, they did not publish this treebank.
[6]`https://universaldependencies.org/treebanks/akk_pisandub/index.html`
[7]`https://universaldependencies.org/treebanks/pcm_nsc/index.html`
[8]`https://universaldependencies.org/treebanks/sa_ufal/index.html`
[9]`https://universaldependencies.org/treebanks/wbp_ufal/index.html`

Cantonese belongs to the Chinese language family. Although there is not any language resource in the training data which shares the same language family with Laz language, our treebank has the third best attachment scores. The low average token count per sentence (approximately 4 tokens per sentence) in our treebank has an impact on these relatively high scores. However, the results suggest that we need to manually annotate more data from scratch before taking advantage of a dependency parser as a pre-annotator. We see that there is an immense need to improve the parsing scores of our treebank and we hope that the parsing accuracy of the Laz language will greatly benefit from the presence of training data as we continue to annotate more sentences manually in the Laz language.

5   Conclusion

This paper reports the development of the first Laz Treebank ever. Considering that there is no Laz corpus or treebank that precedes this work and no treebank from the South Caucasian language family, we believe our work will be an important contribution to the field and support the further development of typological studies that utilize the UD framework. In addition, our work is also a gold standard for both syntactic and morphological annotation which will help many future studies on both Laz and Georgian. Our treebank currently consists of 576 sentences extracted from linguistic research. This paper discusses three topics of Laz grammar which can contribute to the UD framework in the future. Additionally, we report dependency parsing results with a multilingual parser: UDify. The parsing accuracy of our treebank in a zero-shot learning setting are found to be similar to other low-resourced treebanks with no training data.

The main aim of our work is to create treebanks for the minority languages spoken in Anatolia, including Cappadocian Greek, Pontic Greek, Pomak, Ladino, and many others. We believe that these series of treebanks can promote future research in language contact studies as well as NLP studies in these languages. Additionally, we hope to contribute to the revitalization efforts for these languages, including Laz. In the near future, we will expand our treebank to include 1,500 sentences before annotating any other language.

References

Maria Jesus Aranzabe, Aitziber Atutxa, Kepa Bengoetxea, Arantza Diaz de Ilarraza, Iakes Goenaga, Koldo Gojenola, and Larraitz Uria. 2015. Automatic conversion of the Basque dependency treebank to universal dependencies. In *Proceedings of the fourteenth international workshop on treebanks an linguistic theories (TLT14)*, pages 233–241.

Hagen Blix. 2020. Spans in South Caucasian agreement. *Natural Language & Linguistic Theory*, May.

Ömer Demirok, Deniz Özyıldız, and Balkız Öztürk. 2019. Complementizers with attitude. In Maggie Baird, editor, *NELS 49: Proceedings of the Forty-Ninth Annual Meeting of the North East Linguistic Society: Volume 3*. Amherst, MA: GLSA, Dept. of Linguistics.

Ömer Demirok. 2013. Agree as a unidirectional operation: Evidence from Pazar Laz. Master's thesis, Boğaziçi University.

Ömer Demirok. 2014. The status of roots in event composition: Laz. *Lingue e linguaggio, Rivista semestrale,* (1/2014):83–102.

Ömer Demirok. 2018. A modal approach to dative subjects in Laz. In Sherry Hucklebridge and Max Nelson, editors, *NELS 48: Proceedings of the Forty-Eighth Annual Meeting of the North East Linguistic Society*. CreateSpace Independent Publishing Platform.

Ömer Demirok. 2020. Non-linear blocking of portmanteaus: a case study on Laz. Talk given at NanoLAB, Masaryk University, Brno.

Jacob Devlin, Ming-Wei Chang, Kenton Lee, and Kristina Toutanova. 2019. BERT: Pre-training of deep bidirectional transformers for language understanding. In *Proceedings of the 2019 Conference of the North American Chapter of the Association for Computational Linguistics: Human Language Technologies, Volume 1 (Long and Short Papers)*, pages 4171–4186, Minneapolis, Minnesota, June. Association for Computational Linguistics.

Cheikh Bamba Dione. 2019. Developing universal dependencies for Wolof. In *Proceedings of the Third Workshop on Universal Dependencies (UDW, SyntaxFest 2019)*, pages 12–23, Paris, France, August. Association for Computational Linguistics.

Kira Droganova and Daniel Zeman. 2019. Towards deep universal dependencies. In *Proceedings of the Fifth International Conference on Dependency Linguistics (Depling, SyntaxFest 2019)*, pages 144–152, Paris, France, August. Association for Computational Linguistics.

Betül Emgin. 2009. *Finiteness and complementation in Laz*. Ph.D. thesis, Boğaziçi University.

Belma Haznedar. 2018. The living Laz project: The current status of the Laz language and Laz-speaking communities in Turkey. Talk given in LINGDAY, Boğaziçi University, Turkey.

Olájídé Ishola and Daniel Zeman. 2020. Yorùbá dependency treebank (YTB). In *Proceedings of The 12th Language Resources and Evaluation Conference*, pages 5178–5186.

Dan Kondratyuk and Milan Straka. 2019. 75 languages, 1 model: Parsing universal dependencies universally. In *Proceedings of the 2019 Conference on Empirical Methods in Natural Language Processing and the 9th International Joint Conference on Natural Language Processing (EMNLP-IJCNLP)*, pages 2779–2795, Hong Kong, China, November. Association for Computational Linguistics.

Joakim Nivre, Marie-Catherine de Marneffe, Filip Ginter, Yoav Goldberg, Jan Hajič, Christopher D. Manning, Ryan McDonald, Slav Petrov, Sampo Pyysalo, Natalia Silveira, Reut Tsarfaty, and Daniel Zeman. 2016. Universal dependencies v1: A multilingual treebank collection. In *Proceedings of the Tenth International Conference on Language Resources and Evaluation (LREC'16)*, pages 1659–1666, Portorož, Slovenia, May. European Language Resources Association (ELRA).

Atul Kr. Ojha and Daniel Zeman. 2020. Universal Dependency treebanks for low-resource Indian languages: The case of Bhojpuri. In *Proceedings of the WILDRE5– 5th Workshop on Indian Language Data: Resources and Evaluation*, pages 33–38, Marseille, France, May. European Language Resources Association (ELRA).

Esra Önal and Francis Tyers. 2019. Building a morphological analyser for Laz. In *Proceedings of the International Conference on Recent Advances in Natural Language Processing (RANLP 2019)*, pages 869–877, Varna, Bulgaria, September. INCOMA Ltd.

Balkız Öztürk and Markus A. Pöchtrager. 2011. *Pazar Laz*. Lincom Europa München.

Balkız Öztürk and Eser Erguvanlı Taylan. 2013. Omnipresent little v in Pazar Laz. Talk given at Little v Workshop, University of Leiden.

Balkız Öztürk. 2016. Applicatives in Pazar Laz. Talk given at The South Caucasian Chalk Circle 3, Paris.

Balkız Öztürk. 2019. The loss of case system in Ardeshen Laz and its morphosyntactic consequences. *STUF - Language Typology and Universals*, 72(2):193 – 219.

Niko Partanen, Rogier Blokland, KyungTae Lim, Thierry Poibeau, and Michael Rießler. 2018. The first Komi-Zyrian universal dependencies treebanks. In *Second Workshop on Universal Dependencies (UDW 2018), November 2018, Brussels, Belgium*, pages 126–132.

Jack Rueter and Francis Tyers. 2018. Towards an open-source universal-dependency treebank for Erzya. In *Proceedings of the Fourth International Workshop on Computational Linguistics of Uralic Languages*, pages 106–118.

Binyam Ephrem Seyoum, Yusuke Miyao, and Baye Yimam Mekonnen. 2018. Universal dependencies for Amharic. In *Proceedings of the Eleventh International Conference on Language Resources and Evaluation (LREC 2018)*.

Guillaume Thomas. 2019. Universal dependencies for Mbyá Guaraní. In *Proceedings of the Third Workshop on Universal Dependencies (UDW, SyntaxFest 2019)*, pages 70–77, Paris, France, August. Association for Computational Linguistics.

Tak-sum Wong, Kim Gerdes, Herman Leung, and John Lee. 2017. Quantitative comparative syntax on the Cantonese-Mandarin parallel dependency treebank. In *Proceedings of the Fourth International Conference on Dependency Linguistics (Depling 2017), September 18-20, 2017, Università di Pisa, Italy*, number 139, pages 266–275. Linköping University Electronic Press.

Dependency annotation of noun incorporation in polysynthetic languages

Francis M. Tyers
Department of Linguistics
Indiana University
Bloomington, IN
ftyers@iu.edu

Karina Mishchenkova
Institute of Linguistics, RAS, Moscow
Institute for System Programming, RAS, Moscow
School of Linguistics, HSE, Moscow
karinam6@mail.ru

Abstract

This paper describes an approach to annotating noun incorporation in Universal Dependencies. It motivates the need to annotate this particular morphosyntactic phenomenon and justifies it with respect to frequency of the construction. A case study is presented in which the proposed annotation scheme is applied to a corpus of Chukchi, a highly-endangered language of Siberia that exhibits noun incorporation. We compare argument encoding in Chukchi, English and Russian and find that while in English and Russian discourse elements are primarily tracked through noun phrases and pronouns, in Chukchi they are tracked through agreement marking and incorporation, with a lesser role for noun phrases.

1 Introduction

This paper addresses the question of noun incorportion in Universal Dependencies. It gives an overview of the phenomenon and some current challenges with its representation in Universal Dependencies. It then describes an annotation solution requiring minimal changes to the existing annotation guidelines. A case study is then given in which a corpus of an endangered polysynthetic language that exhibits noun incorporation is annotated and a comparison is drawn between how this language encodes arguments and how two more well-studied and better-resourced languages do.

There are many definitions of polysynthetic languages, and there is no agreement in the literature as to what precise features of a language merit its inclusion within the category of polysynthetic languages (Fortescue et al., 2017). A common definition is a language is polysynthetic if its verbal morphology is extremely complex and a single verb is capable of expressing all of its arguments internally, through agreement or incorporation, i.e. *holophrasis.*

In comparison to more familiar morphological types such as isolating, fusional and agglutinative languages, vanishingly little computational work has been done on languages of this type, although note the recent workshop on polysynthetic languages (Klavans, 2018). This is largely as a result of the fact that these languages are usually spoken by communities that are either comprised of a small number of speakers, have limited economic and political power or both. Geographically, there are few if any in Europe or most of Asia, but they are spoken by many indigenous communities in the Arctic region, the Americas, Australia and Papua New Guinea (Fortescue et al., 2017).

We present the first work on annotating noun incorporation in a language[1] using the Universal Dependencies guidelines — and probably the first medium-scale computational annotation work of any kind of a language of the noun-incorporating type.[2]

---

[1]Senuma and Aizawa (2017) present a treebank of Ainu, a language that is recorded as exhibiting noun incorporation. The treebank contains 36 sentences. The authors state that noun incorporation for Ainu is only used in poetry and fixed expressions but provide no quantative evidence. Note that this existence of incorporation as a marginal phenomenon is not the case for all languages that exhibit incorporation.

[2]We note that Bick (2019) presents a dependency formalism for Greenlandic, which has a phenomenon similar to noun incorporation, but that we distinguish as lexical affixing — a large, but closed, set of verbalising affixes that can be attached to nouns to make complex predicates.

In passing we address two issues that are often brought up when discussing the phenomenon of noun incorporation. The first is a matter of frequency: is this a core part of the language, or is it a marginal phenomenon? This matters because if we are to propose changing annotation guidelines that may have an effect on hundreds of existing treebanks, then our approach will be more convincing if the phenomenon is frequent and the change is minimal. The second is a matter of level of representation: is this syntax, morphology or something else? This matters because (typically) if it is grouped within the syntactic phenomena then it should have an expression in the syntactic annotation, but if it is grouped with morphology then it should be expressed in the morphological annotation.

2 Noun incorporation

Noun incorporation is a phenomenon whereby a noun and a verb are combined to produce a complex verb. It forms part of a wider group of incorporation phenomena such as nominals being incorporated with other nominals, a process often called *compounding*. In this paper we are specifically concerned with the incorporation of core arguments into verbal predicates. Or put another way, the 'saturation' of argument slots in the verb by compounded lexical material.

	Ынӄэната	гакиноратјенатъым	клюпчыко.
(1)	*ənqenata*	*ɣakinoratłenatʔəm*	*kłupsəko*
	ənqena-ta	*ɣa-kino-rat-łena-t=ʔəm*	*kłup-səko*
	this-INS	PF-film-bring-PF.3SG-PL=EMPH	club-LOC

'They brought the film to the club by this transport.'[3]

We can illustrate this process with Example 1 from Chukchi, the form гакиноратјенатъым [ɣakinoratłe-natʔəm] is composed of two lexical roots, *кино* 'film' and *-рэт-* [ret] 'bring'.[4] The process of incorporation in this case renders a transitive verb, intransitive, with the concomitant effects on agreement inflection — Chukchi has separate inflectional paradigms for transitive and intransitive verbs. Here, the circumfix for third-person plural subject in the perfect aspect of the stative paradigm is *гэ- … -јинэт* [ɣe- … -łine-t].

There is a question in the literature as to what extent the incorporated noun can have definite reference, which overlaps with the discussion of if noun incorporation should be considered primarily a syntactic phenomenon or a lexical phenomenon. There has been a substantial amount of lively debate in the literature written about this with authors such as Baker (1996) positing that noun incorporation is a syntactic movement rule which takes a direct object and moves it inside the verbal complex leaving a trace. In this analysis, the incorporation of nouns with definite reference is permitted, and in some cases obligatory.

Dunn (1999) in his description of Chukchi draws a distinction between lexical incorporation, or compounding (see above) and *syntactic incorporation*, noting that syntactic incorporation leads to a rearrangement of valency in the verb and that there can be "distinguished dependency relationships between the two stems" (Dunn, 1999, §12.1).

On the other end of the scale, incorporation has been treated as a lexical phenomenon (Mithun, 1984; Rosen, 1989; Anderson, 2001), although they also acknowledge the discourse and pragmatic usage of noun incorporation and the part it plays in the argument structure of predicates. Mithun (1984) in particular provides a four-way categorisation of noun incorporation ranging from the more lexical to the more syntactic. Different languages may exhibit different kinds of incorporation. In this paper we are primarily concerned with Mithun's 'TYPE III' incorporation, or that incorporation which is used to manipulate the discourse structure, with the incorporated noun having low discourse salience.

Noting that discussion of the issue has been caught up in various debates surrounding theoretical syntax, we prefer to take a practical approach. Noun incorporation is a wide-ranging phenomenon with effects in morphology — the form of the word, syntax — the arrangement of clause and argument structure, and discourse — the arrangement of information structure. Thus we find a purely lexical approach, or the 'all verbs with incorporated nouns should be annotated as separate lexemes' to be untenable.

---

[3] INS – instrumental; PF – perfective; 3SG – third person singular; PL – plural; EMPH – emphasiser; LOC – locative. Hyphens denote morpheme boundaries, while the equals sign denotes a clitic boundary.

[4] The transformation of the vowel in the verb stem *-pəm-* [ret] 'bring' to *-pam-* [rat] is a vowel harmony process. For a short description of vowel harmony in Chukchi, refer to §4.

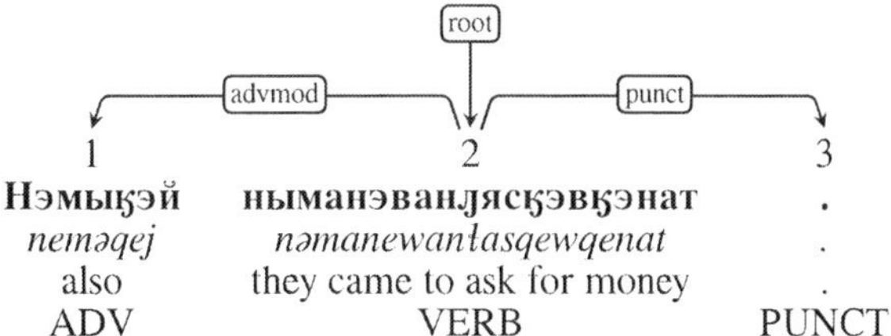

Figure 1: A simple dependency annotation scheme. The transitive verb *-ванӊ-* [wanɬa] 'ask' has been combined with the lexical stem *манӭ* [mane] 'money' to produce a new intransitive verb, to which is added intransitive agreement morphology.

3 Proposed annotation scheme

In order to develop and test annotation guidelines for these phenomena, we decided to approach a particular language, Chukchi (see Section 4), and develop them iteratively during an annotation project. For the base annotation guidelines we used those of the Universal Dependencies project (Nivre et al., 2020) and extended them following the six principles of *Manning's Law*:

1. UD needs to be satisfactory for analysis of individual languages.

2. UD needs to be good for linguistic typology.

3. UD must be suitable for rapid, consistent annotation.

4. UD must be suitable for computer parsing with high accuracy.

5. UD must be easily comprehended and used by a non-linguist.

6. UD must provide good support for downstream NLP tasks.

Within the current guidelines for Universal Dependencies, a suggested approach for annotating noun incorporation is of the strong lexicalist type. Relations are between syntactic *words*. For a language exhibiting noun incorporation this would result in trees such as in Figure 1.

Here, 'to come to ask for money' would be represented a single verb. We argue that this is not a satisfactory analysis (1), and that it is not useful for downstream NLP tasks (6). As a result of the lack of information in the annotation, it would be suitable for rapid, consistent annotation (3) and high-accuracy parsing (4). While in terms of comprehensibility for non-linguists (5) and use for linguistic typology (2) various arguments may be made, there is not much to understand in the annotation, and it may be useful in terms of illustrating that certain languages have very long verbs, but not in terms of looking at anything more than morphology from a typological point of view.

It is worth presenting for a moment the lexicalist hypothesis to which Universal Dependencies subscribes. Broadly stated it is that syntactic structures or relations hold between *words*, that is there is a separate component (in the human mind) for building words — the *lexicon* — and for building sentences — the *grammar*. The strong variant of this hypothesis states that all production of word forms happens in the lexicon, and that this contains lexemes, derivational rules,[5] and inflectional rules. Syntactic rules may not interact with derivational rules. This is often described as the 'Lexical Integrity Principle' and is adopted by formalisms such as Head-Driven Phrase Structure Grammar (HPSG; Bresnan and Mchombo (1995)) (although see also (Emerson and Copestake, 2015)) and Lexical-Functional Grammar (LFG; Dalrymple (2001)). A weak variant of the lexicalist hypothesis states that lexemes and derivational rules belong in the lexicon, while syntax operates on structures composed of lexemes and features, to which subsequently are applied inflectional rules. Finally, there is non-lexicalism, in which syntax applies directly to simple lexemes and morphemes, a popular approach in contemporary theoretical syntax.

The Universal Dependencies project as a whole subscribes to strong lexicalism, that is syntactic structures and relations hold between syntactic words, although there is flexibility with how the notion of *word*[6] is defined. For example, clitics are often, but not always, tokenised as separate syntactic words.

---

[5] Here we refer to morphological derivation, these rules are sometimes called *word-formation rules*.

[6] We note here that there is discussion as to if the word should be a unit of analysis at all. For an informative overview, see Haspelmath (2009).

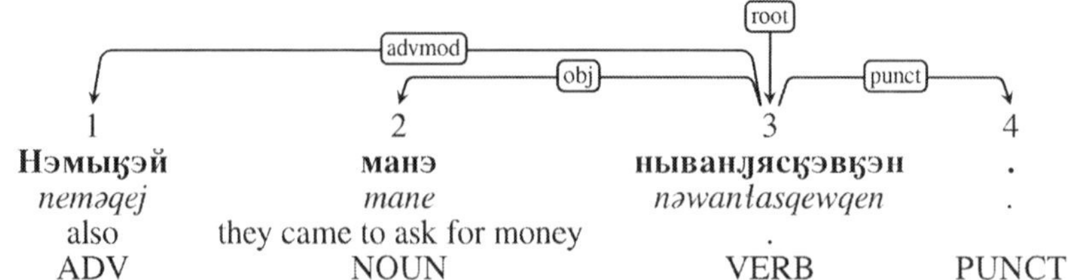

Figure 2: An annotation scheme where the intransitive clause post-incorporation has been rewritten as a transitive clause with no incorporation. Note that in addition to moving the incorporated element out of the verb, the agreement circumfix also must be modified. The intransitive stative habitual agreement circumfix for the third-person plural subject is *n*-STEM-*qinet*, whereas the transitive agreement for third-person plural subject and third-person singular object is *n*-STEM-*qin*. Thus, producing this annotation would necessitate the reinflection of the verb by the annotator.

```
# sent_id = Money:10
# text = Нэмыӄэй ныманэванӆясӄэвӄэнат.
# text[phon] = neməqej nəmanewanɬasqewqenat
# text[rus] = Тоже приходили просить денег.
# text[eng] = They also came to ask for money.
1     Нэмыӄэй             _    ADV    _    _    4    advmod    _    _
2-4   ныманэванӆясӄэвӄэнат _    _      _    _    _    _         _    _
3     манэ                _    NOUN   _    _    4    obj       _    _
4     ныванӆясӄэвӄэн      _    VERB   _    _    0    root      _    _
5     .                   _    PUNCT  _    _    4    punct     _    _
```

Figure 3: Partial CoNLL-U representation of the tree in Figure 2 illustrating the encoding of the verb as a multi-token syntactic word. The contents of the FEATS column has been omitted for reasons of space.

If we accept that noun incorporation should be encoded in the annotation, the question then becomes, where should it be encoded? A morphological encoding would see the incorporated noun become part of the morphological features, possibly with a expression like `Incorporated[obj]=манэ` for 'the object of this verb has been incorporated and the lexeme is *манэ*'. An advantage of this method would be that it is minimally disruptive to the existing guidelines, adding additional language-specific `Feature=Value` pairs is directly permitted by the guidelines. However, it has some unsatisfactory consequences, typically the `Value` portion of `Feature=Value` pairs are considered a finite set. There is a fixed number of possible `Values` for each `Feature`. Noun incorporation does not follow this. In languages that permit it, any noun — semantic and pragmatic conditions permitting — can be incorporated as an object.

A second option is to include it in the basic dependencies, using the existing solution for 'multiword' tokens, clitics, and contractions. This would involve splitting the token into sub-tokens and annotating as the underlying construction, for example an intransitive clause would be annotated as if it were transitive with a free-standing object. This is primarily unsatisfactory from a descriptive point of view, there is every indication, regardless of the theory subscribed to, that the surface structure of a transitive verb with incorporated object is intransitive.[7] Additionally, it would require substantial effort on the part of annotators, who would need to be both fluent in the language (to be able to generate the non-incorporated equivalents of clauses with incorporation), and expert in the annotation scheme. For many (if not most) under-resourced and marginalised languages, this does not obtain. Furthermore, the information structure of the incorporated and non-incorporated forms are different, so further processing would need to distinguish unconverted transitive clauses and converted ones.[8]

Our proposal is to encode it in the *enhanced* dependency structure (Schuster and Manning, 2016). The enhanced structure is built on top of the basic dependencies and may include:

---

[7]For simplicity we restrict discussion of antipassivising verbs (Dunn, 1999, §12.2.1) here, where the incorporation of an object does not reduce the valency, and some other non-patient role is promoted to the object slot.

[8]To aid the reader, one could imagine a hypothetical annotation scheme whereby analytic passives must be rewritten as non-passive with a feature indicating passivisation.

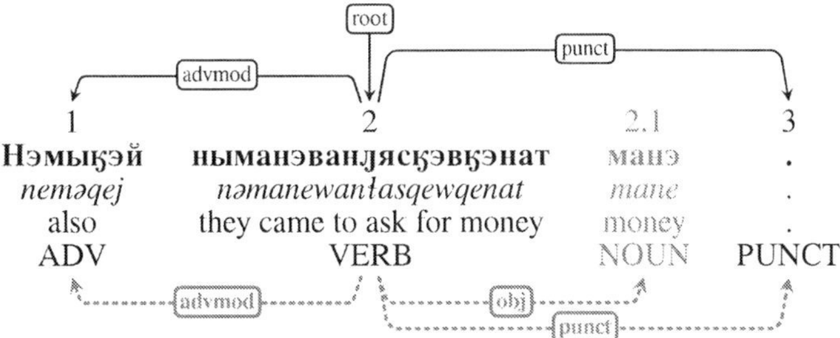

Figure 4: Dependency tree for the sentence in Figure 5. The enhanced representation is shown in grey. As for morphological features, the verb is marked with a feature `Incorporated[obj]=Yes` and a feature `Valency=1` to indicate the intransitive nature of the verb. The incorporated noun in the enhanced representation receives the feature `Incorporated=Yes`.

1. Null nodes for elided predicates

2. Propagation of conjuncts

3. Additional subject relations for control and raising constructions

4. Coreference in relative clause constructions

5. Modifier labels that contain the preposition or other case-marking information

We propose extending the guidelines for the enhanced representation to allow *additional* nodes for core arguments of predicates, which are expressed via incorporation of lexical material.[9] Note that these are not strictly *null* nodes — such as those used for elided predicates — as they could only be permitted to represent incorporated lexical material, which by its nature is not *null*. This would allow the annotation of trees such as that in Figure 4 where the incorporated object becomes a node in the enhanced graph.

In an outward sense, the annotation of incorporation has some relation to the annotation of *pro-drop* languages, where arguments required by the predicate may not have any form in the syntax and only appear as agreement markers on the verb. However in one important sense it differs in that while for pro-drop languages the potential list of pronouns is from a finite set and can often be inferred mechanically from the verbal agreement, with incorporation the arguments are not a finite set and, barring additional annotation, cannot be recovered from the predicate.

4 Case study

In order to test our proposed annotation guidelines, we decided to approach a particular language, Chukchi. Chukchi (ISO-639-3: `ckt`) is a highly endangered and polysynthetic language spoken in the sparsely-populated Chukotka Autonomous Okrug in the far north east of the Russian Federation. The total population of Chukotka was 50,526 in 2010. According to the 2010 census it was spoken by 5,095 people, or around a third of the ethnic population. Today most speakers are over the age of 50, and, even by the 1990s intergenerational transmission had been disrupted (Dunn, 1999). The language exhibits polypersonal agreement, ergative–absolutive alignment, and a subject–object–verb basic word order in transitive clauses. The language is severely under-resourced and there has been very little computational work on this language. We are only aware of a description of a finite-state morphological analyser (Andriyanets and Tyers, 2018). There have been a number of theoretical and descriptive linguistic works on noun incorporation in Chukchi, including Spencer (1995) who gives a general overview and Polinsky (1990) who covers subject incorporation.

We used the Amguema corpus, available through the «Chuklang»[10] site, which is a corpus of spoken Chukchi in the Amguema variant. The corpus consists of both audio recordings and transcriptions with glosses and translations in Russian and English. There are a total of 65 texts, most of which are elicited

---

[9]This is the most conservative variant of our proposal, the most essential part. We also think it is worth opening up a discussion about *null* nodes for core arguments expressed morphologically, such as subject and object in languages with polypersonal agreement.

[10]https://chuklang.ru/

1.10	neməqej	nəmanewanɬasqewqenat				
	neməqej	nə-	mane	wanɬa	-sqew	-qena	-t
	тоже	ST	деньги	просить	MCP	ST.3SG	PL
	also	ST	money	ask	MCP	ST.3SG	PL
	'Тоже приходили просить денег.'						
	'They also came to ask for money.'						

Figure 5: An annotated sentence in Chukchi from the Amguema corpus, text *Деньги* 'Money'. The sentence includes an ID, a phonetic transcription, morpheme segmentation, gloss in Russian and English and a free translation in Russian and English. The sentence demonstrates object incorporation, the object *-mane-* 'money' is combined with the transitive stem *-wanɬa-* 'ask' to make an intransitive verb which is then conjugated with subject conjugation for 3rd person plural *nə-* ...*-qena-t*.

stories and tales, comprising 1,004 sentences/utterances with 6,124 tokens. The corpus was created between 2016 and 2018 by Chukchi speakers and researchers from *Higher School of Economics* in Moscow.

Figure 5 presents an example of a sentence from one of the texts in the Amguema corpus. In this sentence, the noun *мане* [mane] 'money' has been incorporated as an object of the verb *-ванʌя-* [wanɬa] 'ask'; the derivational affix, *-cҕeв* [sqew] 'GOAL', is suffixed, and the inflectional agreement morphology is circumfixed.

The tokenisation in the corpus follows the scheme set out by Dunn (1999) and others, in that the formal boundary of a word is indicated by the vowel harmony process. For an extensive description the reader is referred to Dunn (1999, §3.4.1), but in brief: In Chukchi vowels are split into two groups, recessive, *u* /i/, *ə* /e₁/ and *y* /u/ and dominant *ə* /e₂/, *a* /a/ and *o* /o/. The two variants of /e/ are phonetically identical but phonologically behave differently. If any vowel in any morpheme in a word is dominant, then any recessive vowels harmonise to their dominant counterparts.

Nouns incorporated into verbs, as with all other morphemes in the verb form, participate in this process. Consider the example *таунырэҙҕыпатҕэнат* [taŋnəreɬqəpatqenat] 'They cooked porridge'. The incorporated nominal object *-рэҙҕ-* [-reɬq-] < *риʌыҕ* [riɬəq] 'porridge', which is harmonically recessive, undergoes *u* /i/ → *ə* /e/ harmony as a result of the dominant vowel /a/ in the verb stem *-nam-* [pat] 'cook'.

The corpus was annotated for dependency structure by two linguists over a period of around two months. Each linguist took a disjunct set of texts to annotate. After the dependency structure was annotated, a program was written to convert the glosses into parts of speech and sets of morphological features.

There were a total of 79 incorporated elements in the corpus, which leads to a per token percentage of 1.2%, and a per utterance percentage of 7.8%. If we look at the percentage of verb forms with incorporated elements, the percentage is 6.6%.[11] Around half of all texts contained no incorporations, and around half contained more than one with the minimum being 0 and the maximum being 14. We aim to show with these statistics that although the per token percentage may appear to be marginal, if we look at the level of predicates and discourse, the phenomenon is far from marginal and is a core part of the language.

By and far the most productive type of incorporation was object incorporation, with 50 out of 79 examples. Following this was incorporation of verb stems as adverbial modifiers, which we do not treat here. More marginal, under five examples each were incorporation of obliques, subjects and adverbs.

Figure 4 presents a CoNLL-U representation of the tree in Figure 4. Lemmas have yet to be included, and the morphological features are `Aspect=Hab` 'Habitual aspect', `Deriv[goal]=Yes` 'Goal derivation', `Incorporated[obj]=Yes` 'Incorporated object', `Mood=Ind` 'Indicative mood', `Number[subj]=Plur` 'Plural subject', `Person[subj]=3` 'Third-person subject', `Valency=1` 'Intransitive', `VerbForm=Fin` 'Finite verb form', `Voice=Stat` 'Stative verbal paradigm'. The goal derivation indicates motation towards a goal.

5 Comparison

To illustrate some differences between how Chukchi encodes arguments and how English and Russian do, we selected a short story from the corpus and categorised how different entities (principally subjects and objects)

---

[11] We note that this percentage far exceeds that than phenomena such as reflexive pronouns in English, which account for under 1% of all pronouns, but without which an annotation scheme for English could hardly be considered complete.

```
# sent_id = Money:10
# text = Нэмыӄэй ныманэванӈясӄэвӄэнат.
# text[phon] = neməqej nəmanewanɬasqewqenat
# text[rus] = Тоже приходили просить денег.
# text[eng] = They also came to ask for money.
1      Нэмыӄэй                    _    ADV      _    _    2    advmod    2:advmod    _
2      ныманэванӈясӄэвӄэнат  _    VERB     _    _    0    root      0:root      _
2.1    манэ                       _    NOUN     _    _    _    _                   2:obj    _
3      .                          _    PUNCT    _    _    2    punct     2:punct     _
```

Figure 6: Partial CoNLL-U representation of the tree in Figure 4 illustrating the encoding of the incorporated object *манэ* 'money' in the enhanced representation. The contents of the FEATS column has been omitted for reasons of space. The 2.1 notation is usually used for elided predicates, but here we extend it to incorporated objects.

are encoded. These were split into four categories: Non-incorporated nominals, incorporated nominals, agreement affixes and pronominals.

The annotation is shown in Figure 7. The motivation behind this comparison is to demonstrate in a visually interpretable way the necessity of an annotation scheme that includes information about incorporated nouns.

In this comparison we can clearly see that English and Russian both have strong tendencies towards encoding arguments with free pronouns. The majority of sentences have at least one pronominal argument. In addition, Russian makes use of verbal agreement markers to encode the subject. English also uses agreement markers, but sparingly. Most verb forms are not inflected for person and number.

In Chukchi however, fewer than half of all sentences contain an explicit pronoun or external noun phrase argument. Arguments are either encoded via incorporation, agreement or by a combination of these two processes. As Dunn (1999, §7.2) observes, personal pronouns are "textually rare and pragmatically marked", and "in unelicited texts [...] are not used for anaphoric specification of arguments in clauses".

This clearly has implications for language technology applications and further linguistic analysis. Annotation schemes for predicate–argument structure such as PropBank (Palmer et al., 2005; Haverinen et al., 2015) are often annotated over the tree structure, and systems for co-reference resolution such as *Xrenner* (Zeldes and Zhang, 2016) rely on the dependency structure to add co-reference information. Semantic parsing systems such as *Universal Semantic Parsing* (Reddy et al., 2017) also rely on the dependency structure. If incorporated objects are kept out of the tree structure, then specific language-specific solutions will have to be made in each downstream application for the languages that exhibit incorporation. It is our belief that the most adequate place to represent this information is in the morphosyntactic structure as part of the dependency tree.

6 Future work

We have been able to obtain permission to annotate a further corpus of Chukchi. This corpus contains an additional 1,000 sentences (approx. 11,500 tokens) of parallel text in Chukchi and Russian from the Chukotkan newspaper *Крайний Север* 'Kraynyj Sever'.[12] It is reported by Comrie (1981) that incorporation in Chukchi is on the wane, and by Dunn (1999) that this may be the case for written Chukchi, but not spoken Chukchi, there has to our knowledge been no empirical study of this.

An additional aspect of future work is how to represent lemmas. The problem being that if we use the lemma from the basic representation then it should include the incorporated item, but then in the enhanced representation the object will be doubled: once in the lemma and once in the tree. However if we use the base lemma, then in the basic representation the lemma will not match the word form. Ideally for the verbal predicate we would like to have a different lemma in the enhanced representation to the basic representation. This would leave the basic representation with the lemma of the verb + incorporated element, and the enhanced representation with the root lemma of the verbal predicate.

Finally, in many polysynthetic languages, including Chukchi, there is a related process which also makes

---

[12] https://www.ks87.ru/

	Language	Argument(s)			
	Chukchi:	Nom	Inc	Agr	Pro
1	Ҡонпы **ны**вичвэтчыҡивҡинэтъым **ны**манэванляскъэвҡэнат.	-	+	++	-
2	Ҡынвэт [Ирана] инэльуҡин [чиниткин экык] эймэвылъын инныкагтым.	++	-	+	+
3	Ҡъыръыйылҡынноҡэн ынңин вай.	-	-	+	-
4	[Эккэтэм] ынңин ынҡэн инэгитэҡинъым.	+	-	+	-
5	Ҡынвэт ҡынвэт тытанңыткоңноҡэн.	-	-	+	-
6	«[Нымэмы] ҡэнаманэлпынрыгэ.»	+	+	+	-
7	«Ынкы ҡээҡынъым **мы**вичвысҡиквъэк автомат.»	-	-	+	-
8	Эээ ҡэлюҡъым нэнаманэлпынрыҡэн.	-	+	+	-
9	[**Мургинэт**] нэмыҡэй **ны**етҡинэт [ңинҡэгти].	+	-	+	-
10	Нэмыҡэй **ны**манэванляскэвҡэнат.	-	+	+	-
11	«Э'тки вай ҡээҡын **мы**тылгирывичвэнңыркын.»	-	-	+	-
12	Ну ҡэлюҡъым [ытдыгэ] нэнаманэлпынрыҡэнатэ амъянра наҡам.	-	+	+	-
13	Нэмэ ынҡэн комната **ны**йъоҡэн.	-	+	-	
	Russian:	Nom	Inc	Agr	Pro
1	**Они** постоянно ходил**и** играть, постоянно просил**и** [денег].	+	-	++	+
2	И тут [Ира] вид**ит**, как [**её сын**] приближа**ет**ся к ней.	++	-	++	+
3	Она ста**ла** делать вид, что она сп**ит** вот так.	-	-	++	++
4	[**Сын**] ста**л** вот так разглядывать её.	+	-	+	+
5	Наконец, она нача**ла** смеяться.	-	-	+	+
6	«[Мама], дай **мне** [денег].»	++	-	-	+
7	«**Я** пойд**у** ещё там поигра**ю**.»	-	-	++	+
8	Конечно, она **ему** да**ла** [денег].	+	-	+	+
9	[**Наши сыновья**] тоже подходил**и**.	+	-	+	-
10	Тоже просил**и** [денег].	+	-	+	-
11	«**Мы** ужас как хот**им** поиграть ещё.»	-	-	+	+
12	Ну конечно, [отец] да**л** [денег], причём каждому отдельно.	++	-	+	-
13	И опять [**эта тройка**] направля**ет**ся к комнате.	+	-	-	-
	English:	Nom	Inc	Agr	Pro
1	**They** constantly went to play, constantly asked for [**money**].	+	-	-	+
2	And then [Ira] see**s** [**her son**] approaching her.	++	-	+	+
3	[She] began to pretend that she was sleeping like this.	-	-	+	++
4	[**Her son**] began to look at her like this.	+	-	-	+
5	Finally, she began to laugh.	-	-	-	+
6	"[Mum], give **me** [**some money**]."	++	-	-	+
7	"**I'll** go and play there again."	-	-	-	+
8	Of course, she gave **him** [**the money**].	+	-	-	++
9	[**Our sons**] also came.	+	-	-	-
10	**They** asked for [money].	+	-	-	+
11	"**We** really want to play more."	-	-	-	+
12	Well, of course, [their father] gave **them** [money], separately.	++	-	-	+
13	And once again [**these three boys**] **are** heading to the room.	+	-	+	-

Figure 7: Argument encoding in a short story: A comparison between encoding strategies in Chukchi, Russian and English. Entities are colour coded, inflectional agreement markers are <u>underlined</u>, noun phrases are in square brackets [...] and pronouns are unadorned. False starts have been removed from the Chukchi example. The columns on the right show four strategies for argument encoding, as a (Nom)inal, as (Inc)orporation, as (Agr)eement and as (Pro)nominal. In Chukchi, answering a question like "What did their sons want to do with the money?" would require a model of both inflection and incorporation, whereas in Russian and English the question could be answered on the level of tokens. Note that in (9) in Chukchi, [*Мургинэт ...ңинҡэгти*] 'our ...son' is a discontinuous constituent. The glossing of this story can be found in https://chuklang.ru/media/ texts/Money.pdf and the Latin transcription of Chukchi can be found in Appendix A.

compound predicates, lexical affixing. In this process a grammaticalised set of verbalising lexical affixes can be added to nouns to make verbs where the noun fills one of the valency slots. This is widely used in Chukchi and in other polysynthetic languages, such as Greenlandic and Yupik and has been treated before in formalisms such as HPSG (Malouf, 1999) and LFG (Grimshaw and Mester, 1985). The challenge with this construction is which verb to consider the head, as unlike with canonical noun incorporation it is not clear. The morphological head is certainly the root (the affixes are bound morphemes), while the semantic head is the verbalising affix (supplying the argument structure).

In addition to continuing work on Chukchi, we plan to work with other languages which exhibit incorporation, such as Western Sierra Nahuatl and Mapudungun.

7   Concluding remarks

In this paper we have presented an approach to dependency annotation of the phenomenon of noun incorporation within the Universal Dependencies framework. The approach modifies the existing guidelines by allowing core arguments expressed by noun incorporation to be included as additional nodes in the enhanced representation. Additionally we perform a case study using our annotation scheme by annotating the Amguema corpus of Chukchi and show that noun incorporation is not a marginal phenomenon.

Acknowledgements

We would like to thank the Universal Dependencies community for very informative and useful discussions. We also thank the anonymous reviewers, Robert Pugh, and Kevin Scannell for their helpful and insightful comments. This article contains output of a research project implemented as part of the Basic Research Programme at the National Research University Higher School of Economics (HSE University).

References

Stephen R. Anderson. 2001. Lexicalism, incorporated (or incorporation, lexicalized). In *Proceedings of the 36th Annual Meeting of the Chicago Linguistics Society*, pages 13–34.

Vasilisa Andriyanets and Francis M. Tyers. 2018. A prototype finite-state morphological analyser for Chukchi. In *Proceedings of the Workshop on Computational Modeling of Polysynthetic Languages*, pages 31–40, Santa Fe, New Mexico, USA, August. Association for Computational Linguistics.

Mark Baker. 1996. *The Polysynthesis Parameter*. Oxford University Press.

Eckhard Bick. 2019. Dependency trees for Greenlandic. In *Proceedings of the 15th Conference on Natural Language Processing (KONVENS 2019)*, pages 140–148.

Joan Bresnan and Sam A. Mchombo. 1995. The lexical integrity principle: Evidence from Bantu. *Natural Language and Linguistic Theory*, 13(2):181–254.

Bernard Comrie. 1981. *Languages of the Soviet Union*. Cambridge University Press.

Mary Dalrymple. 2001. *Lexical Functional Grammar*. Academic Press.

Michael Dunn. 1999. *A Grammar of Chukchi*. Ph.D. thesis, Australian National University.

Guy Emerson and Ann Copestake. 2015. Lacking integrity: HPSG as a morphosyntactic theory. In Stefan Müller, editor, *Proceedings of the 22nd International Conference on Head-Driven Phrase Structure Grammar*, pages 75–95. CSLI Publications.

Michael Fortescue, Marianne Mithun, and Nicholas Evans. 2017. The Oxford Handbook of Polysynthesis.

Jane Grimshaw and Ralf-Armin Mester. 1985. Complex verb formation in Eskimo. *Natural Language and Linguistic Theory*, 3:1–19.

Martin Haspelmath. 2009. The indeterminacy of word segmentation and the nature of morphology and syntax. *Folia Linguistica*, 45(1).

K. Haverinen, J. Kanerva, S. Kohonen, A. Missilä, S. Ojala, T. Viljanen, V. Laippala, and F. Ginter. 2015. The Finnish Proposition Bank. *Language Resources and Evaluation*, 49:907–926.

	Language	Argument(s)			
	Chukchi:	Nom	Inc	Agr	Pro
1	Qonpə nəwiswetsəqiwqinet?əm nəmanewanłasqewqenat.	-	±	++	-
2	Qənwet [Irana] ninet?uqin [sinitkin ekək] ejmewəł?ən ənəkaxtə?m.	+±	-	±	±
3	N?ər?əjəłqəŋŋoqen ənŋin waj.	-	-	±	-
4	[Ekkete?m] ənŋin ənqen nineyiteqin?əm.	+	-	±	-
5	Qənwet qənwet natanŋətkoŋŋoqen.	-	-	±	-
6	«[Ommemə], qenamanełpənrəyе.»	±	±	±	-
7	«Ənkə qeeqən?əm məwiswəsqikw?ek avtomat.»	-	-	±	-
8	Eee qełuq?əm nenamanełpənrəqen.	-	±	±	-
9	[Muryinet] neməqej nəjetqinet [ŋinqeхti].	+	-	±	-
10	Neməqej nəmanewanłasqewqenat.	-	±	±	-
11	«?etki waj qeeqən mətəłyirəwiswenŋərkən.»	-	-	±	-
12	Nu qełuq?əm [otłaye] nenamanełpənrəqenate am?janra naqam.	-	±	±	-
13	Neme ənqen komnata nəj?oqen.	-	-	±	-

Figure 8: Argument encoding in a short story: Chukchi have been orthographically transliterated into Latin script.

Judith L. Klavans, editor. 2018. *Proceedings of the Workshop on Computational Modeling of Polysynthetic Languages*, Santa Fe, New Mexico, USA, August. Association for Computational Linguistics.

Robert Malouf. 1999. West Greenlandic noun incorporation in a monohierarchical theory of grammar. In Gert Webelhuth, Andreas Kathol, and Jean-Pierre Koenig, editors, *Lexical and Constructional Aspects of Linguistic Explanation*, pages 47–62. CSLI Publications.

Marianne Mithun. 1984. The evolution of noun incorporation. *Language*, 60(4):847–894.

Joakim Nivre, Marie-Catherine de Marneffe, Filip Ginter, Jan Hajič, Chris Manning, Sampo Pyysalo, Sebastian Schuster, Francis M. Tyers, and Dan Zeman. 2020. Universal Dependencies v2: an evergrowing multilingual treebank collection. In *Proceedings of the 12th Conference on Language Resources and Evaluation (LREC 2020)*, pages 4027–4036.

Martha Palmer, P. Kingsbury, and D. Gildea. 2005. The Proposition Bank: An annotated corpus of semantic roles. *Computational Linguistics*, 31(1):71–106.

Maria Polinsky. 1990. Subject incorporation: Evidence from Chukchee. In Katarzyna Dziwirek, Patrick Farrell, and Errapel Mejias-Bikandi, editors, *Grammatical relations: A cross-theoretical perspective*, pages 349–364.

Siva Reddy, Oscar Täckström, Slav Petrov, Mark Steedman, and Mirella Lapata. 2017. Universal Semantic Parsing. In *Proceedings of the 2017 Conference on Empirical Methods in Natural Language Processing*, pages 89–101, Copenhagen, Denmark, September. Association for Computational Linguistics.

Sara Thomas Rosen. 1989. Two types of noun incorporation: A lexical analysis. *Language*, 64:294–317.

Sebastian Schuster and Christopher D. Manning. 2016. Enhanced english universal dependencies: An improved representation for natural language understanding tasks. In Nicoletta Calzolari (Conference Chair), Khalid Choukri, Thierry Declerck, Sara Goggi, Marko Grobelnik, Bente Maegaard, Joseph Mariani, Helene Mazo, Asuncion Moreno, Jan Odijk, and Stelios Piperidis, editors, *Proceedings of the Tenth International Conference on Language Resources and Evaluation (LREC 2016)*, Paris, France, may. European Language Resources Association (ELRA).

Hajime Senuma and Akiko Aizawa. 2017. Toward Universal Dependencies for Ainu. In *Proceedings of the NoDaLiDa 2017 Workshop on Universal Dependencies (UDW 2017)*, pages 133–139, Gothenburg, Sweden, May. Association for Computational Linguistics.

Andrew Spencer. 1995. Incorporation in Chukchi. *Language*, 71(3):439–489.

Amir Zeldes and Shuo Zhang. 2016. When annotation schemes change rules help: A configurable approach to coreference resolution beyond OntoNotes. In *Proceedings of the NAACL2016 Workshop on Coreference Resolution Beyond OntoNotes (CORBON)*, pages 92–101.

A Transcription

Universal Dependency Treebank for Xibe

He Zhou, Juyeon Chung, Sandra Kübler, Francis M. Tyers
Indiana University
{hzh1,juychung,skuebler,ftyers}@iu.edu

Abstract

We present our work of constructing the first treebank for the Xibe language following the Universal Dependencies (UD) annotation scheme. Xibe is a low-resourced and severely endangered Tungusic language spoken by the Xibe minority living in the Xinjiang Uygur Autonomous Region of China. We collected 810 sentences so far, including 544 sentences from a grammar book on written Xibe and 266 sentences from *Cabcal News*. We annotated those sentences manually from scratch. In this paper, we report the procedure of building this treebank and analyze several important annotation issues of our treebank. More specifically, we look at loanwords from Chinese, at the attributive function of the case marker *i*, at the topic marker *oci*, and at relative and adverbial clauses. Finally, we propose our plans for future work.

1 Introduction

The Xibe language (ISO 693-3:sjo) is a Tungusic language spoken by members of the Xibe minority group of China. Based on the 2010 population census of China, the population of the Xibe minority is no more than 200,000[1]. Xibe people are mainly distributed in northeastern China, including Heilongjiang, Jilin and Liaoning, and northwestern Xinjiang Uygur Autonomous Region. However, active native speakers mainly live in Cabcal Xibe Autonomous County and adjacent regions in Xinjiang. The number of native Xibe speakers has dropped below 40,000 and continues to decrease. Therefore, the Xibe language is considered a severely endangered language by UNESCO[2].

There is a limited amount of linguistic studies pertinent to the Xibe language. Gu (2016) provides a survey on Xibe language research since the 1970s. Most of the previous studies are either theoretical description of this language or comparative studies with other languages, including Chinese, Manchu, and Mongolian. However, there is no corpus or any computational tool available for this language so far. In Cabcal Xibe Autonomous County, there is a single newspaper written in Xibe, *Cabcal Serkin* 'Cabcal News', which provides an invaluable resource for linguistic research. Therefore, to start the process of building NLP applications for this low resourced language, we first aim to create a syntactically annotated treebank based on texts from this newspaper.

We choose the Universal Dependencies (UD) framework (McDonald et al., 2013) to create a dependency treebank for the Xibe language. The UD project has been developed for consistently constructing treebanks for many different languages cross-linguistically, aiming to capture similarities as well as idiosyncrasies among typologically different languages (Nivre et al., 2016). The existing universal guidelines[3] have been widely used for a wide range of typologically different languages. Thus, we expect that they will be usable for Xibe without much adaptation. Xibe is an agglutinative language with rich morphological inflections. We decided that annotating word features as detailed as possible will allow us to make available as much syntactic and semantic information as possible.

[1]http://www.stats.gov.cn/tjsj/pcsj/rkpc/6rp/indexch.htm
[2]http://unesco.org/languages-atlas/index.php
[3]https://universaldependencies.org/guidelines.html

Proceedings of the Fourth Workshop on Universal Dependencies (UDW 2020), pages 205–215
Barcelona, Spain (Online), December 13, 2020

The remainder of this paper is organized as follows: In Section 2, we provide a comparison of Xibe and Manchu, and explain the differences between written and spoken Xibe. We introduce details of the corpus, including transliteration and pre-processing, in Section 3. In Section 4, we discuss several important annotation issues in part-of-speech and syntax. We summarize our work in Section 5.

2   Background

2.1   Xibe and Manchu

The Xibe minority used to reside in northeastern China and had a close relationship with Manchurian and Mongolian in both lifestyle and language. The Xibe people used to be one of the Manchu Eight Banners; therefore, they were considered a part of Manchu. Around 1764, the Xibe troops and their families left their hometown of Mukden (now Shenyang, China) and headed west towards the Ili Valley in Xinjiang to strengthen the border under the decree of Emperor Qianlong. Since their settlement there, they have continued using their own language and there still exists an active language community now.

Since the Xibe language is highly similar to Manchu, the question whether Xibe is an independent language or a Manchu dialect has been the focus of a controversial discussion among historians and linguists. In 1947, the Xibe minority conducted a language reform and determined the modern Xibe writing system, which is based on Manchu with slight modifications. However, modern Xibe has developed characteristics that set it apart from Manchu, as a result of language contact with adjacent languages such as Uygur, Kazakh, Russian, and Chinese. Most of the changes originate from Xibe absorbing a large amount of new words in the political domain from Chinese.

We mainly used *Xiboyu Yufa Tonglun* (General Introduction to Xibe Grammar) by Setuken (2009), a comprehensive description of written Xibe grammar, to guide our annotation decisions. Additionally, although Manchu is rarely used in daily life, there are many more accessible reference works for Manchu than for Xibe. Because of the similarity between the two languages, we have also consulted Manchu materials, such as *the Comprehensive Manchu-Chinese Dictionary* (Hu, 1994) and *Manchu Grammar* (Gorelova, 2002), when making annotation decisions.

2.2   Written and Spoken Xibe

Spoken Xibe is a collection of dialects, and there is no standard. Thus, spoken Xibe differs to a certain point from the written form. Most previous studies are concerned with documenting Xibe dialectal variation or studying spoken Xibe phonology or morphology (Norman, 1974; Li, 1979; Li, 1982; Li, 1985; Li, 1988; Jang, 2008; Zikmundová, 2013). The language data in those works are not written in Xibe script but are collected by recording native speakers' pronunciation and transcribed with IPA or transliterated in Roman alphabet since the goal is documenting the dialectal differences. Considering the variation of spoken language among the Xibe communities and the difference between the written and spoken language, we take written Xibe as the research object, and our data are mainly based on Xibe language publications, that is, a newspaper and a grammar.

3   Corpus

3.1   Data Collection

In our present work, we have collected written Xibe sentences from two data sources. The first part originates from *Xiboyu Yufa Tonglun* (General Introduction to Xibe Grammar) (Setuken, 2009). We extracted all 544 example sentences from the grammar, only excluding examples from poetic language. Using sentences from a grammar has the advantage that they comprehensively cover all grammatical constructions. The 544 sentences contain a total of 5,773 tokens, and the average sentence length is 10.6 tokens per sentence.

The second part was collected from *Cabcal News*. Each issue of the newspaper has four pages, the first two pages are news, the remaining two pages are essays or poems written by native speakers. To keep the genre consistent, we only extracted news. We collected 266 sentences from 9 issues, including 9,716 tokens. The longest sentence has 92 tokens and the average sentence length is 36.5 tokens per sentence. After combining the two parts, our complete treebank consists of 810 sentences, or 15,489 tokens.

vowels (5)	a[a]	e[ə]	i [i]	o [o]	u[u]
consonants (19)	n[n]	k [q]/[k]	g [ɢ]/[g]	h [x]/[χ]	b [p]
	p[pʰ]	s [s]	š[ʂ]	t [tʰ]	d [t]
	l[l]	m[m]	c[tʂʰ]	j[tʂ]	y[j]
	r[r]	f[f]	w[v]	ng[ŋ]	
foreign letters (10)	ck[kʰ]	cg[gʰ]	ch[xʰ]	z[z̩]	ts[tsʰ]
	dz[ts]	sy[sz]	tsy[tsʰz]	cy[tʂʰz]	jy[tʂz̩]
Manchu vowel(1)	v [u]				

Table 1: Xibe alphabet, with transliterations and IPA.

3.2 Pre-processing

Before converting each sentence into CoNLL-U format, we Latinized each Xibe sentence and translated it into English. We manually transliterated the first 544 grammar book sentences and automatically transliterated the news data using a python script. After the conversion to the CoNLL-U format, each sentence has its original text written in Xibe script, the transliteration, and the English translation. Tokenization assumes that all words are separated by spaces or punctuation. We annotated each word with its lemma, UTS part of speech tag, morphological features, and dependency annotation.

For the first 544 sentences, the annotation work was carried out by two annotators. The first annotator annotated 464 sentences, and the second annotator annotated 80 sentences. The 80 sentences by the second annotator were checked by the first annotator to keep the annotation consistent. As for the second part of the data, the annotation was performed by the first annotator. We used UD Annotatrix (Tyers et al., 2017) to facilitate our annotation.

3.3 Transliteration

The writing system of Xibe is untypical in that its writing direction is from top to bottom, from left to right. The Xibe script is based on Manchu script with slight modifications, which uses traditional Mongolian letters. Xibe letters have different forms: Most of the letters have three forms at initial, medial, or final position, but some letters just have one or two forms. In Table 1, all letters but *ng* ᠩ are the initial forms. For *ng* ᠩ, we show the final form since it cannot occur in initial position.

Modern written Xibe has 5 vowels, 19 consonants, and 10 foreign letters, shown in Table 1 (Setuken, 2009; Xinjiang Ethnic Language Work Committee, 1992). Additionally, the 10 foreign letters are constructed on the basis of elements from which the letters of the Xibe alphabet are formed. They are only used for foreign words, mostly Chinese loanwords. The additional vowel ᠸ listed in the table is one of the Manchu vowels, it is not part of the official Xibe script. However, since Xibe and Manchu have a large amount of words in common, this letter is frequently used in Xibe texts. It has a similar pronunciation to the Xibe ᠣ *u*, thus to differentiate the two, we used *v* to transliterate this vowel.

4 Annotation Issues

Xibe is one of the Tungusic languages. Like other Tungusic languages, it has agglutinative morphology. Xibe morphology mainly focuses on verbs in that verbs are marked for tense, aspect, mood, and voice, but also for converbs and participles. Xibe phrases are head-final, both on the phrasal and the clausal level. The canonical word order is Subject-Object-Verb (SOV) (but see Section 4.3), and arguments are marked for case.

Figure 1[4] shows a Xibe sentence in canonical order, in which *muse* 'I' is the subject, *mini juwe gala* 'our two hands', in instrumental case (marked by *i*), is an adjunct to the main verb, *ice usin tokso* 'new

---

[4]Because of space limitations, we show short example trees in vertical form with Xibe text and long example trees in horizontal form with transliteration only.

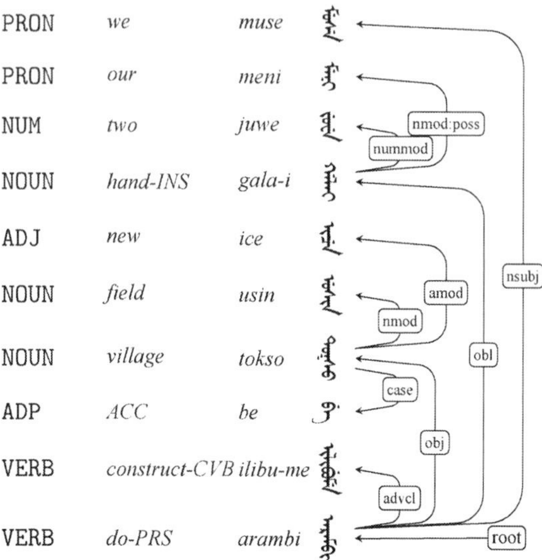

Figure 1: Dependency Tree for 'We construct the new countryside with our two hands'.

18–20	᠊᠊ ᠊ ᠊	_	_	_	_	_	_	_	_
18	᠊	᠊	X	_	_	22	nsubj	_	Translit=gung
19	᠊	᠊	X	_	_	18	flat	_	Translit=he
20	᠊	᠊	NOUN	_	_	19	flat	_	Translit=cgo

Figure 2: Fragment of the multi-word expression ᠊ ᠊ ᠊, *gung he cgo*, 'republic' in CoNLL–U format.

countryside', marked for accusative case *be*, is the direct object, and the verb phrase *ilibume arambi* 'construct' is the main verb.

In the following sections, we will discuss several language phenomena in Xibe, with a focus on the annotation decisions we have made for these phenomena.

4.1 Loanwords from Chinese

In UD annotation, the smallest unit is defined to be the syntactic word rather than morphemes or constituents smaller than words; morphological features can only be encoded as properties of words. However, an issue arises because of the frequency of Chinese loanwords: Xibe adapts Chinese loanwords in different ways, but in most cases, they are handled as phonemic loanwords, i.e., Chinese syllables are transliterated into Xibe letters with similar pronunciation. As a consequence, each Chinese character is written as a separate word in Xibe. Thus, it is necessary to combine these elements into a single syntactic word in the UD annotation scheme.

Figure 2 shows an example. Here the sequence ᠊ ᠊ ᠊, *gung he cgo*, 'republic' corresponds to the tri-syllabic Chinese word 'gòng hé guó'. The three syllables are directly transliterated into three Xibe syllables and written separately as three tokens. In Chinese, the first two tokens are bound morphemes while the third token is a free morpheme. Therefore, we could not find proper part-of-speech tags for the bound morphemes. Here our strategy is to assign X to the bound morphemes and the proper part-of-speech to the free morpheme according to the syntactic function of the complete word. In the example, the first line depicts the whole word. The following lines represent the syllables: ᠊ *gung* and ᠊ *he* are the bound morphemes, and ᠊ *cgo* the free morpheme. On the syntactic level, we treat this type of structure as a multiword expression (MWE) and annotate it with a flat internal structure.

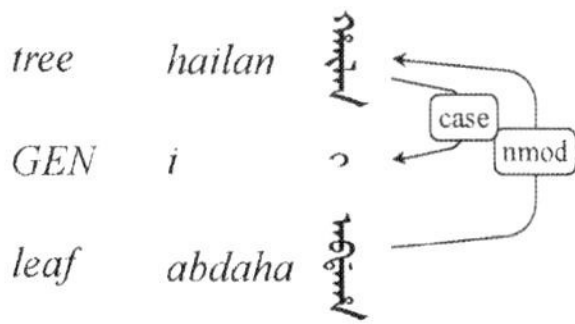

Figure 3: Dependency Tree for noun phrase 'leaf of tree'.

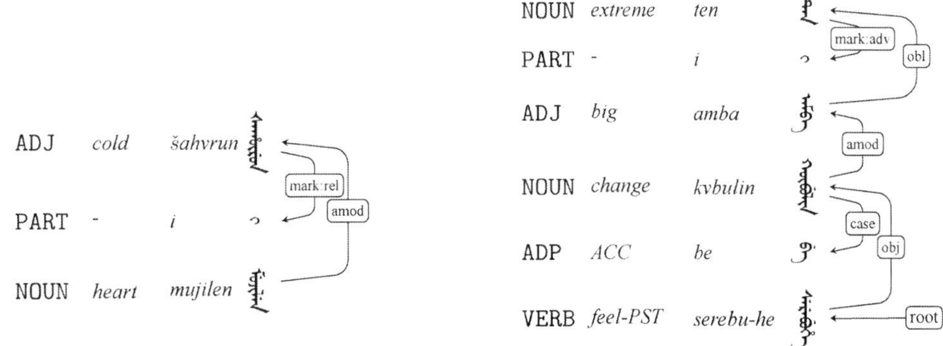

Figure 4: Dependency tree for 'cold heart'.

Figure 5: Dependency tree for '(someone) experienced extremely big changes'.

4.2 Attributive Function of *i*

ᠴ *i* is one of the case markers in Xibe, and its primary syntactic function is to express genitive and instrumental case. Figure 1 shows an example of the usage of *i* as instrumental case marker: *i* is attached to the head of the noun phrase *meni juwe gala* 'our two hands'. Figure 3 shows an example of *i* as genitive case maker, which connects *hailan* 'tree' and *abdaha* 'leaf'. Besides these two case, *i* is also used in other syntactic contexts, as an attributive function. We consider this usage a homograph of the case marker, assuming that it is influenced by Chinese. I.e., *i* is a modifier particle PART instead of a case marker ADP. The attributive function of *i* occurs frequently in *Cabcal News*.

There are two types of attributive functions: In the first case, *i* marks adjectival modifiers. In Figure 4, *šahvrun* 'cold' is an adjective and directly modifies *mujilen* 'heart', but there is an *i* without obvious function. We assume that this is borrowed from Chinese. We follow the Chinese-HK UD treebank (Leung et al., 2016; Wong et al., 2017) and annotate the adjective as the head of the particle *i*. The particle *i* is treated as a mark:rel dependent of the adjective.

In the second case, *i* marks adverbial modifiers. In Figure 5, *ten* is a noun, meaning 'pole, extreme'. The following particle *i* marks it to be an adverbial modifier of the adjective *amba* 'big', describing the degree of the adjective. Thus *ten* is an adjunct depending on the adjective with the relation obl, and *i* depends on *ten* with the relation mark:adv indicating that the noun functions as an adverbial modifier.

4.3 Topic Marker *oci*

Xibe uses the canonical word order of subject-object-verb (SOV). Rearranging the word order is possible to a certain degree, the syntactic functions and semantics of the sentence are still clear because of the government by case markers. The topic of a sentence tends to occupy sentence-initial position and is marked via topic markers. In written Xibe, *oci* is one of these topic markers, but it shows signs of changing to a copula, influenced by Chinese. *oci* derives from the verb *ombi* 'to become' in its conditional converb form, and it literally means 'if becoming somebody or something'. As a topic marker, *oci* is similar to the Japanese topic marker は *wa* and the Korean topic marker 은 *eun*/는 *neun*. We consider it an ADP, and it assigns nominal case to the subject, but it has the function of topicalization in terms of information

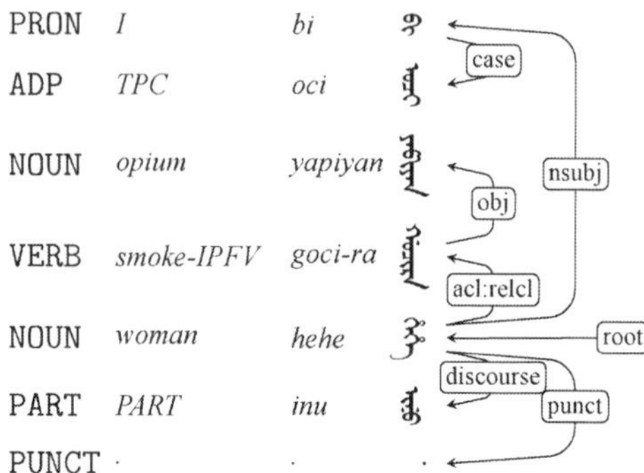

Figure 6: Dependency tree for 'I am an opium smoking woman'.

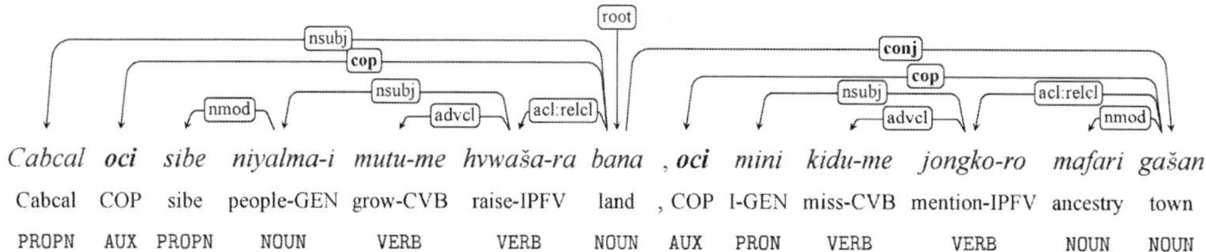

Figure 7: Dependency tree for 'Cabcal is the place where Xibe people grow up and the hometown that I miss'.

structure. In addition, when a topic marker is used, a modal particle *inu* is optionally added at the end of the sentence denoting modality.

In Figure 6, *oci* follows the subject *bi* 'I', functioning as topicalizer for the subject. *inu* – located at the end of the sentence – functions as a modal particle and indicates that the sentence is declarative. The modal particle is a dependent of the head of the sentence, marked as `discourse`, following the Classical Chinese UD Treebank (Yasuoka, 2019).

It is worth noting that *oci* seems to be in the process of changing from a topic marker to a copula, which we assume to be influenced by Chinese since it literally corresponds to the Chinese copula 是 shì . In this usage, *oci* is frequently found in *Cabcal News*, typically in equational constructions. In Figure 7[5], *oci* is used in an equational construction where it functions as a link between the main subject *Cabcal* to each nominal phrase introduced by *oci*. The head of the first conjunct in the coordinating construction is the `root`, and the head in the second conjunct depends on it via the `conj` relation. In each conjunct, *oci* as a copula depends on the nominal head via the `cop` relation. This is the only case we find so far that counters the typical SOV structure in Xibe, and we assume that it is highly influenced by Chinese.

4.4 Relative Clauses

Similar to many Tungusic languages, relative clauses in Xibe are pre-nominal, and there is no relative pronoun. The main device to render relative clauses in Xibe is via the predicate verb in a relative clause, which takes participle form and modifies the following noun or noun phrase. Xibe has imperfect and perfect participles, which express the temporal meanings present or past. The imperfect participle has the suffix *-ra/re/ro*, and the perfect participle has the suffix *-ha/he/ho*.

Under UD guidelines, a relative clause is an instance of an adjectival clause, which is characterized by finiteness and omission of the modified noun in the embedded clause. Therefore the modified noun should be an argument in the clause. In other word, there should be a gap in the clause which the head noun or noun phrase can fill in. Based on this criterion, Xibe has two types of relative clauses, subject-gap

---

[5]Please note that subjects in relative clauses take genitive case and are not marked for topic. Thus, *sibe niyalma-i* 'Xibe people-GEN' and *mini* 'I-GEN' are the subjects of the relative clauses.

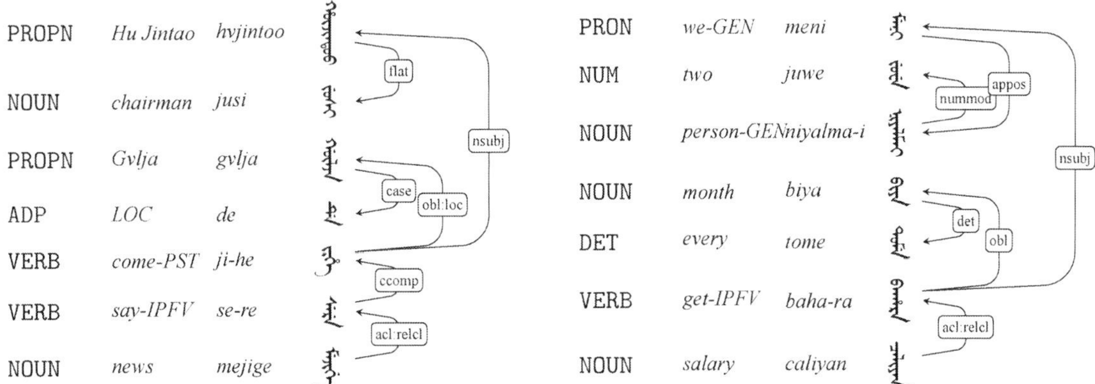

Figure 8: Dependency tree for 'the news that Chairman Hu Jintao came to Gvlja'.

Figure 9: Dependency tree for 'the salary that we two people get every month'.

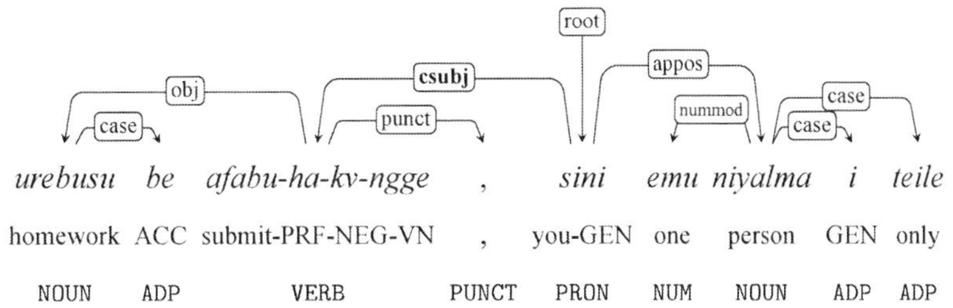

Figure 10: Sentence with headless relative clause 'The only person who did not submit the homework is you'.

and object-gap relative clauses. For a relative clause, the participle is a dependent of the modified noun or noun phrase, and their relation is `acl:relcl`.

In subject-gap relative clauses, the head noun should be able to be filled into the subject position of the clause. In Figure 8, *sere* is the imperfect participial form of *sembi* 'to say', whose object is the sentence complement prior to it. This phrase literally means 'the news which is saying that Chairman Hu Jintao came to Gvlja'. *mejige* 'news' is the subject of *sere* in relative clause.

In object-gap relative clauses, the head noun can be filled in the object gap. In Xibe, the subject noun of the relative clause must take genitive case, which puts the subject noun and the participle morphologically in a possessive relation, but semantically it is the agent. In Figure 9, *bahara* is the imperfect participle of *bahambi* 'to get' and requires two arguments. The subject consists of an appositive phrase, and both of the appositive constituents take genitive case.

In addition to these two basic types, there is a construction that can be considered a special form of relative clause. Instead of modifying a nominal constituent, the participle in the relative clause adds suffix *-ngge*, converting the participle to a verbal noun (VN). *-ngge* semantically denotes an abstract concept of an action, or an object to which the action is applied, or a person (Gorelova, 2002). In Figure 10, '*urebusu be afabuhakvngge*' is such a construction. *afabuhakv* is the negated perfective participle of verb *afabumbi* 'to submit'. By adding the suffix *-ngge*, it changes to a verbal noun and refers to a person according to the context, meaning 'the person who did not submit'. It functions as a clausal subject of the sentence, and the verbal noun '*afabuhakvngge*' depends on the nominal predicate with relation `csubj`.

Xibe also has adjectival clauses that are not considered relative clauses. The modified nominal constituent cannot be filled into either subject or object position of the clause. The participle is dependent on the head noun, and their relation is `acl`. In Figure 11, *toksimbi* 'to knock' requires two arguments in which the subject typically has the semantic feature of animacy. The head noun of this phrase *asuki*

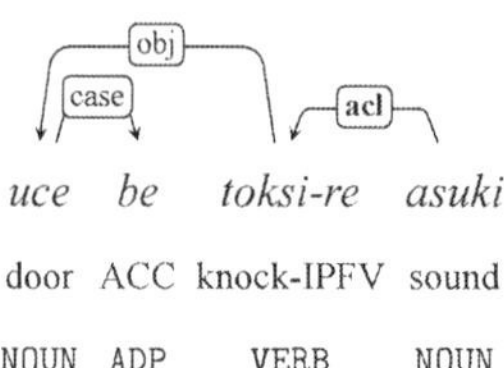

Figure 11: Dependency Tree for noun phrase 'the sound of knocking on doors'.

-me	imperfect converb, denoting simultaneity of subordinate and main actions
-fi/-pi	perfect converb, indicating the reason for performing the main action
-ci	conditional converb, indicating the subordinate action precedes the principal action in time, meaning 'if'
-cibe	concessive converb, usually collocates with adverb *udu* 'although'
-tala/tele/tolo	terminal converb, indicating the main action continues until the final completion of the subordinate action, meaning 'until...'
-nggala/nggele/ nggolo	denote the subordinate action before which the main action takes place, meaning 'before...'
-tai/tei	denote an extreme degree of an action
-hai/hei/hoi	denote the action that is durative and intermittent, meaning 'continually, constantly'

Table 2: Xibe converb suffixes.

'sound' does not meet the semantic criterion, it is the result of the action. We treat such case as `acl` as shown in the example in Figure 11.

When an adjectival clause modifies nouns such as *turgun* 'reason', *ba* 'place', *erin* 'time', or *fon* 'period', they function as adverbials, that is, causal, locative, and temporal, by adding dative case markers. We will explain these cases in the next section.

4.5 Adverbial Clauses

There are two main devices to express adverbial clauses: converbs and a certain type of adjectival clauses. Converb is a separate subclass of verbal forms, and they function as the means of subordination of one verb to another. Converbs cannot serve as predicates of a simple sentence but can function as adverbs or predicates of adverbial clauses (Gorelova, 2002). A Xibe converb is formed by the verb root and one of the eight types of converb suffixes listed in Table 2. The converb is the predicate of the adverbial clause, and it is dependent on the main predicate, their relation is `advcl`. For example, in Figure 12, *wajinggala* is the converb form of *wajimbi* 'to finish', meaning 'before finishing something'. It serves as predicate of the adverbial clause and modifies the main predicate *yabuha* 'left'.

However, converbs cannot explicitly express adverbial clause types such as locality, time, or causality. Such meanings are expressed by specific constructions, as described in Section 4.4. The constructions are syntactically adjectival, but semantically express adverbials. The construction is formed by an adjectival clause modifying a noun and a case marker, mostly dative case *de*. The participle is the predicate of the adjectival clause, modifying nouns including *ba* 'place', *erin* 'time', *fon* 'period', *turgun* 'reason'. In the dative case, these constructions express locative, temporal, and causal relations with the main predicate. Therefore, the cased nouns *bade*, *erinde/fonde*, *turgunde* tend to serve as the corresponding subordinating conjunctions. In Figure 13, the imperfective participle *yabure* modifies *erin*, *erin* then takes the dative case, which turns the modified noun phrase into an adverbial attached to the verb, with relation `obl`. The phrase literally translates as 'at the time of going on the road'.

Postpositions in Xibe are uninflected words denoting syntactic relationships between nouns or a noun and a verb. Postpositions govern nouns, pronouns that they follow. However, such words can also function as a subordinate conjunct when they follows a participle, and the participle serves as the predicate of the clause and is dependent on the main predicate with relation `advcl`. The subordinate conjunct func-

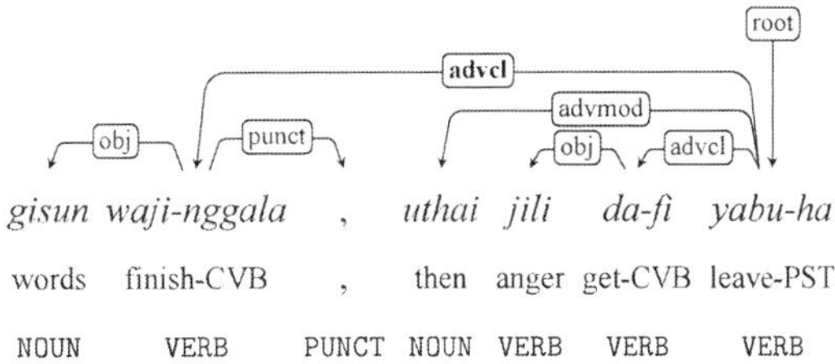

Figure 12: Sentence with adverbial cl.: 'Before (someone) finished the words, (he) got angry and left'.

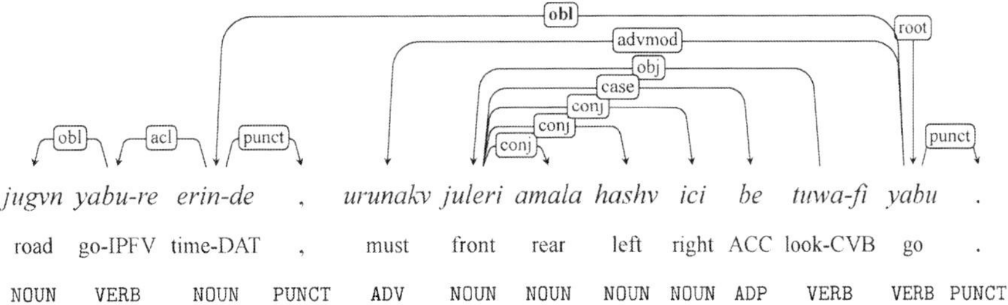

Figure 13: Dependency tree for 'When you go on the road, you must look around your surroundings'.

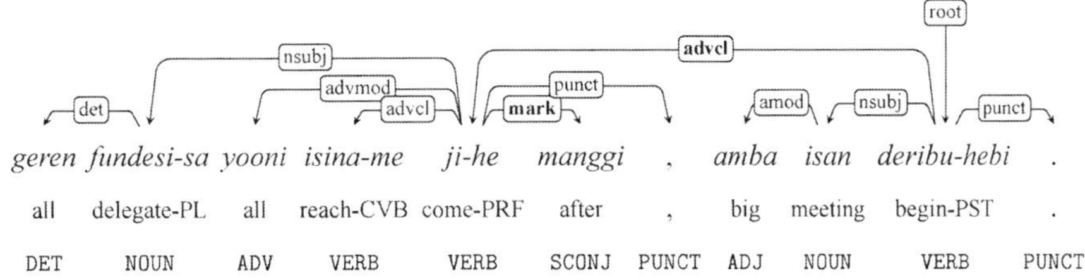

Figure 14: Dependency tree for 'After all the delegates arrived, the conference began'.

tions as a marker, and it is dependent on the clausal head. In Figure 14, *manggi* 'after' is a subordinate conjunct and follows an adjectival clause with the perfective participle *jihe* as head. *jihe* depends on the main predicate *deribuhebi*, having relation advcl.

5 Conclusion

In this paper, we have shown the procedure of building the first Xibe treebank using Universal Dependencies. This is an important step towards the documentation of Xibe, for which little previous research exists due to its low number of language resources. Along with the treebank construction, we document several language specific phenomena. For future work, we will continue collecting and annotating sentences from *Cabcal News* and Xibe elementary textbooks to expand our treebank. At the same time, we will also conduct corpus-based linguistic research on the language, and we will start investigating parsing approaches that will work for such a low resource language.

Acknowledgments

We are grateful to Jonathan North Washington, He Ma, and several native Xibe speakers (who want to remain anonymous) for their discussion and assistance. We would also thank the two anonymous reviewers for their helpful comments. He Zhou is supported by China Scholarship Council.

References

Liliya M Gorelova. 2002. *Manchu Grammar*. Brill.

Songjie Gu. 2016. A literature review on Sibe language. *Manchu Studies*, 2(2):83–87.

Zengyi Hu. 1994. *A Comprehensive Manchu-Chinese Dictionary*. Xinjiang People's Publishing House, Urumqi, Xinjiang, China.

Taeho Jang. 2008. *Sibe Grammar*. The Nationalities Publishing House of Yunnan, Kunming, Yunnan, China.

Herman Leung, Rafaël Poiret, Tak-sum Wong, Xinying Chen, Kim Gerdes, and John Lee. 2016. Developing universal dependencies for Mandarin Chinese. In *Proceedings of the 12th Workshop on Asian Language Resources*, pages 20–29, Osaka, Japan.

Shulan Li. 1979. A survey on the Sibe language. *Minority Languages of China*, 6(3):221–232.

Shulan Li. 1982. Possession category in Sibe. *Minority Languages of China*, 6(5):50–57.

Shulan Li. 1985. Adverbials in Sibe. *Minority Languages of China*, 6(5):12–25.

Shulan Li. 1988. Auxilaries in sibe. *Minority Languages of China*, 6(6):27–32.

Ryan McDonald, Joakim Nivre, Yvonne Quirmbach-Brundage, Yoav Goldberg, Dipanjan Das, Kuzman Ganchev, Keith Hall, Slav Petrov, Hao Zhang, Oscar Täckström, Claudia Bedini, Núria Bertomeu Castelló, and Jungmee Lee. 2013. Universal dependency annotation for multilingual parsing. In *Proceedings of the 51st Annual Meeting of the Association for Computational Linguistics*, pages 92–97, Sofia, Bulgaria.

Joakim Nivre, Marie-Catherine De Marneffe, Filip Ginter, Yoav Goldberg, Jan Hajic, Christopher D Manning, Ryan McDonald, Slav Petrov, Sampo Pyysalo, Natalia Silveira, et al. 2016. Universal dependencies v1: A multilingual treebank collection. In *Proceedings of the Tenth International Conference on Language Resources and Evaluation (LREC'16)*, pages 1659–1666.

Jerry Norman. 1974. A sketch of Sibe morphology. *Central Asiatic Journal*, 18(3):159–174.

Setuken. 2009. *General Introduction to Xibe Grammar*. Xinjiang People's Publishing House, Urumqi, Xinjiang, China.

Francis Tyers, Mariya Sheyanova, and Jonathan Washington. 2017. UD Annotatrix: An annotation tool for universal dependencies. In *Proceedings of the 16th International Workshop on Treebanks and Linguistic Theories*, pages 10–17.

Tak-sum Wong, Kim Gerdes, Herman Leung, and John Lee. 2017. Quantitative comparative syntax on the Cantonese-Mandarin Parallel Dependency Treebank. In *Proceedings of the Fourth International Conference on Dependency Linguistics*, pages 266–275, Pisa, Italy.

Xinjiang Ethnic Language Work Committee. 1992. *nei fon sibe šu tacin gisun i arara kooli (Modern Literary Xibe Orthography)*. Xinjiang People's Publishing House, Urumqi, Xinjiang, China.

Koichi Yasuoka. 2019. Universal dependencies treebank of the four books in Classical Chinese. In *DADH2019: 10th International Conference of Digital Archives and Digital Humanities*, pages 20–28, Taipei, Taiwan.

Veronika Zikmundová. 2013. *Spoken Sibe: Morphology of the Inflected Parts of Speech*. Karolinum Press.

A Tagset, Relations and Features

This treebank uses 17 Universal POS Tags, 30 Universal Dependency relations, relation subtypes, and 20 features.

A.1 Universal POS Tags

ADJ	ADP	ADV	AUX	CCONJ	DET	INTJ	NOUN	NUM
PART	PRON	PROPN	PUNCT	SCONJ	SYM	VERB	X	

A.2 Universal Dependency Relations and Subtypes

A.2.1 Universal Dependency Relations

acl	advcl	amod	advmod	appos	aux	case	cc	ccomp
clf	compound	conj	cop	csubj	det	discourse	fixed	flat
iobj	mark	nmod	nsubj	nummod	obj	obl	parataxis	punct
root	vocative	xcomp						

A.2.2 Relation Subtypes

acl:relcl	flat:name	mark:adv	mark:plur	mark:rel
nmod:poss	nmod:range	nsubj:pass	obl:loc	obl:tmod

A.3 Features

feature	value	feature	value
Abbr	Yes	Polarity	Neg
Aspect	Imp, Perf, Prog	Polite	Elev
Case	Abl, Acc, Cmp, Com, Dat Gen, Ins, Lat, Loc,Nom	PronType	Dem, Ind, Int, Prs, Tot
Clusivity	Ex, In	Poss	Yes
Degree	Cmp, Pos	Reflex	Yes
Foreign	Yes	Tense	Fut, Past, Pres
Mood	Cnd, Imp, Ind, Sub	Typo	Yes
Number	Plur, Sing	VerbForm	Conv, Fin, Inf, Part, Vnoun
NumType	Card, Frac, Mult, Ord, Sets	Voice	Act, Cau, Pass, Rcp
Person	1, 2, 3		